ECOLOGUE

THE ENVIRONMENTAL CATALOGUE AND CONSUMER'S GUIDE FOR A SAFE EARTH

Edited by Bruce N. Anderson

PRENTICE
HALL
PRESS

NEW YORK · LONDON · TORONTO · SYDNEY · TOKYO · SINGAPORE

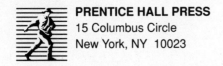

PRENTICE HALL PRESS
15 Columbus Circle
New York, NY 10023

Copyright © 1990 by Bruce N. Anderson

PRENTICE HALL PRESS and colophons are registered trademarks of
Simon & Schuster, Inc.

Library of Congress Cataloging-in-Publication Data

Anderson, Bruce, 1947-
  Ecologue: the environmental catalogue and consumer's guide for a
safe earth / edited by Bruce N. Anderson.
        p.   cm.
    Includes index.
    ISBN 0-13-084518-3
    1. Environmental protection — Citizen participation.
  2. Environmental protection — Equipment and supplies — Catalogs.
  3. Household supplies — Catalogs. 4. Consumer education. I. Title.
  TD171.7.A53   1990
  363.70525—dc20

                                                    90-7501
                                                      CIP

Printed on recycled paper.

An Ecologue book from International Environment Group, Inc. All profits from
royalties on this book are contributed to environmental organizations.
Designed by communication**design**
Manufactured in the United States of America

1 0   9   8   7   6   5   4   3   2   1

First Edition

To my daughter Karina,
who learned patience at the tender age of five
while her daddy was on the telephone or at the computer.
This book is dedicated to you and to all future generations.

ACKNOWLEDGMENTS AND THANKS

Who Says I Can't Change The World?

Doing this book has been one of the most rewarding experiences of my life because all of the dozens of truly wonderful and professional people who worked on it believe they can change the world! And we all believe that *Ecologue* will!

The editorial and production teams were just great — hard working, professional, and committed to making the world a better place. My warm and hearty thanks go to my assistant editor, Lonny Brown, a stalwart rock and friend who did whatever, wherever, whenever, however; Mona Anderson, unflappable sister and products editor, who remained organized despite the hundreds of companies and products we worked with; Ellen Ruggles, gatherer and editor of the hundreds of tips and facts, and her supporting staff at Sunplace, Inc.; editor Sharon Smith, who turned spaghetti-pile-like content into flowing prose and organization; eagle-eyed Lida Stinchfield and Anna Larson, copy editor and proofreader respectively, who brought flawless consistency and accuracy; and Barry Rhodes, who performed miracles first with data management and then later as he healed from brain surgery.

The creative organization of the book you are holding is due to the loving professionalism of Ellen Klempner-Béguin, design and production director; Jill Shaffer, who handled design and pasteup; and Linda Ottavi, computer guru, typesetter, and pasteup person. Thank you!

For so many different writers to provide exceptional information on time and in a somewhat consistent format is nothing short of phenomenal. Thank you, authors!

- Jennifer A. Adams, energy engineer and author for the Write Design: "Fuel Savers."
- Mary Allen, freelance writer, mother, and owner of four cats: "Pet Care."
- Ray E. Ashton, Jr., former Director, Natural History Travel for Massachusetts Audubon Society: "Ecotourism."
- Lisa Braiterman, businesswoman and diaper queen: "Baby Care."
- Lonny Brown, Ph.D, holistic health counselor and book author: "Personal Care."
- Lonny Brown with David Litwak and Paula Perlis, grocery industry consultants: "Grocery Shopping."
- David Del Porto, President, Water Conservation Systems, Inc.: "Water Purification" and "Water Conservation."
- Leda Hartman, writer, gardener, cook, musician, and swimmer: "Household Cleaners," "Clothing," "Batteries," "Other Household," "Appliances," "Transportation," and "On the Job."
- Richard Katzenberg, environmental businessman and advocate since 1974: "Environmental Investing."
- Steven S. H. McFadden, organic gardener, writer, and earth befriender: "Organic Yard & Garden."
- Steven Maviglio, writer who heats his home solely with wood and a little help from the sun: "Wood Heat."
- Tom Minnon, 15-year veteran of sunspace design and sales, energy instructor, and gardener: "Sunspaces."

- John Quinney, former Director, New Alchemy Institute: "Environmental Organizations."
- Barry Rhodes, data base management consultant and homeowner: "Radon."
- Wendy Smith, fanatical Recycling Coordinator, Southwest Solid Waste Management District of N.H.: "Recycling."
- Jay Stein, HVAC energy engineer: "Heating and Air Conditioning."
- Catherine Werth, mother and consultant for innovative ventures: "Education/Fun."
- Alex Wilson, energy specialist and writer, West River Communications, Inc.: "Lighting," "Environmental Construction," "Photovoltaics," and "Hydro Power."

Thank you to the many other contributors: Hank Huber, architect: "The Kitchen Recycling Center"; Rodger Martin, poet, writer, and teacher: "The Home That Happened to Be Solar"; Penny Uhlendorf, proprietor, Conservatree retail environmental store, Martha's Vineyard: numerous reviews; Johnny Weiss and Steve McCarney, teachers at Red Rocks Community College, Colorado, and solar masters for ten years: numerous reviews; Thelma Babbitt, living her beliefs for more than 70 years: miscellaneous lifestyle tips; Richard Crowther, architect: various contributions and support; and Suzanne Rametta, Amy Huckins, and Katrina Hall: product reviews.

Many thanks to all who pitched in at the last minute to help the rest of the team collect and identify photos: Anna Messa, Trisha Beattie, Robin Cook, Donna Wohlfarth, Sue Dunholter, and, of course, my mother, Sylvia Anderson.

Thank you, Ellen Klempner-Béguin, for giving me the idea for the name *Ecologue*, and to Joel Wollner, who gave it to you.

Many thanks to the dozens of people who tested various products, reviewed various chapters, passed along tidbits and suggestions, gave untold moral support, and promised to buy the book when it was done. (It's done . . .)

Many thanks to the hundreds of companies, environmental organizations, and other groups who cooperated with us by sending literature, product samples, and/or photos. We honor you for your commitment to working for a safe earth. We welcome others to join them and to send us the same for future editions of *Ecologue*.

Thank you to Sandy Taylor, who helped as literary agent and had confidence long before anyone else.

Many thanks to the team at Prentice Hall Press, particularly to Sheila Curry, my editor, who was always there when I needed her and always confident in the outcome.

Thank you to the many people at International Data Group, Inc., who helped directly or indirectly, especially Patrick J. McGovern, Chairman and CEO, who also helped to make International Environment Group, Inc., possible.

Finally, many thanks, reader, for buying *Ecologue* and for sharing the information with others. Even more thanks for living your life differently as a result.

Bruce Anderson, Editor

Contents

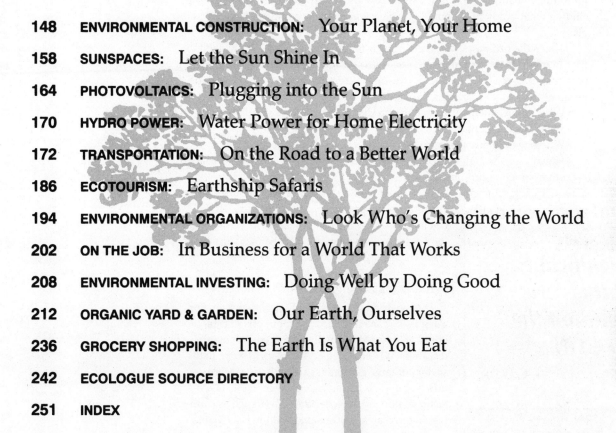

Who Says You Can't Change The World?

You, me, we — all five billion of us around the world — already have profoundly changed the world. Our thousands of individual daily actions — including what products we buy — are damaging the environment. None of us is blameless.

That's the bad news. The good news is that by changing our daily habits, we can improve the environment. *Ecologue* is designed to help us do just that. In particular it is designed to help us consume differently. Specifically it helps determine:

- What environmentally damaging products we no longer should buy
- What environmentally safe products we can buy instead
- Where we can buy these products
- How to see through some of the hype and exaggerated claims and be smart environmental consumers

> *Whatever you do may seem insignificant, but it is very important that you do it!*
>
> — GANDHI

We don't need to feel powerless because of the enormity of the problems; on the contrary, we can be empowered by the fact that, if each of us changed the world for the worse, we can change it again — positively — now that we know better.

What Does *Ecologue* Cover?

We've tried to include in *Ecologue* every major category of consumer products, but not all categories are created equal. Extensive environmental research has been going on for years in some fields, such as organic gardening; authoritative information is abundant there. But environmentalists are just beginning to explore other areas, such as clothing; in those areas far less information is available. The different lengths of the chapters reflect this.

How did we select the products? In essence, we asked ourselves whether the earth would be happy if the product in question were to be used by 10 billion people, which is what the global population could well be in 30 or so years. Would the earth smile, or would it frown? Would it laugh with delight, or would it have death spasms?

The actual process of deciding which products to include in *Ecologue* in many cases was easy and in others was neither easy nor scientific. Certain categories such as fuel-efficient cars and energy-saving devices are the easy ones. The fact that a car is built of plastic to make it lighter for getting better mileage was not a consideration in our evaluations because the benefits of the improved mileage vastly outweigh the disadvantages of using plastic. And it's easy to recommend composting and organic fertilizers over chemicals for your yard and garden, even if the organics are shipped in non-recycled packaging, although we noted this shortcoming when we could.

But it got tougher when selecting, let's say, a shampoo. Are its ingredients natural or man-made? Are the natural ingredients safe for people when they use the shampoo? For the environment when it's washed down the drain? Were the ingredients tested on animals? Was the shampoo? Is the manufacturing process environmentally sound? Is the shampoo packaged in a recycled or recyclable container? Is the company that makes it committed to improving the environment? (Does it recycle at its offices? Is its promotional material on recycled paper? Does it contribute to environmental causes?)

And oh, yes, does the shampoo work? We had people like you use many of the products we reviewed, and we eliminated some because they didn't work well enough.

Then, of course, there are the "two sides to every issue" questions that confuse us all and about which we are still learning. For example, had we published this book in 1989, we might have promoted biodegradable plastic. But we've learned enough so that *Ecologue* doesn't even include degradable diapers.

So we tried to ask all the right questions, and we got help from many excellent authors, reviewers, and other experts in making the final decisions about what to include and what to leave out. Are we always right? No way! We tried hard and did our best. Have we made mistakes in our selections? Absolutely! We hope they're not dangerous ones, and we eagerly welcome your scoldings . . . and your evidence.

We're objective, we hope. We don't sell any of the products; we care about people and about the earth.

Price? Yes, some environmentally safe products cost more, though we tried to stay away from pricey ones. But if you can afford to buy an environmental product that is more expensive than what you are buying today, we urge you to; there are too many people who can't afford to.

Fun? Of course. We chose some products for your enjoyment, some of them even tongue in cheek. We wanted to entertain, too, not just inform.

Society's knowledge about environmental products will continue to grow, manufacturers will make false claims, and you may often be confused about who's right. When you are, you may have to depend on your own judgment. If you do, just ask yourself if you think that the earth would be happy if the product in question were to be used by 10 billion people — would the earth smile, or would it frown? Would it laugh with delight, or would it have death spasms?

What It Took To Do This Book

A few words about the effort that went into making this book will give you a better sense of its strengths and weaknesses.

None of the 50 or so people who worked on this project commuted to a central office; all the work was done free-lance out of people's homes, saving precious resources and reducing auto emissions. Hooray for the telephone, fax, modem, mail, overnight delivery services, and yes, occasional car trips to deliver things or to talk. And computers saved countless trees in avoided paper shuffling, not to mention time and error.

The entire focus of everyone working on *Ecologue* has been on helping you, the reader, change your buying habits as well as other lifestyle habits. A lot goes into a buying decision. You don't necessarily want enough shopping information to earn you a Ph.D for having learned it; you just want to know which products to avoid and which ones to buy instead. You want to make sure that environmental product alternatives perform satisfactorily, that you can afford them, and that they're worth the price. And you want to know where to order them.

To achieve this, we started *Ecologue* by first creating a detailed outline of what we considered the ideal book. Then for several months we researched products, companies, and environmental information. We wrote to more than 600 companies, asking for product literature and product samples and photos. We followed up with further letters and phone calls. We commissioned 30 top-notch authors, sent them the material we'd collected, and worked with them in gathering additional information.

Other people tried, tested, and evaluated dozens of product samples while still others maintained the vast data base of information, compiled "What You Can Do" tips and the facts that are on the bottom of each page, collected photos and other art, and reviewed the written material for accuracy and clarity.

In the middle of all this, the tidal wave of change in products and companies hit us. Five years ago there might have been little or no change in product information, but today's news story can date yesterday's information, as it did many times during the final weeks of production.

How to Use This Book

Because of this constant state of change, some of this information may be wrong! To avoid frustration, we advise caution.

When you see a product you want to buy, find the company listed with the product or find a catalogue source mentioned in the same section. Turn to the Source Directory at the back of the book to find ordering addresses and phone numbers. They are listed by chapter; within each chapter grouping, they're alphabetical by company.

Call or write before sending money for a product. The product may have been dropped or the design may have been changed. The company may have moved or the price may have gone up. Ask about shipping and handling charges; they're usually extra.

If you find that the supplier we've listed no longer carries the product, ask who the manufacturer is. Contact the manufacturer directly for the name of another supplier. By doing this you and *Ecologue* are helping the company develop its distribution system, which is important if more and more people are to have easy access to these important products.

Write and let us know when you learn about a change in ordering information.

Talk to Me!

The best way for you to use this book is to talk to me. This is your planet and *Ecologue* is your book. I want to help you make the best possible decisions you can to help the environment.

- So if you need help, write me.
- If something is confusing, write me.
- If you need more information, write me.
- If you have some experience with any of the products or companies or lifestyle tips, write me.

Yes, there will be a new edition, not to replace this one but to supplement it. If you have ideas for new products, lifestyle tips, or facts that we should include, write me.

If you need a reply, please enclose a stamped, self-addressed envelope. I will write back!

Product suppliers, manufacturers, and creators: we cannot be bought, but we cheerfully welcome product samples, literature, and — a requirement for publication — high-quality black-and-white photos, preferably with people in them.

Closing Words

Am I writing this as an environmental saint? Hardly. I drive 30,000 miles a year in a 1983 car that burns gasoline and gets just 24 miles a gallon. To heat my house, which could be more energy efficient, I burn hundreds of gallons of oil each year and a couple of cords of wood. The electricity I buy is generated by coal, oil, and nuclear power. I separate my trash but buy two or three newspapers every day and subscribe to dozens of magazines. I'm trying hard to buy environmentally safe cleaning and personal care products, but sometimes it's just plain easier to buy the old-fashioned stuff off the supermarket shelves.

But I'm trying. A thousand-mile journey begins with the first step, the Chinese tell us. One foot in front of the other, I console myself.

There are those who say that consumerism is the real culprit of our environmental destruction, that we have to cut back fundamentally on our wasteful, greedy consumption patterns, and that a book like this does as much to promote consumption as it does to change our buying habits. There are others who argue that we can have it all — that we can keep consuming at the rate we have been as long as we change what it is we consume.

Both views are right. Both are wrong. And both miss the most important point.

The U.S. represents five or six percent of the world's population, yet we consume up to a third of some of its resources such as energy. In the next 30 to 40 years the world's population will double, to perhaps 10 billion. All of those people are going to want the economic fruits of freedom and democracy. The resulting strain on the world's resources is going to make today's problems seem like a Sunday picnic.

Unless. Unless we redefine what's important in life. Unless we can "love our neighbor as ourselves" — whether that neighbor be our immediate family or people on the other side of the planet. Unless that kind of caring means we also have the capacity to love the earth. Unless we take care of it now, so it will be there for our children and our grandchildren.

No, we cannot continue to buy the same products we've been buying if we are to save the earth; the products in this book represent alternatives that we can buy instead.

No, we cannot continue consuming at the same rates as we have been; we must cut back.

Yes, both of these changes *can* make a difference.

So love your earth — you can change it for the better if you do.

April 22, 1990
Bruce Anderson, President
International Environment Group, Inc.
71 Sargent Camp Road
Peterborough, NH 03458

P.S. If you'd like to receive two free *Ecologue/Updates*, full of late-breaking information about new environmental products, see page 246.

Editor's Choice Awards

Every product we've reviewed in this book is "environmentally safe." They all deserve recognition, and they all deserve our support as consumers. But not all of the products in *Ecologue* rank equally in terms of environmental safety. Here are the best.

— *Bruce Anderson*

HUG-A-PLANET

The first step in solving our environmental problems is to love the earth, and the second is to instill that love in our children. If you want the feeling of embracing the earth and want the same for your children, I recommend this soft fabric globe. It even seems to hug back. See pages 88-97 for other "love your earth" ideas.

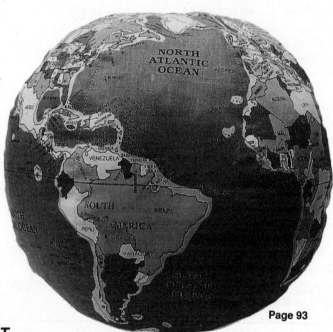

Page 93

COMPACT FLUORESCENTS

Twenty dollars for a light bulb? You've got to be kidding! The new compact fluorescent light bulbs cost about that but last ten times longer than ordinary bulbs and use one-fourth the electricity. The yearly dollar savings from buying fewer bulbs and less electricity is four to six dollars per bulb. Over its life, each bulb saves the combustion of 500 pounds of coal at a power plant.

SEVENTH GENERATION   **Pages 120-23**

HONDA CIVIC

No question about it: our single biggest environmental problem is the amount of energy we use, and the biggest villain on that front is the automobile. The easiest and most important thing any of us can do about the environment is to drive less and to substitute walking, bicycling, public transportation, and carpooling. But if we must drive, then the best thing each of us can do is to operate a more fuel efficient car — which saves money, too.

Some car companies are working on prototypes that get nearly 100 miles per gallon, but our favorite on-the-road winner is the Honda Civic CRX. Yes, the Geo Metro XFI gets better mileage (58 mpg on the highway versus 49 for the Civic), but our testers tell us that it does so at the expense of power (the engine is 33 percent smaller) and general handling performance.

Most cars dump roughly their own weight in carbon into the atmosphere every year. The Honda takes several years. And if you drive 15,000 miles, your annual gasoline bill will be about $320. That doesn't rank the Honda above trains, buses, bicycles, and foot power, but it's the next best thing.

Page 177

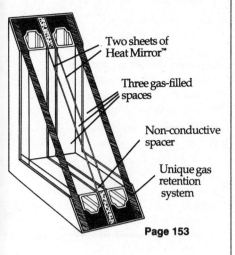

Two sheets of Heat Mirror™

Three gas-filled spaces

Non-conductive spacer

Unique gas retention system

Page 153

THE HURD INSOL-8 WINDOW

Windows are the big heat losers and gainers in any building. (They are also, of course, the simplest form of solar collector.) An ordinary, single-layer window's resistance to heat flow is measured as R-1. The new Hurd InSol-8 has an R value of 8. In other words, each square foot loses only one-eighth the heat of that same area in an ordinary single pane of glass. The reverse is true during air-conditioning weather; each square foot of the InSol-8 lets through only one-eighth the heat of a single pane.

In fact, these windows are so efficient that the days of small-windowed houses as the best means of saving energy are past. Instead, in almost any climate and facing in almost any direction, the InSol-8 lets as much light and heat into the house on a winter day as it loses back out at night.

PHOTOVOLTAIC CELLS

The big car companies are scheduled to introduce electric cars soon — a move that sounds promising until you realize that those vehicles will run on batteries that are recharged using ordinary electricity. If that electricity is generated by burning fossil fuels at power plants, these cars surely will not mean environmental salvation.

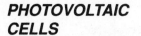

Pages 164-69

Solar cars, on the other hand, are covered with photovoltaic cells that absorb the sun's energy to recharge their batteries. I look forward to the day when my car can recharge itself, and when, if that's not enough, I can make up the difference using excess electricity generated by PV cells on my house — or, better yet, sell the excess back to the power company.

CLEAN PELLET FUEL

Besides solar energy, how else can we heat our homes without using oil, gas, and electricity? Try wood. Yes, wood. Modern stoves make wood heating environmentally clean, and pelletized fuel from pulverized wood makes it convenient. The advantage of pellets is that they can be fed into a burner automatically.

Our favorite wood pellet stove is the Whitfield WP-2 from Pyro Industries. It gives you the convenience of pellets with the ambience of a wood stove.

Page 147

JUST THINKING

"Examine each question in terms of what is ethically and aesthetically right, as well as what is economically expedient. A thing is right when it tends to preserve the integrity, stability, and beauty of the biotic community. It is wrong when it tends otherwise."

— *Aldo Leopold*

CAULK AND WEATHER STRIPPING

How could we leave out caulk and weather stripping? Most of our houses are so full of holes they're virtual sieves in terms of heating; just as fast as we pump heat into them, it leaks right out again. There is nothing you can do that is more cost effective for reducing heating and cooling bills than to thoroughly caulk and weather-strip. Page 113 covers some of my favorites among these products.

SUNFROST REFRIGERATOR

Our major appliances are energy guzzlers, and most so-called energy-efficient versions are only modest improvements over their conventional counterparts. The Sunfrost is the stellar exception.

The Sunfrost uses about one-fifth the energy of the old-fashioned rig in your kitchen corner. Is it magic? Nope. Just common sense — in the form of thicker insulation and *tight* door seals.

Page 229

© BAT CONSERVATION INTERNATIONAL

BAT HOUSES

There are few animals that more fully demonstrate how uncomfortable we are with nature — and how foolish this discomfort is — than the bat. And boy, can I relate to that! Like most other children, I had a couple of frightening experiences with bats flying around in the church basement or the bedroom. The thought of a bat flying into my face gave me the willies! Of course, as a grownup, I'm not afraid of bats, right? Wrong. I just don't show it.

But I've learned a lot about bats. The first is that they have extraordinary "radar," and the last thing they want to do — or will do — is fly into me. The second is that most bat species are voracious bug eaters — consuming up to 600 mosquitoes per hour.

Since I hate pesticides as much as I do mosquitoes, putting up a bat house to encourage these mammals to move into my neighborhood was irresistible.

The thought of a bat flying into my face still gives me the willies, but I know it will never happen. And I'm happy to overcome this unfounded fear, to help the earth by avoiding pesticides . . . and to reduce the mosquito population.

GROCERY TOTE BAG

"Which is better for the environment," I'm frequently asked, "paper bags or plastic?" The easy answer is paper. A good case can be made for plastic, too, but I'm still not convinced. In fact, neither is acceptable.

But it took me a long time to figure out how to avoid using either plastic or paper shopping bags. The fishnet, string bags from Europe collapse into a pocketbook for ready availability, but I'm afraid my toothpaste will fall through — and I don't carry a pocketbook! Besides, when I shop, I need ten bags sometimes and just one other times. Do I have to carry ten bags around with me? If so, how can I do that gracefully?

Page 33

I finally figured it out when Sayward Ayre sent me a grocery tote bag made by her company, Signature Art. Voilà!

Why did this tote zap me when others hadn't? Simple. It has an inside pocket that holds other bags, whether canvas, paper, or plastic. Now, the tote rides in my trunk at all times, so it's always there when I shop — for groceries or for anything else. I carry lots of bags in the pocket of this carryall and pull out whatever I need at the counter. And it's beautiful.

What would winners be without some losers? Here are my selections for top-ranked environmental disasters:

Styrofoam and Paper Cups

Why does tea taste so awful in a Styrofoam cup? Because some of the styrene has dissolved into the water — from either the heat, a chemical reaction with the tea, or both. For all that is said in defense of Styrofoam, the fact is that most of us already have styrene in our fatty tissue. We don't have the scientific knowledge yet to know the consequences of adding to that — and it may be decades before we know more.

So is paper the better alternative? Almost certainly, it is. Almost. Most paper contains dioxins from the bleaching process, although techniques are being developed to avoid this. Also, coated cups are very difficult to recycle.

The best solution, of course, is washables — glasses and coffee mugs. More and more churches, businesses, and homebodies are rediscovering the cost savings that come with avoiding both Styrofoam and paper. Next time you walk into McDonald's, bring your own mug. They *will* fill it up!

Turn to pages 30-37 to read more about these issues.

Toothpaste Pumps

Toothpaste pumps are prime examples of packaging gone awry — using too many resources to do the simple and effective job that tubes have done for years. And too much plastic! Not only can the tube be compressed for disposal, but it also contains at least 50 percent less packaging. So love tubes and avoid pumps. Or mix your own toothpaste with baking soda and a few drops of peroxide (recommended by dentists).

Throwaway Diapers

If you find someone trying to make an environmental argument favoring disposable diapers over cloth, have that person try to make the same case for disposable shirts, pants, dresses, socks, and underwear. It can't be done. With a diaper service, cloth diapers are no more expensive than disposables. Wash the cloth version yourself and they're cheaper and far more environmentally friendly than either the diaper service or the disposables. The big reason we can recommend cloth without apologies for inconvenience is the spate of new, innovative covers that have revolutionized the chore of changing cloth diapers. See pages 76-81 for details.

The Five-Gallon Flush

Few dinosaurs that remain with us from society's early development are more in need of fundamental change than our procedures for handling human waste. It makes no sense to go to the great environmental and financial expense of purifying and delivering five or more drinkable gallons of water to our homes only to have us flush it into a mammoth collection system that removes the waste at great environmental and financial expense.

A step in the right direction is the currently available array of low-flush toilets, each of which uses a gallon or so of water per flush. Favoring these units, individual states are beginning to outlaw the old-fashioned variety in new construction — but the next logical step is the composting toilet. It uses no water and turns the waste into usable compost. Yes, this may sound bizarre, but there was a time when flush toilets seemed pretty strange. Check out the modern alternatives on pages 106-09.

Plastic Beverage Containers

If your family is typical of most American households, beverage containers account for more than half of all the packaging you throw away. Only the glass and aluminum varieties are widely recycled.

The major obstacle to recycling plastic containers is that they are made of so many different kinds of plastic, and it's hard to tell them apart and to separate them for recycling.

So stick to glass and aluminum — and recycle! (Learn more about recycling on pages 16-41.)

Chemical Oven Cleaners

One of the most difficult cleaning jobs around the house is scrubbing out the oven. When we use souped-up chemical sprays, the fumes drive us from the kitchen. When we resort to self-cleaning ovens, their super-high temperatures mean super-high energy use.

I know it's hard to believe, but a shallow pan of ammonia sitting in your oven overnight will loosen the black carbon enough to let you wipe it off pretty easily. As a last resort, products such as Shaklee's At-Ease scouring cleanser do a great job without the fumes.

If we can accomplish this most difficult cleaning job without health threatening and environmentally damaging measures, we should be able to clean just about anything else more safely than we do today. See pages 42-49 for more clean earth product ideas.

Reuse It Or Lose It

W E SO OFTEN FEEL HELPLESS to do anything about ocean dumping, the depletion of the ozone layer, oil spills, and global warming. But there is no other action through which you and I can assert so direct and powerful an impact on the environment as in our buying and recycling.

The beauty of recycling is its simplicity. Throwaway materials are remade back into themselves. Some of these products can be recycled many times — a few, like aluminum, almost indefinitely. Recycling saves resources and energy, preserves land and wildlife habitat, decreases water and air pollution, and saves tax dollars.

What exactly can be recycled? Here are some ideas.

Aluminum Beverage Cans

Aluminum beverage cans are the success story of recycling. Because the conversion of raw aluminum (bauxite) takes an enormous amount of energy, 1.2 billion aluminum cans were recycled annually as long ago as 1972.

> *"Use it up, wear it out, make it do, or do without."*

By 1988 this had grown to 31 billion or over one-half of all aluminum beverage containers. The energy savings from avoiding the need to produce new cans is impressive — enough to supply the residential electric needs of the city of New York for six months.

But recycling only half is not good enough, particularly when aluminum cans are one of the easiest things to recycle.

Collecting aluminum cans is a wonderful activity for schools, churches, and Scout troops. There are about 27 aluminum cans in a pound, and prices have held steady at between 30¢ and 50¢ a pound. For this reason aluminum cans are the cornerstone of most recycling and litter collection programs.

To be certain that a can is all aluminum, test it with a magnet. If the magnet sticks, the can is *not* all aluminum and cannot be recycled with aluminum cans; it should be treated as a steel can.

Aluminum Foil and Pie Plates

Aluminum foil and aluminum pie plates are recyclable, but may not be included in your municipal program. Encourage your program

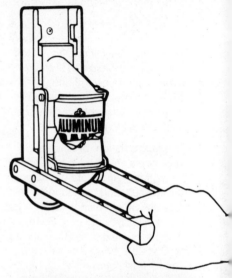

If all the aluminum beverage cans Americans throw away in one month were stacked on top of each other, they would reach to the moon.

WB RECYCLER™

An all-steel flip-top recycling bin for high traffic areas. Twenty-gallon can is 16"x29". You can stencil on the side the type of recyclable being collected. —W.S.

$49, Windsor Barrel Works

What You Can Do

✔ Learn to recognize the recycling logo and, whenever possible, buy those products that display it.

WINDSOR BARREL WORKS

TRASHCYCLE

The Trashcycle holds 2 trash containers and has a shelf for newspapers beneath. Contained in a sturdy, epoxy wire cabinet. Use at home or office, indoors or outdoors. Comes in 2 models for holding different-sized containers. Small (27"Lx 32"Hx19"W) holds up to two 11½"x 15"x24½" containers. Large (48"Lx35"H x24"W) holds up to two 21½"x29¼" containers. —W.S.

$99.95 Small; $119.99 Large; $35 Casters, Better Environment, Inc.

Before ordering from any mail order suppliers, please check with them to determine shipping and handling charges.

STEEL RECYCLING CART WITH PLASTIC BINS

These wheeled carts are available in 2- and 3-container versions. Each container holds approximately 24 gallons and is partially made of recycled plastic. Available in a variety of colors. Carts are adjustable and are constructed of tubular steel. Your order includes a choice of stickers to label the containers for different types of recyclables. May be more suitable for office than home use. —W.S.

Less than $200, White River Paper Co.

WHITE RIVER PAPER CO.

Every second we are losing an area the size of a football field through the cutting and burning of rain forests.

organizers to begin accepting these items; while recycling them is not as lucrative as recycling cans, there is still money to be made.

Aluminum foil items should be free of large amounts of food when you recycle, but they don't need to be spotless.

Steel Cans

Steel cans are used for staples such as soup, canned meat and fish, and pet food. During World War II cans were crushed and recycled by the millions for use in the war effort. Today steel can recycling programs are just beginning to take off, largely stimulated by promotion by the industry. Steel cans are actually coated with tin. When recycled, cans are de-tinned, and tin and the remaining scrap metal are recycled separately. Many scrap-metal dealers will now accept tin cans from municipal recycling programs. Typically, cans must be rinsed and labels removed. Crush them for more convenient storage and transport.

Glass

Glass was the predominant packaging material in the U.S. until very recently; now plastic has replaced it in practically every food and sundry line. Glass is made of sand, soda ash, and limestone, all of which are abundant resources. It is readily recycled back into itself and into fiberglass for insulation and construction.

Today 25 percent of the glass used to make containers is recycled. Glass recycling programs have been very successful, experiencing a 450 percent increase in the last ten years. Today over five billion glass containers, or 1¼ million tons of glass, are recycled annually in the U.S.

Glass recycling programs typically require that glass be separated by color. Caps and rings may have to be removed. Paper labels can be left on, but all plastic and polystyrene labels must be removed.

Paper

Most paper is made from virgin timber, whole trees that are cut down specifically to be turned into paper. This destroys wildlife habitat and reduces the number of carbon dioxide "sponges" (trees) available to help avert global warming. The bleaching process used to make paper white creates dioxins and other toxic materials. We will always need to cut some trees to make paper, but recycling most of the paper we use can significantly reduce the amount of forest we cut.

The best thing you can do to encourage paper recycling is to buy recycled paper; by doing this, you help to create the market for waste paper, which makes recycling pay for itself. Sometimes, however, recycled paper is not easy to identify. To find the real thing, look first for the fiber content. "Recycled paper" might be made from 100 percent recycled fiber, but it is far more likely that 40 to 60 percent of its fiber content is recycled; you need to ask what percentage the paper contains because too often the supplier will claim "recycled" when the percentages are lower than an acceptable 40 to 60 percent.

(All paper can't be 100 percent recycled because higher-quality papers require new wood. Many manufacturers contend that consumers desire the higher quality that the virgin paper ensures. Sometimes this may be true, but more and more people are finding that recycled paper is just fine for most purposes and that virgin paper is needed for far fewer purposes than they used to think.)

The second thing to look for is the origin of the recycled fiber. Some

Up to one million sea birds and 100,000 marine mammals are killed each year by plastic trash such as fishing gear and six-pack yokes.

HOME RECYCLING SYSTEMS

Recycling Kit No. 3 is a stacking system on wheels, with 3 stackable containers and a top tray to hold newspapers. This looks like an excellent, compact, and inexpensive setup for home recycling. The company is set up to work primarily with municipalities. 14"x17^1/$_2$"x30^1/$_2$". –W.S.

$19.96, Cancelor Corp.

WHAT IS RECYCLABLE?

What exactly is the potential for recycling in this country? How much of our trash could be recycled instead of going into landfills and incinerators? Here's how it all breaks down (figures are rounded).

The starred (*) items are commonly recyclable in municipal programs. Those marked with a dagger (†) are also recyclable, but are more difficult to market and so are sometimes not included in recycling programs.

	% of waste
ALUMINUM	
* Beverage containers	.8
Other packaging (plates, foil, misc.)	.3
Total Aluminum	**1.1**
STEEL CANS	
Food and beverage containers	1.6
Nonfood uses	.4
Barrels, drums	.1
Total Steel	**2.1**
GLASS	
* Beer and soft drink containers	3.5
* Food and other containers	4.0
* Wine and liquor	1.5
Total Glass	**9.0**
PAPER	
* Newspaper	8.0
* Office paper	6.0
†Mixed paper (magazines, junk mail, paperboard packaging)	15.0
* Corrugated cardboard	12.0
Total Paper	**41.0**
PLASTIC	
* Plastic food and household containers (laundry, motor oil, etc.)	1.8
Other plastic packaging (shrink wrap, polystyrene)	1.8
Miscellaneous plastic (toys, disposables)	3.8
Total Plastic	**7.4**
YARD WASTE FOR COMPOSTING	**18.0**
TOTAL, ALL OF THE ABOVE	**78.6**

In a recent Gallup poll nearly 90% of those polled were willing to pay more for environmentally safer products and packaging.

of it is virgin or "preconsumer" paper that comes from the floors of print shops and paper manufacturers and would otherwise be thrown away. It's great that such paper is reused, but to help push recycling forward, ask for paper that contains a high percentage of "postconsumer" or "minimum-impact" waste. This is paper that has been used and then recycled. It can be office paper, newspaper, magazines, paperboard, etc.

Once you've bought recycled paper, you can help the environment still more by continuing the recycling cycle — but here, too, all paper is not the same. It's important to distinguish among these kinds.

High-grade office paper. This is one of the most easily recyclable commodities, and the market for it is growing rapidly. White stationery, envelopes (without plastic windows), copier paper, index cards, white lined and notebook paper, ledger paper, and computer paper can all be recycled into paperboard, new office paper, construction paper, and protective paper packaging. Once you begin an office paper recycling program (see page 205), you will be amazed at how much less trash you have. Recycled office paper earns good money and reduces collection, hauling, and disposal costs.

Mixed paper. This is paperboard from cereal and other food boxes, shoe boxes, magazines, catalogues, and most junk mail. This is the largest single category of paper in household trash, but because of the glossy material and varying types of fiber included, it can sometimes be difficult to recycle. It can be remade into several kinds of paperboard and multilayer paper packaging, such as laundry detergent and cracker boxes, cones for yarn spinning, and forms for concrete construction.

Cardboard

In separating for recycling, cardboard refers only to heavy, double-walled (with an inner mesh) packing-box material, not light paperboard such as shoe boxes. This is one of the most sought-after recyclables; it can be incorporated into any company or municipal recycling program. (Most cardboard waste comes from businesses, not homes.)

A considerable amount of cardboard already is recycled; the amount will approach 80 percent by the year 2000. It is recycled back into itself and into other, similar types of paperboard packaging.

BURNING PAPER

It is environmentally safe to burn any of the following in your wood stove or fireplace:
• black and white newsprint.
• waxed paper (such as a bag from fresh bread or baked goods).
• white office and letter paper (including white, nonglossy pieces of junk mail).
• noncolored paperboard containers (such as from generic brands of baking soda).
• used white tissues and paper towels.
• used cotton swabs (if they have wooden or paper rather than plastic sticks).

• used white paper tampon applicators and wrappers.
• cardboard.

Other than newspaper, don't burn items listed above until the fire is relatively hot; wait until it's been burning vigorously for about half an hour.

Don't burn:
• glossy or colored paper (which release toxic heavy metals from the dyes).
• envelopes with windows (unless you know the windows are not plastic).
• any nonpaper or nonwood items, particularly plastic.

Americans throw away a total of 2.5 million plastic bottles every hour.

OLD NEWS BINDERY

The best (and the most expensive) of these products is made of naturally stained solid wood and has a handy spindle for the ball of twine. When it's full, just wrap the twine (which comes with it) around the papers, tie, and remove. You could make your own, but why bother at this price? Our biggest objection to it is the space it takes up, 14"Hx 15"Wx18"D. We also wish the twine were stronger. *–Bruce Anderson*

$35.95, including postage and handling, Seventh Generation **$29.95, Plow and Hearth Slightly different model, walnut finish, $28.95,** Gardener's Supply **Another variation is available from The Chef's Catalog**

SEVENTH GENERATION

BARGAIN BINDER

The real bargain is this clever 6-arm vinyl-clad steel wire rack that folds flat for shipping and storage. Comes in dark brown only and is compact, not much larger than the newspapers it holds. No place to conveniently keep twine and not really attractive or sturdy either, but it'll do the job fine. *–B.A.*

$6.98; 2 for $12.98, Lillian Vernon

LILLIAN VERNON

WHY RECYCLE?

When we recycle, we are:

- **decreasing our total volume of trash**
- **saving energy — in manufacturing, transportation, exploration, and excavation**
- **saving resources — trees, petroleum, metals**
- **saving land and wildlife habitat — reducing the need for new landfills and incinerators, excavating and deforesting fewer acres to tap resources, and reducing erosion**
- **conserving water (much less water is needed to produce products from recycled rather than raw materials)**
- **reducing air pollution (manufacturing emissions are significantly less using recycled materials).**

You can save a tree with each four-foot stack of paper that you recycle.

GETTING THE FAMILY INTO THE RECYCLING ACT

Involving your whole family in recycling — along with as many friends and neighbors as you can convert — is a great way to help them learn about their environment. Here are some ideas that worked for my family.

• Establish a special place for recyclables, one that doesn't take up much room and is out of the way. A closet-sized space is usually adequate.

• If space is limited or if your family is small, don't bother with separate containers for every recyclable. People in apartments, for example, may have one trash can for garbage and one for recyclables (labeled, of course). The recyclables are mixed together and separated at the recycling center or separated as you put them out at the curb.

• To create and sustain interest in recycling, get the whole family to make and decorate recycling containers. Get large cardboard boxes, packing crates, or pails. Then paint, crayon, or paste collages of gift wrap on them. Cut out holes on the sides and draw faces around them to make it easy for little ones to put things in the containers.

• Grab every chance to explain to others the energy and resource savings that result from recycling. One day at the post office I nearly attacked my postmaster as he tossed an aluminum can into the trash. "Don't you realize that you just threw out half a can of gasoline?" I exclaimed. The next day he handed me a small bag of aluminum cans over the counter.

• Don't give up! As a recycling radical living with a "lay" person, I've been repeatedly challenged by my husband's casual attitude toward this essential household duty. But he's coming around. Through recycling, composting, and smart shopping, we have reduced our trash to one paper grocery bag every two weeks. When my formerly blasé spouse saw the reduction in volume and realized that the recyclables were all going to be remanufactured, the battle was won.

• Relate recycling to whatever is meaningful. A child who loves birds will understand that there will be fewer of them if we continue to cut down trees they nest in instead of reusing waste paper. Someone who likes water sports or who fishes can appreciate the problems caused by plastic debris in a favorite lake.

— *W.S.*

What You Can Do About Aluminum

✔ Buy aluminum containers instead of glass or plastic.

✔ When you buy aluminum cans, try to purchase them in a cardboard or paperboard container (both of which are recyclable) rather than a plastic six-pack yoke.

✔ Encourage retail stores, offices, and snack shops to place aluminum can recycling bins next to vending machines. Kick off the program by earmarking revenues for an office party or outing.

✔ Suggest to retail, mall, and shopping center management that "reverse vending machines" be installed near exits and in parking lots. These machines accept aluminum cans and return money to the recycler. They also draw a lot of interest to shopping areas — a good selling point.

✔ Encourage the recycling of scrap aluminum — aluminum siding, gutters and downspouts, storm doors, window frames, and lawn furniture — at your local recycling center or through a scrap dealer. This material also fetches a good price; a construction-worker friend of ours buys his wife jewelry with the money he earns scrounging aluminum from job sites and dumpsters.

✔ Reuse your own aluminum foil as many times as you can. You can use it to store leftovers, to place at the bottom of a baking pan, and in lunch boxes ten to 15 times before it gets holes in it. Wash it along with your dishes and air dry.

About Glass

✔ Sterilize (by washing in the dishwasher or by placing in boiling water for 5 minutes) and save glass bottles and jars to store spices, flour, cereal, and grains. Kept in the refrigerator, these items can last for months.

✔ Use small glass jars to hold nails, screws, and other hardware.

✔ Buy glass instead of plastic when possible, whether it be packaging or kitchenware. In addition to being a better resource choice, glass is superior because it does not absorb its contents as readily as plastic — as anyone knows who's tried to microwave spaghetti sauce in a plastic container.

✔ Of course, in states that have bottle bills, take returnable bottles back to the store whenever possible.

About Newspaper

✔ Get into the habit of recycling your newspapers. Load them into paper grocery bags for stacking, or use a newspaper bundler (see the accompanying product reviews).

✔ Use newspapers as an excellent organic mulch in the garden. Simply lay sheets down around the base of plants to keep moisture in. Sprinkle crushed egg shells on top to keep cutworms and slugs away — they can't crawl over the sharp edges.

✔ Urge your local newspaper to switch to vegetable-based inks and to use recycled newsprint.

About Office Paper

✔ Make memo pads from discarded white paper that is blank on one side. Cut to size and then staple or put into small boxes.

✔ Try to limit your use of "stick-em"-type notes, which are colored and hard to recycle; go back to using old-fashioned paper clips.

✔ Reuse brown mailing envelopes. For use on the bottom of ours we have a stamp that says, "Please recycle this envelope by using it again."

✔ Shred your office paper and use it for packaging instead of polystyrene "peanuts." If you can't use it, offer it to local mail order companies.

✔ Urge your company and other businesses and utilities you deal with to stop using envelopes with plastic windows. The plastic makes it impossible to recycle the envelope in most high-grade paper recycling programs.

About Other Paper

✔ Locate local paper mills that will accept mixed paper. Although they usually will not pay you for it, it's worth recycling because of the sheer volume of material. Look in the Yellow Pages under "Paper" or "Paper Manufacturers."

✔ When you place orders by mail, apply for or receive a credit card, order a subscription, or donate to a charity, state clearly on the order blank, "Please do not give my name out to other mailing lists." Most companies and charities will honor this request.

✔ If there is a postage-paid return envelope with the junk mail solicitation, return it with your name and address crossed out and with "Please take my name off your mailing list" written on it. We know someone who, when confronted with a repeat offender, fills the postage-paid envelope to the brim with everything she can find to make it as heavy as possible.

✔ If a piece of unwanted mail says, "Address correction requested," ask your postmaster to return it to the sender at the sender's expense with the message that you wish to be removed from the list.

✔ Share magazine subscriptions. Give used magazines to nursing homes and hospitals, particularly if you don't have access to mixed paper recycling.

✔ Because it's easier to recycle, use white paper rather than colored paper.

Almost every Sunday morning my son and I head for the town landfill, slowly but surely becoming the town recycling center. I've noticed that 75 to 80% of our unpleasant cargo comes from the kitchen. Our friends report the same experience. It's clear that the kitchen is the number one target for solid waste reduction efforts. It's also the highest energy-use room in the house and thus has the greatest potential for energy conservation measures.

Here are some fun and profitable things you can do to turn your kitchen into an energy-efficient recycling center.

- Set aside a kitchen drawer for aluminum foil and plastic bags and wraps that you can use again. In the same drawer, keep a container of twist ties as well as new rolls of foil and plastic wrap for those occasions when reusables won't work. Reserve another drawer or pantry shelf for containers to be used for storing leftovers.

- If your state has a bottle bill, you may want to store returnables in sturdy cardboard boxes that can be easily taken to the store. Mud rooms, closets, and garages are good places to keep these.

- Divide your recyclables into the most common categories: glass bottles, plastic bottles, aluminum cans, cardboard, and newspaper.

- Avoid using a garbage disposal. Septic tanks and municipal wastewater treatment systems weren't intended to handle garbage.

- If you have a wood stove or fireplace, and if you can't recycle, consider burning any relatively clean paper rather than throwing it out with the trash. (See page 20.) Paper in landfills resists biodegradation, and if your community incinerates its trash anyway, you might as well get the heat benefit.

- If you prefer to store bulky newspapers and cardboard out of the kitchen, we've found that all you need in a separate location are baling twine and a simple wood box to put the recyclables in.

- Set up a mini recycling area, like the one in the illustration, that can fit into existing cabinets or a nearby pantry. If you

are building something new, try putting the lower buckets on pull-out slides or tilt-down doors hinged at the bottom just above the toe kick. The recycling buckets will work in a lower shelf area of a nearby walk-in pantry or an underused kitchen closet. If you diligently recycle, your "trash basket" won't have to be larger than the recycling buckets.

- Take the buckets from your household collection area directly to the recycling center or empty them into an intermediate, larger container outside the kitchen.

— *Hank Huber*

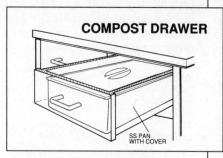

COMPOST DRAWER

SS PAN WITH COVER

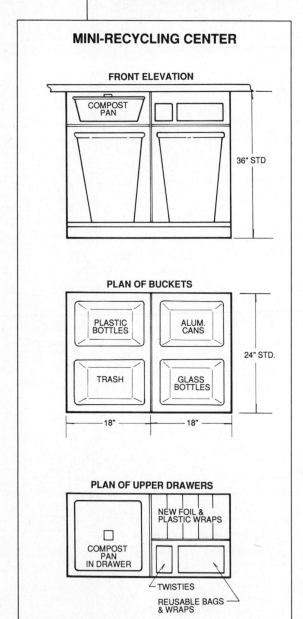

MINI-RECYCLING CENTER

FRONT ELEVATION

COMPOST PAN

36" STD

PLAN OF BUCKETS

PLASTIC BOTTLES

ALUM. CANS

TRASH

GLASS BOTTLES

24" STD.

18" 18"

PLAN OF UPPER DRAWERS

NEW FOIL & PLASTIC WRAPS

COMPOST PAN IN DRAWER

TWISTIES

REUSABLE BAGS & WRAPS

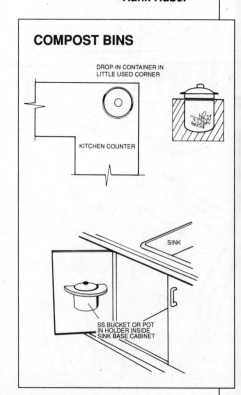

COMPOST BINS

DROP-IN CONTAINER IN LITTLE USED CORNER

KITCHEN COUNTER

SINK

SS BUCKET OR POT IN HOLDER INSIDE SINK BASE CABINET

TOILET TISSUE AND NAPKINS FROM RECYCLED PAPER

Toilet papers with artificial fragrance and colored dyes may irritate the sensitive areas they are supposed to clean and are toxic in the environment. Use only white, fragrance-free brands. Better yet, try unbleached varieties like those from Seventh Generation. The absorbency is the same, and as tester Mona Anderson reported: "It was hard getting used to brown toilet paper, but other than that, I can't tell the difference."–W.S.

PAPER SERVICE LTD.

This company manufactures 100% recycled paper products — all unbleached and all produced in an environmentally sound manner. Wastewater treatment, frequently a problem at paper recycling facilities, is accomplished through a series of water-treatment ponds that serve as homes to otters and ducks.

Top marks; good quality without being luxurious. Napkins are of institutional quality only, but highly absorbent and attractive. Toilet tissue is light enough in color to please; it is not, however, the soft quilted product available in the grocery store. Write for complete catalogue. –W.S.

100% unbleached toilet tissue: $6 for 12 rolls
Napkins: $11.25 for 10 pkg.

SEVENTH GENERATION

SEVENTH GENERATION

This mail order firm offers a full line of recycled paper products, including toilet tissue, facial tissue, dinner napkins, and stationery. It also carries office products such as copier and computer paper. Some of the products are bleached.

Seventh Generation has zoomed to the forefront of suppliers with a wide range of environmentally safe products. Product selection is becoming increasingly more environmentally discriminating. Catalogue is informative and helpful about environmental issues. The company gives 1% of gross sales to not-for-profit environmental groups. –W.S.

Toilet paper from 100% recycled paper: $7.50 (Sampler of 12 rolls)
Paper towels from 100% recycled paper: $6.95 (Sampler of 6 rolls)
2-ply facial tissue from 100% recycled paper: $6.75 (Sampler of 6 boxes)

PAPER SERVICE LTD.

H. T. BERRY CO.

This company distributes a full line of 100% recycled products, including toilet tissue, paper towels, boxed facial tissue, and napkins. All the paper used is recycled, mostly "postconsumer" (from consumers, not from industry). Sold by case only. One case toilet tissue is 96 rolls. One case paper towels is 12 rolls. Call for prices. –W.S.

Most of the plastic now being recycled comes from states with bottle bills.

SUCCESS STORIES: ONE VOICE IN THE WILDERNESS

In addition to rewarding companies whose packaging and products you approve of (through discriminating purchasing), take a minute to let a manufacturer know if something bothers you. I keep a package of recycled paper postcards in my top drawer for just such a purpose. Here are just two instances of success.

• Red Rose Tea began to manufacture tea bags with plastic, rather than cotton, strings. I halfheartedly wrote to them about this, never expecting results. A few months later the tea bags were on the shelves with cotton strings again. A note inside the package said that the change was made in response to consumer demand.

• In 1989 the *New Yorker* began arriving in subscribers' mailboxes in a plastic wrapper. This was a major bone of contention in our home, and I argued for cancellation. I lost the battle. In early 1990 it arrived in a plain brown wrap. A message on the inside from the CEO, Steven Florio, said the change had been made for environmental reasons.

Here's sample wording for a complaint letter:

Dear Mince Brothers:
I note with extreme annoyance that your lemonade, which has always come in a recyclable metal canister, is now being marketed in a plastic jar. I find this unacceptable. The increasing use of plastic for packaging is an enormous environmental problem. This change indicates your insensitivity to our solid waste crisis and is sufficient reason for me to no longer purchase your product.
Sincerely,

If enough of us make a commitment to buying for recyclability today, we can affect the decisions manufacturers will make tomorrow. — *W.S.*

YOU SHOULD KNOW

Reports in the *New England Journal of Medicine* show that certain foods, particularly those that are acidic or fatty, such as hot tea with lemon, actually cause foam cups and dishes to erode into the food itself, from which the foam enters your body tissue.

What You Can Do

✔ If you drink soda, choose recyclable aluminum or glass instead of plastic one-liter bottles.

✔ Switch brands of ketchup, maple syrup, or cooking oil if your favorite companies begin to package in plastic.

✔ Substitute paper bags for plastic garbage bags. See the product reviews in this section.

✔ Bring your prescription bottle back to the pharmacy for refilling, rather than taking a new one.

✔ Take your cardboard boxes to local mail order businesses if they can use them.

✔ Ask your grocer if he returns his cardboard to the distributor (many do) and if he would be willing to take cardboard from his customers. If your grocer does not recycle cardboard, let him or her know the savings to be achieved from not having it hauled away with the trash, plus the money that can be earned from recycling.

✔ Try to establish a cooperative system of recycling among retail stores and businesses.

✔ If your local recycling center accepts cardboard, flatten it before turning it in. If your center doesn't accept cardboard, encourage it to.

✔ Encourage your workplace to buy recycled products for packaging.

Thirty-five percent less water pollution results from producing recycled paper compared to non-recycled paper.

RECYCLED WRITING AND OFFICE PAPER

EARTH CARE PAPER

This company offers a very large line of writing papers, gift wrap, greeting cards, lined writing pads, and postcards, plus children's books and games. We have ordered from this company for years and think it is the best around. Products are of top quality, attractive, and competitive with traditional brands. Some are 100% recycled (Minimum Impact), but most are only partially of recycled materials. Samples are available. We have used Earth Care's

Christmas cards, postcards, gift wrap, and high-quality stationery. Not only are the products and service excellent, but the company devotes finances, catalogue space, and effort to environmental education about saving the planet. Service and environmental attitude are exceptional.

Earth Care products are sold through other catalogues, including Co-op America, as well as their own. See pages 31 and 202 for reviews of specific Earth Care products. –W.S.

CONSERVATREE PAPER CO.

Conservatree is a unique organization whose goals are both to sell recycled paper products and to act as an environmental advocate to develop recycled paper markets. Although it is a profit-making company, a considerable amount of its income is devoted to working with paper mills to develop new products using more postconsumer paper waste, to developing nationwide recycled paper markets, and to helping write legislation for pro-recycled procurement guidelines. It strives continually to change its product line to offer the most environmentally sound paper available.

Conservatree sells to wholesale customers only, with a minimum order of $100. The product line consists of text and cover printing papers (for brochures, letterhead, and business cards), copy paper, bond and rag bond (for letterhead), computer paper, plain envelopes, and envelopes with glassine, rather than plastic windows. (Glassine is a recyclable wood-fiber product.) Most of their products, including the glossy papers, are identical to virgin paper in appearance and texture.

Conservatree has some regional distribution arrangements with several companies nationwide. Contact Conservatree directly for a source near you. –W.S.

RECYCLED PAPER COMPANY, INC.

Recycled Paper Company offers a full line of copier paper, stationery, envelopes, computer paper, and printing paper sold only in cartons to retailers in the Northeast. This is an excellent firm with a good reputation and a commitment to the environment. Stationery is competitive in both price and quality with even the deluxe grades of virgin stock. –W.S.

At least one state (Maine) has outlawed juice boxes altogether because they can't be recycled.

HELP FIGHT DEADLY DIOXINS

When paper mills bleach wood pulp, they discharge tons of toxic materials into waterways. The best known of these are dioxins, a by-product of paper making and among the most dangerous of cancer-causing substances.

Dioxins cause birth defects, cancer, and immunological problems. Dioxins poison the fish and birds that live downstream from paper mills. Those same poisons are also present in the bleached paper products themselves, including diapers, sanitary napkins, paper plates and cups, toilet paper, coffee filters, and office paper.

To avoid dioxins in recycled paper, look for brands that haven't been bleached.

What You Can Do

✔ Rather than wait for Uncle Sam to recycle unwanted junk mail, become your town's postal recycler. I have observed that much of this material never even comes home but is discarded by postal box patrons right at the post office. I keep three or four large heavy-duty boxes available near the public boxes, then transfer the contents on my weekly trip to the recycling center. Think of the impact if this practice were adopted in every post office in the country.   — H.H.

TRASH BAG ALTERNATIVES

DANO ECOLOBAGS

Ecolobags are *the* alternative to plastic garbage bags. Made of 2-ply, heavy-duty (50-pound) brown kraft paper, they are known as "wet-strength" bags, meaning they can stand up to rain and snow for up to 2 weeks. These bags are actually much sturdier than plastic bags, which can be easily pierced by roving animals or by a wayward twig or tin can. They are self standing, with a square, gusseted bottom, so no garbage can is required. Capacity is 30 gallons or 50 pounds, and they are appropriate for recyclables, household garbage, and yard waste, such as leaves and grass clippings. Ecolobags have been used for 18 years by Brookhaven Township, New York, in its leaf collection programs and are widely used by other municipalities. Made of 100% wood fiber and biodegradable in 9 to 14 months, they measure 16"Wx12"Dx35"H.

This 20-year-old company has worked hard over the years for the passage of good environmental laws. Its goals are more ecological than financial. Companies such as this deserve our support. –W.S.

$30 for 50 bags
Dano Enterprises, Inc.

DANO ENTERPRISES, INC.

PAPER TRASH BAGS

What's 3 feet tall, holds 30 gallons, is made of paper, and is 100% biodegradable? The most environmentally versatile trash bag on the market today! Big enough to line a standard trash can, strong enough to withstand all kinds of rubbish abuse, these heavy-duty, wet-strength paper bags can tackle a multitude of cleanup jobs. No more fighting to keep the bag open as you stuff in the leaves, and no more 200 plus years to degrade where you dump it. "It's sturdy and waterproof, and I'm not adding any more plastic into the ground," says tester Marion Burke, who is using the 30-gallon trash bags for her weekly rubbish collections. (I'll second this! –B.A.) Also in 8- and 13-gallon sizes. –Penny Uhlendorf

$9.95 for 20 (30-Gallon)
Seventh Generation

SEVENTH GENERATION

BAGIT

This is a wonderful idea and a great alternative to plastic. Woven polypropylene bags (yes, petroleum based, but using much less material and permanent) have drawstrings and hold about 25 gallons of material. They slide onto a holding rack made of wood and vinyl-covered metal. Racks come in floor models or wall-mounted ones. The bags are very sturdy and washable, and stand up well to the elements.

These bags are suitable for use in the home, placed at curbside, and for office waste (placed next to the copier or wastebasket). They are the mainstay of many curbside recycling programs nationwide. Available in 1- and 2-bag versions for freestanding and wall-mounted models. –W.S.

Regular 3-oz. Bags:
$1.35
Heavyweight Bags:
$2.50
Freestanding Holders:
$12.95
Wall-Mounted Holders:
$5.95
The Bag Connection, Inc.

ONCE IS NOT ENOUGH
RECYCLE

What You Can Do

✔ When shopping, don't bag large items, such as paperboard containers of sodas or dog food, but place them right into the car.

✔ Suggest to your grocer that a stand be set up just inside the store entrance where people can return bags for others to use.

✔ Alternatively, suggest that your grocer sell tote bags, as many chains have started doing.

✔ Don't hesitate to say, "Thanks, but I don't need a bag," if you're buying a greeting card, a magazine, or other small thing.

More than 100,000 gallons of diesel fuel spilled in the Antarctic last year.

Plastic

This has been the wonder material of the last 20 years; no other single substance has made such enormous changes in virtually everything we buy and use. Plastic has made many innovations and extraordinary accomplishments possible — in medicine, aerospace technology, household appliances, and more. In a discussion of the serious problems of solid waste and environmental pollution, however, plastic must take center stage.

The virtues of plastic in other areas are precisely what make it inappropriate as a packaging material. It is light, permanent, and virtually indestructible. But the essential concept behind packaging is convenience and a brief lifespan — the opposite of plastic's eternal durability.

There are several reasons why we should reduce our use of plastic:

- It is a petroleum product. Petroleum is a non-renewable resource that is most urgently needed for such necessities as heat and transportation. It's dangerous to transport (1989 was the "Year of the Oil Spill"), and its use sustains an unhealthy American dependence on volatile foreign markets.

  Of course, the best example of the flip side of this argument is in the auto industry. The principal reason that cars get better mileage today is their lighter weight — a result, primarily, of the replacement of metal with plastic. The savings in gasoline use and auto emissions more than offsets plastic's other drawbacks.

- Plastic creates hazardous waste when manufactured and again when burned in incinerators.

- A glass bottle can be recycled back into a new glass bottle. A plastic bottle can be turned into part of a fencepost, a flowerpot, carpet backing, fiberfill for sleeping bags, etc. — all better ends than throwing the stuff away. But it can't be recycled back into a new plastic bottle. So recycling that plastic bottle doesn't eliminate the environmental costs of creating new plastic bottles.

- Many plastic containers look alike but actually are made of different kinds of plastic or layers of different plastics. The resulting mix cannot be "same-use" recycled. For example. . .

  HDPE (high-density polyethylene) plastic is solid colored or opaque white (you can't see any light through it). It typically holds soap products or bleach. Milk, water, and cider jugs are the only non-opaque plastic also in this category.

  P-E-T (polyethylene terephthalate) plastic is used exclusively to package soda.

  These two types of plastic can be recycled and are worth money. However, it takes an enormous amount of plastic to make a ton, the minimum amount most recyclers will accept. This makes storage at recycling centers a problem.

What You Can Do

✔ Ask your takeout restaurant to wrap your burger in paper, rather than in an elaborate plastic foam clamshell.

✔ If you patronize a local coffee shop or are on the road a lot, take your own mug.

✔ When grocery shopping, avoid using plastic bags for your produce. Take your purchases right to the checkout and load them onto the counter loose. Bring along your own bag, or ask for a paper one.

✔ Reuse your plastic shopping bags; turn them into trash can liners, laundry bags, freezer bags, moisture-proof travel bags, lunch bags, or beach bags.

✔ At the deli counter, request that prepared meats and cheeses be wrapped in old-fashioned butcher paper, which is still used for wrapping fish at most counters.

✔ Bring back your deli containers to be refilled with salads.

✔ Instead of plastic wrap, try a shower cap (nicely covers leftovers or a pitcher of juice); a piece of cloth held on with an elastic band or ribbon; glass refrigerator containers with lids; or waxed paper. If you must use plastic, use permanent plastic containers with lids.

✔ Avoid plastic foam completely. Polystyrene is non-biodegradable, and many kinds still contain ozone-damaging chlorofluorocarbons.

In 1987 alone, the United States produced more than 50 billion pounds of plastic.

CELLULOSE STORAGE BAGS

These environmental alternatives to plastic bags are made entirely of plant fiber and are fully biodegradable and compostable. They contain none of the carcinogens found in plastic bags that can leach into your stored food. They may not be strong enough for all uses, but where strength is not critical, they offer the same storage and convenience benefits as plastic. –W.S.

SEVENTH GENERATION

BORN-AGAIN BAGGIES

Now you can bag your sandwiches and store leftover food without adding to the mountain of plastic trash that's already in our landfills. These food storage bags are made from cellulose, the chief component in the cell walls of plants, which has been used to make paper for almost 2,000 years. These bags are strong, waterproof, and transparent and totally disintegrate in 1 to 3 years. Twist ties are included. –*Leda Hartman*

$18.50 Food Bag Economy Pack (100 sandwich, 50 freezer), including postage and handling Seventh Generation

ECCO BELLA CELLULOSE BAGS

This company offers cellulose bags in sandwich sizes and storage sizes (large enough to cover leftovers or a small loaf of bread). The bags are brittle in texture, but quite sturdy and stand up well.

Ecco Bella donates 20% of its profits to environmental groups. It has given us excellent service, and its commitment to the environment is impressive. –*W.S.*

$4.50 for 50 sandwich bags; $6 for 50 storage bags Ecco Bella

EARTH CARE PAPER, INC., CELLULOSE BAGS

Its cellulose bags come in spice, sandwich, bread, and product sizes. We purchased some for bagging bulk foods in our food co-op and found they could not stand up to weight of any magnitude. However, this was beyond their intended use, and they will likely perform well in your home. The company is an excellent one. –*W.S.*

$8.50 for 100 sandwich bags with ties; $15.80 for 100 product bags with ties, Earth Care Paper, Inc.

One Sunday edition of the *New York Times* requires the equivalent of over 63,000 Douglas fir trees.

What You Can Do About Grocery Shopping

✔ Whenever possible, purchase foods and other supplies in bulk to avoid excessive packaging.

✔ If you can, store bulk purchases in a walk-in pantry. A cool, dry basement storage area also works for less frequently used supplies.

✔ Store many bulk-purchased food items such as grains, noodles, and beans in clear glass or plastic containers. Displaying them on open shelves or behind clear glass doors in full view can add to your kitchen decor.

✔ Buy eggs in paper rather than foam containers.

✔ Ask your grocer to consider using paper rather than foam trays for meats, carryout trays, and cakes.

✔ Don't buy individually wrapped cut melons, cubed cheese, or other so-called "convenience" items.

✔ Don't buy disposable razors, batteries, diapers, and flashlights. They hurt the environment more than they help you.

✔ Buy juice in concentrate rather than in plastic or cardboard containers. It is much less bulky and much less expensive. (I just wish that concentrate containers were of just one material for easy recycling! — B.A.)

✔ Purchase butter or margarine in sticks, rather than in plastic tubs, and in boxes that are waxed paper, not foil covered.

✔ See pages 236-41 for more grocery-shopping tips.

About Packing Lunches

✔ Instead of plastic sandwich and storage bags, use cellulose bags, which are made entirely from plant materials and are biodegradable.

✔ Resist buying the individually boxed juices that come with straws. These contain paper, plastic, foil, and wax, making them completely unrecyclable. Use an old-fashioned Thermos or pack aluminum cans or individual serving-size glass bottles.

✔ Use a metal lunch box or canvas bag instead of paper bags or plastic lunch boxes.

About Cooking

✔ Avoid single-serving, cook-in-a-disposable-dish-or-bag food. If you're in a hurry, make sandwiches, spaghetti with bottled sauce, casseroles with noodles and soups as a base, or any number of other quickie meals.

✔ If you have a family that won't be satisfied with the above, cook ahead in large quantities, if possible, and store in the freezer.

CARRY-ALLS

Reusable bags are the classic answer to disposables. Instead of taking new bags each time you go to the store, bring your own tote. Fill it with additional bags. It's permanent, washable, and far sturdier than any retail carryout bag. After using carry-alls for over 15 years, the one design characteristic that we would particularly look for is a gusset, a square-stitched portion at the base and sides that helps the bag to stand up by itself. This makes bagging much easier and eliminates the need for a paper bag insert, which defeats the purpose. –W.S.

THE SHOPPING BAG DILEMMA

When faced with a choice between paper and plastic bags at checkout time, which should the environmentally conscious shopper choose? Is the answer plastic, which uses 1/3 the energy used in making paper bags and which produces far less sulfur dioxide, carbon monoxide, and hydrocarbon emissions when it's made? Or is it paper, which comes from a renewable source and breaks down quickly in moisture and sunlight but which, nevertheless, we discard as waste?

The best solution is neither of the above. Get into the earth-friendly habit of taking your own cloth or string bags with you. Choose canvas or woven string bags, or return to the store with your used paper or plastic bags.

Every glass bottle or jar on the supermarket shelves contains at least 20% recycled glass.

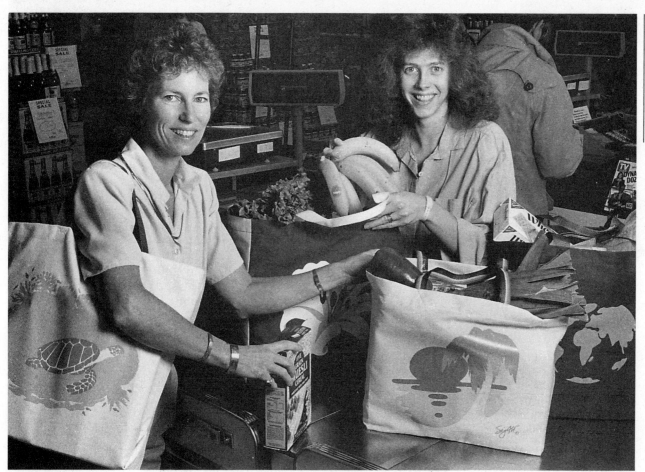

SIGNATURE ART

SIGNATURE ART TOTES

This is a one-woman cottage industry in Vermont that makes For-the-Earth bags from 100% canvas. They are all-around totes designed specifically for grocery and clothes shopping; each has an interior pocket large enough to hold 6 to 8 folded brown paper bags. Four sizes. The designer researched shoppers' preferences and found that the larger sizes were preferred for groceries; they hold as much as a grocery-sized bag, without crushing the contents.

These bags are absolutely beautiful, multicolored with silkscreened designs that celebrate nature and the earth. They're very well made, sturdy, and washable with leather strip handles for easy carrying. Quantity orders can be imprinted with your group's logo. Ten percent of profits are donated to environmental groups. –W.S.

$14.95 large; $11.95 small
Signature Art

What You Can Do

✔ When ordering by mail, request right on the order blank that your purchase not be packaged in plastic foam products, either peanuts or sheets. Ask the company to contact you if they can't accommodate the request.

✔ When shipping a package yourself, use shredded newspaper, computer paper, or molded pulp paperboard for cushioning.

Surely we can give as well as take, recycle and return as well as consume.

What You Can Do

✔ If you wash dishes by hand, wash your recyclables last. They don't have to be spotless, just considerately clean. A stiff vegetable brush with a handle is useful for this task. Or run recyclables through the dishwasher with your dishes.

✔ Keep a separate small dish drainer (we found ours at a yard sale) off in a corner of the sink and use it just for recyclables. An old refrigerator rack works well, too. When items are dry, take the entire drainer into the sorting area and separate the recyclables there.

✔ Instead of paper towels, use newspaper to wash windows — no streaks! — and to line the cat box.

✔ To reduce your use of paper, use rags for cleaning instead of paper towels; they are free, more absorbent, and cost just pennies to wash.

✔ When you need a sponge, try a cellulose variety, made from natural plant extracts.

✔ Use cloth napkins instead of paper.

✔ Use handkerchiefs instead of tissues. Keep a small stack of them in a basket next to the bed or chair.

✔ Use cloth dishtowels instead of paper ones.

✔ Use vinegar instead of fabric softener in the final laundry rinse.

✔ Clean windows with alcohol, vinegar, or ammonia.

✔ Clear a clogged drain with baking soda, vinegar, salt, and boiling water.

✔ Keep a sturdy dish towel inside the cabinet door under the sink to clean up spills and wipe hands.

✔ At church and community gatherings, use an assortment of mugs instead of paper cups. You can find them for pennies at local thrift stores.

✔ Buy toilet tissue individually wrapped in tissue paper rather than in large plastic bags.

✔ See pages 42-49 for additional cleaning tips and for environmentally safe cleaning products.

YOU SHOULD KNOW

Even substances that are biodegradable have a tough time degrading. Dr. W. Rathje, a garbage "archaeologist," has found thirty-year-old landfilled newspapers that are still perfectly legible!

BIODEGRADABLE: IT'S NOT

"Biodegradable plastic." There simply is no such thing. In fact, the idea has been denounced as a sham and a marketing ploy by scientists and environmentalists alike, including Greenpeace and the Natural Resources Defense Council.

Biodegradation is nature's way of returning materials to soil, sand, and other natural earth elements. But the term has been grossly misused, and it has no legal definition. As a result, anyone who wants to call something "degradable" or "biodegradable" can do so with impunity.

"Biodegradable plastics" are made of plastic molecules that are interconnected with a natural, biodegradable additive, such as cornstarch. However, once this additive degrades, millions of plastic particles remain. These are sometimes referred to as plastic dust, and they pass intact into soil and water, where they are eaten by bacteria and wildlife and pass into the food chain.

Plastic products labeled "biodegradable" actually contain five to ten percent more plastic than traditional versions; in order to maintain the strength necessary for bags, they have to compensate for the poorer bonding abilities of the natural additives. Besides, only six percent of a "biodegradable plastic" bag is the additive; the other 94 percent is plastic.

Meanwhile, what should you do? Try to avoid using plastic. But if you can't get by without it, stick with the traditional "nondegradable" type.

STRING BAGS

These collapsible knit bags have been used for hundreds of years in Europe. Suitable for all kinds of purposes, they stretch beyond one's imagination, yet shrink conveniently into a pocket or handbag when idle. They are now widely available at upscale houseware and gourmet stores nationwide. –W.S.

FISHNET SHOPPING BAGS

Fresh from France in several color choices, these versatile bags may be used for shopping, picnics, gathering vegetables — even carrying a basketball. As much as I objected to carrying a string bag as a teenager growing up in England, it's great to see its comeback and contribution in the fight to save the environment. –P.U.

$3.95 each, Nichols Garden Nursery
4 for $21.95, including postage and handling, Seventh Generation

SEVENTH GENERATION

JETTISON THE JUNK

One of the best ways to cut down on wasted paper is to reduce the volume of junk mail you receive. Write to the Mail Preference Service (c/o Direct Marketing Association, 11 West 42nd Street, P.O. Box 3861, New York, NY 10163; 212-689-4977). Send them all the different ways your name and address are printed on mailing labels; better yet, send the labels themselves. Do this every few months if you need to. The organization is pleasant to work with and claims as high as a 75 percent reduction in junk mail.

What You Can Do

✔ Instead of buying spray cleaners, buy one sturdy spray bottle, such as one for misting plants. Mix one part soap to three to four parts water, and use as you would the more expensive, chemically laden cleaner.

✔ Don't start using plastic bags again when your recycling center begins accepting them. Recycling is the best answer to what to do with your trash, but it's far more important not to bring the plastic into your home in the first place.

✔ Check labels on aerosol cans. VCR head cleaners, boat horns, spray string, photo-negative cleaners, and drain plungers are still allowed to contain the most dangerous CFCs. Although labeling is not required on these products, many do state whether they contain CFCs.

The paper industry is the largest single industrial user of fuel oil and the third largest consumer of energy in the U.S.

KITCHEN COMPOSTING

Kitchen composting can cut your trash by up to 30 percent. Some friends of ours swear by their covered bucket that sits in a hole in the counter. When it gets full of kitchen scraps, they lift it out and take it to the compost pile or to a galvanized bucket in the shed. Then, when that's full, they empty the bucket into the compost. Other people use a shallow pan in a drawer under the food chopping counter.

A stainless steel container doesn't absorb smells as plastic does, but if the lid is tight, it really doesn't matter. You might ask a local restaurant for a free pail with a lid. The restaurant will be pleased to have you take the container, and you'll know it's safe to use because it's held pickles, ketchup, etc.

A more complicated scheme uses a steeply inclined tube that runs from the counter, or from some other spot in the kitchen, directly into a compost pile located outside, right next to the kitchen. Keeping the tube clean and sealed against the weather are some concerns about this approach.
— *H.H.*

JUST THINKING

"The 'degradable' point is largely moot. Landfills are technologically engineered tombs that will not allow anything to degrade, including grass clippings."

— *Edward J. Stana, executive director of the Council on Plastics and Packaging in the Environment*

What You Can Do

✔ If you have a wood stove, save some of the ashes in a pail to place around tender seedlings in the spring; slugs don't like to cross a line of ashes.

✔ Add wood ashes to your compost pile, too.

✔ Save other wood ashes for traction on slippery walks and driveways in the winter. They have none of the chemicals, harmful to plant life and groundwater, that are found in rock salt.

✔ Set up a flea market/exchange at your refuse or recycling dropoff center, or make arrangements to use a small room at the fire house, town hall, church, or school. This will not only be a great way to exchange books, clothes, kitchen items, and furniture, but will become a gathering place as well.

✔ Locate a handy retired person who's interested in repairing bicycles and small appliances. Set up a system where these broken items are brought directly to this individual; after fixing, the repair person can sell the merchandise for a modest sum or give it to charity. (Enlist the help of local churches and senior citizens to get started.) Through a program in our area, bicycles are repaired and sent to Nicaragua.

✔ Reuse clear plastic takeout trays (clamshell variety, such as those from salad bars) as minigreenhouses to start seeds. Fill with soil starter, plant, place in a warm and sunny spot, and return in a week or so. Your seeds will have sprouted and can then be transferred to larger containers.

✔ Use plastic liter bottles in a similar way: Pull off the solid-colored bottom portion. Take the clear bottle portion and cut off the lower two or three inches. Stick the top portion back inside the solid-colored bottom and plant as above.

✔ Try paper or plastic berry trays for plant beds. Place soil-filled and planted trays inside a plastic bag or waxed paper, then seal. Old dry-cleaning bags are excellent for this.

✔ Use plastic milk and water jugs to cover and protect tender young plants in the garden. Cut off the bottom inch or so, and place firmly into the soil around the plant. Leave cap off. Remove if temperature gets above 60 degrees.

✔ Use old pantyhose to stake up tomato, pepper, and other non-bush plants. They will hold plants firmly without cutting into the stems.

FOR FUN & HOME FASHION

MOTION MUGS

Granite Lake Pottery is a small, two-person pottery works. Its Motion Mugs are beautifully crafted and perfect for setting on car dashboards, seats, or floors. The bottom of each is flat; the lid, flip-top and secure. There is no lead in the paints, service is excellent, and packaging is recycled and environmentally aware. Use these instead of polystyrene or paper takeout cups. Most restaurants and coffee shops will be pleased to fill them for you.

I bought one of these for my husband, who uses it every day and absolutely loves it. He says the mug stands up to even the bumpiest winter driving. –W.S.

$9 with lid; $8 without
Granite Lake Pottery

DESIGNER SHADES

This company makes floor and table lamps using designer shopping bags as shades. Suitable largely for contemporary uses. Featured in *Omni* magazine, these are sure conversation pieces. –W.S.

Prices start at $195
American Things

GRANITE LAKE POTTERY

YOU SHOULD KNOW

Recycling two weeks of daily newspapers saves the equivalent of one full-grown tree. Recycling one ton of newspapers saves 17 trees, 7,000 gallons of water, and 4,200 kilowatt hours of energy, enough to power the average home for six months.

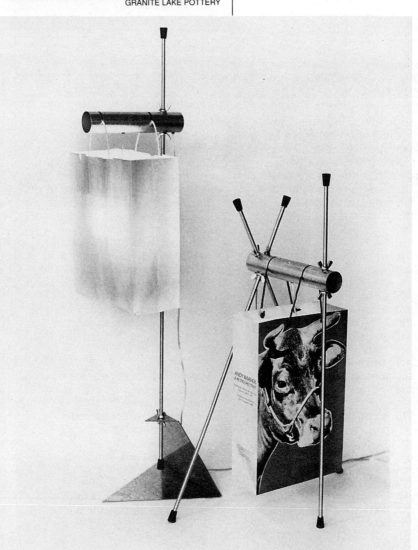

Household Hazardous Waste

Most people think hazardous wastes are primarily produced by industry. However, many things that we all have in our homes, workshops, and garages are just as hazardous as industrial wastes. They include oven cleaners, nail polish remover, auto products like motor oil and transmission fluid, and paint — all of which should be used and disposed of with care. Pouring these toxic substances down the drain or throwing them away with your household trash can contaminate drinking water and kill helpful organic microorganisms in septic systems.

Inappropriately dumped into landfills, household hazardous wastes leak into soil, into groundwater, and ultimately into our water supplies. They can also come into contact with other reactive substances and lead to possible ignition and corrosion. Some produce dangerous emissions when burned in a refuse incinerator.

It All Comes Around

In the end, no matter what the substance, the rule is the same: If we don't buy it, if we don't use it, or if we recycle it, it won't be manufactured and it won't become trash. It's that simple.
—*Wendy Smith*

What You Can Do

✔ Use a rechargeable flashlight to avoid disposing of batteries and thus releasing toxic heavy metals such as mercury and lead into the environment.

✔ Keep a small container of used motor oil to coat and protect the surfaces of metal, instead of virgin oil. Or try beeswax.

✔ Use castor oil or mineral oil as a lubricant on hinges, doorknobs, and latches.

All company addresses and phone numbers are listed in the Ecologue Source Directory beginning on page 242.

HAZARDOUS WASTE: HANDLE WITH CARE

- Never place hazardous waste in unlabeled containers or repackage hazardous waste in containers whose shapes suggest the contents are edible. Children have died from drinking substances that were stored in empty soft drink bottles.

- Do not mix hazardous-waste products.

- Try to use up all of a hazardous product before you throw the container away. It's safe to dispose of an empty container with other household trash if it contains less than one inch of material in the bottom.

- Work with your local community center or public works department to develop a waste exchange where those who need paint and auto products, garden chemicals, etc., can put their names on a list to be matched with those who wish to dispose of those items.

- Save and bring your materials to a household hazardous-waste collection. These collections are held by many states and municipalities to provide safe, insured hazardous-waste disposal. A special contractor is hired to transport and dispose of the wastes in ways that must meet strict environmental standards. If your town does not have such a program, contact your state department of health or environmental services (listed under state agencies in your phone book) to find out how to set one up.

- Alternatively, ask your state environmental protection agency for guidelines on proper disposal of hazardous waste in your area.

- Reduce your use of hazardous-waste products when possible. Use basic ingredients and make your own cleaning products (see page 46).

YOU SHOULD KNOW

Household toxins can cause respiratory problems, burns, poisoning, nausea, headaches, and dizziness. Swallowing some of these substances can be fatal and serious medical problems can arise from simply breathing their vapors. The Consumer Product Safety Commission reports over 100,000 cases per year of injuries resulting from misuse of household toxins that required emergency room treatment. Many of these victims were children.

WHEELS OF FORTUNE

THE EHMI WASTE WHEELS

The Environmental Hazards Management Institute (EHMI) of Durham, New Hampshire, has created 3 highly informative and useful guides. The Household Hazardous Waste Wheel leads you from products containing potentially hazardous ingredients to safe alternatives, including many you can produce yourself by using vinegar, salt, baking soda, or lemon juice. It also has waste management information for your community. The Water Sense Wheel helps you to investigate your own water quality and pursue treatment options. Both these guides, plus the newest EHMI addition, the Recycle Wheel, can help you, your community, and local organizations to encourage a positive change in consumer habits. "It's the best, most durable, and most accurate guide I've found — and I've looked into many," says Alice Robinson, Facilitator for the Resource Recycling Coalition on Martha's Vineyard, Massachusetts. –P.U.

$2.75 each, Conservatree (contact EHMI for bulk orders)

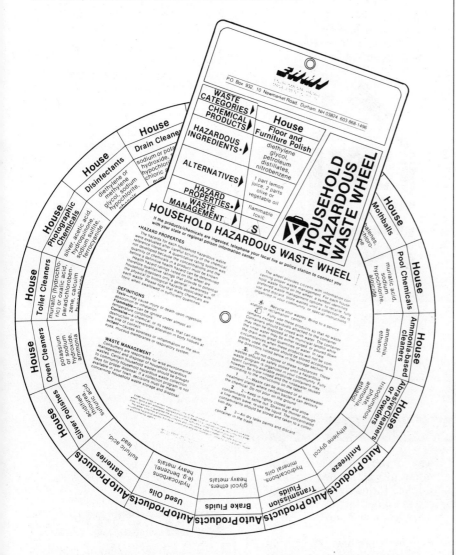

MY ENVIRONMENTAL GOALS FOR THE NEXT YEAR

- **To encourage the federal government to switch to recycled paper and to other recycled products. Uncle Sam consumes 22 percent of the gross national product. Can you imagine what would happen to the markets if our government switched to recycled materials?**

- **To pressure corporate America to reduce its use of bleached paper materials and thereby reduce the ominous and growing threat of dioxins.** — *W.S.*

YOU SHOULD KNOW

A rule of thumb for glass recycling: The only glass that is recyclable is a container that once held food or drink. Light bulbs, drinking glasses, eyeglasses, fish tanks, and mirrors are not recyclable.

Producing one ton of glass generates 384 pounds of mining wastes and 27.8 pounds of air pollutants.

WHAT TO TAKE TO HAZARDOUS-WASTE COLLECTION SITES

These common household products require special disposal:

FROM THE GARAGE
Antifreeze
Brake fluid
Wax polish
Engine degreaser
Carburetor cleaner
Creosote
Radiator flushes
Asphalt
Roofing tar
Air conditioner refrigerants
Car batteries (will be recycled)

FROM THE HOUSE
Drain cleaners
Oven cleaners
Furniture polish
Metal polish
Window cleaners
Expired prescriptions
Arts & crafts supplies
Photography chemicals
Floor cleaners
Chemistry kits
Mothballs
Rug & upholstery cleaners

FROM THE WORKBENCH
Rust preventatives
Wood preservatives
Wood stripper
Wood stains

Paint thinner
Oil-based paint
Solvents
Degreasers
Sealants
Varnish

FROM THE YARD
Pesticides (including DDT & Chlordane)
Herbicides
Insect sprays
Rodent killers
Pool chemicals
No-pest strips
Fertilizers
Cesspool cleaners
Silvex, Weed-B-Gone, Penta Wood Preservative

CAMBRIDGE GARDEN CLUB

READ MORE ABOUT IT

RECYCLING: 101 PRACTICAL TIPS FOR HOME AND WORK

By Susan Hassol and Beth Richman. Using this booklet, you can help create a healthier world without sacrificing your quality of life. It's divided into the 3 Rs of waste: Reduction, Reuse, and Recycling. You'll learn how to reduce the amount of waste you generate through better shopping choices, how to reuse wherever possible, how to choose long-lasting over disposable products, and how to recycle what you can back into useful products. Recycling is the major focus here, but plastic and hazardous wastes are also discussed.

The publishers practice what they preach. All the booklets in the Windstar EarthPulse series, of which this is one, are printed on 100% recycled paper. *–Jennifer A. Adams*

$3.95
The Windstar Foundation

HOPE FOR THE FUTURE

• Many municipal recycling programs are starting to recycle plastic food containers (principally polystyrene) and household product containers (detergent, dish washing liquid). These programs have been developed and promoted by the plastics industry, as it recognizes the problems posed by these products.

• Promising research is underway for recycling a mixture of different plastics back to their original forms by first separating the different plastic polymers from each other.

• Scientists are now working on a nonpetroleum plastic, which is grown by bacteria feeding on glucose cultures. If it works, these plastics would be completely natural and biodegradable.

YOU SHOULD KNOW

America is drowning in its own trash. We produce 160 million tons per year — 3.5 pounds per person per day. A family of 3 averages 350 bags per year.

Currently, recycled paper makes up about 25% of the fibers used in the U.S. paper industry.

GARBAGE: THE PRACTICAL JOURNAL FOR THE ENVIRONMENT

This is a tremendous compilation of information and analysis for the homeowner on trash, packaging and source reduction, water use, hazardous waste, pesticides, etc. A beautiful and glossy publication testifying to the beauty of recycled paper, which it's printed on. —W.S.

$21 (6 issues)
Old-House Journal Corp.

JUST THINKING

"The man who fights for his beliefs is the man who is truly alive."
— Cervantes

COMPLETE TRASH: THE BEST WAY TO GET RID OF PRACTICALLY EVERYTHING AROUND THE HOUSE

By Norm Crampton. If you're looking for a way to get rid of something, with no apologies for using it in the first place, then this book's for you. Crampton is the secretary of the Institute for Solid Wastes of the American Public Works Association. Here, from aluminum cans to deceased pets to smoke detectors (did you know they contain radioactive material?), he offers "solutions" to garbage disposal.

Don't look for easy answers here; "burn or bury" is often Crampton's answer. If you don't have a hazardous-waste collection network in your area, many of his other solutions won't do you any good. And some of what he says may rub you the wrong way if you're a purist. 136 pages. —J.A.A.

$8.95, M. Evans and Company, Inc.

A glass bottle must be reused at least ten times to equal the energy saved when recycling an aluminum can.

Clean Cleaners for A Clean Earth

T HE "WHITER THAN WHITE" refrain from Madison Avenue for the past four decades has brainwashed us into thinking that the First Commandment is "Cleanliness is next to godliness." The Second has been that if it doesn't smell lemon clean, it isn't.

> *Most cleaners are actually pretty dirty — and so poisonous that they endanger not only your family's health but also that of the planet.*

But from an environmentalist's point of view, most cleaners in today's supermarket are actually pretty dirty and smelly, containing chemicals so powerful and poisonous that they endanger not only your family's health but also that of the planet. When you pour them down your drain or flush them down your toilet, they leach into lakes, rivers, and soil — and could even come back through your own kitchen faucet.

Clean Up Your Act

There are plenty of alternatives to environmentally hazardous cleaners. So it should be possible to avoid the following dangerous components in common cleaners.

Detergents often are made from petroleum, a non-renewable resource containing impurities that are toxic and difficult to break down.

Phosphates, which are added to powdered detergents to boost their cleaning power, end up in our rivers and lakes, where they cause excessive algae growth. The algae eat up all the oxygen in the water, suffocating fish and other marine life.

Chlorine bleach, when it breaks down, can produce toxic and even carcinogenic compounds. It also kills bacteria that many sewage treatment systems depend on to break down waste material.

Optical whiteners, found in laundry detergent, create an illusion that clothes are "whiter than white." They can cause skin allergies, and they biodegrade poorly, accumulating in the tissues of fish and roots of plants.

Enzymes, added to laundry detergent to remove stains, can cause skin and respiratory allergies in some people.

CLEAN CLEANING PRODUCTS

If you, like most people, don't have the time or the energy to make your own cleaners, take heart. There are plenty of products on the market that are safe for both you and the environment. And they work. Many of these products are available in stores, but contact the companies listed if you can't find them.

ECOVER: ECOLOGICALLY OUT IN FRONT

When it comes to cleaning your home, Ecover biodegradable household cleaners are truly on the cutting edge. They're mean to dirt but nice to the planet.

Ecover products are based mainly on vegetable-oil cleaners; they also contain citrus and other oils, which leave a clean, fresh scent. They avoid all the no-no's: no petroleum-based detergents, phosphates, chlorine bleach, optical whiteners, enzymes, synthetic perfumes, or colorings. None of the products or their ingredients are tested on animals, and all ingredients are fully biodegradable within five days.

The company has paid attention to ecology down to its packaging. For powdered products, Ecover mainly uses recycled cardboard cartons. The company packages liquid products in bottles made of polyethylene, which is slow to biodegrade but is recyclable and creates no chemical pollution.

Manufactured in Belgium, Ecover products are available in many natural food stores and natural product catalogs, such as Seventh Generation. Or contact the distributor, the Mercantile Food Company, for the name of your nearest supplier.

Here's a sampling of Ecover's products. –L.H.

WOOL WASH LIQUID
Especially formulated to clean and condition delicate fabrics such as wool or silk. Use in your washing machine or in sink for washing by hand.

$4.50 (33.8 oz.)

ECOVER

FABRIC CONDITIONER

A nontoxic formula with a coconut-oil derivative that softens fabric. Ecover isn't crazy about fabric conditioners in general because they increase the amount of cleaner needed in future washes; instead, the company recommends drying your clothes outside. But for people who want to use fabric softener, this is a gentler alternative.

$3.50 (33.8 oz.)

DISHWASHING LIQUID

Easy on your hands and the environment. Contains a coconut-based cleaner, sea salt, and milk whey, which not only boosts the cleaning power, but also stabilizes the pH level of the liquid to the pH of your skin. Chamomile and calendula oils help heal small cuts and scratches. This dishwashing liquid cleans well without showy suds, so you can use just a little to wash a lot. (If you like "squeaky clean," this is for you. It works! –B.A.)

$3.89 (33.9 oz.)

CREAM CLEANER

A nonabrasive cleanser that contains finely ground chalk and liquid soap made from palm, coconut, and linseed oil. Works on a variety of surfaces, including acrylic, fiberglass, stainless steel, porcelain, and chrome.

$3.35 (33.8 oz.)

TOILET CLEANER

Works while you don't. Squirt a small amount under the rim and around the bowl of your toilet and leave overnight; then use a toilet brush in the morning before flushing. This cleaner, which contains vinegar and oils of pine, citrus, lavender, citronella, and eucalyptus, has no strong acids, so it won't affect your septic tank.

$4.45 (33.8 oz.)

FLOOR SOAP

Mixed with warm water, works on any type of floor. Its secret is liquid soap made from coconut, palm, and linseed oils, which give your floor a deep, natural shine with regular use, and the oils of pine, eucalyptus, citronella, and rosemary, which give off a penetrating scent.

$3.35 (33.8 oz.)

A CLEANING POTPOURRI

WINTER WHITE

A cruelty-free laundry detergent in liquid and powdered form. It is biodegradable, works in all temperatures, and is economical, too, because the liquid detergent is 3 times as concentrated as other commercial brands and the powder is 10 times as concentrated. This laundry detergent does contain optical whiteners, which may cause allergies in sensitive people. In many natural foods markets. –L.H.

Liquid: $6.65 (32 oz.), $11.95 (64 oz.), $19.95 (128 oz.)

Powder: $9.35 (48 oz.)
Mountain Fresh

What You Can Do

✔ To help protect septic systems and groundwater, use nonchlorine bleach.

✔ Since even small amounts of chlorine will kill fish, never empty chlorinated swimming pool water into streams, ponds, or oceans.

✔ If you must use detergent instead of soap, look for liquid detergent packaged in recycled and/or recyclable plastic containers. Spic-and-Span, Pine, Tide, and Cheer use some recycled plastic.

Household hazardous-waste collections cost $15,000 to $100,000 per day, depending on participation and how the waste is then managed.

The Secret Is To Simplify

Despite these problem ingredients, you do not have to unnecessarily compromise your cleanliness standards in order to protect the environment. Instead, try these make-it-yourself alternatives; they're safer to use, easier on the environment, and will meet almost all your cleaning needs.

Soap cleans it all, apples to zoot suits. (If your skin is sensitive to the harsher agents in soap, try a no-soap hand cleaner, such as Shaklee's.)

Vinegar cuts through mildew, stains, and wax buildup.

Baking soda cleans, scours, deodorizes, polishes, removes stains, and softens fabrics.

Borax disinfects, deodorizes, removes stains, and adds to the power of other cleaners by softening water.

Washing soda, or sodium carbonate, cleans and also boosts other cleaners. But it's moderately toxic and could irritate your mucous membranes, so wear gloves and use it in a well-ventilated area.

Ammonia is a powerful cleaner for carpets, linoleum, copper, enamels, and appliances. But it's also moderately toxic, so use the same precautions as with washing soda.

Finally, there's one other ingredient you shouldn't forget: elbow grease. It works, it's free, and it's good exercise! — *Leda Hartman*

Recycling one aluminum can saves the amount of energy you'd get from half of that same can full of gasoline.

ALLENS CARES

Allens Naturally makes a variety of cruelty-free, nontoxic, and biodegradable home care products. The company's motto is, "For people who care about the world and the animals in it." All Allens products come in recyclable plastic bottles. –L.H.

ALLENS DISHWASHER DETERGENT

A concentrated formula that softens water, prevents spotting of glass-ware, and cuts grease.

$8.90 (4-lb. container)

ALLENS DISHWASHING LIQUID

Washes dishes and fine hand washables without phosphates or alcohols.

$3.50 (1 qt.)

ALLENS MULTIPURPOSE SPRAY CLEANER

Cleans most washable surfaces, including countertops, walls, and even white-wall tires.

$2.50 (1 qt.)

ALLENS GLASS CLEANER

Also cleans chrome, Formica, and enameled surfaces.

$2.50 (1 qt.)

ALLENS ALL-PURPOSE CLEANER

Cleans heavily soiled hard surfaces and can be added to laundry to treat heavily soiled clothes and stubborn spots.

$3.75 (1 qt.)

ALLENS LIQUID SOAP WITH ALOE

A mild hand and body cleanser that contains aloe vera and almond oil.

$5.90 (1 qt.)

ALLENS CONCENTRATED FABRIC SOFTENER

A perfect companion to Allen's laundry detergent. Phosphate free, prevents static cling, and softens clothes.

$8.50 (1 gal.), $3.10 (1 qt.)

What You Can Do

✔ Read the label before you buy a product, and make sure it will do what you want. Whenever you buy a product, you take on the responsibility to use and dispose of it properly.

✔ Don't buy environmentally expensive disposable plastic dispensers for liquid soap. Go back to hand soaps wrapped in paper.

Thirty-five thousand square miles of rain forest (an area larger than the state of South Carolina) are cut down each year.

EASY HOMEMADE SUBSTITUTES FOR COMMON HOUSEHOLD CLEANERS

Bleach. Use one that doesn't contain chlorine, or use baking soda and water. Or use borax. It will clean, disinfect, deodorize, whiten, and soften water and is gentle to the environment.

Carpet cleaner. Sprinkle carpet with two parts cornmeal and one part borax, leave on for one hour, and vacuum thoroughly. Baking soda also does the job. For small spills, clean with vinegar and soapy water, rinse with clean water, and pat dry.

Cleanser. Use a mixture of baking soda, soap, and salt for abrasion; or rub the area with half a lemon dipped in borax, and rinse dry.

Drain opener. Use a plunger or a snake, or pour down 1/2 cup baking soda, 1/2 cup salt, and 1/4 cup vinegar in that order. Close the drain until the fizzing stops, then flush with boiling water. (To avoid the problem in the first place, use a drain sieve to prevent clogging, and never pour grease down the drain.)

Floor cleaner. Mix 1/4 cup vinegar in 1 gallon of warm water.

Glass and window cleaner. Mix 2 tablespoons of white vinegar in 1 quart warm water; after washing, dry glass with newspaper.

Laundry soap. Synthetic laundry detergent causes much of the toxic contamination found at home. Substitute scentless, colorless soap flakes or liquids that are toxin-free and completely biodegradable. Add 1/3 cup of washing soda (sodium carbonate) to lift out stubborn grease and stains. When you first make the switch to a soap cleanser, wash all laundry once in pure washing soda to remove the synthetic detergent residues that collect on clothing and cause yellowing. By the way, liquid laundry soaps never contain phosphates.

Fabric softener. Add 1 cup of white vinegar to the final rinse cycle.

Oven cleaner. Place 1/4 cup ammonia in a shallow, non-aluminum pan and add enough water to cover the bottom of the pan. Heat the oven for 20 minutes, turn it off, and place the pan in it overnight. This will loosen baked-on grime, which can be scrubbed off in the morning with baking soda and water. But be sure to ventilate your kitchen well while you're scrubbing!

Spray starch. Mix 2 tablespoons cornstarch and 1 pint of cold water in a spray bottle and shake well.

Floor or furniture polish. Mix 1 part lemon juice and 2 parts vegetable or mineral oil. Apply beeswax afterward for a glossy finish.

Brass polish. Lemon juice.

Copper polish. Lemon juice and salt.

Silver polish. Baking soda or toothpaste.

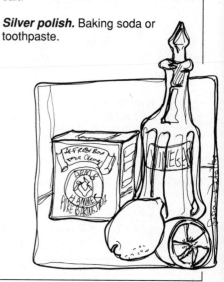

"LIVOS" MEANS LIFE, LIGHT, AND SHEEN

Livos, an innovative company, markets furniture and floor waxes, soaps, and wood-finishing products that use only high-quality natural ingredients, such as clarified organic plant oils, tree resins, and herb extracts. (See the review of the company on page 52.) –L.H.

LATIS NATURAL SOAP

A liquid soap derived from pure plant ingredients. Ideal for cleaning clothes and dishes on camping trips because it's biodegradable and effective when mixed with cold water.

$6.65 (33.8 fl. oz.)

BEKOS BEE AND RESIN OINTMENT

A clear paste furniture wax. Stable, resists dirt, and can be applied to many areas not exposed to excessive moisture: furniture, interior window frames, architectural woodwork, and stone, metal, and plastic laminates. Bekos also helps maintain handles on tools — provided the tools aren't left out in the rain.

$6.50 (6.8 fl. oz.)
$11.85 (13.5 fl. oz.)

In 1986 the United States produced 525 million tons of hazardous waste, most of it in wastewater.

SHAKLEE

Shaklee was in the vanguard for 30 years with a variety of earth-friendly household cleaners. Its products are still good, but most of the other companies reviewed here have surpassed it recently from an environmental point of view. The company has lost ground, too, because ingredients, which are not listed on all of the containers, do not meet the higher environmental standards of companies such as Ecover. The packaging and literature are not made of recycled materials and may not be recyclable.

Having said that, all Shaklee cleaners are biodegradable and free of toxic fumes, corrosive chemicals, solvents, and phosphates. They can be purchased only from local distributors who will come to your home. The many we've met are friendly, knowledgeable, and concerned about the environment. And the company is working hard to regain its environmental leadership. –*Bruce Anderson*

SHAKLEE BASIC-H

A powerful, all-purpose cleaner. So concentrated you need to add only one teaspoon per gallon — or one teaspoon per quart, if you want something a little stronger. This cleaner can handle everything from windows, floors, walls, and bathtubs to awnings, countertops, and even barbecues. –*L.H.*

$6.40 (1 qt.), $22.35 (1 gal.)

SHAKLEE BASIC-L LAUNDRY CONCENTRATE

Cleans your clothes gently but thoroughly in all temperatures. As effective at removing grime in cold water as other detergents that contain phosphates. Contains zeolite, a natural water softener that helps the biodegradable cleansers work even in hard water. –*L.H.*

$19.95 (10 lbs.)

SHAKLEE LIQUID-L LAUNDRY CONCENTRATE

If Liquid-L could make the ubiquitous black stains on a white cotton sweater disappear, we decided, it would have our blessing. So we tried it as a prewash stain remover and then in the laundry. And the sweater came out white again. –*L.H.*

$5.95 (1 qt.)

SHAKLEE CONCENTRATED FABRIC SOFTENER

This liquid softener can be used in the wash cycle, rinse cycle, or in the dryer. Without phosphates, it softens fabrics, smoothes wrinkles, and reduces static cling. –*L.H.*

$5.10 (1 qt.), $17.50 (1 gal.)

SHAKLEE BASIC-D DISH-WASHING CONCENTRATE

Works in your dishwasher even in the hardest water. Leaves glassware spotless and plates shiny. –*L.H.*

$8.95 (47 oz.)

SHAKLEE SATIN SHEEN DISHWASHING LIQUID

We did the old comparison test, the kind you used to see on TV commercials. We scrubbed one side of a grimy baking pan with our usual dishwashing liquid and the other side with Satin Sheen. And Satin Sheen cut the grease better.— *L.H.*

$4.75 (22 fl. oz.), $23.95 (1 gal.)

SHAKLEE AT-EASE HEAVY-DUTY SCOURING CLEANSER

Uses natural abrasives that eliminate grease and dirt on ceramic tiles, ovens, and grills. Has a pleasant scent and is free of ammonia, toxic fumes, and volatile solvents. "This is a remarkably effective and easy-to-use cleanser," says our tester, Sylvia Anderson. –*L.H.*

$4.75 (9 oz.)

BILO FLOOR WAX

The strongest wax in the Livos line, able to resist scratches, dirt, and general wear and tear. This wax is especially designed for use on wood, stone, brick, terra cotta tiles, and linoleum floors. It's also helpful on old wooden floors in need of a new shine. Some surfaces, including new wooden ones, should be pretreated or cleaned beforehand.

$2.50 (sample)
$10.95 (13.5 fl. oz.)
$42 (68 fl. oz.)

LAVENOS HAND SOAP

Mild and versatile, formulated to clean skin without drying it out. Made of pure plant oils; unscented and uncolored.

$4.85 (16.9 fl. oz.)

GLEIVO LIQUID FURNITURE WAX

Cleans as it buffs surfaces made of wood, stone, metal, and plastic laminates. Especially good for refinishing and for areas that are frequently waxed. Can be applied over previously waxed and oiled furniture.

$5.95 (8.5 fl. oz.), $12.50 (25.36 fl. oz.)

AVI SOAP CONCENTRATE

A highly concentrated cleaner made from pure plant ingredients to use on tiles, window frames, and furniture. It can be used diluted in water or full strength for very tough jobs and can even be mixed with sand for a potent hand-washing paste.

$18.75 (100 fl. oz.)

Every two weeks we throw away enough glass to fill the twin towers of the World Trade Center in New York City.

PARKER'S PERFECT POLISH

Parker's has been on the market since 1917 when C. W. Parker, a dealer of Steinway Pianos who lost patience with the furniture polish available at the time, concocted his own.

Unlike other commercial polishes that must have safety caps or warnings, Parker's products contain no linseed oil, silicones, petroleum distillates, or harmful solvents. The polishes are clear or white, odorless, nonaerosol, noncombustible, and nonflammable. And they come in recyclable plastic containers.

Parker's will deduct $1 from your order and pay shipping when you mention this book. –L.H.

PARKER'S LEMON OIL

Polishes, protects, and preserves fine furniture, antiques, and other wood surfaces, penetrating to replace lost moisture and helping to prevent drying, cracking, and peeling.

$9.95 (1 bottle, 16 oz.)
$8.50 (each, 2 to 5 bottles)
$6.50 (each, 6 to 11 bottles)
$5.50 (each, 12 or more bottles)

PARKER'S SCRATCH-FREE FORMULA FOR ALUMINUM AND STAINLESS STEEL

This polish has no abrasives, so it won't mar the surface of your aluminum and stainless items or leave a gritty residue. What's more, it's fine to use on many other surfaces, including stoves, sinks, faucets, refrigerators, counter tops, shower doors, and bathroom tiles. This formula won't clean heavily soiled or rusted areas, but it will help prevent those conditions.

$9.95 (1 bottle, 16 oz.)
$8.50 (each, 2 to 5 bottles)
$6.50 (each, 6 to 11 bottles)
$5.50 (each, 12 or more bottles)

PARKER'S WOOD FINISH CREME

A concentrated, oil-based liquid cleaner and polish that can be used on all wood-finished surfaces. Repels dust, keeping the finish cleaner longer. After 72 years on the market, this product has developed a loyal core of followers. "It's the best I've ever used," says our tester, Sylvia Anderson. "Really cleans all the buildup from other cleaners."

$9.95 (1 bottle, 16 oz.)
$8.50 (each, 2 to 5 bottles)
$6.50 (each, 6 to 11 bottles)
$5.50 (each, 12 or more bottles)

HAND IT OVER

Williams Sonoma has developed three products that will cleanse and condition your hands.

WILLIAMS SONOMA LIQUID GLYCERINE SOAP AND GLYCERINE KITCHEN HAND CREAM

Made in Spain by an experienced soap maker, both products are unscented and hypoallergenic and contain no coloring agents. The soap lathers softly, and the hand cream softens your hands with a nongreasy milk extract. –L.H.

Soap: $9 (11.8 oz.)
Cream: $9 (11.8 oz.)
$13 (set of 2)

WILLIAMS SONOMA GLYCERINE HAND SOAP

A soft lather and a delicate scent. Contains no animal tallow, relying instead on pure vegetable oil, which has a naturally high glycerine content. –L.H.

$10 (set of 6), $16 (set of 12)

"The planet is a unit. No one nation can solve the problem. We're all in the greenhouse together." — *Robert Redford*

TRIED & TRUE

MURPHY OIL SOAP

A favorite, all-purpose household cleaner for 75 years. Murphy's is great on all wood surfaces, no-wax floors, painted walls, washable wall coverings, leather and vinyl, auto upholstery and vinyl tops, and even on laundry stains. It's based on vegetable oil, contains no harsh detergents or strong alkalis (so it's kind to your hands as well as the planet), and has a mild, pleasant scent. Comes in a plastic jar, bottle, or spray bottle and can be found in most supermarkets. –L.H.

$2 to $5 depending on quantity
Murphy-Phoenix Company

THE BEGINNER'S SAMPLER

THE RESPONSIBLE ALTERNATIVE SAMPLER KIT

Contains just about everything you'll need for most household cleaning. All products are nontoxic, nonfuming, and nonflammable. They're safe enough to use without gloves or protective clothing, yet powerful enough to cut through even oil and grease.

This sampler includes: Clean and Safe (a powerful, all-purpose cleaner that biodegrades fully within a week); Gordon's Miracle Shine (a cleaner that resists scratches and rust, for glass, plastic, metals, and jewelry); D-Grease II; GP-10 Window Cleaner; Pumice Scouring Stick; and a Cleansing Applicator.

The pumice alone is a nifty little wonder. We're no cleaning freaks, but we came to see the light (and white). First we tried it with mild curiosity on a porcelain kitchen sink (with stains that, no doubt, date back to the day the house was built), then with increasing enthusiasm on the stovetop, and finally, with the devout radiance of newly converted disciples, on the oven, which was caked with months of unfriendly, if venerable, food stains. The pumice cleaned the oven quickly and thoroughly. And we could breathe at the same time. –L.H.

$12, Co-op America, Chip Distribution Co.

READ MORE ABOUT IT

Here are 2 terrific books to help you capture that fresh bouquet fragrance for your house without having to use chemical sprays and aerosols.

NATURAL FRAGRANCES: OUTDOOR SCENTS FOR INDOOR USES

By Gail Duff. Do you yearn for a breath of country air in your home? Then open the delightful pages of *Natural Fragrances*. Using the precise directions (all with lovely photographs and illustrations), you'll learn how to cultivate herbs and flowers, dry and prepare them, and then whip them into delicious-looking (and smelling!) potpourris, toiletries, sweet sleep pillows, candles, and other gifts. Don't have a garden? Never mind, this thorough book includes a list of suppliers. 1989, 153 pages. –*Suzanne Rametta*

$22.95, Garden Way Publishing, Storey Communications, Inc.

THE BOOK OF POTPOURRI: FRAGRANT FLOWER MIXES FOR SCENTING & DECORATING THE HOME

By Penny Black. This luscious, elegant book deserves a spot on anyone's coffee table. But it won't stay there for long — expect to be inspired again and again to explore different methods and recipes for mixing your personal blend of natural scents. 1989, 128 pages. –S.R.

$19.95, Simon and Schuster

What You Can Do

✔ Scent or freshen the air by leaving out a dish of potpourri. Boil sweet herbs such as cinnamon, or place an open dish of baking soda in a room. Keep houseplants, which are great for purifying the air.

✔ Try wiping soiled surfaces with a cloth dampened in water, before resorting to stronger cleansers.

✔ Keep rags in the kitchen to wipe up spills. Unlike paper products, they can be rinsed and reused often.

✔ Use nontoxic automatic dishwashing powder (found in natural food stores) or the lowest-phosphate detergent available.

✔ Soften used paintbrushes with hot vinegar.

✔ Use a heat gun rather than toxic solvents to peel off paint.

Good Earthkeeping

IT'S NO ACCIDENT THAT PROCTER & GAMBLE has started to test-market Tide laundry detergent in recyclable plastic bottles or that Melitta is selling unbleached coffee filters. "Green" — which can mean anything that's recyclable, biodegradable, or otherwise environmentally sound — is the latest catchword in consumer products.

> **Bleached white coffee filters have been banned in Sweden, because hot water leaches cancer-causing dioxins into the coffee.**

Here are some signs of the times:

- A recent survey of 1,000 adults found that 77 percent would pay more for a product packaged with recyclable or biodegradable materials. Fifty-three percent of those surveyed also said they'd chosen not to buy a product recently because they considered it environmentally harmful.
- The sale of aerosol products, which often contain chlorofluorocarbons that damage the earth's ozone layer, has declined. Aerosol antiperspirants, for example, fell from 85 percent of the market in the 1970s to just 25 percent today. Manufacturers of plastic bags worry that their products could face a similar fall.
- Wal-Mart, the third largest retailer in the nation, is encouraging its suppliers to develop environmentally sensitive products.
- The Canadian Loblaw company, which owns about 100 U.S. supermarkets, in June of 1989 introduced a complete line of "green" consumer goods to its stores. The products include foam plates that contain no chlorofluorocarbons, a dishwasher detergent that is free of phosphates and other harmful chemicals, and motor oil made from recycled or re-refined oil. Everything sold like gangbusters — more than double projections.

You don't have to wait for corporations to catch up with you, however, in order to be an environmentally responsible consumer. In this section you'll find all sorts of suggestions for keeping the planet healthy while you're making your home a pleasant place to live.

— *Leda Hartman*

DEBUGGING PRODUCTS

Bugs bugging you? It's no secret that pesticides contain carcinogens and other toxic substances. But did you know that mothballs are no great shakes either? They contain paradichlorobenzene, which can irritate the nose, throat, and lungs and may even induce depression or kidney or liver injury over prolonged periods of exposure. Mothball vapors are absorbed by clothing and bedding, so the exposure is direct. And mothballs are a particular hazard for children, who may swallow them because they look sugar coated. Here are safer ways to deter moths and other pests:

NATURAL MOTH REPELLENT

This natural moth repellent combines lavender and rosemary with tansy, peppermint, and other traditional repellents. The mix comes in cotton pouches that you can place in your bureau drawer, trunk, or closet. It'll keep working for as long as a year. –L.H.

$9.95, Vermont Country Store

What You Can Do

✔ Freeze clothing or expose it to hot sun for two days to kill moth larvae.

Every ton of paper that's recycled saves 7,000 gallons of water that would have been used to manufacture virgin stock.

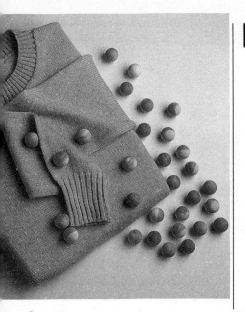

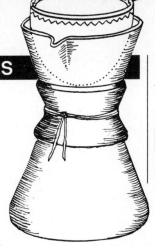

COFFEE FILTER ALTERNATIVES

For years, people have been putting white paper filters into their coffee makers each morning without a second thought. But now it's time to wake up and smell the brew: white coffee filters can be dangerous to your health and the environment because the bleaching process leaves dioxins, a known carcinogen, in the filter's fibers. The hot water leaches it into your coffee and then into your body.

CEDAR BALLS

Cedar is another traditional material used against moths. Cedar oil discourages female moths from laying eggs and also helps stop the spread of mildew. Lillian Vernon makes cedar balls that can be placed around garments and linens in closets, chests, and drawers. –L.H.

$12.98 (set of 30), Lillian Vernon

THE HUMMERS

The Hummers make a variety of moth repellents from aromatic Texas juniper cedar, using pieces of wood left over by other industries in the Texas hill country. Cedar Friends come in animal shapes that can be hung or strung. Texas Moth Balls (without the nasty ingredients found in commercial versions) are good in your linen closet, drawers, and suitcases. The Hummer Juniper Closet Set includes 4 repellent pouches (which slip over the hook of clothes hangers) and 2 closet fresheners. –L.H.

$10 Cedar Friends; $12 Texas Moth Balls; $15 Juniper Closet Set Co-op America, The Hummers

UNBLEACHED COFFEE FILTERS

Two companies, Melitta and Rockline, have come up with an alternative: unbleached coffee filters. They're brown, the same color the white ones become when you use them, and they work the same. They come in different sizes to fit most coffee makers and are available in supermarkets and natural food stores. –L.H.

$1.29 to $1.89 per package

ECO FILTERS

Want to be even more conscientious? Try one of Co-op America's Eco Filters. They are washable, reusable, and good for coffee or tea. Each filter is made of durable cotton and will last a year or 2. They come in 3 sizes and cone, Melitta, round, or square styles to fit regular drip coffee makers. –L.H.

$3.75 to $4.75, Co-op America

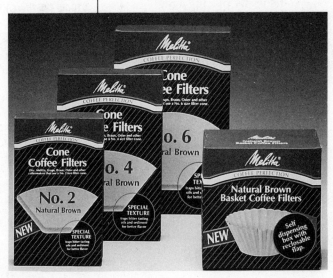

GOLD MESH FILTERS

You need never buy another package of filters if you buy a Krups gold mesh coffee filter. This Swiss-made filter, with a 23.7 karat gold finish, is a cinch to clean under running water. –L.H.

$20 to $24, Williams Sonoma

What You Can Do

✔ Seal cracks and other pest entry areas, and fix plumbing leaks and other excessively moist areas.

✔ As a barrier for ants, sprinkle salt or red pepper on counters and across doors or windowsills.

✔ Wipe a solution of vinegar and water on your kitchen counter to repel flies. Or use clove or citrus oil. And use a flyswatter!

✔ Trap cockroaches or silverfishes by placing a rag soaked in beer (or a mixture of ½ baking soda and ½ powdered sugar) into a shallow dish overnight.

LIVOS, THE NATURAL CHOICE

Livos is a creative company from New Mexico that specializes in nontoxic paints, shellacs, varnishes, primers, and waxes derived from plant oils and tree resins. They'll protect your lungs as well as your furniture. All of these products, once they've dried, are harmless to humans, animals, plants, soil, and water.

We're intrigued by this company's unusual product names. They're all ancient Celtic words with special meanings. The name Livos, in fact, stands for life, light, and sheen — that's what these products will give your good woods. Here is but a sampling:

KALDET RESIN AND OIL FINISH

Kaldet preserves, stains, and finishes. It is water resistant for interior and exterior use and provides a subtle satin shine. Kaldet can be applied to almost any wood, stone, or metal surface, including architectural woodwork, clay pots, and masonry. This finish comes in many different shades, including clear, pine, walnut, oak, and white. –L.H.

$10.95 (25 fl. oz.); $98 (2.5 gal.)

STAIN PASTES

These oil-based earthen and mineral pastes are good for staining wood and stone surfaces, especially when you want to match a particular color. The pastes come in a spectrum of colors. –L.H.

$12.85 (16.9 fl. oz.); $49.50 (set of all colors)

TREBO ALL-PURPOSE SHELLAC

Shellac has the advantage of sealing up to 80% of the fumes emitted by particle board, plywood, and other chemically treated building materials. Trebo contains a milder alcohol than most shellacs, so it can be tolerated by sensitive users. It's for interior use, but should not be used on objects that come into contact with food. –L.H.

$12.75 (25 fl. oz.); $38.50 (84.5 fl. oz.)

DUBRON NATURAL RESIN WALL PAINT

This fast-drying wall paint can be used on wood, stone, or drywall. It contains no chemical additives, only the fragrances of plant extracts and essential oils. Unlike conventional paints, Dubron emits no fumes once it has dried. Comes in bright white or off-white; Livos also carries 11 different stain pastes for tinting. –L.H.

Paint: $5.85 (25 fl. oz.); $98 (4.5 gal.)
Stain Pastes: $4.85 (3.4 fl. oz.); $12.85 (16.9 fl. oz.)
Set of all colors: $45

LEINOS CITRUS THINNER

Leinos is extracted from citrus peels at a relatively low temperature, which stops pesticides and other chemicals used in growing oranges from contaminating the thinner. Leinos works like turpentine, but it's less flammable and dries faster. It also has a lemon fragrance that makes it pleasant to use. People with allergic sensitivities will find this thinner easier to use than most conventional ones, but Livos still recommends wearing protective gloves. –L.H.

$4.85 (16.9 fl. oz.); $32.50 (1.25 gal.)

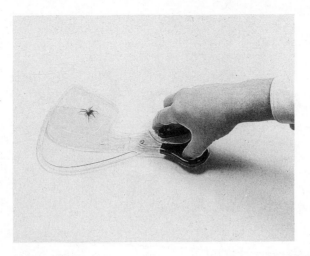

MISCELLANEOUS DISCOVERIES

THE GOOD AEROSOL

Conventional aerosol cans filled with chlorofluorocarbons damage the earth's ozone layer. But now you can spray away to your heart's content with a rechargeable aerosol spray can that contains no hazardous chemicals. You simply fill the can half-full with whatever liquid and pressurize it with any bicycle pump or air hose. It's good for use with paints, lubricants, cleaners, and other household helpers, and it's refillable time after time. –L.H.

$29.95, Abbeon Cal, Inc.

INSECT SAVER

How often have you tried to return spiders, moths, and other uninvited house guests — in one piece — to the outdoors, using either your hands or the age-old cup-and-paper trick? Well, now you can make that job effortless and even fun: Just place the cupped part of the plastic Insect Saver "scissor" over the insect and carefully slide the flat part underneath it. Then safely release your captive outside. No more close calls with a harassed bumblebee! We wouldn't be without ours, especially in the summer, when the honeybees are drawn inside by the smell of beeswax products. –Penny Uhlendorf

$6.95, Kinsman Company, Inc.

In the U.S. alone, over 1,000,000 gallons of used motor oil are released into the environment every day.

Dressing for The Earth

AT FIRST GLANCE, you might think it's better to buy clothes made from natural materials, such as cotton, wool, silk, or linen, because they biodegrade and also let your skin breathe. Besides, most synthetic materials, including polyester, are derived from petroleum, a non-renewable resource. And making synthetics is a smokestack industry, replete with toxic pollution. Isn't "natural" always better?

Not necessarily.

There's more to the question of ecologically sound clothing than meets the eye. Consider that natural fibers are often grown, processed, dyed, and cleaned with a hefty helping of harmful chemicals. The wool industry uses fewer chemicals than other parts of the clothing industry, but cotton growers are the third-largest users of pesticides in the world. And silk and linen often require dry cleaning, a process that uses toxic chlorinated solvents that damage the atmosphere's ozone layer.

All of this means there's a real need for clothing fibers that are grown and processed organically, just as there's a need for organic food. We wonder whether there are farmers who grow "organic clothing" . . .

The Fuss over Furs

Wouldn't you know, it's a "natural" material — fur — that's at the crux of the fiercest controversy in the clothing industry today. The fur industry says that mink — which compose 75 percent of domestic fur sales — are raised on farms where they're treated humanely and killed painlessly. Furriers remind us that the production of fur can be an ecologically integrated process, as farming at its best is. It should cause little or no pollution and use few fossil fuels. In sharp contrast is the pollution that results from the creation of synthetic fibers, most of which are made from non-renewable resources such as petroleum.

The cotton industry is the third-largest user of pesticides in the world.

But fur opponents say there can be mistreatment on mink farms. And they point to the use of painful steel-jawed leg traps for bobcat, coyote, fox, lynx, and wolf to argue that wearing animal fur supports cruelty to animals.

Even royalty hasn't been able to withstand the pressure against wearing furs. Amid a storm of protest Prince Andrew, the Duke of York, returned a full-length mink coat he had ordered for his wife, Sarah Ferguson, on their first anniversary. And Diana, the Princess of Wales, has publicly announced that she'll no longer wear furs.

What You Can Do

We don't have solutions yet for all of the issues that may arise just as you get yourself dressed in the morning. But here are a few tips to keep in mind that may help matters just a little. And if we all followed them, they'd help a lot.

✔ When possible, avoid having clothes dry-cleaned; the process involves the use of toxic chlorinated solvents. If the label says "dry clean or hand wash," opt for the latter. (See pages 42-47 for suggestions regarding environmentally safe cleaning materials.)

✔ If your clothes are still good but you've grown tired of them, have a clothing swap with your friends.

✔ Give old clothes to a charity rather than creating more garbage. If they're too far gone, try using them as cleaning rags or polishing cloths. It's better than buying wasteful paper towels.

✔ Avoid faddish clothes that can be worn only a short time.

✔ Make use of thrift shops, especially for clothes for young children who outgrow clothing before they wear it out.

✔ Avoid toxic pest controls by placing lavender, rosemary, or cedar chips in your clothing drawers. Cedar oil discourages female moths from laying eggs and stops the spread of mildew.

Buying and selling endangered species and the products made from them is a $5-billion-a-year illegal business.

AN ALTERNATIVE TO IVORY

Scrimshaw is a true American folk art, born when sailors on long whaling voyages killed time by etching designs onto ivory whale teeth. But nowadays environmentalists have turned thumbs down on the craft, fearing that it will lead to the slaughter of more whales, walruses, and elephants.

Artek, Inc., is doing something to keep both the art of scrimshaw and the whales alive. Its proprietary ivory is so indistinguishable from the real thing that a growing list of museums is asking Artek to reproduce their scrimshaw collections for sale in museum shops.

Artek makes no bones (pardon the pun) about its product — each piece is clearly marked as an ivory alternative. That makes Artek the only known producer of an "honest" line of reproduction scrimshaw, according to the director of the Kendall Whaling Museum.

Its 200-item gift line, which will appeal to that hard-to-buy-for person on your list, includes carved whale teeth, jewelry boxes, puzzles, buttons, thimbles, buckles, pendants, and even kits for the novice scrimshander.

You can find Artek's products at the Metropolitan Museum of Art, the Museum of Fine Arts in Boston, Nantucket Whaling Museum, and Mystic Seaport Museum in Connecticut. Or write Artek directly. –*Mary Allen*

$2 for Christmas ornaments to $180 for a reproduction of the famous Starbuck Tooth. Scrimshaw kits (including a scrimshaw blank, etching tool, ink, and instructions) start at $25.

Once the question of the acceptability of fur is raised, do we forsake all clothing derived from animals, including goose down and leather? Environmentally, should we prefer synthetics? We don't know the answers . . . at least not yet.
— *Leda Hartman*

JUDGMENTS ON JEWELRY

We do know that if you really want to clothe yourself conscientiously, you should pay attention to the kind of jewelry you wear.

Ivory, which comes from the tusks of the endangered African elephant, is the most obvious material to avoid. Recently Lord & Taylor and Macy's joined the ranks of department stores trying to help the elephant by proclaiming ivory out of fashion. Yet there are other, less obvious, precious metals and gems that are best avoided because their production is devastating to the environment.

A large amount of cyanide is used in processing gold, for instance. Cyanide can cause widespread water pollution and is especially toxic to fish. Later in processing, burning off the sulfides in the gold produces sulfur dioxide, causing acid rain that damages lakes and forests. The mining of diamonds and other gemstones also has its environmental hazards, including deforestation, soil erosion, the accumulation of silt in rivers, water and air pollution, and excessive water use.

The African continent in particular has felt the effects of gold and diamond production. In South Africa, where gold mining is a major industry, pollution and safety problems abound. And in Botswana a future diamond mine may disrupt the water system that much wildlife depends on.

Production of these and other precious gems is surely not friendly to the environment.

Scrimshaw kits, part of Artek's "Save the Whale" collection, promote the "American art of scrimshaw."

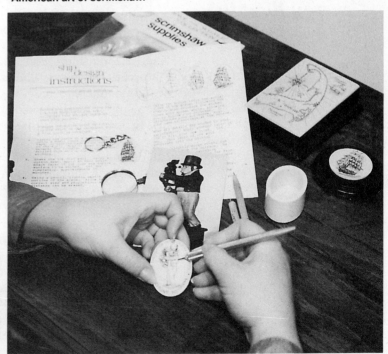

Reproduction of Japanese powder box from the Mystic Seaport Museum Collection. Made exclusively by Artek to simulate real ivory, using no animal parts.

Getting Recharged

E ACH DAY OUR HEALTH is placed more at risk from the poisonous heavy metals that escape from batteries once they've been discarded. Batteries leach toxins into the soil, the water, and the food chain if they've been buried in a landfill, or into the air if incinerated.

There's no perfect battery on the market, but you do have some options. You can learn how to choose the best battery for your purpose, how to get the most out of it, and how to dispose of it properly.

Read the Ingredients List

The contents of the batteries you buy are usually identified on the package. These are the most common types:

Zinc carbon and *alkaline manganese* batteries, made by manufacturers like Eveready and Duracell, are designed for general use in items such as radios, smoke alarms, flashlights, and clocks.

Mercuric oxide, silver oxide, and *zinc air* batteries are button cells that are used in small devices such as hearing aids, calculators, cameras, and watches.

> *Manufacturing batteries can consume up to 50 times more energy than the batteries produce.*

All five types listed above contain mercury in varying amounts. Mercuric oxide batteries, for instance, contain 30 to 50 percent mercury by weight, while zinc carbon batteries contain just 0.01 percent. No amount of mercury is good for you, however. When ingested by humans (in contaminated air, drinking water, or fish) mercury can cause severe brain and kidney damage and the loss of motor function.

Nickel cadmium batteries are more expensive than the other kinds, but they can be recharged hundreds of times, which saves buying hundreds of disposables. They are particularly good for such things as children's toys that go through batteries as though they were chocolate chip cookies.

Unfortunately, nickel and cadmium are both toxic. Cadmium is a suspected carcinogen and may cause permanent kidney damage, anemia, emphysema, and birth defects. Nickel can destroy nasal tissues and cause asthma after chronic, concentrated exposure.

Batteries can also contain other heavy metals such as silver, lead, lithium, manganese, and zinc, which can accumulate and concentrate in the food chain if they escape into the environment. — *Leda Hartman*

What You Can Do

✔ When you do use batteries, use rechargeable ones, especially for devices that use lots of power.

✔ To get the longest possible life from your rechargeable batteries, be sure to charge them completely each time you recharge them. This is particularly important the first time because they take on a "memory" of their first charging experience.

✔ Similarly, and for the same reasons, drain them completely when you use them, especially the first time. The more fully you drain and recharge them the first time, the more power they will store and the fewer times you will need to recharge them.

✔ Use a small, inexpensive battery tester to double-check your battery's charge. It's quick and easy.

✔ To save money, use disposables while recharging the others.

✔ Teach your kids to recharge their own batteries. This saves you time and money and is a good earth-loving lesson for them.

✔ Use electricity instead of batteries when possible since batteries consume much more energy than they produce.

✔ Don't mix a new battery with an old one (by using them together in a flashlight, for instance), because the new battery will try to recharge the old one and thus cut its own life short.

✔ Recharge your batteries using solar energy (see product reviews).

In 1979 there were 1.3 million elephants trodding the African savanna. Today there are only 625,000 remaining.

A PLUG FOR RECHARGEABLES

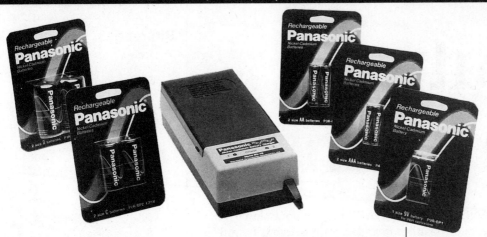

PANASONIC RECHARGEABLE BATTERIES

Long lasting and intended for industrial use. These will work in everything from radios to toys to flashlights. They can be recharged up to 500 times. –L.H.

$5.95 for 2 AA batteries
$14.95 for 2 C batteries
$24.95 for 2 D batteries
Panasonic

NICD BATTERY CHARGER

If you go through a lot of batteries for flashlights, toy trucks, portable radios, and cameras, the SunWatt NiCd battery charger might be the best deal on the market. It will charge C, D, and AA batteries using PV cells mounted on the lid. Just put the dead batteries in it and set the unit in the sun. Because it slowly trickle-charges the batteries, it's safer than plug-in NiCd chargers. –Alex Wilson

About $25, SunWatt

Before ordering from any mail order suppliers, please check with them to determine shipping and handling charges.

BATTERYMATE™ SOLAR BATTERY MAINTAINER

If your car runs the risk of a dead battery when it sits unused for days or during cold weather, you can solve the problem by plugging a Solarex Batterymate into the cigarette lighter and putting it on the dashboard.

The Batterymate's 4"x12" PV panel is mounted in a sturdy plastic housing. It comes with an eight-foot cord; in case the sun is shining through only the rear window, the cord should be long enough to reach there, too. At $39.95 in auto parts stores, it's about the same price as an AC battery charger. Before running out to buy one, though, check to make sure that your cigarette lighter will work with the ignition off — if not, neither will the Batterymate. Solarex is a pioneer in PV development. –A.W.

$39.95, Solarex (also available from auto parts stores)

HOW TO SAY GOOD-BYE

It is critical that you keep batteries out of ordinary landfills and out of incinerators. Take them only to a double-lined landfill or to a hazardous-waste collection site. Battery recycling facilities extract and reuse mercuric oxide, silver oxide, and nickel cadmium so they won't enter the waste stream.

Some jewelry stores, pharmacies, and hearing aid stores collect button batteries and sell them to battery recycling facilities. One such facility is the Mercury Refining Co.

For information about battery recycling programs, contact the Environmental Action Coalition.

If you're concerned about possible hazards in your community, call the working group on Community Right-To-Know at (202) 546-9707.

Beauty & The Earth

T HE PERSONAL AND THE PLANETARY meet at your skin. Multiply your "private" health care and grooming habits by millions, and you realize that the individual act of choosing a lotion or shampoo has significant ecological implications.

Beauty preparations can be cruel to the earth — and to your health. Ingredients in hair dyes can harm eyes and lungs. The bleaching process that creates lily-white plastic cosmetic packages also creates highly toxic dioxins.

A shampoo's testing may have entailed the painful slow burning of the eyes of thousands of rabbits. A skin oil may be leading to the extinction of whales. A non-biodegradable mascara can poison our rivers and lakes. Hair spray aerosol cans are choking our landfills.

In previous generations, virtually all personal hygiene and beauty care products for skin, hair, and teeth were natural, organic, and relatively benign. Today, modern science and Madison Avenue have sold us a huge selection of highly refined chemical agents for use in our bedrooms and bathrooms. Many of those products have little to do with human well-being. In fact, some of them may be downright lethal. We'll look at safe personal care products, which companies are making the best, and where and how to get them. But first, some motivation.

A study of more than 58,000 beauticians found they developed multiple myeloma at 4 times the rate of the general population.

– CONSUMER'S DICTIONARY OF COSMETIC INGREDIENTS

Warning: Existing Laws Do Not Require That Personal Care Products Be Proven Safe

In fact, the converse is true: no product can be restricted unless proven harmful, and products can be released before being tested. Don't rely on the government to protect you and your family.

It is disturbing that many of the very products that contact the most sensitive and vulnerable areas of the body — the mucous membranes of the eyes, nose, lungs, and vagina — are the least regulated.

HAIR PRODUCTS

Shampoos

Shampoos are the personal care products most frequently cited in complaints to the FDA. Many detergent-based shampoos (particularly antidandruff) contain toxins that can be easily absorbed through the scalp. Try these more benign alternatives.

TOM'S OF MAINE NATURAL SHAMPOO

The delicious fragrance here is from almond oil and lemongrass oil. Tester Sue Kennedy says, "It left my hair shining and manageable . . . and without using a conditioner." Besides that, you can pick it up with your groceries!

$3.60 to $5.25 (12 oz.)
Tom's of Maine; Feather River Co.

REAL PURITY MOISTURIZING SHAMPOO

Raspberry nectar essence makes this shampoo smell good enough to eat, and the ingredients are more natural than those in many processed foods. A heavy plastic tube with nozzle top protects freshness.

$7 (113.4 g), Real Purity

It takes 95% less energy to produce an aluminum product from recycled aluminum than from raw aluminum.

PAUL PENDERS JASMINE, ROSEMARY, AND PEPPERMINT SHAMPOOS

An impressive list of herbal and vegetable ingredients, plus a trace of paraben preservative. Natural separation requires shaking before use. Smells exotic, feels great.

$4.95 (8.8 oz.), Paul Penders Co.

Conditioners

Home versions of hair conditioners include henna, olive, sesame, or corn oil, honey, mayonnaise, and avocado. Experiment with any of these, but make sure you rinse thoroughly.

NATURE'S GATE RAINWATER AWAPUHI CONDITIONER

A creamy rich after-shampoo. All our testers loved it going on and felt it gave a "full body" effect to the hair. It smells absolutely delicious — like whipped tangerines.

$4.50 (18 oz.)
Nature's Gate Herbal Cosmetics

Hair Coloring

Unfortunately, thanks to a milestone in special interest lobbying, hair dyes have enjoyed a congressional special exception to all ingredient controls since 1938. So, consumer beware! *Consumer Reports* has named 20 different potential human carcinogens used in many commercial hair dyes. That's at least 20 different reasons to try one of these benign alternatives.

PAUL PENDERS COLOUR CONDITIONERS

Natural colors made from minerals and salts. You won't find chemicals, peroxides, or irritants in these products. They're water-soluble; the color will wash out after three shampoos.

$9.75 (6 oz.), Paul Penders

VITAWAVE ALL NATURAL HAIR COLOR

Made from fruit, vegetable, and herbal sources in spirits of ammonia. No chemical dyes. Eighteen colors can be mixed to individual preferences at home or in your favorite salon. Instructions included.

$9.75, Ecco Bella

Hair Sprays

We have not yet found a hair spray that's safe for both people and the environment. Even the "natural" brands are predominantly synthetic agents. Aerosol hair sprays contain hazardous propellants, carcinogenic plastics, formaldehyde, and artificial fragrances. Also, aerosol cans are very resource intensive.

Mousses & Gels

We haven't discovered any environmentally safe mousse or gel. But the tube that gel comes in uses fewer resources than the pressurized cans that mousse comes in. This one is the closest. Let us know if you're using one we haven't heard about.

THE BODY SHOP MOSTLY MEN SLICK HAIR STYLER

We use this because it works well and is a gel rather than mousse. It does, however, contain non-biodegradable synthetics (PVP/VA, triethanolamine, carbomer 940, and three preservatives).–*Bruce Anderson*

$4.95 (3.5 oz.), The Body Shop

Perms

Commercial permanent hair-waving lotions contain PVP plastic as well as formaldehyde, glycols, and mineral oil. Avoid them.

VITAWAVE ALL NATURAL PERMS

Made from plant sources only, in four types: Resistant, Normal, Bleached/Tinted, and Mild. And, of course, instructions are included.

$11, Ecco Bella

Nineteen countries, including the Soviet Union (but not the U.S.), have committed to cutting their sulfur dioxide emissions by 30% by 1993.

TO PRESERVE OR NOT TO PRESERVE?

The hottest debate in personal care is over preservatives: whether to use them, and if so, which and how much? It is a built-in irony of cosmetics that the more organic a product, the more susceptible it is to dangerous bacteria, yeast, and fungus. The fact is, the best way to preserve truly "natural" personal care products is refrigeration. Such inconvenient precautions being unlikely to gain popularity, many "natural" brands contain one or more of 60 different synthetic preservatives.

The purists maintain that microbe-killing chemicals also kill beneficial skin bacteria and our own living cells, and are more harmful than the organisms they destroy. This camp's answer to spoilage is comprehensive: clean, organically whole ingredients, plus purity in manufacturing, protective packaging (small sizes, narrow openings), rapid shipping, and plant-based preservatives (such as propionic acid from fruits, leaves, and wood pulp). But most distributors, stores, and consumers do not limit themselves to strictly 100% preservative-free products. In fact, very few such products exist.

Although people disagree about their safety, the paraben family of synthetic preservatives (methyl, propyl, and butyl) are, after water, the most common ingredients in cosmetics. The parabens have been around for decades, and are widely considered the most acceptable preservatives currently available.

The skin itself is permeable and absorbs chemicals directly, yet ingredients in skin lotions and cosmetics go untested, unlabeled, and unregulated. To this day, hair dyes are completely exempt from federal labeling requirements, as are antiperspirants, sunscreens, shampoos, and soaps.

Enforcement of the few regulations that do exist can't keep up with the hundreds of new products that come out every year. And when warning labels have been required, manufacturers have been known to replace proven carcinogens with other ingredients that, on testing, prove equally deadly. It can take years for that testing to be completed and for the FDA then to propose new warning labels.

Looks Can Kill

Few people who learn about the brutality and agony involved in the testing of cosmetics on animals wish to support it. In some tests, caustic detergents, dyes, and other toxic agents are applied repeatedly to open wounds or poured into the eyes of immobilized, unanesthetized rabbits. Other tests involve the forced feeding of deadly doses of toxic chemicals to guinea pigs, rats, mice, dogs, monkeys, and horses. The poisoned and mutilated animals are discarded after testing, dead and alive, like used rags. Tens of thousands of helpless creatures are tortured and killed in these ways each year, in the name of product safety. Yet these gruesome procedures are not required by law!

Animal by-products in beauty aids include stearic acid, amino acids, cell and tissue extracts such as DNA, and gelatin from cattle and horses, lanolin from sheep, spermaceti from whales, and squalene from sharks. There are several categories of animal-based products: slaughterhouse by-products, those derived from living animals, and those from animals killed specifically for their "by-products." The last cate-

SKIN PRODUCTS

Be good to your skin. It's your largest sense organ and your largest organ of elimination. It excretes toxins, regulates moisture and temperature, keeps out bacteria and ultraviolet rays, and protects sensitive nerve endings.

Soaps and Facial Cleansers

All hand soaps clean just fine, so the main issue is ingredients. Unfortunately, most soaps don't list them. Shop for informative labels, not sexy wrappers.

Virtually all mass-marketed soaps are made with beef tallow. For alternatives, look for "vegetable based," "plant based," or "cruelty free" on the label. Avoid detergent/deodorant soaps. Their potent germ-killing chemicals break down the skin's defenses against harmful ultraviolet rays and destroy beneficial bacteria in soil and water. And, finally, avoid alkaline soaps, alcohol in skin toners, and artificially scented soaps. Synthetic fragrances and their fixatives can cause dry skin, redness, and rashes. Here are some products to try instead.

CLEARLY NATURAL GLYCERINE SOAP

The first pure glycerine "see through" soap and the sole product of a small, eco-conscious company that has refused to raise its price since 1978, Clearly Natural has earned a loyal national market in spite of zero advertising. The label is now the first to claim "good for sensitive skin," without animal testing. Not only that, but we found it in our local supermarket!

60¢ to 90¢ (4 oz.)
Clearly Natural

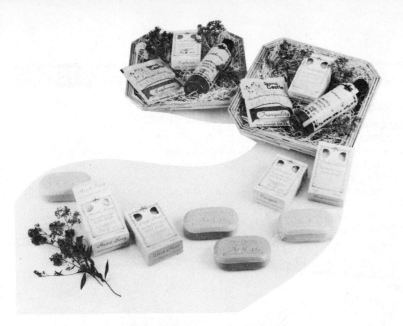

AURA CACIA AROMATHERAPY BATH SOAP

Contains pure cocoa butter, essential oils, and absolutely nothing synthetic. Highly aromatic, but all natural. Said to be long lasting, although bars are soft when wet.

$2.25 (3 oz.), Aura Cacia

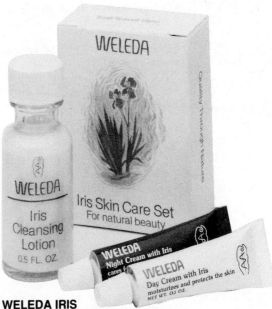

WELEDA IRIS CLEANSING LOTION

A mild facial cleanser/moisturizer/skin tonic. Looks like milk, smells like the Garden of Eden! Use this lotion and feel like royalty. Comes in a clear glass bottle.

$5.50 (4 oz.), Weleda; Feather River; Meadowbrook Herb Garden

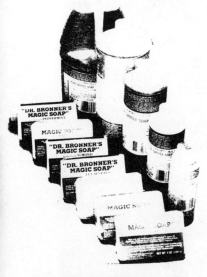

DR. BRONNER'S PURE CASTILE LIQUID SOAP

Our favorite liquid all-purpose body soap. Concentrated, zesty and tingly, yet safe enough for dentures, babies, and the family pet. From the eccentric "Master Chemist & Essene Rabbi," Dr. Emanuel H. Bronner. This soap is so good it's a health food store standard in spite of its legendary, small-type religious labels. An ecological choice because it can substitute for shaving cream, shampoo, deodorant, and dishwashing liquid! One-hundred percent biodegradable.

$3.50 (16 oz.), Dr. Bronner All-One-God-Faith, Inc.

HOME HEALTH ALMOND GLOW NOURISHING BEAUTY BAR

This earthy-looking bar contains almond meal with a subtle fragrance from sweet almond oil and rosemary oleoresin. No detergents or animal tallow; completely biodegradable.

$2.75, Home Health Products, Inc.

We use 40 million acres of forest each day for the production of paper.

BEWARE OF COSMETICS BEARING THESE

PETROCHEMICALS
- Are non-renewable.
- Are non-biodegradable.
- Can be mutagenic and carcinogenic to humans.
- Are polluting when released into the environment.
- Generate toxic by-products in their production.

FORMALDEHYDE (preservative sometimes called "Quarternium-15")
- Is toxic to humans.
- Is toxic to fish and wildlife.

TALCUM POWDER (found in body powders)
- Is a lung and eye irritant.
- Is often contaminated with cancer-causing asbestos.
- Can be dangerous to babies.
- Poses serious occupational hazards to miners of talc.

ARTIFICIAL COLORS
- Contain irritating, dangerous chemical dyes.
- Have been carcinogenic when tested on animals.
- Contain non-renewable, non-biodegradable petrochemicals.

ARTIFICIAL FRAGRANCES
- Many contain untested, unregulated, new chemicals.
- Can be skin irritants.
- Can contain volatile fumes.
- Are non-biodegradable.
- Can contain toxic petrochemicals.

FLUORIDE (in toothpastes)
- Carcinogenic (according to Debra Lynn Dadd, author of *Nontoxic and Natural*).
- Poses numerous other serious health threats.
- Is banned as a water additive in ten European countries.

MINERAL OIL (lubricant)
- Is a suspected human carcinogen.
- Prevents skin from breathing.
- Dissolves skin's germ-fighting sebum.
- Interferes with vitamin absorption.
- Is phototoxic (becomes an irritant in sunlight).
- Is non-biodegradable.

gory includes such ingredients as musk, carmine, keratin, placenta, collagen, tallow, elastin, and mink oil. The practice is most unacceptable when the animal is an endangered species, as when whales are killed for their oil.

Animal-Friendly Alternatives

"Cruelty-free" and "vegetable-based" products are intended for the growing number of consumers who find animal exploitation in the name of beauty unacceptable. They use traditional, time-proven safe, whole, plant-derived ingredients, or test new ones on human volunteers or microorganisms.

Changing their testing policy for the nineties, top cosmetic firms like Avon and Revlon have bowed to animal rights pressure and agreed to cease animal testing, while — as of early 1990 — Gillette and Procter & Gamble continue to hold out, and Estée Lauder refuses to stop using shark oil in its perfume.

SKIN PRODUCTS

Moisturizers

After 20 years of New England wood-heat winters, we've just discovered the benefits of moisturizers. Oil or wax based, moisturizers don't put water into your skin — they keep it from coming out. Our favorites dissipate nearly completely into the skin, but leave a clean, refreshing smell.

AUBREY ORGANICS MANDARIN MAGIC MOISTURIZER

Made with eight Chinese herbs and nothing else. Very rich and aromatic. The best scent of all the moisturizers we've tried. Comes in a clear glass bottle.

$12 (1 oz.), Aubrey Organics

AUTUMN-HARP PURE PLANT BODY LOTION

A sweet, oil-based lotion with an ingredients label that spells natural: "Distilled spring water, olive oil, sweet almond oil, peanut oil, aloe vera juice, rose petals, comfrey root, vegetable glycerin, unbleached beeswax, gum benzoin, & true fragrance oils for scent. Nothing more — nothing less."

$6.95 (6 oz.)
Autumn-Harp; InterNatural

ALEXANDRA AVERY ALMOND CREAM

Sweet almond, sesame, wheat germ, vitamin E oils, plus lecithin, distilled unbleached beeswax, plant essences. Absorbs nicely. Subtle scent.

$5.95 (1 oz.)
Alexandra Avery; InterNatural

Skin Protection

AUTUMN-HARP UN-PETROLEUM JELLY

At last, "veggie-vaseline"! From pure plant oils only. Baby mild, with a faint, earthy scent. Recyclable plastic container.

$6 (4 oz.)
Autumn-Harp Inc.; InterNatural

LAKON HERBALS COMFREY SALVE

A "healing salve" for baby rash, bruises, blisters, chapped skin, and insect bites. The closest thing to a medicine recommended in this book. It contains organic olive oil, fresh comfrey, chickweed, burdock, plantain, sage, red clover, benzoin (a natural preservative from gum plant resin), beeswax, essence of rosemary, and lavender.

$4.50 (2 oz.), Lakon Herbals

SHAVING

The modern environmental insults resulting from the ancient vanity of shaving include high-tech aerosol containers, synthetic ingredients harmful to man and the environment, and mounting millions of non-biodegradable disposable razors. Many shaving creams and foams contain propane, a harsh petrochemical. Many also contain animal ingredients, and are routinely tested on animals. Try these instead.

Shaving Creams

TOM'S SHAVING CREAM

A low-lathering cream from 100% coconut and olive oil. Concentrated: use a dab a day. You squeeze it from a tube. (We've been known to mistake it for toothpaste, so we're glad Tom's is all natural!) An old favorite.

$4.50 (3 oz.), Tom's of Maine and many supermarkets

SPEICK SHAVING CREAM

A spicy herbal, foamy "soap cream" made from beeswax, glycerine, and the aromatic Speick plant.

$4.20 (2.25 oz.)
Meadowbrook Herb Garden

After-Shave Lotions/Astringents

Caution: After-shave lotions can be unfriendly to your skin. Read labels! Don't put harsh chemicals like formaldehyde on your freshly shaven face.

AUBREY ORGANICS MEN'S STOCK GINSENG MINT AFTER-SHAVE/HERBAL SKIN BRACER

Our favorite. A thin, smooth fluid. Strong, fresh sting with cool after-feel. Very clean smelling. Preserved with citrus seed extract only.

$5.75 (4 oz.), Ecco Bella

PAUL PENDERS AFTER-SHAVE LOTION

Contains skin-healing wheat germ oil (vitamin E). Witch hazel gives the quick brace, while chlorophyllin leaves the wonderful smell. Paul Penders also makes skin cleanser and toner.

$7.50 (6 oz.), Feather River Co.

What You Can Do

✔ Refuse to purchase any product with ingredients you don't recognize or cannot pronounce. If it sounds as if it was born in a test tube, it's probably non-biodegradable, animal tested, of questionable safety, or unnecessary.

✔ Watch out for terms like "made with" and "derived from." A product can be called "herbal" when it has only the slightest percentage of herbs in it. Only the words "ingredients" or "composition" indicate full disclosure.

Companies That Do Not Test Their Products On Animals . . .

As of early 1990 the following companies do not test their products on animals, nor do they use in their products ingredients that are tested on animals. Some do offer products with ingredients derived from animals or insects; these are marked with asterisks.

Abkit *
Abracadabra, Inc.
Aditi Nutri-Sentials
Adwe Labs
African Bio-Botanica
Alba Botanica
Alexandra Avery
Allens
Amway
Ananada Country Products
Andalina
Arbonne International
Aroma Vera
Aubrey Organics *
Aura Cacia, Inc.
Auromere
Autumn Harp, Inc.
Aveda
Avon
Baby Massage
Baby Touch, Ltd.
Bare Escentuals
Baudelaire, Inc.
Beauty Naturally
Beauty Without Cruelty
Benetton
Biokosma
Bioline *
Body Love
Body Shop
Bon Ami
Bonne Sante
Borlind of Germany
Chenti Products, Inc. *
Clearly Natural
Clientele
Colour Quest
Comfort Manufacturing
Community Soap Factory
Country Comfort
Creature Care
Desert Essence
Dr. E.H. Bronner
Dr. Hauschka Biodynamic Formulations
Earth Healing Arts
Earth Science
Ecover
Essentials
Everybody
Fashion Two Twenty *
Four-D Hobe Marketing
Freemans
A.J. Funk & Co.
Future Perfect
General Nutrition
Giovanni Cosmetics
Golden Lotus
Goldwell Cosmetics *
Granny's Old Fashioned
Green Ban
Gruene Kosmetik
Hain Pure Food Co. *
Heavenly Soap
Home Health Products
Home Service Products

Huish Chemical
Humphrey's Pharmacal
I & M Natural Skincare
Irma Shorell, Inc.
Jacki's Magic Lotion *
Jason Natural Products *
Jeanne Rose Herbal Body Works
Jurlique
Kiss My Face
KMS
KSA Jojaba
Lakon Herbals
L'Anza Research Labs
L'Arome
Life Tree Products
Loanda Herbal Products *
Magic American Chemical
Michael's Health Products
Mountain Fresh
Mountain Ocean, Ltd.
Murphy's Oil Soap
Naturade
Nature Cosmetics, Inc.
Nature De France *
Nature's Colors *
Nature's Gate
Nature's Plus

Naturessence
Nevada Nutritional
New Age Products
New World Minerals
Nexxus *
No Common Scents *
North Country Soap *
Nu Skin
Nutri-Metics International
O'Naturel, Inc.
Oriflame International *
Orjene Natural Cosmetics
Passion (Elizabeth Taylor's)
Patricia Allison
Paul Mitchell Systems
Paul Penders
Peelu Products
Pets 'N People
Professional/Technical Services *
Rachel Perry *
Rainbow Research Corp.
W. T. Raleigh Co. *
The Real Aloe Co. *
Real Purity & Co.
Reviva Labs, Inc. *
Rokeach & Sons, Inc.

Sappo Hill Soap Works
Schiff *
Shahin Soap
Shikai Products *
Sierra Dawn
Sirena
Sombra (C&S Labs)
Sunshine Scented Oils
Tom's of Maine
Tonialg
Trans India
Uni Pac Laboratory
Uninhibited (Cher's)
Velvet Products
Victoria's Secret *
Vita Wave Products
Wala-Heilmittle *
Walter Rau "Speick" Soaps & Toiletries
Warm Earth Cosmetics
Weleda, Inc.
Woods of Windsor *
Wysong *
Youthessence
Zia Cosmetics

—Source: New England Anti-Vivisection Society

. . . Companies That Still Test on Animals

Many — if not most — of the common ingredients found in body products today were at one time animal tested, and even cruelty-free companies use them. The following companies, however, as of late 1989, have refused to cease testing their products or new ingredients on animals.

Alberto-Culver
American Cyanamid
Andrea Rabb
Aramis
Armour-Dial
BeautiControl Cosmetics
Beecham Cosmetics
Bonne Bell
Boyle-Midway
Breck
Bristol Myers
Carter-Wallace
Chanel
Chesebrough-Ponds
Church & Dwight
Clairol
Clarins of Paris
Clinique Laboratories
Clorox
Colgate-Palmolive
Cosmair
Coty
Dana Perfumes
Dell Laboratories
Diversey Wyandotte
Dorothy Grey
Dow Chemical
Drackette Products

Economics Laboratory
Eli Lilly
Estée Lauder
Francis Denny
Gillette
Givaudin
Helena Rubenstein
Helene Curtis Industries
Houbigant
Jean Patou
Jergens
Johnson & Johnson
S.C. Johnson & Son
Johnson Products
Jovan
Lamaur
Lancome
Lever Brothers
L'Oreal
Maybelline
Mennen
Neutrogena
Nina Ricci
Pfizer
Physicians Formula Cosmetics
Procter & Gamble
Purex

Quintessence
Richardson-Vicks
Schering-Plough (Maybelline)
Sea & Ski
Shulton
Squibb
Sterling Drug
Syntex
Texize
Vidal Sassoon
Warner Lambert
Wella
Westwood Pharmaceuticals
Zotos International

—Source: PETA (People for the Ethical Treatment of Animals).

Nearly a third of the trash we generate is empty containers and packages.

DEODORANTS/ANTIPERSPIRANTS

Antiperspirants work by closing down the sweat glands — not necessarily a good thing since this keeps waste products in. Deodorants work by masking odors or killing the bacteria that cause them. Underarm products have a bad safety record. Even the not-always-vigilant FDA found it necessary to ban eight different deodorant/antiperspirant ingredients in the 1980s.

The most dangerous ingredient in antiperspirants is *aluminum chlorohydrate,* which can irritate skin, infect hair follicles, or — in sprays — poison the lungs. Antiperspirants can also contain aerosol propellants, ammonia, alcohol, zirconium, formaldehyde, and/or triclosan, which can cause liver damage when absorbed through the skin. Silicone lubricants like dimethicone can be toxic. Here are some alternatives.

ALVERA ALOE UNSCENTED ALL NATURAL ROLL-ON DEODORANT

Seventy-five percent aloe vera gel and preserved with grapefruit seed extract. No alcohol, dyes, or artificial preservatives. Just quietly does the job, without endangering your skin or the ecosystem.

$4.45 (3 oz.)
Home Health Products

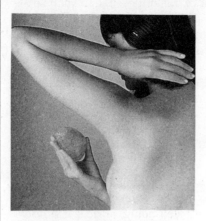

LE CRYSTAL NATUREL MINERAL ROCK DEODORANT

Something really different: a fist-size rock crystal deodorizer, made of 100% natural mineral salts. Just moisten and slide around under your arms. Le Crystal leaves a thin, nonsticky, invisible layer that prevents bacteria (the real cause of odor). Non-staining. Odorless. A long-term investment, one rock lasts up to a year. According to tester Audrey McKnight, it "works just fine, even when I'm exercising." Beware that this contains potassium alum and is toxic if swallowed. Keep away from children.

$14.95 (5.35 oz.)
Self-Care Catalog

BATH PREPARATIONS

Bubble-bath preparations present the greatest hazard of all bath products, causing skin rashes as well as urinary tract, bladder, and kidney infections. Try this natural and safe alternative.

AURA CACIA SAND CASTLE AROMATHERAPY MINERAL BATH

A true experience: hot bath, special scents, and soothing minerals from the ocean and desert, all skin and water friendly.

$2.25 (3 oz. — 3 baths)
Aura Cacia

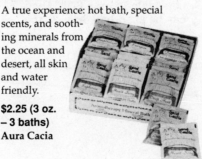

What You Can Do

✔ Use alternatives to aerosol sprays whenever possible, like squeeze bottles, pumps, and roll-on applicators. Even ozone-friendly propellants can carry harmful substances into your lungs. If you must use aerosols, empty cans completely, and recycle them.

✔ Lather for shaving using a thin layer of plain soap or aloe vera gel. Shaving cream often contains ammonia and ethanol.

✔ Condition hair by generously applying either sesame or corn oil. Wrap in a hot damp towel for 20 minutes, then shampoo.

✔ Create a shampoo from nontoxic ingredients by mixing one cup liquid castile soap with half a cup of distilled water and one-quarter cup of olive or avocado oil.

✔ Use vegetable oil to remove makeup.

✔ Try witch hazel extract, sold in pharmacies and supermarkets, for skin care. It tones, soothes, and refines oily or blemished complexions and also deodorizes. Just apply and rinse off.

You should know that even some products claiming to be non-animal tested actually contain synthetic ingredients that have been tested on animals, usually by the supplier. Since it is impossible to analyze every source of every ingredient in all products, the integrity of the manufacturer may be your only guide in shopping for animal-friendly products. Watch for more companies to go cruelty-free in the nineties.

Contact PETA (People for the Ethical Treatment of Animals) for updated lists of companies that do and do not test on animals, and (for a $15 donation) "The PETA Guide to Compassionate Living."

Do I Really Need This Particular Product?

In the face of cruel animal testing, personal health risks, dwindling non-renewable resources, and factory and packaging waste, the first question to ask when considering a personal care product is, "Is this really necessary?" Will it truly enhance my well-being, or does it simply cater to my vanity or fear of aging? And at what price to the world around me?

Another good question: Is there a simpler, more natural substitute for this ingredient? Cornstarch, for example, is a safe and inexpensive replacement for talc, which is subject to contamination with cancer-causing asbestos. Witch hazel makes an excellent and safe after-shave astringent. Jojoba can substitute for whale oil. And the gooey juice of the common house cactus, *Aloe vera*, is a natural skin protector.

You do have choices. If do-it-yourself doesn't do it for you, try any of the products recommended on these pages. — *Lonny J. Brown, Ph.D*

BUYER BE WISE

- Only a handful of FDA toxicologists are responsible for evaluating and inspecting 20,000 different cosmetics products. Five hundred new products are introduced annually in the United States.

- It's also "buyer beware" in natural food stores, where commercial co-opting of "new age" health language runs rampant. So-called expert opinions differ widely about the significance of minerals, pesticides, processing, and certain concentrations and combinations of ingredients. There is no legal definition of the word "natural"; at least one company (Borlind) main-

tains that petroleum is natural since it comes from the earth.

- The word "fragrance" can stand for any of up to 4,000 synthetic additives, some of which can cause headaches, dizziness, rashes, discoloration, coughing, and skin irritation.

- "TEA" and "DEA" (triethanolamine and diethanolamine), detergents found in hundreds of bath products, were contaminated with cancer-causing nitrosamines in half the products tested by the FDA. They can be absorbed through the skin.

What You Can Do

✔ Be suspicious of "natural" products that are brilliant white or "pearlescent." Few organic substances look like that, and it probably took a high-tech, environmentally expensive chemical process to achieve it.

✔ Read labels. Many bath and body product manufacturers do not reveal ingredients unless required by law. You can exercise your right to full disclosure by patronizing only those conscientious companies that list all ingredients on their packages and literature.

✔ Choose personal care products with labels that best inform you of the origins, purposes, concentrations, and biodegradability of their ingredients. If you can't find a detergent-free soap or a preservative-free moisturizer, then pick one with the smallest concentration of synthetics and with additives low on the list. If the first two or three ingredients are synthetic, the rest don't matter.

BODY POWDERS

Many body powders contain the dangerous mineral talc. Keep away from babies. Better yet, buy plant-based alternatives.

AURA CACIA NATURAL BODY POWDER

Cornstarch (instead of talc), plus absorbent floral substances like powdered patchouli and oils of lavender and lemon peel (test for skin sensitivity). Very absorptive.

$7.95 (4 oz.), Aura Cacia

ALEXANDRA AVERY PURELY NATURAL MOONSILK BODY POWDER

So mild, it's fine for babies. A good deodorant, too. Contains baking soda and the powders of arrowroot, sandalwood, ginger, comfrey, and myrrh. Not superfine, it has some texture. Natural tan color (not fake white).

$5.95 (4 oz.), Alexandra Avery; InterNatural

BODY/MASSAGE OILS

High-quality skin oils are concentrated. Avoid eye contact. When massage oils are used in sexual activity, ingredients become especially critical. Even vegetable oils that go rancid can be toxic when introduced internally. *Avoid:* mineral oil, artificial fragrances, synthetic lubricants, and alcohol astringents.

WELEDA MASSAGE OIL WITH ARNICA

Strong outdoor smell and warm feeling. Ingredients: peanut oil, olive oil, arnica extract, birch leaf extract, natural fragrance. Glass bottle.

$6.50 (4 oz.), Weleda; InterNatural; Meadowbrook Herb Garden

HOME HEALTH ALMOND GLOW SKIN LOTION

A light oil with a truly delicious scent. Ingredients include lanolin oil and vitamin E.

$4.95 (8 oz.) Home Health Products, Inc.

SUN LOTIONS

Man-made deterioration of the ozone layer in the atmosphere has made prolonged exposure to sunlight an even greater skin-cancer risk. Furthermore, antibacterial soaps, cosmetic dyes, antibiotic drugs, and vitamin supplements of riboflavin all increase your skin's sensitivity to sunlight. The fairer your skin, the higher the sun protection factor or SPF (from 1 to 20) you need in a sunblock product. Don't go sunbathing or snow skiing without proper skin protection.

AURA CACIA SUN BUTTER

Low sun protection factor (4) allows even tanning without drying. Not for the highly sun sensitive. Low-tech ingredients: sweet almond oil, pure cocoa butter, coconut oil, natural vitamin E oil, PABA (a natural plant-based sunscreen).

$5.95 (8 oz.), Aura Cacia

ALEXANDRA AVERY GARDENIA SUN OIL

Sesame is the natural sunscreen ingredient. Gardenia lends a fabulous misty-sweet aroma.

$7.45 (8 oz.), Alexandra Avery; Feather River; InterNatural

Each Sunday 500,000 trees are made into newspapers that aren't recycled.

OUR FAVORITE PERSONAL CARE COMPANIES & CATALOGUES

Since there are far too many personal care products on the market today to review them all here, we also review the best companies in order of preference — based on their products, their policies, and their people. The premise is that if you can trust the company, you can have confidence in their entire product line.

What are the criteria for inclusion in this list? We've recommended only those companies that currently manufacture products without testing them on animals. Most use only plant-based ingredients, but some use ingredients that come from living animals. In most cases, these companies avoid preservatives. Exceptions are noted.

Finally, we recommend personal care companies that have all ingredients listed on their product labels and whose products have:

- no artificial colorings
- zero or very low percentage of chemical preservatives
- no harsh detergents
- no man-made fragrances

PERSONAL CARE COMPANIES

(In order of preference)

Look at the end of each company review for these symbols:

♣ means that the company either lists ingredients on its products or packaging or makes that information available on request.

◯ means that the company uses recycled, recyclable, and/or biodegradable packaging.

More and more of these companies' products are now available in your local drugstore or supermarket. But in case some of them haven't reached your area yet, catalogues that carry the company's product line follow each review. (All reviews by Lonny Brown, except where noted.)

AUTUMN-HARP

This is *the* industry leader in people-and-planet-conscious business practices. Autumn-Harp's high-quality products were the first to be packaged in coded, easily recyclable plastic containers; the company also uses recycled paper and recycled packing materials. Two percent of its sales revenues go directly to environmental causes.

♣, ◯ — **Feather River Co.**

TOM'S OF MAINE

The "natural" pioneer in the mainstream market, Tom's is available in many supermarkets. Tom's uses safe, biodegradable ingredients that, on testing, prove as effective as their artificial counterparts. Seven and a half percent of their pre-tax profits go to charity and to environmental causes. This is the only producer that lists all ingredients, sources, and purposes on its products. Thanks, Tom!

♣, ◯ — **Feather River Co.**

DESERT ESSENCE

Skin, hair, and oral products based on the oils of two traditional healing plants: jojoba and tea tree. Known for its simple, whole ingredients. Paraben is used as a preservative.

♣ — **Feather River Co; Lion & Lamb**

ORAL HYGIENE

Toothpastes & Powders

Commercial, mass-market toothpastes typically contain artificial sweeteners, preservatives, and chemical dyes. Also found in the worst offenders: plastic resin (the kind used in hair spray), paraffin, and saccharin — all potential health threats and all irrelevant to oral hygiene. In addition, most big name brands are whitened with the highly processed chemical titanium dioxide.

Fluoride *on* teeth prevents tooth decay, but too much fluoride *in* your body is toxic. If you're concerned that your intake may already be exceeding safe levels from fluoridated water and food made with it, frequent brushing is an alternative to choosing a fluoride toothpaste.

Finally, avoid products containing the popular foaming agent sodium lauryl sulfate. It's a known irritant, but it's found in many "natural" toothpastes, shampoos, and creams.

DESERT ESSENCE NATURAL GUM TOOTHPASTE WITH TEA TREE OIL

We love this stuff. Tea tree oil is delicious! When we find a product this good, we don't even look at the price. The label speaks for itself, eloquently: "Ingredients: calcium carbonate, vegetable glycerin, Australian tea tree oil, soft water, carrageenan (seaweed extract), sodium bicarbonate (baking soda), sea salt, calcium ascorbate (vitamin C), natural mint flavor. No artificial preservatives, artificial sweeteners, or coloring. No harsh abrasives. Animal ingredients: not tested on animals."

$2.90 (3 oz.)
Desert Essence; Feather River; Lion & Lamb; Wishing Well

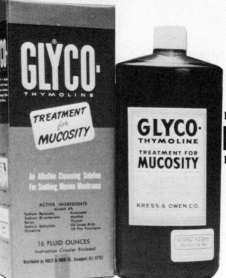

GLYCO-THYMOLINE

A technical-sounding name for an old natural mouthwash recipe with glycerine, sodium salts, eucalyptol, menthol, pine oil. Alkaline cleansing. Mild, sweet taste. 4% alcohol.

$6.95 (16 fl. oz.)
Home Health Products

OXYFRESH

Uses a pure, stabilized form of the natural oxidizing agent chlorine dioxide to fight bacteria, deodorize, and whiten teeth. (The EPA recommends $Cl\text{-}O_2$ as a safe alternative to chlorine in drinking water). Leaves a cool after-tingle. The ingredients are natural, nonallergenic, biodegradable, noncarcinogenic, and listed on the tube.

$6 (5.5 oz.), Red Rose Gallerie

VICCO HERBAL TOOTHPASTE

An amazing 20-herb Ayurvedic recipe from India. Leaves an unusual aftertaste. Not sweet. Concentrated, so you use about 1/3 the amount of whipped toothpastes. No fluoride, harsh abrasives, or refined sweeteners. Nothing artificial.

$2.99 (3 oz.), Auromere Ayurvedic Imports; Home Health Products

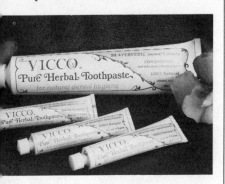

Floss

TOM'S NATURAL FLOSSING RIBBON

Vegetable waxes substitute for synthetic paraffin in this natural dental floss. Propolis is a mixture of tree resins, rich in bioflavanoids, which bees gather to line the hive. Most testers found Tom's flat ribbon design superior to string floss: "Wrapping it around your finger doesn't cut circulation."

$4.55 (40 yds.)
Tom's of Maine; local supermarket; Feather River Co.

Mouthwashes

Most mouthwashes are between 14% and 26% alcohol, which can be dangerous if swallowed. These alternatives have none or very little.

What You Can Do

✔ Use baking soda as an effective toothpowder to polish teeth and freshen breath. Mix in peppermint extract for refreshing flavor if you wish.

OXYFRESH SPEARMINT MOUTHRINSE

A mouthwash with stabilized chlorine dioxide as the active ingredient. Said to inhibit bacteria, viruses, fungi, and odors. It's biodegradable with no alcohol, dyes, or sweeteners.

$6 (16 oz.), Red Rose Gallerie

Eight million hectares of rain forest — an area about the size of Austria — were burned in 1987 in the Amazon basin.

OUR FAVORITE PERSONAL CARE COMPANIES & CATALOGUES

WELEDA
Quality Through Nature

WELEDA PRODUCTS

Weleda organically grows and then processes and packages its own ingredients to the highest standards of purity. The unique formulas, known for their exquisite natural fragrances, are made in small batches, preservative free. We use Weleda products with near reverence.

❖, ○

Meadowbrook Herb Garden

AURA CACIA

Aura Cacia's plant-oil soaps are colored with natural iron oxides, and its body powders use cornstarch in place of talc. You won't find synthetic fragrances or colors here. One percent of this company's proceeds goes to rain forest conservation.

❖, ○ — **InterNatural**

JURLIQUE

A new company with a 15th-century secret process and uncompromising natural purity and freshness. Jurlique uses organically cultivated herbs from Australia (for the clean air and mineral-rich soil); then they're processed and packaged on site, air shipped, and distributed in six days!

○ — **Jurlique**

new *I & M* age
NATURAL SKINCARE
Made in Germany

I & M NATURAL SKINCARE

Highly concentrated hair and skin products, handmade to order, packaged in small containers with instructions on extending freshness. I & M allows natural color variations, and its low-lather shampoos have no foaming agents. It uses no mineral oil, synthetic additives, or added colors. High marks for purity.

❖ — **I & M**

ALEXANDRA AVERY

Only home-grown organic herbs from Oregon are used in Alexandra Avery's primo quality skin care and perfume products.

❖ — **Earthen Joys; Feather River Co.; InterNatural**

AUBREY
ORGANICS

AUBREY ORGANICS

Aubrey Hampton has been making fabulous natural hair, skin, and body care products for 21 years. He also creates consternation in the industry by labeling his products "the only 100% natural, organic hair and skin care line." He uses no petrochemicals, hydrocarbons, emulsifiers, or artificial anything. Aubrey's answer to preservatives is citrus seed extract, itself a controversial ingredient. He'll send a free, 4-page "Dictionary of Cosmetic Ingredients" on request.

❖ — **Ecco Bella**

Breath Fresheners

TIB 100% BREATH FRESHENER

Concentrated, from pure essential flavor oils. Strong, almost stinging feeling, followed by a cold rush. Our favorite is Orange Cinnamint.

$1.95, Liberty Distributing

COSMETICS

Makeup

Mascara often brings formaldehyde, alcohol, carcinogenic coal-tar dyes, and plastic resin in contact with ultrasensitive eye tissue. Many eye shadows and face powders contain talc, which is sometimes contaminated with carcinogenic asbestos and is readily inhaled into the lungs.

Lipstick is particularly dangerous, since it is easily ingested with food. Lipsticks frequently contain PVP plastic, paraffin wax, saccharin, mineral oil, and artificial colors that are known to cause cancer in animals. Unfortunately you have no way of knowing if they are in your brand because lipstick is exempt from labeling requirements.

BARE ESCENTUALS

Eye shadows, pencils, and mascara with "absolutely no chemical ingredients or animal derivatives," formulated entirely from selected herbs, plant extracts, and vegetable oils. Bare Escentuals uses only "naturally occurring" titanium dioxide for white colors. It does not use mineral oil, talc, perfume, alcohol, artificial dyes, binders, fillers, or additives.

From $4 shadows to $12.50 face powders, Bare Escentuals, Inc.

Most of Massachusetts' approximately 700 landfills are polluting surface and groundwater or are threatening to do so.

COSMETICS

DANIEL GRAE

IDA GRAE SKIN CARE

Ida Grae is a purist and expert on hypo-allergenic cosmetics. Chemically sensitive, she has been making her own cosmetics for ten years. She does not use synthetic preservatives, detergents, emulsifiers, or petrochemicals.

Ida Grae Nature's Colors Cosmetics; InterNatural

DR. HAUSCHKA DECORATIVE COSMETICS

The finest of natural plant color "day creams," eyelid tones, and lip and cheek shades. Healthy cosmetics from herbalist skin scientists.

Prices range from $23.50 for a .16-oz. pot of lip cream to $25 for a 1-oz. tube of face cream
Meadowbrook Herb Garden

Lip Protectors

Sun, wind, and dryness are good reasons for using lip protectors. Unfriendly ingredients are a reason to look before you lick. Avoid glosses with mineral oil, a long-term irritant.

MOUNTAIN OCEAN LIP TRIP

High sun protection from pure beeswax, plus apricot kernel oil. The "allantoin" is from comfrey root (not uric acid). SPF (sun protection factor) is 15.

$2.75, Mountain Ocean

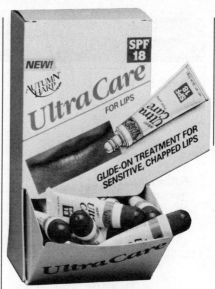

AUTUMN-HARP ULTRA CARE

Pleasant-tasting, petroleum-free, vegetable-based glide-on treatment for sensitive, dry, or chapped lips. The Feather River catalogue defines the sun-blocking ingredient oxybenzone used here as a "synthetic organic compound."

$1.89 (10 g plastic tube)
Autumn-Harp; Feather River Co.

PERFUMES

Animal oils are used in many perfumes to bind the scent, including oils from musk deer and sperm whales, both endangered species. Civet cats and beavers are also sacrificed for many perfume recipes. Synthetic substitutes are available, but are generally animal tested, and their safeness is questionable. Perfumes may also contain formaldehyde, phenol, trichlorethylene, and cresol, all toxic solvents. Allergic reactions to fragrances include skin irritation, headaches, and nausea. The high alcohol content of perfumes makes them potentially lethal to children.

The best alternative to chemicalized fragrances is natural essential oil extracts or floral "absolutes." Highly concentrated, they should not be applied to mucous membranes and must also be kept away from children who might ingest them.

The average American uses between 10 and 45 pounds of soaps, toiletries, and cosmetics every year.

OUR FAVORITE PERSONAL CARE COMPANIES & CATALOGUES

PERFUMES

LAKON HERBALS

Lakon organically cultivates or wild harvests its own fresh botanicals in central Vermont. Even the beeswax is native. Lakon's products show a reverence for the land.

○ — **Lakon Herbals**

DR. HAUSCHKA BIODYNAMIC FORMULATIONS

This meticulous German company oversees every stage of cosmetic production from soil care and cultivation to processing and packaging.

❖, ○ — **InterNatural; Meadowbrook Herb Garden**

WALTER RAU SPEICK SOAPS & TOILETRIES

A 60-year-old company with a skin care line based on the legendary healing plant "Speick" (*Valeriana celtica*). Pure and simple with no artificial or synthetic anything.

❖ — **Meadowbrook Herb Garden**

BORLIND OF GERMANY

Making high-quality skin, hair, and makeup products in the Black Forest area of West Germany for 35 years, Borlind uses purified water and the first pressings of organically grown plant ingredients. Shelf life is guaranteed for three years with parabens used as preservatives.

Self-Care Catalog

PAUL PENDERS

Natural body products made in small, hand-blended batches. Paul Penders skin, bath, cosmetic, and men's products are very popular in health food stores. Labels stand up well to a naturalist's scrutiny, with the exception of triethanolamine — an irritant — in some products. Parabens are used as preservatives. Natural separation shows that emulsifiers are left out. Shake well.

InterNatural

TONIALG SEAWEED-BASED SKIN & HAIR CARE

Active enzymes and hormones from seaweed are extracted by a special freezing process in sterile laboratory conditions. A preservative-free, three-year shelf life is achieved with a specially designed "airless" lined dispenser. No added color or perfumes are used.

Feather River Co.

REVIVA LABS

Scientifically designed skin care line based on Hawaiian seaplant gel. Uses some synthetic preservatives, with explanations. The company also publishes a "Cosmetic Ingredient Manual."

❖, ○ — **Feather River Co.**

AURA CACIA ESSENTIAL OILS & ABSOLUTES

True botanical perfume oils and natural essential oils from aromatic flowers, fruits, herbs, roots, leaves, barks, and resins. Beautiful exotic scents (like Nile Spice and Temple Santal), ranging from subtle to sensational. The only natural fragrances we've found with full ingredients on the label. Aura Cacia Pure Floral "Absolutes" are highly concentrated non-oil extracts of fragrant flowers like rose and jasmine.

$1.95 to $11.95 (Essential Oils, 1/2 oz.); $7.95 to $11.95 (Perfume Oils); $19.95 (Rose) to $29.95 (Jasmine) (Absolutes, 2 ml.)
Aura Cacia

NAIL CARE

Many nail polishes are toxic, yet have no warning labels. They contain the highly volatile and harmful chemicals phenol, toluene, and xylene along with formaldehyde. Almost all nail polish removers contain the solvent acetone. Breathing it can damage the lungs and affect the brain. Swallowing it can be lethal. Nail polish remover is so dangerous most authorities categorize it as a household hazardous waste.

Twenty-four nations signed a 1988 agreement to freeze nitrogen oxide emission levels.

FEMININE PRODUCTS

Sanitary Napkins/Tampons

Although tampons are worn internally, there's no law requiring listing of their ingredients. Too bad, because production of the rayon used in tampons, like that of the chlorine-bleached paper in sanitary napkins, produces the extremely lethal carcinogen dioxin, which turns up in the effluent of paper pulp mills and in the sanitary products themselves. Johnson & Johnson has announced its intention to switch to chlorine-free pulp.

Another problem is bacteria, the cause of toxic shock syndrome. The more absorbent, the more likely the complaint. The deodorants and fragrances in some commercial sanitary products may also be irritants and allergens. We recommend all-cotton sanitary napkins and tampons over synthetics.

Then there is disposal. Each year millions of bacteria-contaminated tampons and non-degradable plastic applicators pass into the water, rivers, and oceans, even causing the closing of some public beaches.

To avoid as many of these problems as possible, try these products.

FOREVER MAXI PADS & PANTY LINERS

Sanitary napkins and panty liners bleached by a process that uses less wood pulp, without sacrificing absorbency. Ninety-nine percent biodegradable and dioxin free.

$14.50 Maxi Pads (6 boxes); $12.50 Panty Liners (4 boxes, 104 liners), all including postage and handling, Seventh Generation

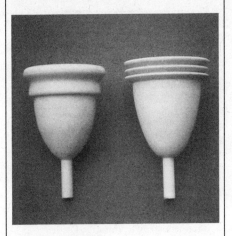

"THE KEEPER" MENSTRUAL CUP

"The Keeper" is an ounce-sized, reusable rubber "menstrual cup" worn internally and emptied several times a day. It looks like a small, deep diaphragm. The product has been quietly marketed for 40 years and is FDA accepted. One size fits all. Pure high-grade gum rubber, it lasts for ten years, an obvious environmental plus.

$25, Keeper Co., Inc.

CALLISTE NATURAL COSMETIC SEA SPONGES

Reusable natural sea sponges are used by many women instead of tampons. They must be sterilized in boiling water monthly.

$1.75, Wishing Well

Feminine Deodorants

Most feminine deodorants contain dangerous talc, benzalkonium chloride, chlorhexidine, and isopropyl myristate. Classified as cosmetics and so exempt from testing and labeling controls, vaginal deodorants have been linked to bladder infections, burning, itching, swelling, rashes, boils, and blood in the urine. Deodorant perfumes can cause rashes, sores, and chemical burns — problems that can also be transferred to sexual partners. Physicians recommend soap and water as the most effective feminine deodorant — and so do we.

Douches

The strong commercial preparations for douching can cause chemical vaginitis: irritation and swelling of delicate vaginal linings. An FDA advisory review panel says there is no need to douche and blames "ignorance and commercial advertising" for the practice.

Regular bathing and loose natural-fiber clothing are the best alternatives to chemical douches. Even natural ingredient douches should be used no more than twice a week.

HYGENIA HYGIENIC CLEANSING DOUCHE

One-hundred percent natural with active lactobacillus-acidophilus yogurt cells in dry vinegar. No chemicals, preservatives, colors, or fragrances.

$4.95 (Eight 5 g envelopes) Home Health Products, Inc.

PAY MORE NOW, LESS LATER

Several factors combine to make "natural" products generally more expensive than their "unnatural" competitors. Real spearmint oil, for example, costs $20 per pound, compared with synthetic oil at $5. As demand increases, prices tend to equalize, but meanwhile keep in mind the real costs of using polluting, non-biodegradable products when our tax dollars are needed to clean up our lakes and streams!

THE BODY SHOP

The Body Shop takes a high-profile stand against animal products and testing in the beauty industry, but uses many man-made ingredients. Its 400 stores in 35 countries feature plant-based, cruelty-free products. The Body Shop compromises its products with petroleum-based preservatives and its reputation by not mentioning it in its literature. They refill containers at their shops.

○ — **The Body Shop**

PERSONAL CARE CATALOGUES

Some body-product catalogues convey more mood than information. Look for full disclosure ingredients lists, and beware of buzz words like "rejuvenating" and "herbal." In alphabetical order, these are some of the catalogues we have found useful.

ECCO BELLA

Ecco Bella is concerned about animals and the environment enough to raise these issues in its exuberant catalogue. A colorful selection of high-quality products from the best names in the business, including Desert Essence, Aubrey, and their own Ecco Bella label. Ingredients are not listed, but the catalogue points out the rare synthetic that is the exception to their organic rule. Ecco Bella supports recycling and biodegradable packaging. Twenty percent of catalogue profits are donated to animal and environmental protection.

FEATHER RIVER CO.

The most conscientious and complete natural cosmetics catalogue: plenty of information on environmentally aware companies, plus complete ingredients listings, a glossary, a bibliography, and informative articles. These folks do their homework. Although they downplay the arguments against the synthetic ingredients they let through, Feather River goes to great lengths to educate the consumer about them.

HOME HEALTH PRODUCTS

Home Health offers unique products developed from the trance health readings of the "Sleeping Prophet," Edgar Cayce, all from naturally occurring herbs, oils, salts, and minerals. Their effectiveness is well documented. For a company with such esoteric connections, they are very no-nonsense, from ingredients to packaging to promotion.

INTERNATURAL

A particularly beautiful catalogue with a wide variety of soaps, lotions, cosmetics, and perfumes from only the most reputable producers. InterNatural discontinued a "natural" brand name (Sleepy Hollow Botanicals) after it was bought out by animal testers.

MEADOWBROOK HERB GARDEN

A high-quality retail store with a mail order catalogue. It carries a small selection of very fine imported body products from Germany. A husband and wife company, these discriminating folks sell only what they use.

SelfCare Catalog

SELF-CARE CATALOG

Forty pages of self-care tools, appliances, books, tapes, etc. Includes home medicine, kitchen, bathroom, bedroom, and baby products, and environmental aids, all researched and tested. No ingredients listing, but a customer service line is provided.

SEVENTH GENERATION

Not primarily for personal care products, but a good source of Tom's Natural line, plus "Forever" brand ecological feminine hygiene items.

BIRTH CONTROL

All forms of artificial birth control carry health risks, some quite serious. The warning labels and long lists of contra-indicators for oral contraceptives and intrauterine devices hardly instill confidence, and many ingredients in oral contraceptives have not been evaluated at all. Which may help explain why, according to the *U.C. Berkeley Wellness Letter*, the most common method of preventing pregnancies in the U.S. is not contraception but sterilization.

The barrier methods (diaphragm, cervical cap, sponges, and male and female condoms) bring synthetic latex, lubricants, and sperm killers in contact with the most sensitive tissue of your body, and their production pollutes our environment.

Of course, the only scientific, natural alternative to man-made contraceptives is systematic abstention, which involves fertility awareness. It requires good instruction, faithful charting of temperature and vaginal secretions, and a patient, supportive partner.

What You Can Do

✔ Avoid tampons and pads that contain dyes, fragrances, deodorants, and superabsorbent fibers. (Kotex Security Tampons by Kimberly Clark and O.B. use cotton and rayon; the Kotex package says there are "no superabsorbent materials.")

✔ Buy tampons with cardboard applicators, not the non-biodegradable, non-renewable plastic kind. (Tampax Original Regular are 100% cotton with a cardboard applicator.)

READ MORE ABOUT COSMETICS

NATURAL ORGANIC HAIR AND SKIN CARE

By Aubrey Hampton. A comprehensive, up-to-date treatise on natural cosmetics, including confusion and deception in the industry. Includes an A to Z guide to ingredients. Encyclopedic in scope, but not overly technical.

$20.95, Organica Press

SECRETS OF NATURAL BEAUTY

By Virgina Castleton, beauty editor of *Prevention* magazine. Home recipes substitute for chemicalized commercial beauty treatments, facial lotions, and cosmetics. Best for those with the time to make their own.

$2.25, Keats Publishing, Inc.

THE COSMETIC INGREDIENT MANUAL

By Stephen Strassler. "What's in a Label?" "The Who's Who & What's What of Cosmetic Ingredients." Plus details not generally known about ingredient functions.

$1.25, Reviva Labs, Inc.

DICTIONARY OF COSMETIC INGREDIENTS

By Ruth Winter. All about "The Harmful and Desirable Ingredients Found in Men's and Women's Cosmetics." More than 300 pages of common ingredients and their uses and effects — but not their origins. Not always complete or technically accurate, but still a welcome compilation of bewildering, important material. Includes bibliography.

$10.95, Crown Publishers, Inc.

What You Can Do

✔ Don't let the hot water run while you're shaving. Rinsing your blade in a filled basin will save energy, water, and money.

✔ Revert to the old-fashioned mug-and-brush system for shaving. It's a lot more ecological than high-consumption disposable shaving cream cans and more fun, too! But avoid shaving brushes with badger bristles or elephant ivory handles.

✔ Try the common supermarket variety of witch hazel as an excellent, safe, and effective replacement for fancy after-shave lotions at one-tenth the price.

✔ For underarm care, use a home substitute that includes rubbing alcohol to kill bacteria and baking soda or cornstarch for absorbency.

✔ Use clear, food-based lip gloss in the absence of reliably safe lipsticks.

✔ Use real cotton balls, not non-biodegradable polyester "cosmetic puffs," for make-up application.

Babying The Earth

WHAT TWO THINGS could be more important to us than our babies and the world they'll inherit? Clearly it's important to every parent to take the best possible care of one without harming the other. Today, with new products entering the market all the time, it's getting easier to baby the earth while loving your baby.

The Diaper Dilemma

If I were to use disposable diapers, my son would contribute about 6,000 diapers — over two tons of trash — to the environment before he is toilet trained. What a first lesson in how to treat our world!

Plastic and paper throwaway diapers, which became popular in the sixties, threaten the environment in many ways. First of all, the production of plastic and paper diapers pollutes our air and water and strips our forests. Bleaching the paper produces dioxins, one of the deadliest substances known to man.

> *Americans throw away 16 billion diapers every year.*

And that's not all. Outer plastic covers inhibit the breakdown of diapers and of the waste inside when it is trashed. Two percent or more of our landfill space consist of disposable diapers. And landfills and incinerators cannot handle human waste safely; only sewage treatment facilities can.

What about "biodegradable" disposable diapers? Do they really degrade in landfills any faster? Their manufacturers claim they do but cannot show conclusively that they degrade completely. Even if the diaper degrades, what about the plastic trash bag in which the diapers are collected and disposed of? And what about the dumping of human waste in landfills? These questions have not been answered to our satisfaction, and we have chosen not to provide reviews and sources for these products in this book. (For more information about "degradable plastic," see page 34.)

The only good answer for the environment is cloth diapers. Real cloth diapers, once made, are used over and over, and the waste created when you wash them is readily handled by our septic and sewer systems.

So they're good for the earth. But are they manageable for you? Actually, using cloth may be simpler than you think. You don't have to be constantly washing diapers and folding laundry and rubber pants — and diaper rash isn't inevitable.

CLOTH DIAPERS & ACCESSORIES

There is enough variety in diapers to please all kinds of parents. From plain bird's-eye cloth to 100% cotton terry velour, from plain unfolded to fitted with elastic and Velcro tabs, the new diapers are eye-openers. The price range is broad, from $9 a dozen for Gerber (available in stores) to $44 a dozen for Snugglups. Like all clothing, the better the quality, the more it costs.

One hundred percent cotton is always the most desirable. Cotton can be washed and rinsed in hot water and dried with heat. Best-quality cotton will go through many washes and get softer each time. The most popular combination of materials in diapers is flannel, which is soft against the skin, and terry cloth, which is superabsorbent.

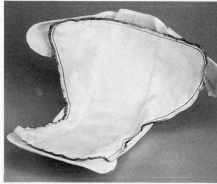

NATURAL BABY

HOURGLASS DIAPERS

Baby Bunz and Natural Baby both make an hourglass-shaped diaper covered with flannel and filled with terry. Both are stitched around the edges with rainbow thread. These diapers fit naturally into a diaper cover without any folding. To get the most absorbency, be sure to wash them a couple of times before the first use. –L.B.

$30 a dozen
Baby Bunz Rainbow Diapers
$27 a dozen
Natural Baby Rainbow Diapers

A disposable diaper is estimated to take 500 years to decompose in a landfill.

TERRY/FLANNEL DIAPER

Diap-Air makes an unfolded diaper with terry on one side and flannel on the other. Baby Bunz also has a terry/flannel diaper. Like their terry velour, this is a well made, thick, soft diaper. –L.B.

$26.95 a dozen, Diap-Air
$33 a dozen, Baby Bunz

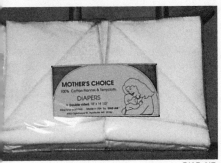

DIAP-AIR

BUMKINS

SNUGGLUPS

This flannel diaper is filled with terry, complete with fitted elasticized waist and legs in two sizes, with or without Velcro tabs. Snugglups work just like the rainbow diapers but need to be tucked into a diaper cover. You are probably better off using Rubber Ducky pull-on pants with Snugglups. –L.B.

Large (over 15 lbs.): $34 a dozen without Velcro; $44 with Lovely Essentials

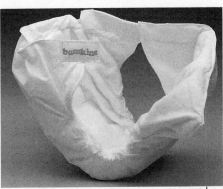

BUMKINS

BUMKINS

Bumkins makes an unusual product, a diaper and cover in one. The diaper is flannel-covered cotton, very thick and soft. The cover is waterproof nylon, and the whole is held on with Velcro tabs. Bumkins recommends washing in hot water with nonchlorine bleach and machine drying, also on hot. Bumkins are available in three sizes and come in a reusable, waterproof, washable bag for travel. –L.B.

$59.95 to $79.95 a dozen, Bumkins

PREFOLDED DIAPERS

Baby Bunz makes a prefolded terry velour diaper that is thick like a fine quality towel. Biobottoms' prefolded diaper is sized for infants or for toddlers. Biobottoms also has a prefolded cotton gauze diaper with Velcro tabs. –L.B.

$36 a dozen, Baby Bunz
$18.50 a dozen for infants; $23 for toddlers, Biobottoms

100%
cotton
flannel

Velcro tabs

elastic legs

thick padding

The energy produced through mass incineration is less than what is saved through recycling.

On the contrary, modern cloth diapers are completely washable, prefolded, 100 percent cotton. You put them on with attractive, convenient diaper covers, and Velcro closures hold them in place. Real cloth diapers are soft, breathable, and comfortable. Real cloth diapers are clothing, not trash.

To use them again, you need only rinse them free of any solid contents, then clean them in your washing machine. Alternatively, a diaper service picks up once a week and delivers fresh diapers. With cloth diapers you also have plenty of soft wipes for drooling little mouths and dirty little bottoms — and great rags after the child is toilet trained.

The modern cloth approach is also cheaper than old-fashioned disposables, at least if you handle the washing yourself. Buying and washing your own diapers and covers costs about $1,000 to $1,500 for the three-year diapering period. Throwaway diapers can cost $1,500 to $2,500, depending on the brand and the number of diapers you use. Diaper service costs $10 to $12.50 per week or about $2,000 to $2,500, including diaper covers.

Diaper service is available in most parts of the country. For the diaper service provider in your area, look in the yellow pages of your phone book or write the National Association of Diaper Services.

The Diaper Cover Revolution

The new diaper covers available today are the biggest factor in making disposables obsolete and cloth the diaper of choice. They make changes quick and painless, and most of them keep wetness off clothes quite well.

A single diaper cover is used through a number of diaper changes, so plan on having six or eight diaper covers available in your baby's size. Simply put the prefolded diaper in the center of the diaper cover, fold the two sides to the middle, and close. The whole operation takes about ten seconds. You can also use the diaper to dry baby after he's been wiped and before folding it into the diaper cover.

If you are too ambitious to use a service, or just a penny-pincher, you can buy your own supply of cloth diapers. A newborn will use about 12 per day. A three-month-old will need only one change per feeding or six per day. If you wash once a week, you will need five to seven dozen.

Used diapers can be stored in a diaper pail until you are ready to wash. Dispose of any solid contents in the toilet, rinse in the bowl, and place in the diaper pail with plain borax and water. (This unpleasant process is made much easier by a cliplike device called a Diaper Duck for holding the diaper.) If the diaper is soiled only by urine, you don't need either to rinse or to presoak it.

Wash diapers in hot water with a mild detergent. Use less detergent for presoaked diapers. For babies with sensitive skin, run the diapers through an extra rinse cycle. Add vinegar to the rinse water if diaper rash is a problem. Machine or line dry.

For short travels carry in your diaper bag a small, rinsable, plastic-lined bag for used diapers. When your child is in child-care, most states allow you as the provider to use cloth if you have a diaper service; you can provide the pail. You can also try the paper diaper inserts called Dovetails that fit inside a standard diaper cover.

In any case, disposables are things of the past. Give new, modern cloth diapers and diaper covers a try.

DIAPERS

DIAPER INSERTS
These flannel-covered terry diaper inserts are washable and provide extra absorbency for nighttime or nap time. –L.B.

$2.25 each, Bumkins
$10.50 for six, Baby Bunz

THROWAWAY INSERTS
Dovetails are biodegradable, chemical-free, throwaway diaper inserts designed for occasional use. They require use of a diaper cover since they can't be pinned closed. Disposing of Dovetails is a little problematic since they don't have the plastic wrapper of a throwaway diaper, and they cannot be flushed down a toilet. We suggest folding and wrapping with a bit of cotton string. –L.B.

$24 per 100 (small), $27 (large)
Baby Bunz; Seventh Generation

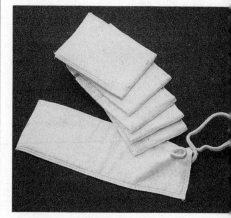

Diaper Duck and pre-folded diapers from Biobottoms

DIAPER DUCK
The Diaper Duck is a cliplike device that holds a dirty diaper while you're cleaning it. –L.B.

Natural Baby; Baby Bunz; Biobottoms

DIAPER COVERS

BIOBOTTOMS

Biobottoms were the first to develop and promote the modern diaper cover, perfecting the art of clothing the diapered baby. A Biobottoms diaper cover is made of high-quality materials, is easily cared for, and fits the baby beautifully. It has a gathered waist, a scooped shell, and liners around the legs to prevent leakage.

Biobottoms come in pure wool, pure cotton, or cotton with a waterproof polyester liner. The advantages of natural-fiber diaper covers are several. Natural fiber breathes, which means it's warm in winter and cool in summer. And nothing fits the body as well as wool or cotton. Natural fibers also release stains and last through many washings. With their superior fit and wide soft Velcro band, Biobottoms are a pleasure to put on a baby. –L.B.

$13 Poly-lined cotton; $16.50 Large all-wool or all-cotton Biobottoms

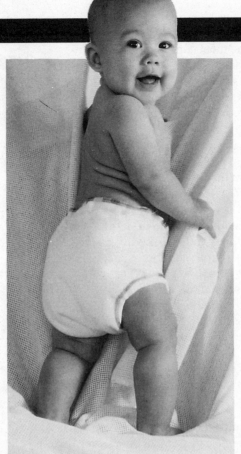

BIOBOTTOMS

NIKKYS

Our next preference is Nikkys. The fit is not quite as exquisite as Biobottoms. They come in a variety of forms including pure wool, pure cotton, and nylon-lined cotton. –L.B.

$8.95 to $14.50 depending upon size, style, and quantity Baby Bunz; Natural Baby; Seventh Generation

RUBBER DUCKIES AND RUBBER DUCKY WRAP-UPS

Rubber Duckies are waterproof nylon pull-on pants; Rubber Ducky Wrap-Ups are nylon diaper covers that close with Velcro. For those who won't give up pins and pull-on pants, Rubber Duckies offer a more comfortable alternative. The nylon is waterproof, but we found that the nylon leg bands tended to wick moisture to the cotton cloth covering some of the more fashionable models like the Jungle Print. The Velcro band across the Wrap-Ups is stiff and tends to roll down the baby's belly. –L.B.

$4 Rubber Duckies; $5.50 each or 3 for $16 Wrap-Ups R. Duck Company

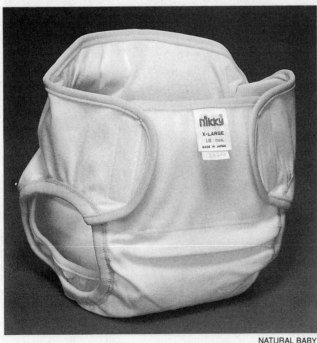

NATURAL BABY

THE GREAT DIAPER COVER-UP

You'll need six to eight diaper covers at a time if you do wash twice a week. Diaper covers can be used a number of times between washings because even if they get damp, they can be left to dry and then used again; you don't need to wash them until they get soiled.

Diaper covers require gentler treatment than diapers. Do not presoak. Let them air dry until you're ready to wash. Wash with other laundry, if you wish, with warm water and detergent. The wool used by Biobottoms and Nikkys stays waterproof by retaining the natural lanolin of the wool. They recommend cleansing in mild soap to avoid removing the lanolin.

A cotton diaper, when it reaches the end of its useful life, will decompose in six months.

Caring for Baby, Caring for the Earth

Like other personal care products, most commercial baby care products are made with petroleum-based chemicals, synthetic colors, fragrances, and preservatives. Some babies and children react to these chemicals, though most tolerate them well. But the main problem with most baby care products is not the products themselves but the waste they create.

Skin products for infants are usually aimed at preventing or treating diaper rash. However, the best prevention is frequent diaper changes and use of a diapering system that breathes. Studies have shown that babies in cloth diapers and natural-fiber diaper covers rarely get diaper rash.

But if it happens, pediatricians usually recommend letting baby's bottom get lots of fresh air. Creams, jellies, and oils usually do little but lubricate and can irritate a rash. Diaper wipes containing alcohol can promote diaper rash by drying baby's skin. Use plain water, and when you bathe a very young baby, use no soap at all.

The best cure for diaper rash is to wipe the baby clean with a washcloth or wipe, dry thoroughly (with a cloth diaper if you have one), and then let him play naked for a few minutes in his crib. Air drying does wonders for any rash!

Food for Thought

As with all food, the making and packaging of baby food and the disposing of that packaging have an impact on the environment. A formula-fed baby goes through about one can a day of concentrate or 365 cans in its first year. And baby food is usually processed from chemically treated vegetables and hormone-fed meat sources.

In addition, scientists at the Natural Resource Defense League say that preschoolers may be at more risk than adults from exposure to many of the most carcinogenic pesticides. The pesticides used on fruit

DIAPER COVERS

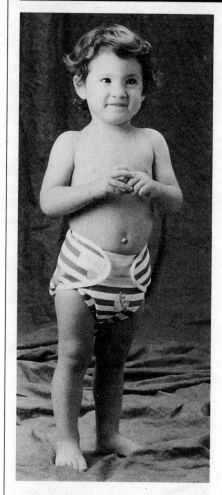

DIAPERRAPS

Diaperraps are cotton-covered foam with Velcro closures. They are not waterproof and have a tendency to disintegrate in the wash. However, Diaperraps have managed to get distribution through the diaper services. They fit moderately well and are inexpensive. –L.B.

$6 each or 6 for $31.50
Diaperraps

AND NOW FOR THE GOOD NEWS . . .

According to Macrofax, the commercial baby foods manufactured by Beech-Nut, Gerber, and Heinz have cleaned up their acts a great deal since Ralph Nader and the Center for Science in the Public Interest went after them several years ago. Their products now contain no preservatives, artificial flavorings, stabilizers, MSG, or colorings, and except in their toddler lines, very little salt. All except Heinz use corn and sugar sweeteners sparingly. Beech-Nut is very careful about monitoring pesticide residues in ingredients and avoids produce grown with carcinogens. For those consumers who may wish and/or need to use commercially produced baby foods as a lower-priced alternative to those sold in natural foods stores, Beech-Nut may be the best choice.

What You Can Do

✔ Instead of using plastic-backed or disposable bibs, take hand towels, stitch down one edge, and run ⅜-inch elastic through. Tie or sew the elastic ends together.

Sixteen billion disposable diapers are dumped into U.S. landfills each year — enough to stretch to the moon and back seven times.

WABBYS

Wabbys are made of Gore-tex, a waterproof, breathable fabric that is used for ski wear and other outdoor clothing. –L.B.

$12.50 each or 3 for $11.95
Diap-Air

DIAP-AIR

BABY CARE PRODUCTS

NATURAL BABY SHAMPOO

Once baby has enough hair so that water alone will not clean it, you may want to use a little soap or shampoo

every few days. Tom's of Maine makes a tearless, natural baby shampoo with a pleasant scent. "Where can I get a case?" tester Dean Parker exclaimed after using it. –L.B.

$5 for 12 oz., Tom's of Maine; many supermarkets

TOM'S OF MAINE

AUTUMN-HARP

Autumn-Harp makes a line of all-natural baby products including shampoo, plant-based baby oil, talc-free powder, and non-petroleum jelly. The shampoo contains only plant-based ingredients and has an unusual, though not unpleasant, smell. Autumn-Harp's containers are marked for recycling. –L.B.

TERRY CLOTH WIPES

The most commonly used baby care product is the baby wipe. Wipes cost about $1 to $3 per container, and you'll go through about $200 to $350 worth (depending upon the brand) before your baby is toilet trained. The plastic containers are not reusable, and the wipes themselves often use preservatives and skin-drying alcohol.

An alternative is washable terry cloth wipes, available in a reusable plastic box of one dozen from Natural Baby or from Baby Bunz. Extra wipes are available by the dozen. Assuming you need four dozen, these save up to $329 plus about 100 to 200 useless plastic containers and 8,760 paper wipes. –L.B.

$7.50 per dozen, Natural Baby
$6.75 for eight, Baby Bunz

What You Can Do

✔ In place of baby powder, use plain cornstarch (which is asbestos-free, unlike talc).

✔ While baby is small, use no soap or shampoo at all. None is necessary, and you avoid allergies and soap in young eyes and ears. Use a clean washcloth and, for baby's head, the kind of brush used for removing cornsilk from fresh corn.

✔ Substitute vegetable oil for baby oil to soften skin.

Although instructions on disposable diaper boxes advise consumers to flush waste matter down the toilet, only 1% ever do so.

are especially dangerous for youngsters because children eat so much more fruit, as a proportion of their weight, than adults do. Although a scare was caused by Alar, sprayed on apples, in fact all pesticides are implicated. Even commonly accepted substances such as colorings, flavorings, and sugar have been linked to such childhood disorders as hyperactivity, attention deficit disorder, allergies, and cancer.

The best solution, of course, is to avoid processed baby foods altogether. Breast milk can provide all of a baby's nutrition for the first six months and most of the nutrition for the second six months at little additional cost to the family. Even working moms can nurse. For more information and support for nursing, call the La Leche League chapter in your area.

Once your baby is ready for solid food, consider organic brands. In addition to reducing your child's exposure to pesticides, buying organically grown food encourages the conversion of more land to pesticide-free growing. Two companies now offer these products; for more information, see the product reviews accompanying this section.

Better yet, make your own. You need not be a superparent to make healthy, wholesome, organically grown food for your infant. You also don't need a lot of containers. First, buy certified organic produce. Then cook fruits and vegetables, using a minimum of water to avoid removing the water-soluble vitamins. Grind the food in a mill or processor, using just enough liquid to achieve a creamy texture. Pour into ice cube trays and freeze. Pop the cubes out and put them into a reclosable plastic bag. Defrost the cubes as needed for baby's meals.

So. . . . use cloth diapers. Be careful in your selection of baby care products. And use organically grown baby foods, or make your own. Your baby will be healthier, and so will the earth.   — *Lisa Braiterman*

ORGANIC BABY FOODS

EARTH'S BEST

EARTH'S BEST

This is the brand currently most widely available in supermarkets. The Earth's Best line includes strained fruits and vegetables, cereals, and juices. Only water and, in some fruits, citric acid (vitamin C) are added. Earth's Best requires its growers to go at least three years without adding chemicals to the soil before marketing.

Its food is tasty, smells good, and includes vegetarian mixtures like brown rice and peas. Its juices contain fruit pulp, and they taste and smell like the real thing. The small juice jars are made to hold a standard nipple. Mostly in glass jars. Contact the company for the name of the supermarket near you that carries the line. –*L.B.*

Seventh Generation

All company addresses and phone numbers are listed in the Ecologue Source Directory beginning on page 242.

SIMPLY PURE

Simply Pure was started by a mom interested in providing her son with organically produced food. The line includes finger foods for toddlers and some unusual items, such as beets and a larger-sized jar of applesauce. Simply Pure adheres to the Maine Organic Farmers and Gardeners standard requiring that the land be free of chemical pesticides for at least three years. Simply Pure foods are certified kosher. They are in some food stores but generally are available only by mail. –L.B.

DO IT YOURSELF

HAPPY BABY FOOD GRINDER

This handy food grinder is the perfect convenience for making fresh, wholesome infant food. –L.B.

$7, Toy, baby specialty, and health food stores

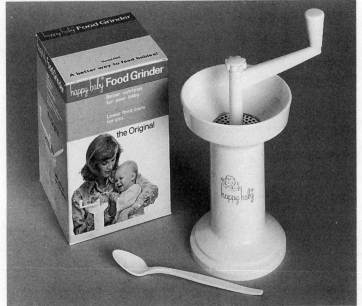

HAPPY BABY

In 1988 treatment, storage, and disposal facilities managed some 300 million tons of toxic waste.

A Man's Best Friend

WE IN THE UNITED STATES share our homes with 50 million dogs, 58 million cats, 425 million fish, and 3 million other assorted furry, feathered, or scaled creatures. We spent $8.5 billion last year on pet care, buying everything for Fido, Fluffy, or Fang from a simple $2 flea collar to a $300 canopied pet bed. Why not use those dollars, when we can, to support an environmentally safe earth?

Fleeing the Fleas

Start with a real sore point for most pets and pet owners: fleas. We get a little crazy when we see fleas — first we panic, then we grab for a chemical to wipe the critters out.

> *Not long ago veterinarians discovered that an over-the-counter flea product was actually killing some of the pets it was used on.*

Flea control can't be taken lightly. Not long ago veterinarians discovered that an over-the-counter flea product was actually killing some of the pets it was used on. It looked as though a combination of EPA-approved chemicals had formed a toxic brew that was absorbed through the animals' skin. That product is now off the market, but it was a hard lesson.

Catalogues and pet stores carry an increasing number of items that claim natural protection from fleas. Our testing shows that some are effective, some are marginal, and some raise other questions.

When it comes to fleas, it's unlikely you'll find a product that's both completely harmless to the environment *and* effective. However, the best recent news for pet owners — and the worst news for fleas — is pyrethrin. Look for this stuff as the active ingredient in a number of flea products. It really works!

Pyrethrin is made from African chrysanthemums, and it's effective in breaking the flea/egg/flea cycle without harming your pet, the environment, or your pocketbook. The nice thing about pyrethrin is that fleas don't seem to build up an immunity to it. You can use it over and over, but you probably won't need to if you follow directions.

Remember, though, that pyrethrin may be mixed with other, toxic ingredients — the greater the amount of pyrethrin, the better.

You'll find pyrethrin in dips, sprays, collars, and house foggers. Read the labels!

— *Mary Allen*

What You Can Do

Fleas can be a problem with many household pets. These steps will help.

✔ Vacuum your pet's bed and the surrounding area frequently.

✔ Feed your pet brewer's yeast, fennel, rosemary, vitamin B, and garlic tablets.

✔ Look for flea products containing methoprene, a growth inhibitor that interferes with flea larvae development.

✔ Make a citrus-oil spray by blending orange or grapefruit skins, then simmering the blend in water. Rub cooled pulp into the pet's fur with your hands.

GREEN BAN CHEMICAL-FREE DOG SHAMPOO

Tested, tried, and true — initially in the Australian rain forest and now in thousands of homes worldwide. It's coconut-oil based with apricot kernel oil, kelp extract, oils of pennyroyal, euca-lypti, and cajuput — all to take care of fleas, ticks, and related skin allergies and keep your pet smelling like a rose — or at least like a eucalyptus tree. One young mother tells us how relieved she is that her children can now play safely around their dog and that the flea problem no longer exists. Another tester, Fred Son-nenberg, says the best thing is that "we don't have to fight any more with a 75-pound dog in the tub. She likes it!" –Penny Uhlendorf

$6.50 (8 fl. oz.)
The Hummer Nature Works

GREEN BAN FOR PETS

Try this natural pet powder containing mint and oils of pennyroyal, eucalypti, and cajuput. Packaged in a special shaker container, it can be used as often as desired, healing existing bites and stopping itching. Vets also recommend it for animals with flea allergies. Once your pet (especially finicky Morris) real-izes it's not getting wet or sprayed, it might willingly yield to the benefits of a full massage. –P.U.

$6.50 (4 oz.), The Hummer Nature Works

FLEA STOP

Flea Stop uses D-limonene, a concentrated citrus oil. We've tested this and judge it not nearly as effective as products made with pyrethrin.

Flea Stop's dip, shampoo, and spray — all products used directly on the animal — seem safe enough, and they leave your pet smelling as though it's just romped in an orange grove. The problem is that it takes too many appli-cations to get ahead of the flea/egg/flea cycle. Beware that Flea Stop Concen-trate, a spray treat-ment for your home, uses piperonyl butox-ide to boost the effect of D-limonene, mak-ing it less benign than the rest of the prod-uct line. –M.A.

$29 Set of dip, shampoo, and spray; $45 Household Spray Animail Pet Care Products

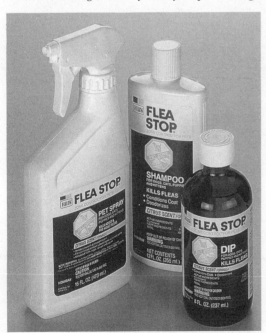

ANIMAIL PET CARE PRODUCTS

SPORTING DOG SPECIALTIES

MICROTECH-2 ELECTRONIC FLEA COLLAR

A high-tech way to chase fleas off your pet using ultrasonic pulses. Manufacturers claim it's safe, but some pet health experts wonder what the constant electrical charge will do to heart and metabolism rates. If your pet likes to chew or lose its collar, this could get expensive. –M.A.

$36 to $39, extra batteries $5 to $6 Pedigree: The Pet Catalog; pet stores

One chlorine atom can destroy as many as 100,000 ozone molecules before it is rendered inactive or removed from the atmosphere.

LION & LAMB CRUELTY-FREE PRODUCTS

These three natural pet care items are from Lion & Lamb, a company that sells products developed without animal testing. We tested them, we like them, and we think your pet will approve; we know the environment will. –*M.A.*

NATURE'S GATE PET SHAMPOO

This lathers nicely, although the scent is a bit medicinal. The manufacturer says it doesn't sting pet eyes.

$4 (12 oz.)

NATURE'S GATE PET COAT CONDITIONER

Creamy, smells like herbs.

$4.50 (12 oz.)

NATURE'S MIRACLE ODOR REMOVER

A liquid enzyme for stains and odors. It can be used on rugs, clothing, and walls. Pleasant scent.

$4.95 (16 oz.)

What You Can Do

✔ Consider raising llamas instead of horses. They are often used as substitutes for horses on ecologically sensitive trails because they move so lightly on the land that they don't damage it. You can shear them once a year for wool, and their dung is so odorless you can use it (composted, of course) on house plants.
— *Mona Anderson*

OTHER PET CARE PRODUCTS

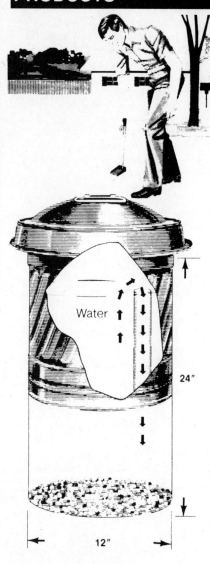

Water

24"

12"

THE DOGGIE DOOLEY

City dwellers, listen up. The Doggie Dooley is the environmental alternative to all that deep doo-doo that political figures refer to.

The Dooley is a small plastic miniseptic tank that installs in the ground. You scoop up the dog stools with a long-handled pooper-scooper and just drop them in. Water and enzymes go to work to liquefy the waste into fertilizer that filters into the ground. This gadget really works . . . and of course the manufacturer likes to quip that "the grass is always greener around the Dooley." –*M.A.*

$39.95 Home Model; $59.95 Kennel Model; $10.95 Extra Enzymes (16 oz.)
Sporting Dog Specialties; Sears; J.C. Penney; pet stores

Landfill closures have caused waste-disposal fees to rise more than 300% in the last five years.

TOO MUCH SCENTS

We like everything we read about the tiny Cedar-äl company — from its decision to use scrap cedar shakes that would otherwise be discarded to the hometown feel of its product literature. But we have a problem . . . our pets and pet experts don't seem to like its products. Maybe our pets are fussy.

Cedar-äl manufactures a pet bed filled with cedar excelsior. Pet owners told us the bed was too stiff (although the bed does loosen in time as the animal paws at it), and some pet experts say cedar products aren't as effective at flea control as the company claims. We also thought the scent of the cedar oil used was far too harsh.

The one exception to our disappointment was the Cedar-äl carpet deodorizer. Our tester Diane said it saved the day when her cat decided to redecorate a bedroom. In this case the overpowering scent was a welcome relief. —M.A.

$19.95 to $38 Pet Pillows (different sizes and covers); $10.95 Carpet Freshener (12 oz.)
Cedar-äl Products, Inc.

CEDAR-ÄL PRODUCTS, INC.

What You Can Do

✔ Compost your cat-box litter in a corner of your yard. Most of it is just clay — a natural ingredient.

✔ Avoid dry dog-food bags that have foil liners. Most dry food is packaged in paper bags, so this is easy.

✔ Shred newsprint to use as animal bedding.

✔ When you purchase tropical animals (such as parrots) or plants (such as orchids), be sure they were raised domestically and not removed from the rain forest.

✔ Watch what chemicals you put on your pet's coat, in its mouth, or into an aquarium. In addition to your concern for your pet's health and safety, consider the environment. If there's a choice, use the product that doesn't cause acid rain or pollute our air or water in its manufacture.

✔ Beware of the growing trade in black-market pets — especially rare birds smuggled out of the tropics. The only way to stop illegal poaching is to put an end to the market.

An estimated 50 million flea collars are used and thrown away every year.

Classroom Earth

JUST IMAGINE. If we were to nurture our children's innate love for nature and teach them to be caretakers of the earth, someday we could virtually eliminate the awesome task of reeducating adults. What progress the planet would make!

But getting there is not a simple task. In my family we recycle, use water-saving showerheads, have solar heat and hot water, and belong to environmental groups. We work at home, saving on ozone damage because we don't commute. So it goes without saying that we want our eight-year-old son, Paul, to value and love the earth.

Wanting is the easy part. Paul says that he's "the last kid on earth not to own Nintendo." And he's developed a passion for cars, insisting that he's going to be a car designer and study with Ferrari in Italy. Will *our* son grow up to design gas-guzzlers?

We had a few discussions about the environment, and now Paul's added alternative fuels to his visions for new car designs. Whew!

Instilling in our children the values we hold is tough. It's a lot easier to relinquish those opportunities to guide the direction of our children's interests, attitudes, and futures to TV and toys. Their lessons include: Plastic is fantastic. More is better. War is play. Violence wins. Creativity belongs to video game programmers.

But we don't have to take this lying down. We can, in fact, teach our children a reverence and love for nature and the planet by our own examples. What a gift to give your child!

We can share current events relating to the environment. We can teach a need for positive action (being careful not to overwhelm the child with fear of a bleak future). We can discuss why we recycle and then do it as a family. We can plant seeds together, put up a bird feeder, walk in the woods, visit a natural history museum. . . .

I hope that the ideas and products here can help us all in our adventure of growing together with our children in our love and caring for our planet. Write to us with your ideas on educating children and ourselves.

— *Catherine Werth*

> *Of several million known forms of life, both plant and animal, one vanishes into oblivion every ten minutes.*
>
> —WILLIAM CONWAY, N.Y. ZOOLOGICAL SOCIETY

CENTER FOR COASTAL STU

THE WHALE ADOPTION PROJECT

Adopt a 40-ton baby! Become a member and choose from over 60 humpbacks. You will receive a certificate of adoption and a picture of the whale. There is a regular quarterly newsletter as well as a child's version of the newsletter. –C.W.

$15, The International Wildlife Coalition

PROJECT LEARNING TREE

Teachers love PLT's programs across the country that train teachers to teach kids about the environment through 175 environmental projects that emphasize how to think. Cosponsored by the American Forest Foundation and the Western Regional Environmental Education Council, PLT has been used by 200,000 educators in the U.S., Canada, Sweden, and Finland. An excellent resource for educators. –C.W.

Free flyer and sample newsletter, Project Learning Tree

CHILDREN FOR OLD GROWTH

This nonprofit group is focusing its efforts on saving the remaining virgin forests on this planet. With membership a child receives a nature poster for coloring and a thank-you for caring for the trees and helping to save them. –C.W.

$10, Children for Old Growth

MAIL ORDER CATALOGUES

Here are some catalogues you can trust for products that encourage love for a safe and healthy earth . . and for each other.

THE MUSIC FOR LITTLE PEOPLE

This catalogue sings with creativity in presenting a broad, carefully chosen selection of videos and cassettes. Also offers storybooks, tapes, stuffed animals, solar and other toys, and T-shirts. – C.W.

HEARTHSONG: A CATALOG FOR FAMILIES

This catalogue is a treasure box Dylan Thomas would have set to lyrical verse. Imagine! A wooden castle blooming with flags and a drawbridge and a real working pulley. Dollhouses and tiny yarn-wrapped dollhouse dolls, china tea sets, and silk scarves for rainy day dress-up. Crystal hearts for windows, beading looms, carpentry books, real baking tins, nesting Russian dolls, and tissue-thin Japanese paper balls to inflate and bat around gently. Wonderful art and music supplies, too.

In our dealings with HearthSong, it has always been courteous and quick to let us know if there will be a wait for anything. Because so many of its items come from Europe, sometimes the delay is up to a month. So do make sure to order well ahead of holidays and birthdays.
–Katrina Hall

THE GEODE CATALOGUE

We highly recommend this catalogue. It has 50 pages, without gloss or color, full of materials to stimulate interest in creative, ecological living and thinking. See other product reviews for details. – C.W.

ANIMAL TOWN: COOPERATIVE VENTURES

Ken and Jann Kolsbun, the powers that be behind this catalogue, write that "Children and Nature . . . have much in common: [they are] sensitive to change, react negatively to abuse, require clean air, water, and food, are irreplaceable. . . ."

The offerings in this catalogue reflect that philosophy. It's chock-full of nature books (Ogden Nash's *Zoo*), cassettes ("Hug the Earth"), and cooperative games (Nectar Collector, Harvest Time). From real children's garden tools to a pop-up weather book, the items in this catalogue will stimulate your child's natural love of the world of plants and animals.
–Mona Anderson

MATTHEW FARRUGGIO, HEARTHSONG

STOCKING A SEVEN YEAR OLD'S POCKETS

The 1990s as the "Decade of the Environment" will increase the demand for alternative stores with products like the ones in this book. Explore these, and let us know about your own favorites.

STORES

At the **World of Science** stores, you'll find ecological educational materials in diverse, bright, well-organized surroundings brimming with color and excitement. The company's motto says, "Whether you're three or 83 . . . science and nature can be fun." Thirteen stores are located in New York, Pennsylvania, Connecticut, Ohio, and West Virginia.

In California you will find stores like **Imaginarium** and **Thinker Things**. In downtown Philadelphia visit **Einstein's**. If you are in Cedar Falls, Iowa, be sure to go to **Galileo's**. In Portland, Maine, visit the **Ecology House**.

At last count the **Nature Company** had 39 stores in California, Boston, Washington, D.C., and places in between. Famed bird-watcher Pete Dune describes the stores as "a cross between a museum, a toy chest, and the contents of a seven year old's pockets!" Not only are the stores a wonderful collection of quality nature products, but they often sponsor free nature activities, too. Get their catalogue if you can't visit.

World Game Players

PHOTO COURTESY LARRY PRICE, PHILADELPHIA INQUIRER

OTHER GREAT PLACES

Science museums, aquariums, zoos, nature centers, and special children's museums are found all over the United States. Locate the ones in your area and search out new ones when you travel. These places offer experiences that cannot be duplicated, and they usually have unique shops as well.

Don't miss the **Exploratorium** when you're in San Francisco. "The whole point of the Exploratorium," according to its promoters, "is to make it possible for people to believe they can understand the world around them." The Exploratorium delights the senses and brings nature to life. Its innovative exhibits — more than 600 of them — are meant to be manipulated, not just admired. Push, pull, open, look through, talk, and listen to exhibits based on light, sound, vision, hearing, touch, motion, waves, animal behavior, heat, and temperature.

The **World Game Institute** in Philadelphia is a research and educational laboratory based on Buckminster Fuller's goal, "to make the world work for 100% of humanity. . . ." World Game programs focusing on global issues, resource availability, and consumption are available for schools at all levels, as well as for corporations, communities, and other groups. The institute presents about 100 on-site programs a year, ranging from an hour to two days in length. A key part of the presentation is a world map the size of a basketball court covered with people and symbols for resources. Players perceive world patterns, problems, and relationships that, through the presentation, become very graphic and involving.

VIDEOS

MAN OF THE TREES

The life story of Richard St. Barbe Baker brings hope and inspiration by showing how one man's vision can help to heal the earth. Through his efforts and the organizations he founded, Baker was instrumental in planting millions of trees throughout the world. $1 from each sale is donated to Children for Old Growth. –C.W.

$19.95 (25 min.)
The Music for Little People

A LINK WITH NATURE

Images from the *National Geographic* archives are accompanied by nature sounds, Andean panpipes, flutes, and vocals from the Chanticleer ensemble. The catalogue suggests this video for infants to age three, but we enjoyed it, too. –C.W.

$19.95 (23 min.)
The Music for Little People

All company addresses and phone numbers are listed in the Ecologue Source Directory beginning on page 242.

AUDIO CASSETTES & CDS

THE NATURE COMPANY'S OWN WILDERNESS SOUND/MUSIC RECORDINGS

Moving wilderness/music adventures by award-winning environmental artist Bernie Krause. "Gorilla" is a portrait of Rwanda's famed mountain ape with songs from neighboring tribes and sounds of the gorilla in its home forest. "Nature," recorded on the North American plains, will mesmerize you with its sounds of morning birds and insects, a midday storm, and owls and coyotes calling at night. *–C.W.*

$9.95 Cassettes; $16.95 CDs
The Nature Company

"FLYING WITH THE SWANS"

With this cassette your children will learn to use relaxation techniques that allow them to become swans, whales, butterflies, and squirrels. Encourages a deep respect for nature. *–C.W.*

$9.95 (60 min.)
The Music for Little People

"JOURNEYS HOME"

What a vivid portrayal of nature's life cycles! Experience the drama of a salmon's powerful call to return home to spawn and meet George the water molecule. Well-known naturalist Garth Gilchrist's expansive vision, insight, and humor make this cassette a must. It's suggested for ages 7-13, but adults will thoroughly enjoy listening to this tape with or without a child. *–C.W.*

$9.95 (90 min.)
The Music for Little People

T-SHIRTS

Wear your attitude on your sleeve — or rather, on your chest. You'll be expressing your convictions and spreading the ecological message, plus supporting hardworking environmental groups. Most T-shirts run $10 to $20.

AERIE DESIGN

One of our favorite sources for T-shirts is operating in the Blue Ridge Mountains of North Carolina. Its wildlife graphics and color combinations are outstanding. *–C.W.*

BOOMER'S

"Attitude T-shirts" is the term used by Boomer's of Boise, Idaho. In addition to Mother Earth slogans they produce shirts with eye-catching prehistoric Zuni and Hopi Indian forms of the Rain Bird. *–C.W.*

GREENPEACE

The Greenpeace catalogue carries a broad selection of T-shirts ranging from an infant shirt with the request, "Please leave me a green and peaceful planet," to youth and adult sizes that remind us to "Save the Roos," "Save the Planet," and "Extinct Is Forever." *–C.W.*

ENVIRONMENTAL DEFENSE FUND

The Environmental Defense Fund has a striking black shirt with an earth-from-space picture and the caption, "If you are not recycling, you are throwing it all away." *– C.W.*

The average life of a passenger car tire has nearly doubled since 1973, as longer-lasting radial tires have come into popular use.

SAVE THE WORLD

Learn about the environmental crisis through a challenging, cooperative board game. Players experience the value of teamwork to find solutions. Two to six players, mature teen to adult. –C.W.

$23, Geode

PREDATOR: THE FOOD CHAIN GAME

This game uses 38 illustrated cards to explore the predator-prey relationship of plants and animals. Available in English, French, or Spanish. –C.W.

$8, Geode

4-IN-1 SOLAR KIT

Choose from models for an airplane, helicopter, watermill, or windmill. Kits include model pieces, wood glue, solar cell, electric motor to turn the propeller, and an outstanding brochure to tell you more about solar energy. Ages five and up. –C.W.

$18.50 including postage and handling, Seventh Generation
$12.98, The Music for Little People

150 SOLAR EXPERIMENTS

Explore the uses of solar energy and have fun constructing all kinds of gadgets and experiments from radios to burglar alarms to solar furnaces. The instruction manual is very informative. For ages ten and up, with full instructions. And no batteries needed! –C.W.

$41.95 including postage and handling, Seventh Generation
$36.98, The Music for Little People

EARTH FLAG

Make a statement of your support for the planet! You can display the 3'x5' flag, a breathtaking image of earth, either inside or out. –C.W.

$39, Earth Flag Co.

BUSHNELL ENVIRONMENTAL SCIENTIST

Be an environmental detective. What is acid rain and is there any where you live? What's in the water that you drink? If you live in the city, are there unsuspected gases in the air? This fascinating kit for kids is a virtual portable laboratory for testing and learning about their environment. Nine separate tests, most usable more than once. Includes fanny pack, containers, log book, tweezers, and complete instructions. Ages ten and up. –C.W.

$45.95 including postage and handling, Seventh Generation
$44.98, Music for Little People

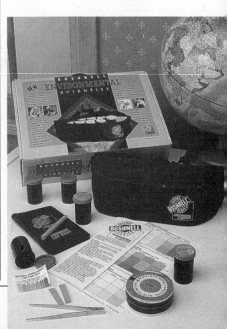

THE WHALE GAME

It's not often you can "become" a migrating humpback whale in the Pacific Ocean! Moving around this challenging board game you are threatened with such dangers as oil spills, capture, and pollution. Each Hazard or Bonus card shares an amazing "Whale Fact." Suggested for ages eight and up. Children may need help until they understand the rules. Ideal to play as a family. –C.W.

$19.95, Wildlife Games

NATURAL ARTS MATERIALS

Environmentally healthy art supplies that use only the highest-quality nontoxic and natural raw materials, such as pigments derived from plants. Products include crayons, watercolors, finger paints, modeling wax in eight colors, and glue. High prices, high quality. –C.W.

**$2.95 to $15.80
Livos PlantChemistry**

JUST THINKING

"We have the know-it-all to feed everybody, clothe everybody, give every human on earth a chance. We dwell instead on petty things. . . . What a waste of time. Think of it. What a chance we have." — *Buckminster Fuller*

ECOLOGUE

93

Education/
Fun

TWO POTATO CLOCK

Uses energy from ordinary potatoes, apples, or soda pop to tell time. A great way to discover energy has sources other than the electric company or an AA battery! It really works — as long as you keep it fueled. –C.W.

$15.95, The Nature Company

HUG-A-PLANET

You'll want to get your arms around this soft fabric globe. While traditional globes are often relegated to a wooden stand or high shelves, Hug-A-Planet invites intimacy. My son has ours on his bed, where at the end of the day it's easy for him to find the rain forest or the latest oil spill location. Even the box design and the informative insert have been given thoughtful, caring attention. –C.W.

$24.95 including postage and handling, Seventh Generation

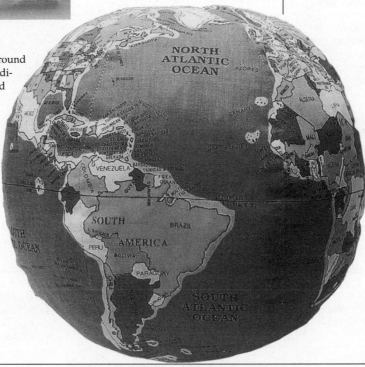

EARTH STICKERS

When an orbiting camera sent back the first full-color picture of the whole earth on November 5, 1967, it became one of the most powerful, consciousness-changing images of all time. You can use these durable stickers in strategic locations as reminders. –C.W.

**$1.50 (package of 8)
California Pacific Designs**

Every year pesticides acutely poison 45,000 people in the United States and up to 2 million people worldwide.

GIFTS/TOYS/GAMES

READ MORE ABOUT NATURE

WILDLIFE PUPPETS

Soar with an eagle that has a 17" wing span. Brown Bear is a cuddly 9". Great for nature stories. –C.W.

$20, Winterland Productions, Sierra Club

SHARING NATURE WITH CHILDREN AND SHARING THE JOY OF NATURE

By Joseph Cornell. These two special books overflow with the joy of nature. They are rightly regarded as two of the best nature-awareness guidebooks available for both adults and children. Cornell's experience is coupled with insight and expansive, uncompetitive activities. The books sing with beauty. Highly recommended by many, including the National Audubon Society. –C.W.

$6.95 each, Dawn Publications; Geode; Music for Little People

KIDS GARDENING: A KID'S GUIDE TO MESSING AROUND IN THE DIRT

Here's a real do-it-yourself book from Klutz Press with 92 durable pages. It includes 14 varieties of vegetable, herb, and flower seeds, guaranteed fresh. Share it with a little friend. –C.W.

$12.95, Klutz Press

LAURIE M. BRIDEFORTH

HUG A TREE AND OTHER THINGS TO DO OUTDOORS WITH YOUNG CHILDREN

By Robert Rockwell, Elizabeth Sherwood, and Robert A. Williams. Based on the philosophy that something special happens when young children explore the out-of-doors. Wonderful activities aimed at ages 3-5 and older with simple-to-follow directions using things you probably already have. –C.W.

$9.95 (103 pages) Gryphon House, Inc.

THE LORAX

A Dr. Seuss classic about the environment. The greedy Once-ler builds a factory to manufacture Thneeds from Truffula trees and destroys the habitat of the area's animals. For ages three and up. And after you've read the book, pick up the video. It brings the story to life. –C.W.

$10, Geode
$14.50 including postage and handling, Seventh Generation
$16.95 Video (30 min.) Music for Little People

Every year 135 billion pounds of toxic waste are discharged into U.S. rivers, lakes, and streams.

CAN THE WHALES BE SAVED?

Why are rain forests important? Are the deserts getting bigger? Can new species be made? This fascinating book from the London Museum of Natural History answers these and dozens of similar questions in colorful style with great illustrations. 96 pages. –C.W.

$16.95, The Nature Company

THE WILD INSIDE: SIERRA CLUB'S GUIDE TO THE GREAT INDOORS

The woods are not the only place to explore nature. Spiders lurk in dark corners; rivers of water roar through the plumbing. This book is full of info and activities for nature adventure inside. –C.W.

$8, Geode

What You Can Do

✔ Let a child help in sprouting seeds such as alfalfa, mung, or radish. Pour seeds over the bottom of a recycled quart or gallon glass jar, cover with a small piece of cheese cloth, and secure with a rubber band. Then rinse the seeds with water. Continue to rinse twice a day until they sprout. In less than a week the seeds can go from bag to salad. Eat. And repeat!

KEEPERS OF THE EARTH: NATIVE AMERICAN STORIES AND ENVIRONMENTAL ACTIVITIES FOR CHILDREN

By Michael J. Caduto and Joseph Bruchac. This beautiful volume has the inspiration, direction, and tools for children to understand that they can be a healing part of their surroundings. Features a collection of North American Indian stories and related hands-on activities. Loaded with great illustrations and activities in creative arts, theater, reading, writing, science, social studies, mathematics, and sensory awareness. 238 pages, hardcover. –S.M.

$22.45, including postage and handling; $9.95 Teacher's Guide (48 pages, large-format paperback), Gaia Catalog Co.

Bubble fun, from HearthSong.

MATTHEW FARRUGGIO, HEARTHSONG

FOCUS ON THE EARTH

Have you ever used your eyes as a camera? Pair up one person as camera and the other as photographer. The photographer gently leads "the camera" — eyes closed — to a shot and adjusts the lens by preparing "the camera" to look at a natural treasure or a broad vista.

Tapped on the shoulder, the camera then opens her eyes for three to six seconds to take the picture. After several shots the pair can change places. Later each develops her favorite picture verbally or by drawing it. (From *Sharing the Joy of Nature*.)

In 1988 only 3% of the plastic waste produced in this country was collected for reprocessing.

SAVE OUR PLANET

By Diane MacEachern. The subtitle of this book is "750 Everyday Ways You Can Help Clean Up the Earth," and that says it all. From home to garage to school to work to apartment, this book covers the many dimensions of good environmental citizenship throughout our everyday lives. We especially like the sprinkling throughout of "Bright Ideas," short anecdotes of inspired success in the fights of individuals to save the planet. Printed on recycled paper. 210 pages. –*Bruce Anderson*

$9.95, Dell Publishing

STATE OF THE WORLD

By Worldwatch Institute. This outstanding compendium has been published annually since 1984 by Worldwatch (see page 201 for a review of this outstanding group). Its team of researchers watches the world, collects and analyzes the facts, and presents programs that we need to heal the environment. If you read no other book about environmental ills and programs for healing them, read each annual edition of this book. About 250 pages. –*B.A.*

$9.95, W. W. Norton & Company

THE EARTHWISE CONSUMER

Editor/publisher Debra Lynn Dadd. This beautifully done newsletter may be just what you need if you want a regular dose of information on everyday products and ideas that are nontoxic, natural, and "earthwise." Printed on recycled paper using soy-based inks. –*B.A.*

**$20 per year for 8 issues
The Earthwise Consumer**

50 SIMPLE THINGS YOU CAN DO TO SAVE THE EARTH

By the Earthworks Group. This best-seller started the tidal wave of environmental book sales in 1989. Yes, its ideas are simple to execute and are presented in manageable bite-sized pieces. 96 pages. Printed on recycled paper. –*B.A.*

$4.95, The Earthworks Press

HOW TO MAKE THE WORLD A BETTER PLACE

By Jeffrey Hollender, the chairman and CEO of Seventh Generation. The 124 suggested actions in this book start with environmental concerns but move into food, social responsibility, peace, and human rights. Be prepared to be inspired to action when you pick up this book. 300 pages. On recycled paper. –*B.A.*

**$9.95
William Morrow and Company, Inc.**

THE GREEN CONSUMER

By John Elkington, Julia Hailes, and Joel Makower. This U.S. edition of the British best-seller with a similar name is packed with facts to make you a more knowledgeable consumer of environmentally safe products. A great resource. 340 pages. Printed on recycled paper. –*B.A.*

**$8.95, Penguin Books
$11.45, including postage and handling, Gaia**

Worldwide, about 100 million square feet of timber surfaces are treated with toxic wood preservatives every year.

Practical Actions For Conscious Living

ONE PERSON'S IMPACT

This excellent newsletter is
jam-packed with practical tips and
products for helping you save the
environment in your everyday life.
Written by folks like you. On recycled paper. –B.A.

**$24 per year for 6 issues
One Person's Impact**

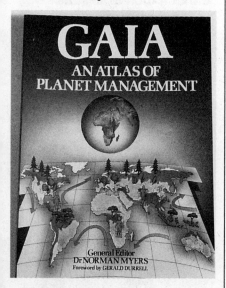

GAIA: AN ATLAS OF PLANET MANAGEMENT

Edited by Dr. Norman Myers. What
a terrific idea for a book! It offers 272
inspiring pages of practical solutions
to the world's seemingly over-
whelming menu of environmental
problems. Under Myers's editorial
guidance, leading ecologists bring
these challenges into sharp focus and
offer positive approaches to the
oceans, forests, and wildlife, as well
as social and cultural evolution. 272
pages. –Steven S. H. McFadden

**$24.95 including postage and
handling, Gaia**

EVERYDAY CHEMICALS: 101 PRACTICAL TIPS FOR HOME AND WORK

By Beth Richman and Susan Hassol.
We hear every day about global
warming and depletion of the ozone
layer. But how about the effect of certain bug repellents on pregnant
women? You use chemicals every
day. But do you use them wisely?
Even if you're not used to thinking
of how the products you use affect
the earth, you'll find this interesting
as well as informative reading.
Printed on recycled paper.
–Jennifer A. Adams

**$4.85 including postage
and handling, The
Windstar Foundation**

Raided by Radon

M Y WIFE, JOANNE, worries a lot, so when we moved into our new home a few years back, it did not surprise me that she began losing sleep after reading about PCB contamination in a town well several miles from our home. I agreed to have our water tested so she could get some sleep.

Every conceivable test was performed, and just as I'd told her, we had no PCBs in our well. In more than a dozen categories, our water was fine. But one category yielded a surprise: radon.

What Exactly Is Radon?

Radon is an invisible, odorless, naturally occurring radioactive gas produced by decaying uranium, itself a common ingredient in granite and other rock. When breathed, it causes lung cancer. Radon enters homes from the ground through leaks in the foundation. In tight, energy-efficient homes that have little natural air exchange, radon can be a major health hazard. Even though it is a gas, radon can remain in water — from which it can be released into the air you're breathing. Some homes have actually been built with radon-contaminated concrete.

If the radon is entering the house through the basement, it can be sealed out or vented with electric fans. If the unwelcome guest has entered through the water, it can be removed by filtration or aeration.

Dangerous radon levels in the home can equal the cancer risk of smoking a pack or two of cigarettes per day.

How Do I Know If I Have a Problem?

Testing for radon is easy and so is understanding the test results. The important key is the "acceptable level" under which you needn't worry. The generally accepted safe level in the air is a score of 4 or less.

Start your testing by using a short-exposure, charcoal-absorbent device for two to seven days to get a preliminary bead on your radon levels. If levels exceed 4, move on to the next, longer test.

Because the longer term "alpha-track" devices require from one to three months, they're more accurate than the preliminary screenings. On one of these tests, two hundred or higher means you should take immediate steps to reduce the radon in your home. Contact your state department of environmental safety for assistance.

WATER RADON STRIPPERS

The two radon stripper aeration units that are the leaders in the field are both priced between $2,400 and $3,000 with an additional $300 to $500 for installation. One is called "The Stripper" from Lowry Engineering, Inc. Lowry is the oldest and best-known company in radon research. The second is called "Clearadon" from North East Environmental Products, Inc. –B.R.

THE LOWRY GRANULATED ACTIVATED CARBON RADON FILTER

This is the only carbon radon filter available. It is noiseless and less expensive than aeration "strippers," but it accumulates and concentrates the radon. Regular testing (three times per year) and filter replacement are absolutely essential for safe, efficient performance. –B.R.

$1,200, Lowry Engineering, Inc.

Heat recovery ventilators can reduce radon levels 50 to 75 percent. See product reviews on pages 138-39.

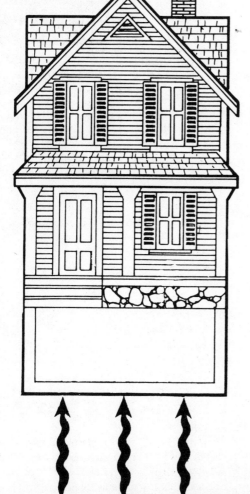

LIFESTYLE ALERT

Radon dangers are multiplied by the co-carcinogen nicotine. Cigarette smokers are more than twice as likely as nonsmokers to get lung cancer if exposed to radon.

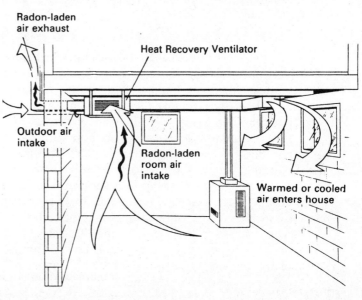

Radon-laden air exhaust

Heat Recovery Ventilator

Outdoor air intake

Radon-laden room air intake

Warmed or cooled air enters house

RADON TESTING

The most reliable radon air testers look like little snuff canisters or oversized tea bags. They are made by many companies and are available at hardware stores for $15 to $50.

The procedure is sensible, though a bit involved. You leave several opened kits sitting around the house in a variety of locations for several weeks. Then you mail them to the manufacturer for analysis, which is included in the price. Sampling should be done only when the house is pretty well buttoned up. For example, opened windows in the summer will really throw the test results off.

Two companies are on everyone's list of approved airborne radon test manufacturers. One is Air Chek, Inc., and the other is Tech/Ops Landauer, Inc. They stand out among some 30 companies for their involvement in radon research since the beginning, for membership in professional scientific associations, and for offering a broad range of products and information. Both sell short- and longer-term devices.
—B.R.

Humanity added 5.5 billion tons of carbon to the atmosphere in 1988. The U.S. was the largest contributor.

What About Testing the Water?

If your air doesn't have dangerous radon levels, that's usually good news about the water, too. Homes with shallow dug wells or publicly supplied water are also safe. You only have to be concerned about water-borne radon if your well is drilled through rock.

To test your water, contact your state department of environmental safety for instructions and referrals to testing labs. The lab you choose will instruct you to run the water for 20 minutes, then bottle samples of freely flowing tap water in sterile jars. The EPA recommends sampling on three different days, but samples must be mailed immediately because radon naturally breaks down rapidly. Analyses cost $15 to $50.

How Do I Get Rid of Radon in My Water?

Our water tested at 25,000 picocuries per liter — many times the safe limit of 2,000 — so now my wife and I were both worried enough to undertake some "radon mitigation" measures.

Deciding to remove the radon from the water, we installed a carbon filter unit in our water line where it enters the house. It worked great for a few months, removing more than 90 percent of the radon.

But that wasn't the end of the story. To know that a radon filter is working, you must periodically retest your water, and we were glad that we did. Over time our tests showed that the rate of removal dropped to 65 percent. The manufacturer explained that a rare, chemical reaction in our water was fouling the carbon and that eventually it would just stop working altogether. This condition, we learned, occurs in only one percent of installations. Lowry Engineering earned our thanks by offering us full credit toward a more suitable system. They even delivered it from Maine.

We switched to a radon "stripper," which contains no carbon filter. It removes 99.6 percent of the radon by aeration (making bubbles) and exhausts it harmlessly outside the house. This device is noisy and expensive ($3,000) and must be installed by a licensed plumber and electrician, but it has the advantage of no radon accumulation and no filter to replace. (Carbon filters must be changed every few years.) And knowing that would make anyone sleep better.   — *Barry Rhodes*

READ MORE ABOUT IT

As of early 1990 there was no national consumer-oriented clearinghouse for radon information or for testing. The U.S. Environmental Protection Agency presently offers technical and some general literature. If you live in one of the 12 radon states, contact your state health department.

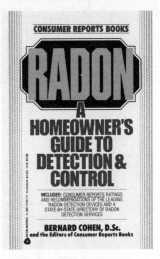

RADON — A HOMEOWNER'S GUIDE TO DETECTION AND CONTROL

By Dr. Bernard S. Cohen and the editors of Consumer Reports Books. Should you worry about radon? Why and how should you test your home? Which tests are available? What should you do if the results indicate a problem? These and many more radon-related questions are answered in this book — arguably the best resource available for understanding radon and what can be done about it.

The book has the usual *Consumer Reports* style product reviews of testing devices, detailed explanations of strategies for radon reduction techniques, results of a nationwide study of radon levels by county and zip code, and a listing of state agency contact persons for information.

This might be the best $10 you could spend on your family's health. –*B.R.*

$10, Available in bookstores

Common Radon Entry Points

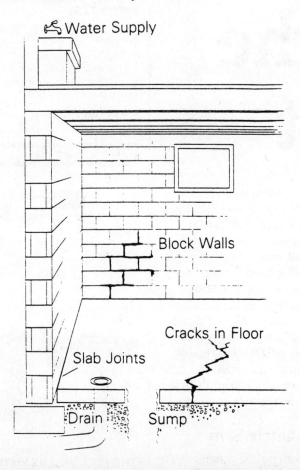

🚰 Water Supply

Block Walls

Cracks in Floor

Slab Joints

Drain

Sump

What You Can Do

✔ Test your air for radon.

✔ If the level is above 4 and your water comes from a drilled well, test your water.

✔ If you can reduce the radon level in the air significantly by treating your water, do it and retest the air before attacking the radon infiltration through the basement. (A generally accepted rule of thumb is that for every 10,000 picocuries of radon removed from water, 1 picocurie will also be removed from the air.)

✔ To keep radon from "infiltrating" your cellar, seal leaks in the foundation with sprayed foam or patching concrete. Holes where pipes and wires enter are typical radon entry sites that should be sealed.

✔ As a last resort, ventilate the ground directly around or under the cellar floor. This is an expensive undertaking. The idea is to reduce the air pressure outside so that radon-laden air doesn't flow into the home. There are companies that will guide you through the process or do it for you. Again, state agencies may be able to recommend contractors.

GOOD NEWS & BAD NEWS ABOUT RADON

The good news: Only 12 states have significant health-threatening levels of radon: Connecticut, Colorado, Florida, Kentucky, Maine, New Hampshire, New Jersey, New York, Ohio, Pennsylvania, Tennessee, and Utah.

The good news: Drinking water with radon in it is generally safe. Only the gaseous emissions of radon absorbed through the lungs are considered dangerous to humans.

The bad news: Radon can be released from water into your airspace easily — at the shower head, in a boiling pot, or even in burps.

The bad news: The five-minute "quickie" radon tests are totally unreliable. The EPA is expected to ban them when it establishes testing standards in the early nineties.

The bad news: Carbon faucet filters, designed to trap organic impurities, also accumulate dangerous levels of radon — another reason for testing your water. Remove all filters for a "clean catch" sample.

Eighty to 85% of CFC consumption for refrigeration and air-conditioning goes to refill existing equipment during servicing.

Getting the Lead Out

CLEAR, SAFE, AND NICE TASTING . . . this is what we expect of our drinking water. But lake, river, and well water is more than just water. It contains many natural and artificial substances that turn it gray or yellow, make it unsafe to drink, and make it taste like . . . well, make it taste terrible.

> *More than 500 billion pounds of hazardous chemical wastes are improperly disposed of every year. Much of that finds its way into our drinking water sources.*

The ingredients of this soup we call "water" include acid rain, pesticides, herbicides, solvents, road salt, fertilizers, lead and cadmium, bacteria, viruses, and parasites. Visualize the ooze leaching into our drinking-water supplies from more than 300,000 toxic-waste sites, 800,000 underground fuel tanks, and millions of dumps and landfills! Clearly, it's time something was done — but by whom?

Don't Leave It to Uncle Sam

Most of us drink from public water systems. Most systems are treated with chlorine — now known to create by-products such as chloroform and trihalomethanes, which are linked to cancer.

Federal regulations require that all public water supplies be tested and that they meet or exceed rigorous standards. However, for whatever reason, the people that supply your water may not correct the problems that arise. You'll have to take matters into your own hands.

Testing the Waters

Have doubts about your water? Call your water supplier and ask for regular reports. Once is not enough because water quality can change overnight due to contamination and natural phenomena.

Then, have your water tested by a reputable lab. The lab can detect any dangerous contaminants the water has picked up as it traveled through the distribution system and into your home.

If you have a private source of water, such as a well, lake, or stream, buy the best water purification system you can afford. Be sure it has a sediment prefilter and disinfection unit. Have your water tested every six months. We recommend a reverse-osmosis filter with added ultraviolet-light disinfection.

We also recommend the following
other activated-carbon water filters:

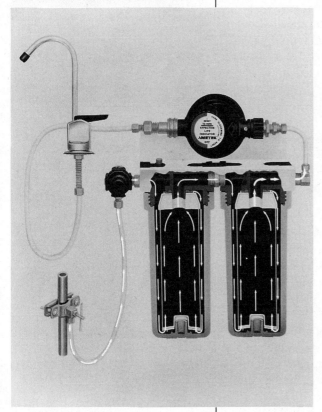

THE AMETEK CCF-210
$160, Ametek

ECOWATER "WATER MASTER"
$250, Ecowater

HURLEY II
$375, Hurley

AMWAY E-9230
$280, Amway

WHAT'S IN THE BOTTLE?

Given all the potential hazards in other water sources, you may decide that bottled water is the way to go. Just remember that all bottled water is not necessarily safe water; its only claim is that it's water in a bottle. Learn how to read the labels.

Spring water is least guaranteed to be safe; it comes from a natural spring, but that's all. It may taste great (watch out for high salt content) and still not be safe. Read the label on the bottle carefully, and consider the source and any testing that was done on it.

Purified water is usually safe; it's gone through a process that removes minerals and contaminants to less than ten parts per million.

Ultrapure (analytical or reagent grade) double-distilled and deionized bottled water contains, for all practical purposes, nothing but H_2O. It's safe but boring. It turns out that minerals and contaminants give water the taste we all like. But if this is your preference, check your yellow pages under "Laboratory Supplies" for a local source.

YOU SHOULD KNOW

One major water filter company asserts that its bacteriostatic filter is registered with the Environmental Protection Agency. Must be OK if the EPA registers the product, right? Not necessarily. The EPA registers the filter because it may put a potentially dangerous compound into the water, and as with pesticides and herbicides, the EPA requires registration of such public health threats!

A 1988 EPA report revealed that industry in the United States released 9.7 billion pounds of chemicals into streams in 1987.

Home Remedies

In-home treatment devices are the best way of making sure that your drinking water is safe. They are categorized by what they do to improve the quality of your water. The vast majority deal with the taste, odor, color, and turbidity (cloudiness) of water. Others reduce organic and inorganic chemicals, heavy metals (lead, cadmium, etc.), and microorganisms that cause cysts and disease.

How Much Is Enough?

Treat the water only to the quality required to do the specific task. For example, you don't need drinking water to wash your socks or flush a toilet, so you wouldn't use the same type of device that mounts on your drinking-water faucet to treat every drop of water you use in your home.

Here are some different types:

Whole-house systems treat all the water that comes into the house. This doesn't make much sense unless the water is contaminated with radon (see pages 98-101 for information and products that cover this) or is too ugly for washing your clothes or showering. Ugly water may have copper, iron, manganese or sulphur in it that turns your toilet bowl green, red, or black or smells like rotten eggs.

A *water purifier* is appropriate when you need only a small amount of pure water for cooking, drinking, and ice cubes. There are two types: One attaches to your faucet or sits on your counter with tubing connections to the faucet. The other taps into the water lines under your sink and pipes water to a separate faucet.

By the way, don't buy small filters that replace your faucet tap aerator. They may be cheap, but they can become a breeding farm for bacteria and viruses and even build up radioactive radon. They're too risky with minimal benefit.

Disinfect Before You Drink

For total safety from bacterial or viral contamination, you must disinfect your purified water before you drink it. Disinfection requires that something be added or done to the water to kill disease-causing organisms, not just filter them out.

You could add chlorine, but that's just another questionable chemical. You could boil the water for 30 minutes, but that's impractical. The best solutions are purifiers that have either ozone or ultraviolet-light treatment.

— *David Del Porto*

DECISIONS, DECISIONS

How do you know which purifier to buy? Consider only those purifiers that are certified by an independent test lab. The only one we would rely on is the National Sanitation Foundation (NSF) of Ann Arbor, Michigan — the Underwriter's Laboratory (UL) for environmental health certification. If the purifier that you are considering has the NSF seal, you can trust that the device and the manufacturing facility have been thoroughly examined to meet rigorous standards of performance.

Buy the best NSF-certified purifier you can afford. Examples include those reviewed here. Service your purifier regularly and test the output once a year to verify the quality.

DISTILLATION DEVICES

THE AQUA CLEAN MODEL-4

Consumer Reports rated the Aqua Clean Model-4 as best overall in organic substance removal, construction materials, and convenience. Well made of stainless steel, with a special float that shuts off the heat to minimize the buildup of scale.
–*Lonny Brown*

$299, Everpure, Inc.

THE SEARS 34555

This performs as well as the Aqua Clean and costs less, but it is built into a plastic housing. In recent studies the solvents in plastic have been reported to leach into the very water you are purifying! –*D.D.P.*

$150, Sears

REVERSE OSMOSIS DEVICES

For home use we recommend four under-the-counter models and two countertop models. These products all effectively remove a wide range of impurities and toxic compounds, as tested by *Consumer Reports* (January 1990) and Rodale product tests (June 1985). Price ranges are from dealers. –*D.D.P.*

Under-Counter Reverse Osmosis Water Purifiers

COAST FILTRATION WS/RO-5
$650 to $850, Coast Filtration

CULLIGAN AQUA CLEAR H-83
$849 (installed), Culligan

ENTING AQUAMATE
$490 to $530, Enting

EVERPURE ULTIMATE 1
$640 to $740, Everpure, Inc.

Countertop Reverse Osmosis Water Purifiers

THE CULLIGAN AQUA CLEAR COMPACT
$499 (installed), Culligan

THE SHAKLEE BESTWATER SYSTEM 50800
$300 to $400, Shaklee

All company addresses and phone numbers are listed in the Ecologue Source Directory beginning on page 242.

TRY A LITTLE REVERSE OSMOSIS

Reverse osmosis (RO) technology is the best for overall removal of all sorts of contaminants from water destined for human consumption. In fact, RO systems are used in hospitals and laboratories to produce ultrapure water that has virtually no impurities, toxic compounds, or trace chemicals. As you might guess, it is also the most expensive water purification method.

In simple terms, reverse osmosis is the filtration of pressurized water through a special penetrable membrane that allows only chemically pure water molecules to get through. The process occurs in nature all the time in the walls of all living cells, but it takes some fancy equipment to duplicate it artificially on a practical scale. Hence the high price.

FILTERS FILL THE BILL

Carbon water filters are metal canisters that take impure water in one end and send it out the other end relatively clean and safe to drink. The key to their effectiveness is the amazing ability of activated carbon to grab and hold onto organic contaminants and inorganic chemicals. (The carbon is "activated" with superheated steam at the factory.)

The more activated carbon in a filtration system, the better, so don't buy a filter that's so small that it resembles a faucet aerator on the end of your spigot.

It's important to replace your water filter cartridge every six months. When that time comes, you'll find there are lots of inexpensive replacements on the market; you shouldn't have to pay more than about $5 for one.

THE DISADVANTAGES OF DISTILLATION

Distillation is a second choice to filtration as a method of purifying water. It is slower, uses a considerable amount of electricity, generates heat, and allows some chemical contaminants to get through.

Distillers work by boiling the water, evaporating it into steam, and then recondensing it, leaving the impurities behind. The process does a good job of removing dissolved solids (inorganic compounds) such as salt, minerals, and heavy metals such as lead. It is not effective against certain volatile organic chemicals, pesticides, and solvents (like benzene) and gases (such as chloroform) that evaporate and recondense along with the water.

To boil the water, a distillation purifier may use up to 3 1/2 kilowatt-hours of electricity to produce one gallon of cleaner water. At present rates that could cost you 20¢ to 35¢ for each gallon you produced. And not all the water distilled reaches your faucet: Stills can waste about two to four gallons of water for every gallon collected. Not a very efficient process, but useful for specific conditions.

DITCHING THE DISPOSAL

Disposing of used water-filter cartridges poses an environmental challenge because all the toxic chemicals removed from the water are now concentrated in the spent charcoal. One approach to dealing with accumulated microbes in water filters is to kill them with ultraviolet (UV) light; therefore some units have built-in UV light bulbs, and some offer them as accessories. If yours doesn't have such a device, take the used cartridge either to your water utility or to a hazardous-waste collection (see page 38).

Slowing The Flow

> *On average, we each use 60 to 75 gallons of water daily indoors. We could cut that amount by half through conservation.*

CONTAMINATED WELLS. CLOSED BEACHES. Poisoned seafood. Sinking water tables. None of us can escape the consequences of our having squandered and poisoned our water for decades. Clean water is becoming as expensive and scarce as petroleum. The difference is, we need gas and oil for our cars — until alternatives are developed — but we need clean water for our bodies. Every day. Forever.

Two-thirds of our planet is covered in water. It falls from the sky and runs underground beneath us. We wash and cook with it and need to consume at least two quarts a day to survive. So when our water goes bad or supplies run short, we have problems of major proportions.

If you still have clean water rushing from your faucet, our first advice is this: Slow the flow. The same advice goes to communities, small businesses, and huge industries. The most immediately available solution, and the only one which is free, is smarter water usage.

Down the Toilet

The American bathroom typifies our confused approach to water use. At five to seven gallons per flush, our common flush toilet consumes up to 40 percent of the water we use indoors.

Then there's the peculiar misnomer of "sanitary engineering," our bizarre propensity to mix human wastes with sources of drinking water — a practice that is the leading cause of death by cholera, typhoid fever, and dysentery in the world. The contemporary solution of adding toxic chemicals such as chlorine to the soup, to kill the disease-causing microbes, creates new cancer-causing compounds such as chloroform.

What Can Be Done

Fortunately, you can do many things to save water. Low-flush toilets, composting toilets, low-flow showerheads, and faucet attachments are some of the options.

LOW-FLUSH TOILETS

All of these toilets are readily available through your plumber or local plumbing supply house. Prices range from $100 to $200. Designer styling and colors can boost prices to $1,000 and more.

THE IFO

The IFO is the best-performing gravity-flush toilet in the world. IFO Sanitar makes the broadest selection of models, including the "Aqua," "Cascade," and "Evak." Water consumption ranges from 1 quart (the Evak vacuum flush) to 3- and 6-liter gravity toilets.

Three liters you say? Yes, 3 liters per flush (about 3.3 quarts). We predict that 3 liters will become the world flush-volume standard by the end of this decade. This is half the volume of the state-of-the-art 1.6-gallon low-flush models. –D.D.P.

IFO Sanitar AB of Bromolla, Sweden; Distributed by Mansfield of Perrysville, Ohio

YOU SHOULD KNOW

Using less water prolongs the life of your septic system because it retains solids, letting bacteria do a more complete job of decomposition.

THE SOVEREIGN

Tapered "rocket" nozzles in the bowl accelerate the water in this Sovereign series of 6-liter flush toilets. This is a higher quality toilet, with solid brass handle and a higher price, too. –D.D.P.

$300 to $400, Fowler of New South Wales, Australia

FLUSHMATE

The Sloan Company pioneered the latest technology in compressed-air flushing — called "Flushmate" — which it licenses to the industry. It uses your home's water pressure to compress air in a tank within the normal toilet tank to deliver a good flush with less water.

These toilets are more expensive, and the flush noise is more abrupt (and even startling) than the gravity models. However, if you like a larger than minimal water surface in your toilet bowl, then this may be the one for you. –D.D.P.

Plumbing supply stores

CRANE TOILETS

Presently Crane Plumbing has more models and colors of Ultra Low Flush toilets than any other American manufacturer. Crane uses both gravity and the "Flushmate" (compressed air) technology for the widest range of choices; the Economiser is one example. You can trust Crane to meet the needs of most every "water closet" installation requirement. –D.D.P.

Plumbing supply stores

MICROFLUSH FEATURES SIMPLE OPERATION

An outstanding feature of the Microflush toilet is the extremely quiet, 12 second flush cycle. Microflush toilets provide a large water surface area and rim wash to assure a thorough bowl cleaning.

■ **FLUSH CYCLE**
When the flush handle is pressed, the flapper opens allowing water to flow from the rim, thoroughly washing the bowl and rinsing the wastewater into the lower chamber.

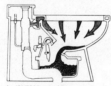

|— 12" (304.8mm) —|
Standard rough-in for downward discharge.

Depth from wall:
|— Round: 24½" (623mm) —|
|— Elongated: 26½" (673.1mm) —|

After several seconds, the flapper closes. Clean water continues to flow into the bowl where it remains until the next flush. When the flapper closes, compressed air is released automatically into the lower chamber, forcing the wastewater over the trap and out the discharge line.

Microflush toilets are listed by the following code authorities.

MICROPHOR

We also recommend products from Microphor, a leader in microflush technologies. These models have their own built-in air compressor. –D.D.P.

$900 to $1,500, Microphor

ENVIROVAC

Envirovac's microflush toilets use a vacuum method to assist the flush. You pay a significant premium in price, but the water savings is phenomenal. –D.D.P.

$900 to $1,500, Envirovac

THE PEARL

The "foam-flush" Nepon Pearl toilet uses only *1 cup* of water per flush! How? A foam generator eliminates friction in the bowl during the flush, and the waste just slips away nearly silently with the smallest amount of water. You see a white foam and hear a slight hum. The foam is made from detergent that you pour into a reservoir about every month and a half. (Please use biodegradable only!) This is truly the "Toyota of toilets" and uses less water than any other WC. Check it out. –D.D.P.

$450, Nepon, Tokyo, Japan

Low Flush

Low-flush toilets are the smart alternative. The best ones look like a regular toilet but flush with only 1.6 gallons or less. These are called "Ultra Low Flush" or ULF toilets. The next best use 3.5 gallons and are called "Water Savers."

Massachusetts has banned the old-fashioned toilets and requires that new "water closet" (tank type) toilets use no more than 1.6 gallons per flush. Many other states are considering the same requirement. By the way, don't believe what you hear about compromises in performance. Low-flush toilets work just as well as conventional models, and you won't be embarrassed by having them in your home.

There are two broad categories of ULF toilets:

Compressed air. These use air pumps to help things move along.

Gravity. These toilets use only gravity to achieve a good flush. They're less complex and so are less costly. We prefer the designs that use tapered water rocket nozzles in the bowl to accelerate the water as it leaves the tank.

No Flush

The premise of dry, waterless toilet technologies is that collecting and treating body wastes where we make them is more effective, ecological, and economical than sending them elsewhere in a huge underground river of precious H_2O.

Dry toilets are categorized by the process they use: packaging, incinerating, or biological. They all have sealed, slide-out drawers for regular emptying. These are the possibilities.

Wrap it. The packaging toilet is a Swedish invention that automatically wraps the solid waste so that it can be transported elsewhere for treatment. It does not treat it in any way. This is a new idea that has not yet caught on in the U.S.

Burn it. Incinerating toilets burn the waste, using electricity or propane. The by-product is a sterilized ash. These are good for sites with no plumbing, but they are more energy intensive than the biological toilets.

Transform it. Biological, or composting, toilets transform urine, feces, and toilet paper waste into a dry soil conditioner, which you can safely add to your garden or take out with the trash.

When a Toilet Becomes an Appliance

Composting toilets are broadly categorized by how they are integrated into the building. The self-contained models that sit on the floor are referred to as appliances. They are small (3'Lx2'Wx18"H at the seat) and weigh about 50 to 90 pounds. These can accommodate up to a four-person family only. In most cases they require added heat to help evaporate liquids and a system to exhaust odor and gases that may require a small electric fan.

A dry toilet that has a conventional-looking toilet seat in the room and a central composting unit below (e.g., in the basement) is called an organic waste treatment system.

Here's how dry toilets work: A small, vented tank holds the waste where naturally occurring aerobic microbes, in the presence of oxygen and heat, rapidly transform it into carbon dioxide, water vapor, and valuable soil-enriching humus. The humus is a dry earthlike material that is safe and portable with a minimum of hassle.

COMPOSTING TOILETS

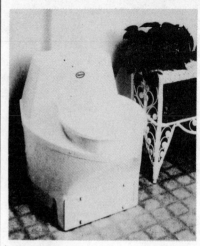

THE HUMUS

This is the best of the appliance dry toilets. It's compact, made of sturdy ABS plastic (the kind used in canoes) and high-grade corrosion-resistant stainless. Reliable and competitively priced. From the largest manufacturer of biological toilets in the world. –D.D.P.

$1,100, Vakuumplast AB of Reftele, Sweden

THE SUN-MAR XL AND N.E.

The Sun-Mar XL is the first appliance dry toilet to be listed by the National Sanitation Foundation (NSF). It has an internal "biodrum" that you crank from time to time to keep air in the decomposing mixture and an electric warmer and fan. The N.E. is the nonelectric version with drainage drying and a larger vent. –D.D.P.

$1,200, Sun-Mar of Ontario, Canada

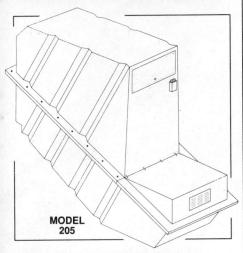

MODEL 205

THE CLIVUS MULTRUM 205

The Clivus is the tried and true system that's been around since the seventies. You can add accessories like extra vent kits or chutes that send kitchen wastes directly to the composting tank. Lends itself to new home construction. –D.D.P.

$5,200, Clivus Multrum, Inc.

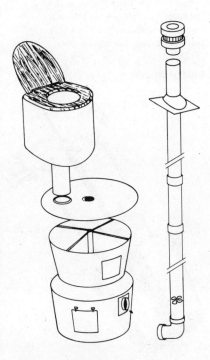

THE CAROUSEL

A compact version of the "upstairs-downstairs" waste treatment systems. –D.D.P.

$2,200 to $3,200 (depending on size), Water Conservation Systems

What You Can Do

✔ Check for a leaky toilet by placing a dozen drops of red or blue food coloring into the tank. Wait 15 minutes. If colored water appears in the bowl, you have a leak. One leaky toilet can waste more than 50 gallons of water a day.

✔ Don't let water just run. If you must let the water run to reach the temperature you desire or to rid the line of copper or lead traces, let it run into a bucket and use it for watering houseplants, for cleaning, or for flushing the toilet.

✔ Use gray water (water that has already been used once for showers, dishwashing, laundry, or cooking) to keep houseplants and garden plants alive during a drought or to reduce excess water use at any time. Be careful of what you put into the water you intend to re-use. Bleach, enzymatic cleaners, and caustic products are hazardous and damage plants.

✔ Promptly replace rubber washers on leaky water valves.

✔ Set houseplants out in a warm-weather rainstorm for a drink.

✔ Take showers, not baths, to cut water consumption.

TAKING A FRESH APPROACH

Morro Bay, California, is short of fresh water, so a moratorium on new buildings was in effect for about a decade. In 1985, however, town officials came up with a unique program. They have tied the approval of new construction to improvements in the efficiency of existing buildings. A builder must install water-saving devices in ten older homes to earn a permit to build one new residence. The result? By retrofitting older homes (at their own expense), builders conserve at least as much water as the new home is expected to use.

LIFESTYLE ALERT

Avoid chemical toilets! These are the worst kind of disposal pollution devices because they add toxins like formaldehyde, quaternary compounds, and artificial fragrances to the organic wastes and send them into the water stream. Designed for boats, recreational vehicles, and campsites, they are illegal in homes and are environmentally dangerous. It's better to properly dispose of untreated wastes than to add chemicals to the problem.

A pinhole water leak can waste as much as 170 gallons of water every day.

Do-It-Yourself Fertilizer

The American engineering community has rediscovered the ancient natural science of composting as the best way to manage organic wastes. Agricultural residues, leaf and yard waste, and sewage sludges are being composted in cities and towns all around the nation.

Modern "ecologically engineered" composting toilets are a far cry from the crude compost privies you might remember from your grandparents' farm and a lot more user friendly, although they do require a modicum of maintenance, such as cranking and emptying. They use a conventional-looking seat in the bathroom and a remote central composting tank below the toilet, usually in the basement.

Tapping the Savings

Increasing the efficiency of your water-using fixtures and appliances reduces your water bill and your water heating bill. It also saves sewage treatment costs.

In the last 15 years we have tried virtually every kind of showerhead and low-flush toilet, and a memorable assortment of Rube Goldberg contraptions that claimed to save water. Most of them in fact do save water, but that really isn't the important issue. The critical issue is: will the device deliver acceptable service? Because if, for example, a showerhead won't rinse the soap from the long brown hair of a five-foot-tall female, then it will most certainly be replaced by a profligate water waster that will. Believe us!

So ultimately the best water-saving devices are the ones that you, the user, find acceptable and therefore keep in place year after year.

— *David Del Porto*

What You Can Do

✔ Turn off the tap while brushing your teeth or shaving. You'll save four to ten gallons of water a day.

✔ Use plain white toilet paper, which degrades faster than decorated, colored paper.

✔ Don't flush the toilet after every use (or "If it's yellow, let it mellow; if it's brown, flush it down").

✔ Rather than washing your car in the driveway, do it on a green area. Wash your car out of a bucket and use the hose for rinsing.

✔ Use a broom, not a hose, to clean off your driveway or sidewalk.

✔ Install sink faucet aerators and water-efficient showerheads, which use two to five times less water but do not noticeably decrease cleansing performance.

✔ Learn to read your water meter so you can detect hidden leaks. Take a reading, then turn off all water-using appliances. (Don't forget the automatic ice maker!) Avoid using any water for half an hour, then take another reading. If there's a change in the reading you have a leak.

✔ If your shower fills a half-gallon milk carton in less than ten seconds you are using too much water.

SHOWERHEADS

In the competitively priced, two-gallon-per-minute range of performance, several showerheads stand out:

MINNCO SHOWERHEAD

After flush toilets, which use 40% of our indoor water flow, water for bathing is next at 30%. Don't buy a showerhead that flows with more than 3 gallons per minute at 50 pounds of water pressure. You can get a really good shower from this one that uses only 1 gallon per minute. This is a hand-held model, but soon the company will have a small, conventional head that will replace your wall-mounted fixture. –D.D.P.

$49.95, Minnco

NOVA SHOWERHEAD

This showerhead gives the most invigorating shower. –D.D.P.

$12.95, Ecological Water Products

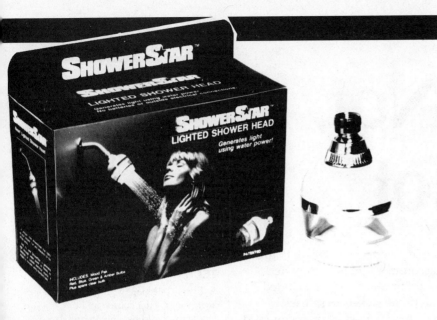

TOILET DAMS

Toilet dams are a simple, inexpensive way to reduce the amount of water your old flusher uses. A dam is a fence that goes inside the tank and reduces the water-filled area. They are readily available in hardware stores for under $5. Get the spring steel kind with gasket seals, rather than the plastic ones, which don't work as well. Be sure not to block the mechanisms inside the tanks. Do not use bricks; they decompose and can clog the drainage pipes. –D.D.P.

THE SHOWERSTAR

This is the most interesting showerhead around. Not only does it give you a water-conserving shower that feels good, but it lights up your shower stall as well. A built-in hydroelectric generator produces 2.5 volts at .31 amps. Not enough juice to be dangerous, but sufficient to light a small but powerful flashlight bulb built into the head. It comes with an assortment of colored light bulbs to suit your mood and create ambience in the shower. It encourages taking showers with a friend, which saves water, too. It's more expensive than most showerheads on the market and uses a lot of plastic in construction, but for the ultimate in cogeneration technology for the bathroom, it's a showstopper. –D.D.P.

$39.95, O'Ryan

LEARN MORE ABOUT IT

THE WATER WHEEL: A GUIDE TO HOME WATER CONSERVATION

Dial the area of home water use, and the window in this paperboard wheel shows the potential water waste and what you can do to conserve. The double-sided display adds up to dozens of water-saving tips. (Example: Clean the tub while you are in it.) Good for getting kids involved. –L.J.B.

$1.50, Water Conservation Systems, Inc.

FAUCET ATTACHMENTS

FAUCET AERATOR

Use up to 60% less water and save on hot water bills with an inexpensive screw-in aerator. It works by mixing air into the water stream. You can't tell the difference at the sink, but you'll notice it in your monthly bills. This one features a handy on-off lever. –Lonny J. Brown

$11.50 including postage and handling, Seventh Generation

YOU SHOULD KNOW

Our porcelain thrones waste from two to three trillion gallons of high-quality drinking water in the United States each year. That's enough water to provide the minimum daily drinking water requirement for the entire world's population for three or four years!

FUEL SAVERS

Waste Not, Watt Not

WONDERING WHERE YOU can find a better investment than any stock, mutual fund, or savings account? Right in your own home! With the few simple tips and handy products we've included here — from weather stripping and water tank jackets to setback thermostats — you can keep the heat where you need it when you need it. You'll be richer and warmer (or cooler in the summer) . . . and saving energy is the most important thing you can do to help the environment.

You can find many of the products on the shelves of your local hardware or building supply store, but if you like to have your fingers do the walking, contact the source that's listed after each product review. In some cases, for specialty items, the listed source may be the only place to find the product.

Stop the Gaps

What should do you do first? Plug those holes. If you can feel air coming in around doors and windows and through electric outlets and light switches on a windy day, you're wasting energy and money. The bad news is that these leaks are costing you a lot of money. The good news is that they're usually cheap and easy to fix. Start saving money and energy here!

Energy-saving measures implemented in the U.S. since 1973 have reduced our national energy bill by $150 billion per year.

Fat cracks may need a heavy dose of fiberglass or foamed-in-place insulation. Use *caulk* to seal those small cracks — around doors and windows, between the top of the foundation and the wood sill that sits on it, and around openings in the walls, ceilings, and floor at wires, pipes, and vents.

Another way to stop the gaps around doors, windows, and hatches is to *weather-strip*. Use a weather stripping that fastens to the stationary side of the crack, like the door jamb, so that the movable surface closes into it and compresses it. But also use common sense. Don't, for example, glue weather stripping to a doorsill.

Gaskets and *plugs* are for "pre-formed" cracks. The best example is the gasket made to fit behind electrical outlets and switches.

Draft dodgers are long, skinny stuffed animals that lie in front of your doorsill to stop the flow of air. They used to be snakes — now they have the heads of ducks, dogs, and cats. They're cheaper than buying a

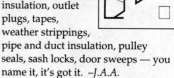
By using energy efficiently we can reduce household energy requirements by as much as 10% to 75%.

STOP-GAP PRODUCTS

BROOKSTONE

ROPE CAULK

Rope caulk can be easily squeezed into place with your fingers. This kind comes in two colors, brown or off-white; choose one to match your window casing. It can be separated into four finer strands for thin cracks or kept together for the wider ones. You can paint it if you like, but we suggest leaving it unpainted to reapply season after season. *–J.A.A.*

$15 (100-ft. rolls), Brookstone

REAL GOODS

CORD CAULK

Cord Caulk stops drafts, window rattles, and moisture damage to sills and floors. The soft, fine fiber yarn is saturated with synthetic adhesive wax polymers so that it can be applied at below-freezing temperatures — an important feature if, like us, you put off sealing up until it's too cold. It can be removed and reused without affecting its usefulness and comes in white or wood grain (dark orange). *–J.A.A.*

$12.95, Real Goods Trading Co.

GARAGE DOOR WEATHER STRIPPING

Usually you can find a neoprene gasket for the garage doorsill, but Brookstone has brush weather strippings for the top and sides as well, made of 3/8-inch bristle weather stripping to seal against the harsh winds of winter. *–J.A.A.*

$47.50 Threshold (10 ft.); $40 Single-Door Weather Stripping; $45 Double-Door, Brookstone

PULLEY SEALS, SWITCH/OUTLET GASKETS, OUTLET CAPS

Energy-saver pulley seals are easy to install and permanently stop window pulley drafts. They come in white or brown and are adhesive backed for easy installation. UL-listed gaskets for light switches and electric outlets and plug sealers (or outlet caps) help reduce drafts. *–J.A.A.*

Niagara Conservation Corp.

OUTLET COVERS

Seal exterior wall outlets with these spring-loaded covers that automatically cover unused sockets. This not only saves energy but also protects little fingers from big shocks. The foam backing keeps leaks from creeping around the edge of the outlet. And they're as easy to install as regular outlet covers. *–J.A.A.*

$3 to $4, We Care; Ace Hardware; Seventh Generation

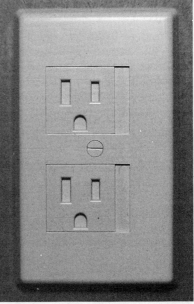

WE CARE

DOORSILL DRAFT DODGERS

A unique three-channel construction makes Hall's draft stopper stay snug against the door, sealing against cold, dust, and dirt and saving on both heating and air-conditioning costs. It's handmade from Guilford of Maine panel cloth in tan or gray tweed and filled with fragrant balsam. *–J.A.A.*

$15.95, Hall's Christmas Tree Farms $9.95 including postage and handling, Seventh Generation

HALL'S CHRISTMAS TREE FARMS

In terms of average annual global temperature, 1987 was the warmest year since such record keeping began 134 years ago.

big dog to do it, and they don't eat as much. Make your own by cutting and sewing a tube shape out of fabric and filling it with sand.

On a larger scale, glass fireplace doors are a kind of gasket that keep house air from leaking around the edge of a loose chimney damper. A layer of insulation, friction-fitted just under the damper, can do the same thing, but that can't be put into place until the fire is completely out.

Speaking of big leaks — don't forget to seal your attic hatchway, through-the-wall or window air conditioner, and bathroom and dryer vents. All of these can leak huge amounts of house air to the outdoors.

Finally, of course, insulate those walls, floors, and ceilings.

Windows of Vulnerability

You can lose a lot of heat through your windows, so if you live in a cold climate, put up a temporary layer of plastic or permanent storm windows during the winter to create a dead-air space — the best insulator available. Products should be readily available at your local hardware or building supply store, and most likely they'll be manufactured by either Macklanburg/Duncan or Frost King Thermwell Products. Prices vary.

Another alternative is the new shrink-wrap plastic storms; they're fast and easy to install. We put one over a picture window five years ago and never took it down — only two people have ever noticed that it's there!

Slightly more expensive are the framed window films that you can use year after year. Both these and the shrink-wrap storms are much cheaper than full storm windows but save the same amount of energy. On the other hand, full storms last forever. If you use a plastic film, remove it carefully at the end of the heating season and try to use it year after year.

Getting Out of Hot Water

If you live in the average home, up to half your energy costs can go to heating water. But why settle for average? Try these fuel-saving tips.

- Turn down the thermostat on your water heater. It takes only a screwdriver and doesn't cost a thing — but the savings are enormous. A dishwasher needs a water temperature of only 120° F; if you don't have one, you can lower your water temperature to 110° F. And you can always turn it up later if you find you need more hot water.

- Use less hot water. How? Experiment with detergents that allow you to wash clothes in cold water. If you use warm or hot water only when you absolutely have to, you'll not only save energy, but your clothes will also last longer. Always rinse your clothes in cold water. Take showers, not baths. Rinse dishes with cold water (you'll have fewer spots on your glasses). And prerinse dishes for the dishwasher with cold water and a sponge.

- Wrap insulation around your hot water tank. Purchase an insulating kit for it — but be sure to buy the right kit for your unit and follow directions carefully. Insulate the hot water pipes while you're at it.

- If you're buying a new water heater, spend a few extra dollars for a better-insulated tank. Your investment will repay you in a year, and that's money back in your pocket every year thereafter.

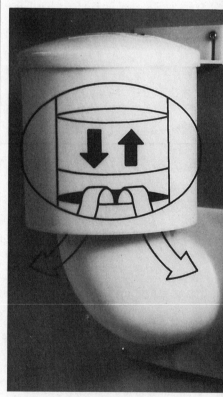
A wall outlet that leaks air can cost $1 per year. If you have 10 outlets on exterior walls, that's $10 in lost heat every year.

BROOKSTONE

FIREPLACE PLUG

When there's no fire, your fireplace flue is a wick, pulling house air up and out the chimney. You can easily trim this closed-cell polyethylene board with a knife for a snug fit up against your damper when you're not using your fireplace. It comes with three finger holes for easy insertion and removal and weighs only 1½ lbs. –*J.A.A.*

$27.50, Brookstone

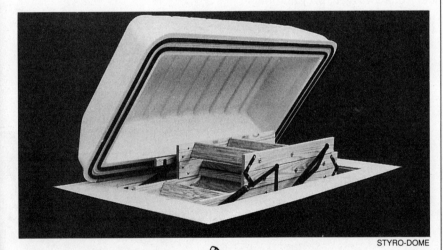

STYRO-DOME

ATTIC HATCHWAY COVERS

It's amazing how much air your house can lose through the crack around the pull-down ladder to your attic. The Energy Lid from People's Energy Resource Cooperative is made of high-density R-5 polystyrene and snaps together in minutes (without tools) to fit on the attic side of most standard attic stairway openings. For colder areas, Styro-Dome's high-impact polystyrene shell is insulated with R-13 fiberglass with double-seal foam weather stripping and a full-length piano hinge for easy operation. –*J.A.A.*

$40.45, People's Energy Resource Cooperative; Styro-Dome Corp.

WATER HEATER PRODUCTS

WATER HEATER INSULATION

One manufacturer claims that 35% of the energy used to heat water is lost through the walls of the tank — but the actual amount depends on the size of your tank and the temperature of the air surrounding it. Several companies distribute vinyl-covered fiberglass water-heater blankets, ranging in insulating value from R-5 to R-13. We use R-11 in an unheated basement. –*J.A.A.*

$7 (R-5); $13 (R-11)
Frost King Thermwell Products Co., Inc.; Niagara Conservation Corp.

NIAGARA CONSERVATION CORP.

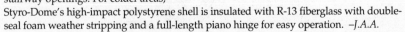

- Put a timer on your tank so that you're not making hot water when you don't need it. Check with your electric company to see if it has off-peak rates (much lower rates if you let the company heat your water when it's convenient for them, usually at night). If it does, your family can save $10 a month or more.
- Going away for several days? Turn off your water heater. Most types will heat very quickly when you return and turn them back on.

Lots of Hot Air

All houses, but particularly older ones, have some rooms that are hotter than others. This is not only uncomfortable, but it is also an energy waster since more heat is lost from a warm room than from a cold one. For example, if it's 90° F in the living room and 20° F outside, heat is lost more quickly than if the room were at 65° F. Try a fan to solve that problem.

Hot But Not Bothered

A programmable thermostat is the way to control the temperature of your house automatically. Your energy savings can be ten percent or more, making this product one of the best investments you can find.

For every degree you lower or raise (for cooling) your thermostat, you can reduce your fuel bill by up to three percent. If your heating bill is $1,000 a year and you lower your thermostat an average of 5°, you can reduce your heating bill by as much as $150. You could do this by, for example, setting your thermostat 10° cooler at night while you're asleep or during the day while you're at work (about half the day). You can do this manually. Or you can install a clock-driven, programmable thermostat that will automatically warm your house back up again before you get up in the morning or get home from work. Put one in your office, too.

— *Jennifer A. Adams*

WATER HEATER PRODUCTS

WATER HEATER TIMER

A timer on your water tank will automatically turn off the electric water heater at a preselected time when you use less hot water and turn it back on again when you need it. You can program the unit for up to 12 on/off periods per day, depending on the number of trippers used, but only two "on" and two "off" trippers are provided. And if you have a sudden hot water demand from unexpected guests, use the manual override switch. —*J.A.A.*

$34.95
Solar
Components
Corporation

FANS

Many companies make small fans that mount in the corner of the doorway between two rooms. Some simply plug into the nearest outlet. Others are mounted and wired in a wall or ceiling. They can be used to move air from the living room to the basement in winter  if the house is overheated; in the summer use them to move the cool air from the basement to the house, also keeping the basement dry. —*J.A.A.*

$20 to $50
Colonial Garden Kitchens; Solar Components Corporation

ALL PHOTOS THIS PAGE
COURTESY SOLAR COMPONENTS

For every 10 degrees you turn down your water heater, you save 6% in energy costs.

PROGRAMMABLE THERMOSTATS

These are available everywhere, but here are some we can recommend:

NUSTAT

This one is compatible with 99% of all furnace systems. It's powered with two AA batteries and is capable of programming for any group of five days and for any two single days you choose as rest days. Has lots of other features to help you save energy. –J.A.A.

$69, Cal-K Inc.

THE HONEYWELL CHRONOTHERM III THERMOSTAT

Our favorite. Easy to program and use, the device remembers different schedules for Saturday and Sunday, as well as for air-conditioning and heating. A small window shows the time, day of the week, and room temperature. –Jay Stein

About $185 (for heating and cooling model), Honeywell, Inc.

HONEYWELL

ELECTRIC THERMOSTATS

The Clark models are designed for use with electric heating. The vacancy thermostat automatically turns down heat in unoccupied rooms and is great for vacation homes. –J.A.A.

$64 to $95, People's Energy Resource Cooperative

SET-BACK THERMOSTAT

This thermostat includes power outage memory and digital time and temperature display and works with air-conditioning or heating systems. –J.A.A.

$59, Seventh Generation

OTHER HEATING PRODUCTS

NONTOXIC ANTIFREEZE

It's always been part of the yearly ritual, when we close up our summer camp, to pour antifreeze into the traps of all the sinks and toilets after  draining the pipes. We never stopped to think that we might be killing off the bacteria that help break down wastes in the septic tank with every springtime flush. Well, there are alternatives. You can use an automotive window washing fluid — cheap and less toxic to the environment. Or you can use the nontoxic antifreezes that are made for solar heating systems. –J.A.A.

$9.95, Solar Components

THERMOSTATIC OUTLET

Many homes have spaces that don't need to be heated but yet shouldn't freeze. For example, we've boxed a water heater, water pump, and water conditioner into a 4'x4' insulated space in a cold basement. If the temperature of that boxed-in space drops below 35° F, this thermostatically controlled electric outlet automatically turns on a little space heater that's plugged into it. The outlets are rated for 1,800 watts and are UL listed. –J.A.A.

$20 to $30 (6 to 15 feet), Brookstone

BROOKSTONE

Three shade trees on the south and west sides of a house can lower air-conditioning bills by 20% to 50%.

OTHER HEATING PRODUCTS

HEAT TAPE

If you have an unheated basement and you're worried about a few pipes, think about wrapping them with heat tape rather than keeping the whole space above freezing. See if you can box the pipes in first to raise the temperature around them. This heat tape gives variable heat along its length, based on the pipe temperature at each point. This is different from the typical tape that gives only uniform heat. –J.A.A.

$20 to $30 (6 to 15 feet)
Brookstone

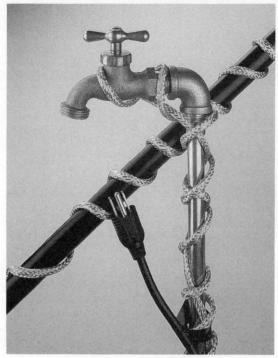

BROOKSTONE

RADIATOR REFLECTORS AND DEFLECTORS

A heating system usually delivers its heat to exterior walls of a building because that's where you lose the most heat. If you have floor registers, air deflectors can help move the air away from the cold wall and into the room. In addition to the obvious benefits of keeping you warmer and saving on energy bills by keeping the wall surfaces cooler, this also keeps the wall cleaner. –J.A.A.

Prices vary, Deflect-O Corp.;
hardware and building supply stores

DEFLECT-O CORP.

DEFLECT-O CORP.

DEFLECT-O CORP.

HEAT REFLECTORS

If you have baseboards, convectors, or radiators, use a foil-faced insulating sheet behind them to reflect the heat into the room where it belongs. You can make this yourself out of builder's foil (or aluminum foil), or buy one of the many products on the market. –J.A.A.

Prices vary, Viking Products;
Niagara Conservation Corp.;
Brookstone; local hardware and
building supply stores

COOLING PRODUCTS

In many climates it's the cooling cost that dominates the energy bill. Insulation, caulking, programmable thermostats, and weather stripping all are as important there as up north, but there are other products developed specifically for saving energy in warmer climates.

RETRACTABLE AWNING SYSTEMS

Stop that hot sun before it enters your windows and overheats your house, or let it in when you want. It's your choice with these beautiful awnings. –J.A.A.

United Textile and Supply Co.

JUST THINKING

"A serious and lasting government commitment to the development and use of energy-efficient and renewable technologies is a prerequisite to stabilizing world climate."

— *Worldwatch Institute,*
State of the World 1989

One million sea birds and 100,000 marine mammals die each year from ingesting or becoming entangled in marine debris.

READ MORE ABOUT IT

ENERGY: 101 PRACTICAL TIPS FOR HOME AND WORK

By Susan Hassol and Beth Richman. Even if you think you've read it all before, you can pick up a few new tips and reinforce the old with this easy-to-read booklet. The tips cover space heating and cooling, water heating, lighting, and appliances. Like all the booklets in this series, it gives tips and resources to help you use energy more wisely, while improving the quality of your life. –J.A.A.

$3.95, The Windstar Foundation

CUT YOUR ELECTRIC BILLS IN HALF

By Ralph J. Herbert. A guide to reducing overall energy use. Some of it's dated (1986), but it does include a good list of energy-efficient appliance manufacturers and data/worksheets to help you figure out how to cut energy costs. –J.A.A.

$9.95, Rodale Press

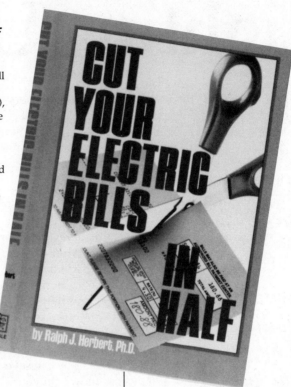

HOW TO WEATHERIZE YOUR HOME OR APARTMENT

Lots of good ideas on common household energy problems, costs, and savings are packed into these 38 pages. You'll find many comparisons of methods and materials for saving energy. –J.A.A.

**$3.50
Massachusetts Audubon Society**

YOU SHOULD KNOW

Energy-efficiency improvements in the next 20 years could lower the amount of carbon being released into the atmosphere each year by as much as 3 billion tons. No approach other than energy efficiency offers as cost effective an opportunity for limiting carbon emissions.

Electricity and heating for the average American home are responsible for nearly 11 tons of carbon dioxide emissions each year.

Lighting Up

H OME LIGHTING IS ONE area where you can very easily help the environment . . . and save money. How? First, of course, by turning off lights you don't need. Second, by using daylight instead of electricity. And third, by replacing your old-fashioned, shamefully wasteful incandescent light bulbs with long-lasting super-efficient compact fluorescent lights and other lighting devices.

> *Over its lifetime, an 18-watt compact fluorescent bulb will save half a ton of carbon dioxide that your coal-burning power company would have given off.*

Cool and Compact

The big, almost revolutionary, news in lighting is compact fluorescents. They're fat looking or are folded into "u" or "s" shapes to take up less room . . . nothing like the old tubular fluorescents. And they screw into sockets like plain old light bulbs.

The big difference is that while these ingenious lights cost much more than ordinary bulbs ($15 to $25), they can save you twice what they cost. How? On your electric bill, because they use only a fraction of the energy to produce the same amount of light, and in the cost of replacement bulbs, because they last ten times longer.

For example, suppose you buy a typical $17, 15-watt compact fluorescent. Because it burns for 10,000 hours, it saves the purchase of ten old-fashioned 60-watt incandescents. At 70¢ each, that's $7 for all ten. Before using the bulbs, then, you're out $10.

But the compact fluorescent uses one-fourth the electricity. Instead of paying up to $60 to light the incandescents, you pay only $15 to light your new investment. The $45 you save more than makes up for the $10 extra you paid for the bulb.

The table called "A Bright Outlook for Savings" (page 124) has more comparisons between these and old-fashioned light bulbs.

There are some minor limitations to these great lights. Compact fluorescent bulbs screw into normal light sockets, but are wider and longer than conventional bulbs and so might not fit your favorite fixture. Consider starting out with one or two, then buying more when you can afford more and when you know more about where and how they'll fit in your home or office.

The only environmental liability of these high-tech lights is the small amount of mercury vapor they contain. A thousand compact fluorescents contain about as much mercury as a home thermometer. Dispose of them as you would any product containing mercury — as a hazardous waste.

— *Alex Wilson*

We have not provided addresses for Sylvania, General Electric, and Phillips because their products are so widely distributed. Addresses of other companies are listed in the Ecologue Source Directory.

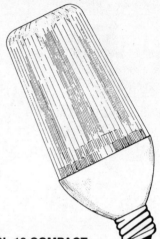

SL-18 COMPACT FLUORESCENT LAMP

Requiring just 18 watts of electricity, the SL-18 produces light comparable to that of a 60-watt incandescent bulb. It combines both lamp and ballast (starter) in one unit and screws directly into standard light bulb sockets. It is bigger than the old bulbs, so make sure it will fit your fixture. For table lamps or standing lamps that have wire hoops, you can buy replacement hoops at lighting supply stores that will raise the shades, making room for the taller compact fluorescent light. –*A.W.*

$20 to $25
Phillips; from most lighting stores

What You Can Do

✔ Turn lights off when they are not being used.

✔ Try the new energy-efficient night lights. One of these uses only ⅓ watt, versus the 7 watts used by old models.

✔ Clean light bulbs occasionally with a vacuum brush. Dirt and dust on bulbs reduces light, wastes electricity, and burns out bulbs.

DULUX® "EL" ELECTRONIC COMPACT FLUORESCENT LAMP

Using electronic ballasts, Osram lamps are silent and flicker free. They turn on instantly and reach full brightness in just a few seconds. (The more common core coils take up to a minute to reach full brightness, are less compact, and are heavier.)

When we installed the 11-watt EL reflector in a kitchen, it seemed brighter than the 75-watt light bulb it was replacing, and even a friend who had never been very fond of fluorescents took to this one. (Her previous experience with fluorescent lighting was with those noisy, flickering, harsh white ones.) Available in 7-, 11-, 15-, and 20-watt sizes. –A.W.

About $25 (standard model), Osram

YOU SHOULD KNOW

"Smartlight," a program started by Municipal Lighting Plant of Taunton, Massachusetts, leases compact fluorescent bulbs to customers for 20¢ a month. Customers are guaranteed to save more than $50 over the life of each lamp, which if burned six hours a day would last approximately five years.

LIGHT CAPSULE™

Panasonic is ahead of the competition in actively marketing its products to homeowners — we can even pick them up at a local small-town hardware store. The T-15 is a tube-style lamp, while the G-15 is a round globe lamp. Both use standard, nonelectronic ballasts.

Panasonic's more advanced electronic-ballast "instant-on" compact fluorescent lamps come in 18, 20, and 27 watts. The smallest of these has a light-diffusing globe over the fluorescent tubes, like its nonelectronic cousins, while the two larger lamps have exposed fluorescent tubes. The 27-watt lamp is the most powerful integral compact fluorescent lamp available and will equal the light output of a 100-watt incandescent light bulb. The larger electronic units are more expensive and less readily available. –A.W.

$15 (nonelectronic), Panasonic

LUMATECH REFLECT-A-STAR COMPACT FLUORESCENT REFLECTOR LAMPS

Here's a great product for recessed ceiling fixtures and track lighting: Lumatech's modular compact fluorescent reflector housing, including ballast.

The Reflect-a-Star takes replaceable quad-tube lamps. Replacements are manufactured by Osram and GTE Sylvania. When the lamp burns out, the diffusing lens is unscrewed, the old 9- or 13-watt lamp pulled out, and a new one plugged in.

Reflect-a-Star units are pretty heavy, so if you plan to use them on track fixtures, make sure a heavy-duty track system is used that will adequately support their weight. Though expensive (expect to pay around $45), Reflect-a-Stars are top quality and built to last. –A.W.

About $45, Rising Sun Enterprises; The Real Goods Trading Co.

The U.S. would reduce its annual energy bill by $30 billion if it used the most efficient lighting possible.

ANOTHER BRIGHT LIGHT FOR THE FUTURE

Compact fluorescents, like ordinary fluorescents, need ballasts as starters. Some integrate the ballast with the bulb into a single unit. When it burns out, the whole unit must be replaced. This is more expensive than the alternative, which is the modular lamps with ballasts and bulbs made separately. Here when the lamp burns out after about 10,000 hours, it can be replaced for just a few dollars. The more expensive ballast component lasts much longer — about 50,000 hours.

Modular lamps can be installed either in screw-in ballasts (available from General Electric and GTE Sylvania), or in specially designed light fixtures with built-in ballasts (see the Lightolier review).

General Electric, GTE Sylvania, North American Phillips, and Osram all make standardized plug-in compact fluorescent lamps to fit into screw-in or fixture-mounted ballasts. They are available in twin-tube and quad-tube configurations. The twin-tube lamps are more common and are available in 5-, 7-, 9-, and 13-watt sizes. In the quad-tube lamps the fluorescent tube is folded in on itself, making the lamp more compact. With higher light output and shorter length, these are often better replacements for incandescent light bulbs. The quads are also available in higher wattages — up to 28 watts.

Currently, all modular compact fluorescents (those with separate ballast and lamp) use standard, core-coil ballasts. You may notice flickering and a slight hum from some. Flicker-free, silent electronic versions will be on the market soon.

What You Can Do

While compact fluorescents are big news, there are also other things you can do to save energy and money with energy-efficient lighting:

✔ Buy fluorescent tubes. Those fluorescent tubes that used to flicker, hum, and look so unnatural are now much quieter and steadier, and are available in mellow color tones that are indistinguishable from incandescent light. All while they save 25 percent or more of the energy.

✔ Look for metal halide and high-pressure sodium lights for outdoor lighting around your home. The lighting quality of high intensity discharge (HID) lights, originally developed for highways and bridges as more efficient than incandescents, is improving.

✔ Don't waste money on those little buttons that go in light sockets. They extend the life of bulbs but cut efficiency.

✔ Shopping for a new lamp? Consider a three-way unit for more lighting control and less energy use.

✔ Save energy by installing (and using) solid-state dimmers with incandescent room lights. Think of them as money valves.

COMPACT FLUORESCENTS

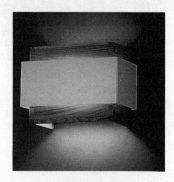

LIGHTOLIER COMPACT FLUORESCENT FIXTURES

Until recently, high-quality residential lighting fixtures with built-in ballasts for modular compact fluorescents simply weren't available. Now Lightolier, one of the best names in residential lighting, offers a complete line of fluorescent-compatible fixtures. They have core-coil ballasts and come with twin-tube plug-in bulbs in place. When the bulb fails, it can be replaced for about $5. The built-in ballasts should last as long as four or five lamps.

Lightolier products are relatively expensive, but they're well built and considerably more attractive than most. As an example, the Lumaframe III, with oak and white glass, retails for about $160. –A.W.

Lightolier

MODULAR COMPACT FLUORESCENT TRACK LIGHTING

Staff Lighting is the only manufacturer we found that produces a track-lighting fixture specifically for modular compact fluorescent lamps. Two of its track fixtures use commonly available 13-watt twin-tube lamps (two per fixture). The other uses longer 18-watt lamps that may be harder to find.

For very bright light from a track system and a really new lighting technology, check out Staff's metal halide Duo Pendant fixtures. These are designed for Osram 70-watt metal halide lamps, which are more efficient than most fluorescent lamps, equal to the best fluorescent lamps in color quality, and put out a remarkable 5,000 lumens, equivalent to about 300 watts of incandescent light. Like all Staff Lighting fixtures, however, they don't come cheap.

Staff Lighting products are not generally carried by retail stores. If you know an architect, ask if he or she has a Staff catalogue. Or check electrical supply houses and building contractors. –A.W.

If everyone switched to compact fluorescent light bulbs, we could close 75 large power plants. — *Amory Lovins*

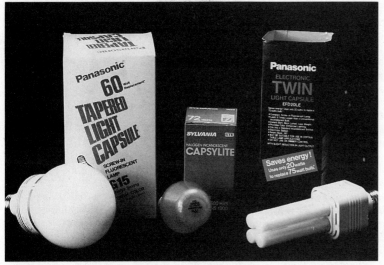

PETER GOLDIE

CAPSYLITE™ TUNGSTEN HALOGEN INCANDESCENT LAMPS

For locations requiring very high quality light, the Capsylite™ could be your best bet. Tungsten-halogen lamps don't save nearly as much as compact fluorescents, but they're still considerably more energy efficient than ordinary light bulbs. Bulb sizes of 42, 52, and 72 watts replace 60-, 75-, and 100-watt incandescent bulbs, respectively. They also come in a wide range of reflector lamp sizes and shapes.

One drawback we have found with these lamps is that there can be a slight flicker, noticeable in your peripheral vision. Apparently this problem can be corrected by installing several different bulbs in the room, which somehow cancels out the modulation. With just one bulb, we found it quite annoying. —A.W.

GTE Sylvania

THE WATT WATCHER AUTOMATIC WALL SWITCH

If you're as forgetful as we are, the Watt Watcher can save you money by turning the lights out when you leave the room. Also available: a light-sensing control. It turns the lights off when enough natural light comes in.

Watt Watcher products were developed for businesses — where lighting expenditures and potential savings are greater — but they make sense at home, too. —A.W.

$30, Watt Watcher

What You Can Do

✔ Do not use light dimmers with fluorescent lamps. This wiring mismatch can lead to fire.

✔ Don't be confused by so-called "energy miser" and "supersaver" incandescent bulbs. They save peanuts compared with compact fluorescents.

✔ Save energy by using one 100-watt light bulb in place of two 60-watt bulbs. It produces about the same amount of light yet consumes 20 fewer watts.

DIMMER SWITCH

Many dimmer switches use a lot of power. This switch uses less than $1/2$ watt of power to control any 4 amp or smaller DC motor or light. It dims lights to save energy — transforming a bright incandescent light into subdued ambience. It can also be used to slow down ceiling fans, preventing papers from blowing away, with a rotary control that operates from full "on" to full "off." You can order an optional forward/reverse switch for reversing directions on ceiling fans (which, if done periodically, is an easy way to clean off that dust). —A.W.

$25; $28 (with forward/reverse) Real Goods

ELECTRONIC DIMMING BALLASTS FOR ORDINARY TUBE FLUORESCENT LAMPS

That annoying hum and flicker of fluorescent lighting can be a thing of the past with electronic ballasts. They also give better quality light and save energy — 15% to 25% over old-fashioned ballasts. A few electronic ballasts are dimmable — until recently an elusive dream of lighting designers.

ETTA offers several top-quality dimming electronic ballasts designed specifically for the energy-efficient T-8 tri-chromatic fluorescent lamps, perfect for recessed indirect (soffit) lighting around a room perimeter. —A.W.

$50 to $60, Rising Sun Enterprises

You can replace the 60-watt bulb in your hall with a 15-watt compact fluorescent and still get the same amount of light.

TUBE FLUORESCENT IMPROVED COLOR LAMPS

If fluorescent lighting still reminds you of those unnatural blue-white buzzing tubes in discount department stores, here's good news. Modern tube fluorescent lamps almost match incandescent lighting in color quality.

The "Color Rendering Index" or CRI of a lamp is a measure of how accurately colors show up under its light, compared with natural light, which has a perfect CRI rating of 100. Incandescent lamps have CRIs of nearly 100, while standard fluorescent lamps have CRIs in the range of 45 to 55. Recently introduced tri-chromatic phosphor lamps, available from the big three lamp manufacturers as well as from Osram and Panasonic, are available in more natural colors and with CRIs as high as 85.

Each manufacturer has a different name for these bulbs, but they are all very similar. As an added bonus these tri-chromatic lamps are significantly more energy-efficient than standard fluorescent lamps (about 90 lumens per watt rather than 60). All tri-chromatic lamps are narrow diameter, and most require special rapid-start ballasts. They cost more than standard cool-white and warm-white lamps. Special order them from your lighting equipment supplier.

A BRIGHT OUTLOOK FOR SAVINGS

Contemplating switching to compact fluorescent lighting? This chart will help you determine how much you will save over the life of the bulb. — *Source: The Energy Federation*

All-in-one compact fluorescent	Replaces	Lifetime Savings*
15-watt	60-watt	$42
18-watt	75-watt	$52

Modular compact fluorescent	Replaces	Lifetime Savings*
7W twin-tube	25-40 watt	$16-$31
9W twin	40-60 watt	$29-$49
13W twin	60-75 watt	$45-$60
9W quad-tube	40-watt	$29
13W quad	60-75 watt	$45-$60
22W quad	75-100 watt	$51-$76

* Assumes electricity cost of 10¢ per kwh

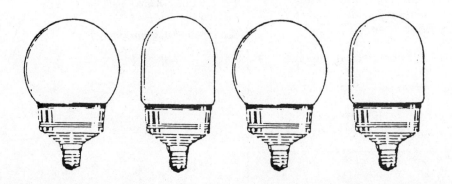

OUTDOOR "HID" LIGHTING

American Scientific manufactures a wide range of fixtures for energy-efficient lighting, including some very attractive fixtures for outdoor high-intensity discharge (HID) lamps. Compared with the HID lighting you've seen along highways, these new versions are quite acceptable outside your home — particularly the high-pressure sodium and metal halide varieties. Low-pressure sodium, the all-time energy-efficiency champ, has terrible light quality and should not be considered for around the house except perhaps for emergency lighting.

The advantage of high-pressure sodium and metal halide over fluorescent lighting outdoors is a much more concentrated light. A single 150-watt high-pressure sodium lamp provides as much light as six 150-watt incandescent flood lights. When you need lots of light outdoors, HID is the answer. For lower light requirements, choose a compact fluorescent fixture. (In cold regions, be sure to buy a "cold-start" type.)

The smallest metal halide lamps available are 70 watts (from Osram); more common sizes are 175 watts and up (from GE, Phillips, and GTE Sylvania). High-pressure sodium lamps are available in smaller sizes — down to 35 watts, though the efficiency drops to levels no better than that of fluorescent lamps at low wattages. *–A.W.*

American Scientific

DAYLIGHT CONTROL

ETTA also makes an energy-conserving state-of-the-art daylight control device for its dimming ballast. In buildings with significant window areas, it maintains room light at a preset level as the sun changes position and intensity throughout the day. When plenty of daylight is coming in, it lowers the electric lighting level, saving as much as 70% in lighting costs in some buildings. *–A.W.*

Rising Sun Enterprises

China plans to double its coal use, which could push it ahead of the U.S. and the Soviet Union as the world's leading carbon emitter.

LIGHTING SUPPLY CATALOGUES

THE ENERGY FEDERATION

The Energy Federation is a nonprofit company founded in 1982 to make resource conservation technologies available to consumers at affordable prices. It ships bulbs from all the major manufacturers (GE, Phillips, GTE Sylvania, Osram, and Panasonic), plus a selection of fixtures for energy-conserving fluorescent and HID lamps. –*A.W.*

REAL GOODS TRADING COMPANY

Long an important supplier of photovoltaic and independent power equipment, the Real Goods Trading Company has recently become a major retailer of energy-efficient lighting equipment. It offers a fairly complete range of compact fluorescent, tube fluorescent, and HID lighting products, including lamps, fixtures, and controls. Call for a catalogue. –*A.W.*

RISING SUN ENTERPRISES

Rising Sun stocks over 150 product lines, from Osram EL lamps to ETTA dimming electronic ballasts for tube fluorescent lamps. It really knows its stuff when it comes to energy-efficient lighting technologies. Its sampler catalogue contains some of the clearest explanations of energy-efficient lighting we've seen. It sells to big companies as well as individuals and knows all about dimming electronic ballasts and occupancy controls for offices and homes. Send $5 for a catalogue. –*A.W.*

A BRIGHTER WAY

A mail order supplier of energy-efficient lighting products and fixtures. Carries several product lines, including Osram. Fairly good prices. –*A.W.*

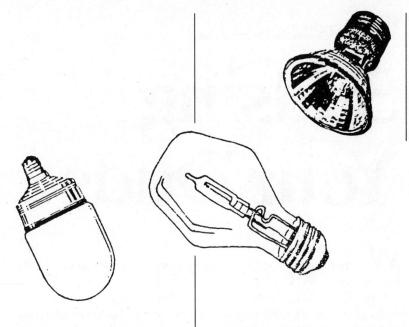

What You Can Do

✔ If you can't find the energy-conserving lighting products you want at your local hardware or lighting products store, talk to the manager. Tell her you want these products. If enough of us ask for compact fluorescents and other energy-saving products, stores will eventually carry them.

✔ By the same token, if a local store does carry energy savers, patronize the store rather than saving a dollar by buying it mail order. Tell the manager that you think it's great that the store carries compact fluorescent lamps and that you'll tell your friends to buy some.

✔ Let the sunshine in. Today's super-efficient glazing (see page 150), window covers, and automatic lighting controls have eliminated the old energy penalties of windows and skylights. Plan additions and new homes to use more natural and less artificial light (see Watt Watcher and ETTA Ballasts reviews).

✔ Before turning on large room lights, consider lighting only the area you will be using, such as a reading corner.

LIFESTYLE ALERT

Beware when you replace the ballast (starter) in old fluorescent light fixtures. Units made before about 1978 are likely to contain PCBs, which are highly toxic. *If the removed ballast does not have a label indicating that it does not contain PCBs, assume that it does.* Put it in a plastic bag, carefully seal the bag, and deliver it to a hazardous-waste collection. (See page 38.)

One compact fluorescent light bulb, over its lifetime, saves enough electricity to avoid burning 400 pounds of coal.

Sudsing Your Duds

WHEN HOUSEHOLD APPLIANCES first made their way into American homes, they were supposed to save you energy by relieving you of work.

But the truth of the matter is that all of the "big ticket" appliances — air conditioners, clothes washers and dryers, dishwashers, ranges and ovens, water heaters, and refrigerators — are energy hogs. And they're pollutants, too, when you consider all the raw material that goes into making them and the difficulty of disposing of them.

Now, we're not suggesting that you go back to sudsing your duds in the river. But there is a lot you can do to choose the most efficient models when you buy new appliances and, in the meantime, to run your old ones in as miserly a way as possible. We'll show you how.

> *Running an average refrigerator for 15 to 20 years typically costs three times as much as it cost to buy it.*

How to Use Energy Guide Labels

Buying an energy-efficient model really makes a difference: With some appliances the most efficient model uses 75 percent less power than the most wasteful.

So for the last decade, the federal government has required manufacturers of major appliances to attach energy guide labels to their products. Read them. These big black-and-yellow signs tell you how an appliance compares in efficiency and true cost with other models of the same type.

Energy guide labels on major appliances have two numbers that are very important to you, the buyer: one is the energy efficiency rating and the other is the operating cost.

The "Energy Efficiency Rating" (EER) is a quick way to know how energy wasteful or energy conserving an appliance is. Typically, ratings range from around 5.5, which is considered very energy wasteful, to over 10, which is excellent and uses lots less energy than most.

The "Operating Cost" on the energy guide label is always given in dollars per year. It is an average that helps you calculate the real cost of your appliance — which is the sale price plus the cost of operation — over time.

The problem with refrigerators isn't just their energy consumption, but their reliance on chlorofluorocarbons for the refrigerant and the insulation. CFCs destroy the ozone layer in the earth's upper atmosphere, which is bad news because ozone protects you from the harmful effects of the sun's ultraviolet rays, such as sunburn, skin cancer, cataracts and other eye disorders, and possible suppression of the immune system. CFCs are also "greenhouse gases," which contribute to global warming.

The U.S. and some European countries have called for the phaseout of CFCs by the year 2000, but the refrigerator industry has had a hard time developing a substitute. Ammonia, which is one option, can be toxic, while propane is explosive. Another alternative is the development of vacuum panels for insulation, similar to what's used in a thermos. And then there's the Sunfrost.

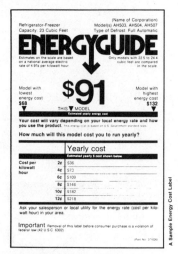

A Sample Energy Cost Label

What You Can Do About Refrigerators

✔ Keep your fridge at the optimum temperature: 38° to 42° in the refrigerator, and 0° to 5° in the freezer.

✔ Wipe refrigerator door gaskets clean so the seal is tight. Replace gaskets when they begin to wear.

Nearly half the world's species of plants, animals, and microorganisms are threatened by the deteriorating environment.

DRY IT, YOU'LL LIKE IT

VERSATILE VERSION

A modern variation on an old standby, this standing clothes-drying rack can be assembled into eight different configurations. Its 4 rack trays can be placed side-by-side for hand washables that need to be dried flat, or they can be stacked atop one another to dry a lot of clothes in a little space. We're not wild about the fact that the rack is made of plastic, but its woven mesh does have the advantage of allowing air to circulate on all sides. –*L.H.*

$36, DLR Design & Development Corp.

SUNFROST

Sunfrost is a modern, state-of-the-art refrigerator that uses superinsulation and other design innovations to reduce energy use 60% to 90% compared with conventional units. You read that right. It takes about 200 kwh per year, compared with the average of 900 to 1,500 kwh. If you pay 10¢ per kilowatt-hour for your electricity, you can save up to $120 per year with the Sunfrost, although your initial investment will be 50% to 100% more than for an old-fashioned refrigerator. If every refrigerator performed as well as the Sunfrost, we could have avoided building one-tenth of the existing U.S. nuclear power plants and saved tens of billion dollars to boot. –*L.H.*

$1,695 (12-cu.-ft. model); $2,500 (16-cu.-ft. model); other sizes available, Sunfrost

ROTA-REEL™

If you don't like the look of an empty clothesline, try this one — it lies flat and out of sight between uses. Its rustproof reel housing mounts with an aluminum bracket that swivels out to dispense a plastic-coated line and to retract it when you're done. Handy for inside drying, too. –*L.H.*

$16, Plow & Hearth

What You Can Do

✔ Get out of the energy-wasting habit of standing in front of the fridge with the door open.

What You Can Do About Refrigerators

✔ Don't buy a separate freezer unless you have a large family and/or do a great deal of bulk buying, gardening, hunting, or fishing.

✔ Let cooked food cool before refrigerating.

Most of the earth's fresh water is frozen in glaciers at the North and South poles.

For example: Refrigerator A costs $600 to purchase, and — with an EER of 7.3 — it will cost $100 a year to operate. Refrigerator B costs $500 to buy, but its lower EER — 6.1 — means it costs $120 a year to operate. In just five years the more efficient refrigerator A "catches up" to refrigerator B in money saved and becomes less expensive to you. Plus it's been better for the environment all along.

The Best & the Worst

Refrigerators. The most efficient mass-marketed refrigerator is the 11-cubic-foot Kenmore single-door manual-defrost model, #86111*2. But it's only slightly better than the others of its size and type. In fact, refrigerator efficiency varies little among those of the same size and type. The real difference in refrigerator performance relates to the basic design — and to size. You can be sure that the larger the model, the more energy it uses. As for model types, an average side-by-side freezer model uses 15 to 25 percent more energy than a refrigerator with the freezer on top. Manual defrost uses slightly less than automatic.

Freezers. The big difference in freezer performance is in the style. Chest freezers use 60 to 90 percent of the energy of the upright models. Also, manual-defrost types use slightly less than automatic-defrost.

Dishwashers. There is no difference in energy performance of dishwashers. The biggest savings come from avoiding the drying cycle.

Clothes washers. The biggest savings come from using cold water rather than hot. However, front-loading washers use less than half the power to operate the motor, and they use less water than top loaders.

It's Cheap. It's Effective. It's Elbow Grease.

Most of us got along pretty well before we had fancy power appliances, and chances are we can still get along without many of them. Maybe better than you think — with new innovations in high-quality tools and appliances that are powered by hand or by a renewable resource, such as sunshine or wood. Though these tools are "powerless" because they don't plug in anywhere, they still pack plenty of punch. And they don't pollute.

Some of these, such as a wooden clothes drying rack, have been around since your grandmother was in swaddling clothes. Others are modern improvements on old favorites. Take the manual food chopper, for instance, that's spring loaded, makes a zigzag cut, and automatically rotates 15° with each push. Who needs electric food processors?

It can be downright empowering to use tools that don't pollute, aren't made with noxious chemicals, and don't require non-renewable energy — because the energy you use is none other than your own elegant elbow grease.

— *Leda Hartman*

YOU SHOULD KNOW

New government standards, which took effect only recently, require all new appliances to be 10% to 30% more efficient than the average models sold in the past. It's estimated that these standards will save consumers at least $28 billion over the lifetimes of the products sold through the year 2000, or about $300 per household.

DRY IT, YOU'LL LIKE IT

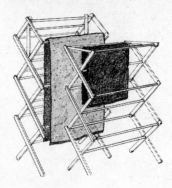

UNFOLD IT

Folding clothes dryers were necessities in every farm kitchen back when air-drying was all we had. This one is made of hardwood and folds out of the way when not in use. The small version has 26' of drying space; the large has 45'. –*L.H.*

$18.95 (small); $37.95 (large), including shipping and handling Vermont Country Store

RETRACTABLE CLOTHESLINE REEL

Here's a spring-loaded, retractable clothesline reel that holds up to 300 pounds of clothes and stretches to 40 feet, indoors or out. The rope is coated with plastic and the housing is waterproof. This reel has a spring hook on the end to attach to a screw eye and can be moved to other spots easily. –*L.H.*

$21.95, including shipping and handling, Vermont Country Store

DRYER HEAT RECLAIMERS

Here's a way to recycle the heat and moisture from your dryer back inside your house. But remember this: make sure you vent the moist air outside the room the dryer is in (or you'll keep circulating moist air through the dryer). Be sure the room the air goes into is big enough and dry enough to absorb that moisture, or your furniture and house may have water damage. And make sure you're capturing the lint before it goes into the air to prevent respiratory problems. –*L.H.*

$5 Lint Trap; $4 Extra-Heat Deflect-O Corp.

More than 25% of the average city apartment dweller's electrical costs are for running the refrigerator.

What You Can Do About Clothes Dryers

✔ Look for two energy-saving features when you buy a new dryer: a moisture-sensor control that automatically shuts off the machine when clothes are dry and a cool-down or permapress cycle that uses cool air to finish the drying.

✔ Make sure, if you buy a gas clothes dryer, that it has an electronic ignition rather than a pilot light, which wastes energy.

✔ Don't run your dryer unless you have a full load — but don't overload, either, because then your clothes won't dry.

✔ Dry one load right after the other to take advantage of residual heat.

✔ Clean the lint filter between loads.

✔ Keep the hose to the exhaust as short and straight as possible.

THIS ONE WRINGS TRUE

Wring your hands over utility bills no longer when you get hold of an old-fashioned James Hand Washing Machine. Washing by hand really isn't that hard with a James machine. You just let your clothes soak for a few hours first in hot soapy water and then swish them around with the agitator for a few minutes. A faucet at the bottom of the washer allows easy drainage. And the rust-proof steel hand wringer, which is optional, squeezes out 90% of the water — compared to 45% with most conventional washers. The James washer handles the same size load as conventional washers, and its sturdy construction guarantees many years of use. –L.H.

**Washer: $175; Wringer: $99.95
Real Goods Trading Co.**

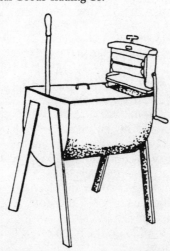

What You Can Do About Clothes Washing

✔ Wash your clothes in cold rather than hot water. Depending on the cost of energy in your area, you could save $100 to $200 a year. In general, the less dirty the load, the less hot water you need to use.

✔ Use a cold rinse cycle if possible. Remember: the temperature of the rinse does not affect the wash.

✔ Go easy on the detergent. Too much of it makes your machine work harder.

✔ Be sure you've got a full wash load. Washers use 32 to 59 gallons of water for each cycle.

✔ Use a liquid soap rather than a powder if your water is especially cold, as it would be from a well in the winter months. Powder may not dissolve in lower temperatures.

✔ Use shorter cycles for small loads, fine fabrics, or less-soiled clothing.

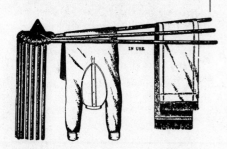

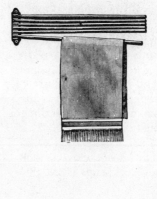

What You Can Do About Cooking

✔ Try to use a gas range instead of an electric one. Though it may cost more to buy, a gas range soon makes up for its higher purchase cost because it's generally cheaper and more efficient to run than an electric range, which uses energy just to heat up.

✔ When buying a gas range, find one with electronic ignition instead of a pilot light. It will use 40% less fuel. Or consider turning off the pilot and lighting your stove with matches or a hand igniter.

✔ Look for these two energy-saving features when you buy either a gas or electric range: a convection oven, which uses a small fan to circulate heat inside the oven, cooking food faster at a lower temperature; and a self-cleaning oven, which is usually better insulated than a manually cleaned oven. Actually using the self-cleaning feature is very energy intensive! If you do use it, do so immediately after baking to take advantage of residual heat.

✔ Avoid joining the mini trend toward installing restaurant-type gas ranges in homes. Most of these units are not very well insulated and not only will tend to overheat your kitchen but may also have oven doors that get dangerously hot.

✔ If you use the oven, cook several dishes at one time.

✔ Cover your pots and pans when cooking, and make sure they fit the size of the burner.

✔ Substitute small appliances for your oven or range when possible. Pressure cookers, crockpots, and steamers use less energy than pans on the stove.

✔ Don't preheat the oven unless you're baking and then only for ten minutes.

✔ Turn burners and oven off early and let residual heat finish the cooking.

✔ Use a microwave oven whenever possible. For most cooking tasks, a microwave uses less than half as much energy as a conventional oven because it speeds up cooking time and uses almost all its energy to cook the food. A microwave is best at cooking small or medium amounts of food that don't have much moisture. And if you do go the microwave route . . .

✔ Don't buy those excessively packaged goods, which microwaving has made popular.

✔ Transfer foods to glass or ceramic dishes before cooking; hot plastic can contaminate your food.

✔ Cover foods with glass, not throwaway wraps.

REFRIGERATOR BRUSH

We must admit that cleaning the coils on the back of the refrigerator is not high on our list of weekend activities. If you don't keep them clean, though, you're reducing the life of your refrigerator motor and the efficiency of the refrigerator —so it's costing you money. Here's a brush made just for this dull chore, with a tapered shape and sturdy bristles to loosen dirt that your vacuum can't. –L.H.

$12, Brookstone

SOLAR SHOWER

This product's been around for a long time. It's a 5-gallon, 4-ply plastic bag that you hang in the sun, and on a warm, sunny day it will warm water to 108°. The shower nozzle has supposedly been improved over the old ones that used to leak. The manufacturer says that the 5-gallon capacity provides ample hot water for at least 4 hot showers. They must be pretty quick showers. . . . –L.H.

$9, Real Goods Trading Co.

SOUL FOOD THE SOLAR WAY

SUNSPOT

One of several solar cookers from Clevlab, this one is lightweight (20 ounces), compact (10"x4"), and relatively simple to use: You set up 4 rectangular reflectors, one on each side of the box, and place your food in a special plastic cooking bag in the center of the oven. Next you aim the box directly at the sun, using a clever chain cross to guide you. If your food isn't cooked in 15 minutes, just re-aim the Sunspot to follow the movement of the sun. –L.H.

$20, Clevlab

MOVE OVER, CUISINART

You don't have to buy a fancy food processor to get your kitchen prep work done. Here are some tools that are easy to use and require no plugs.

VEGETABLE CHOPPER

A Swiss hardware company called Moha makes this spring-loaded vegetable chopper. Its zigzag blade cuts vegetables in a contained cylinder and automatically rotates about 15° with each push of your hand. And the whole works is easy to clean. –L.H.

$17.59, Tarzian West

THE MANDOLIN

Want something a touch more elaborate? Moha also makes a home-use version of the professional mandolin, a classic French tool for slicing and shredding. This one's made of stainless steel and plastic. You can use the mandolin on your countertop, holding vegetables by hand or under a gripper and sliding them back and forth across the blade. The mandolin slices at 3 different thicknesses. –L.H.

**$28.99
Tarzian West; gourmet shops**

What You Can Do About Dishwashing

✔ Try to find a dishwasher with an "air power," "overnight dry," or "energy saver" setting, which automatically turns the machine off after the rinse cycle. If your dishwasher doesn't have this feature, you can turn the machine off after the last rinse and prop open the door to dry the dishes.

✔ Run your dishwasher only when you have a full load.

✔ Use a short wash cycle whenever possible.

✔ Scrub your dirtiest dishes by hand before loading them in the machine to avoid using the longest wash cycle.

✔ When you wash dishes, first scrape them with a spatula. Fill the dish pan with several inches of sudsy water. Don't run the water unless you're rinsing dishes, and then add the rinse water to the dish pan. There are few practices more wasteful than washing dishes with the water running continuously.

If you save all the unwanted mail you receive this year, you'll have the equivalent of one and a half trees' worth of paper pulp.

What You Can Do

✔ Don't buy a halon fire extinguisher, which contains CFCs, for home use. Check the label, and look for an extinguisher that doesn't have CFCs.

✔ Try to run your appliances during off-peak hours (midmorning to midafternoon, or late at night), when utility companies have more energy available than at peak hours. This practice eases the energy crunch during demand times, reducing the need for new power plants. It also may let you take advantage of cheaper rates.

✔ At tea time don't fill your kettle with more water than you need, and turn the kettle off as soon as it boils. Or buy a kettle with an automatic shutoff.

✔ Use a little broom for those quick cleanups. Central vacuum cleaners cost more than twice as much to run as canister-type vacuums.

✔ Avoid hot tubs; they use 200 kwh per month. Or choose a superinsulated model; seal tightly with an insulated cover between uses

✔ Plug your remote control, electronically tuned, or instant-on television set into an outlet that's powered by a wall switch, so you can turn it on and off from the wall. Sets with these features draw up to eight watts of standby power. The equivalent of a large nuclear plant must run continuously to power the nation's television sets — while they are turned off!

What You Can Do About Water Beds

✔ If you have a water bed, keep the bed covered at all times to reduce heat loss. You consume twice as much energy if you leave your bed unmade!

✔ Add a one-inch layer of insulation around the edge of your old water bed; this can save you 10% to 25% of its energy usage. An inch under the bottom can save an additional 10%.

✔ Try one of the new fiber-filled wave-reduction mattresses for your water bed; they use almost 12% less energy than conventional water beds. Or try a soft-sided hybrid bed (with a polyurethane border and cover), which uses almost 25% less than that.

A CLEAN SWEEP

HOKY CARPET SWEEPER

There's no need to sweep dirt under the rug when you have a state-of-the-art Hoky carpet sweeper. The Hoky works efficiently, noiselessly, and effortlessly on a hard floor or carpet. It is lightweight and compact, so it travels and stores easily. Requires only routine maintenance, and all parts are replaceable. –L.H.

$35, Real Goods Trading Co.

YOU SHOULD KNOW

When you wash and rinse clothes in hot water rather than cold, 90% of the energy used by your washing machine goes to heating that water.

All company addresses and phone numbers are listed in the Ecologue Source Directory beginning on page 242.

THE WISH BOOK

Perhaps the most versatile and creative supplier of manual and alternatively powered appliances is Lehman's hardware store, an outfit from Kidron, Ohio, in the heart of the country's largest Amish community. The Amish are experts when it comes to simple and ecological living, and the products in Lehman's Non-Electric Catalog reflect this. The store carries everything from sad-irons — the heavy, flat pieces of iron that were the precursors of modern electric irons — to several kinds of butter churns, logging tools, grain mills, wood cookstoves, and washboards. True to the spirit of combining the best of old and new, Lehman's also carries a solar-powered cattle fence.

Lehman's Non-Electric Catalog ($2) has so many hard-to-find, easy-to-use, old and new necessities and frivolities that we frankly had one heck of a time deciding which products to recommend to you. We did catch a few electric items, mostly self-contained appliances, but we forgave them because the rest of the stuff is so nifty. Besides, everything is packed in used newspaper and shipped in used boxes. Here is but a sampling.

FOLDING TOASTER

This gadget works anywhere — over a wood stove, an open fire, or a gas, oil, or propane stove. It evenly toasts up to 4 slices of bread, yet folds flat into a 9" tin plate for compact storage. –L.H.

$6.95

GRAIN MILLS AND GRINDERS

Lehman's mills range in price from $47.95 to $299. The least expensive is the All-Purpose Mill. It grinds all grains, plus spices, nuts, coffee, corn, soybeans, field beans, and peas — with a capacity as high as 1 pound per minute with coarse grinds. This full-size mill is made of cast-iron with a 10" crank and comfortable wooden grip.

The most expensive is the Country Living Grain Mill. It's made of cast aluminum with a nontoxic enamel coating and has rust-free, cast-bronze burrs that grind finer than most stone-burr mills. This mill is also easily motorized, but it doesn't have to be — its grinding capacity is about 20 pounds per hour. –L.H.

All-Purpose Mill: $47.95
Country Living Grain Mill: $299

HOME-SCALE FRUIT PRESS

Make your own cider! Lehman's carries several fruit presses and grinders, but we picked this one because it's a good starter model. Made of hardwood staves and a cast-iron press, this model will hold up to 8 quarts of fruit. It's so compact (12" round and 19½" high) that you can take it right out to the orchard with you. –L.H.

$117

READ MORE ABOUT IT

THE MOST ENERGY-EFFICIENT APPLIANCES

A complete listing of the energy performance of every major appliance, published each year. 32 pages. –L.H.

$2, American Council for an Energy-Efficient Economy

The standard water bed heater uses about 125 kwh of electricity per month — about the same as a large refrigerator.

House Warming or Global Warming?

Replacing an old furnace that runs at 65% efficiency with one rated above 90% can save as much as four tons of the greenhouse gas carbon dioxide from spewing into the atmosphere each year.

IT PAYS — LITERALLY — TO BE AN ENERGY-EFFICIENCY expert in your own home. By buying efficient furnaces, water heaters, air conditioners, and related products, you can both save money and reduce the world's use of energy. Sometimes you have to spend a little to save a lot — but you're also saving the earth.

Heating the Whole Outdoors

If you're like most people, your furnace or boiler may seem pretty mysterious. But it can be costing you a lot of money and contributing to global warming. Simply keeping it tuned up and cleaned can save many dollars of fuel and many pounds of carbon dioxide. It can make sense to replace it with a more efficient unit. Or, in between those two extremes, you might want to install a setback thermostat instead.

Look to the Rating Label

Just like cars and refrigerators, furnaces come with energy rating labels. To tell how efficient a furnace is, look on its upper right corner for the yellow energy label, or ask your local dealer for the AFUE (Annual Fuel Utilization Efficiency) rating.

The AFUE rating system was devised by the U.S. Department of Energy to show how efficiently a furnace extracts heat from the fuel it burns. The higher the rating, the higher the efficiency.

What You Can Do

✔ Invest in a ceiling fan to distribute warm air in the winter and cooling breezes in the summer. Models with variable speed controls can conserve energy.

✔ Keep windows tightly sealed in cold weather, especially those near thermostats, and use shades and drapes. Even a tight house can feel drafty if cold windows are exposed to the room. And drafts can "fool" a thermostat into thinking the house is colder than it really is.

✔ Replace old-fashioned insulated glass windows with coated "low-emissivity" windows. Doing this throughout an average-sized Massachusetts house using oil heat will reduce carbon dioxide emissions by three-quarters of a ton per year.

✔ Install south-facing awnings. They can lower interior room temperatures 8 to 15 degrees.

✔ When you design a new house, use solar architecture and landscaping.

✔ Investigate the financial possibilities. At least 16 states offer rebates, cash grants, or low-interest or interest-free loans for home energy improvements.

✔ Talk to your utility company. Most utilities are required by law to help their customers conserve energy. Many will conduct free or low-cost home energy audits and then help pay for the recommended changes.

If all the lubricating oil in the U.S. were re-refined, the result would be enough to heat 600,000 homes annually.

THE CARRIER INFINITY GAS FURNACE

The Infinity boasts the highest efficiency rating of all furnaces available: 94% AFUE. (Some others rate as low as 65%.) A computerized microprocessor adjusts gas input and air flow to maintain peak performance. Unlike "dumb" furnaces that go full blast every time the thermostat calls for heat, the Infinity burns less fuel whenever milder conditions allow, which is most of the time. It also saves electricity with lower fan speeds. This is the unit that conservation expert Amory Lovins recommended for his parents' house. –J.S.

$2,400 to $3,100, Carrier Corp.

THE SYSTEM 2000 OIL BURNER

One reason old-fashioned hot-water furnaces are inefficient is that they lose heat to the basement after they shut off. The System 2000 saves oil by keeping the circulating pumps on even after the furnace stops running. This uses the still-hot furnace to continue heating your home, not the basement. An insulated hot-water storage tank adds to the energy efficiency of this model. The System 2000 has a very high AFUE: 87.5%. –J.S.

About $2,600 (not including installation), Energy Kinetics

THE ULTIMA EX-95 OIL FURNACE

If you heat your house with oil, you have a special responsibility to be energy efficient. The burning of oil releases about $1\frac{1}{2}$ times as much carbon dioxide as natural gas and also risks oil spills. This unit has an extra heat exchanger to draw as much energy as possible from the hot gases it produces. The efficiency rating is 90.8%, and like most high-rating furnaces, it wastes so little heat that the flue gases are cool enough to be vented through plastic pipe instead of the usual metal. –J.S.

**Approx. $3,000
Yukon Energy Corporation**

THE INFLOOR® HEATING SYSTEM

We love walking into a home heated with radiant floors on a cold winter day and feeling that pleasant glow of warmth beaming up from the floor. How do radiant floors work? Instead of hot water flowing through radiators or baseboards, warm water circulates through tubing that is laid down before a concrete floor is poured.

The Infloor system comes with a detailed installation manual, and Infloor's parent company, Gyp-Crete Corporation, manufactures a good lightweight topping to cover the tubing on wooden subfloors. –J.S.

**$500 per zone control, plus $4.50 per square foot coverage
Infloor Heating Systems**

THE HEATMAKER GAS BOILER

Seven percent of all homes nationwide use hot-water heating systems. Hot-water heat is comfortable, quiet, and easy to divide into several zones within the house — potentially a big energy-saving feature. Hot water also saves energy because the slender pipes used to convey it around the house lose less heat in cold crawl spaces and attics than the larger forced-air ducts.

The Heatmaker combines two different functions in one compact unit: it heats both your home and your household water. A built-in heat exchanger keeps the two water supplies separate. The system can be set for three output levels, and the annual efficiency rating is a respectable 82% to 87%. A special concentric pipe-venting system allows a single hole in your sidewall to serve for both air intake and exhaust. –J.S.

$1,900, Trianco-Heatmaker, Inc.

Today, every new gas or oil system is required by law to have an AFUE rating. The best rate over 90 percent. The average rating is about 85 percent, compared with an average of about 75 percent for older furnaces. To be truly efficient, a furnace should be just large enough to create heat a bit faster than your house loses it — a rate your dealer or utility company can determine.

Be Cool: Air Conditioners & Heat Pumps

The nature of electrical transmission over power lines allows only 20 to 35 percent of the energy burned at power plants to reach customers' homes. Inefficient air conditioners reduce that figure even more, increasing both waste and pollution.

Room air conditioners are rated with an EER (Energy Efficiency Ratio) number and central air conditioners with a similar SEER (Seasonal EER) number. Both represent the ratio of electrical input to cooling energy. High-efficiency units have EER and SEER ratings of ten and higher. Lower than eight is considered wasteful. Buy the most efficient unit you can afford.

The Air Is Everywhere

Wasted energy isn't the only consideration when you think about the air in your home. You can encounter serious air pollution without leaving your front door. Among the worst hazards:

- *Formaldehyde* and other volatile organic compounds are released from building materials, cigarette smoke, and an alarming number of ordinary consumer products. In low concentrations, formaldehyde can cause eye, nose, and throat discomfort; some highly sensitive people experience more severe reactions.
- *Combustion gases* from gas-fired appliances like stoves should not be a problem if they are installed and vented properly. But sometimes contaminants such as carbon monoxide leak into living areas.
- *Mold and mildew* often develop when indoor relative humidity rises above 40 percent. Over time, excessive humidity can even cause structural failure in buildings.
- *Radon,* the naturally occurring gas produced by decaying uranium, infiltrates homes and causes an estimated 5,000 to 20,000 lung cancer deaths in the U.S. every year. (See pages 98-101 for more information.)
- *Man-made household materials* contribute to indoor air pollution and "sick buildings." Culprits include synthetic carpeting and underlayment, wall boards, furniture glues, and office equipment, such as copiers, that produce fumes.

The best pollution control is prevention. Don't smoke indoors, for example. And do ventilate your living space.

Older homes have natural ventilation in the form of small air leaks. Newer, tighter homes may need vents and fans. Either way, the energy wasted as the air leaves the house can be enormous.

Heat recovery ventilators (also called air-to-air heat exchangers) solve this by forcing the air leaving your house to give its heat to the cold incoming air. They can operate in reverse during the summer. The better ones can salvage 80 percent of the outgoing air's energy. This provides healthy, fresh indoor air without a heavy energy penalty.

COOLING SYSTEMS

THE INTERNATIONAL SERIES™ GM ROOM AIR CONDITIONER

Carrier's Series "GM" features two models with efficiency ratings that are among the highest available. Their EER is from 10 to 12 (most are 8 or 9). They are the only air conditioners that have built-in timers. An energy-saving fan switch adds to the value. –J.S.

$685 and up, Carrier Corporation

What You Can Do

Even the most efficient air conditioners use an enormous amount of energy. So before you plug in the cold, consider these quieter and cheaper alternatives:

✔ Most houses have special devices that improve air-conditioning efficiency and really save on energy bills. They're called shades, drapes, and blinds. Use them on hot, sunny days, and you'll cut air-conditioning costs by 20% and more. Awnings, overhangs, and shade trees are even better because they keep the sun's rays from reaching your windows.

✔ Don't try to cool the entire house. Use room air conditioners only for a few cool oases, like the master bedroom and family room.

ARVIN MASTERCOOL 2-STAGE EVAPORATIVE COOLER

Families in dryer southern and western states (like Arizona and Colorado) have a special opportunity to cool homes ecologically. Evaporative coolers use only one-fourth the electricity of standard air conditioners. They cool by pulling fresh outside air through a water-saturated pad and blowing cool, filtered air into the home. Stale indoor air is pushed out open windows and doors.

Evaporative coolers contain no chlorofluorocarbons and use one-fourth to one-fifth the amount of electricity that regular air conditioners do. If water is in short supply, however, be aware that they can consume up to five gallons an hour or about 100 gallons a day. That's the equivalent of having one extra family member in the house. Evaporative coolers work only in dry climates.

The Arvin is the best evaporative cooler on the market because the cooling pad requires replacement only once every eight years, as compared to annually in other models. (The installation is usually up on the roof.) Furthermore, Arvin offers a unique add-on second-stage that indirectly cools incoming air and drops the temperature an extra five degrees, making its temperature equivalent to the best conventional compressor-type air conditioners. –J.S.

$1,500 to $1,200; $400 to $500 for Second-Stage Cooler, Arvin Air

THE HYDROTECH 2000 HEAT PUMP

Heat-pump owners, try this experiment. This summer, while your unit is working to cool the house, go outside and put your hand over the air stream blowing from it. Feels pretty hot, doesn't it? That's heat being removed from your house and expelled into the atmosphere.

The Hydrotech 2000 takes that wasted energy and uses it to heat your water. A built-in microprocessor varies fan speeds and output to add to its performance, making it one of the most efficient heat pumps on the market, with impressive SEER ratings of 13 and higher. –J.S.

$4,200 to $4,900
Carrier Corporation

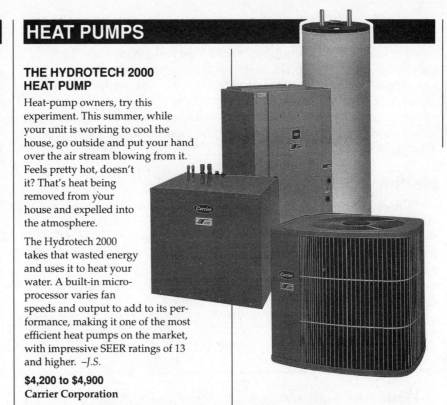

THE WATERFURNACE GROUND-COUPLED HEAT PUMP

Three out of ten new houses are heated and cooled with heat pumps. These devices work like air conditioners in the summer, extracting heat from indoors and expelling it outdoors. Come winter, the cycle is reversed: heat is extracted from outside air and pumped into the home.

The problem with heat pumps is that they give and take heat from the atmosphere — a reservoir that varies widely in temperature through the seasons. The WaterFurnace taps a more stable heat source: the earth beneath your yard. It pumps water through pipes buried in the ground and uses half the electricity of ordinary heat pumps. An additional energy-saving option heats your hot water. Price? The WaterFurnace itself costs about the same as conventional heat pumps, but the necessary ground loop can run up to $2,000 more. –J.S.

WaterFurnace International, Inc.

Housecleaning's in the Air

The alternative to ventilating your house is to remove contaminants with an air cleaner. The best ones are the type that you add to your heating system. Standard furnace filters are designed to protect the furnace, not your family. But air cleaners not only help make your system more efficient by preventing dust and grease from building up in ducts and air-conditioning coils, but they also create a healthier indoor environment.

Heating Water: Gas Beats Electric

Check the energy ratings, and you'll discover that top-model electric water heaters score 90 percent efficiency or higher because nearly all of the electricity they consume gets converted to hot water. But the high rating doesn't reflect the fact that power plants convert fuel to electricity at only 35 to 40 percent efficiency. When that's factored in, the real efficiency of electric water heaters is closer to 35 percent. This compares with an efficiency of around 60 percent for gas heaters.

— *Jay Stein*

VENTILATING SYSTEMS

THE AIRXCHANGE HEAT RECOVERY VENTILATORS

The Airxchange energy recovery systems efficiently ventilate 1,000- to 3,000-square-foot homes. They use a patented wheel that spins 30 times per minute to exchange heat between exhaust and supply air streams. The Airxchange also solves the problem of dry homes in cold climates by exchanging moisture as well as heat between incoming and outgoing air. *–J.S.*

$440 to $750, Airxchange

What You Can Do

Selecting the right furnace is only part of the job of heating efficiently; the other part is proper maintenance. Here are some tips.

✔ Have the efficiency of your oil burner checked annually. If it is below 70% AFUE and cannot be adjusted to bring it up to 80%, then replacement is probably in order.

✔ Check the filter monthly by holding it up to a light. Replace or clean it when dirty — probably about every two or three months during the heating season. A dirty filter can add up to ten percent to your heating or cooling bill.

✔ Brush and vacuum your furnace blower compartment annually. Even with a filter, dust and lint accumulate in the blower. This is also a good opportunity to oil the motor. Check the manufacturer's instruction

manual for details, and remember to turn off power to the furnace before you open any access doors.

✔ Check duct work for leaks by feeling for escaping air, and seal them with duct tape. All ducts that run through cold spaces, such as crawl spaces or the attic, should be wrapped with two-inch-thick fiberglass duct insulation. Forty percent of the output of your furnace or central air conditioner can be lost through an uninsulated, leaky distribution system in an unheated space.

✔ If you have an air system, vacuum and clean the registers. If you have a hot-water system, vacuum and clean the baseboards. Even a thin layer of dust on baseboard heating coils acts as a powerful layer of insulation.

✔ Make sure any dampers in your system are balanced.

AIR CONDITIONER CFCS: DON'T WORRY, BE CAREFUL

We have reason to wonder if the chlorofluorocarbons in home air conditioners are worth the threat to the environment. Our verdict is yes, and here's why. Almost none of them uses the R-11 type of CFC found in refrigerators, aerosols, and auto air conditioners. Instead, most use R-22. This shorter-lived CFC breaks down before it reaches the stratosphere, where CFCs do their damage to the ozone layer. If you choose a durable, high-efficiency model, and use it judiciously, you won't be contributing substantially to CFC pollution. (But we're still looking for industry to find replacements for *all* CFCs!) *—J.S.*

American industry released 2.7 billion pounds of chemicals into the air in 1987, according to a 1988 EPA report.

VENT-AIRE ECS 40

It's not just a heat-recovery ventilator. It's not just a forced-air heater. And it's not just an air conditioner. It's all three. The ECS 40 contains a pure aluminum exchange core that recovers more than 80% of the energy that would ordinarily be lost through ventilation. A built-in heating coil is warmed by a small pump that circulates hot water from your water heater. An air-conditioning coil can be added for summertime cooling. By combining so many functions, the ECS 40 allows you to use your heating and air-conditioning duct work to distribute fresh air from the heat-recovery ventilator, saving you the cost of additional fresh-air ducts. –J.S.

$2,000 (Heating-only Model)
Engineering Development Incorporated

THE HONEYWELL F50 ELECTRONIC AIR CLEANER

The best air cleaners of all are electronic; they remove particulates as small as .01 microns. The F50's high efficiency and competitive price make it our first recommendation for electronic air cleaners. It comes in three sizes for installation on different size furnace systems. –J.S.

$500 to $600 (including installation)

An optional companion device called a performance indicator signals when the cleaner itself needs to be cleaned, which can be as often as monthly. –J.S.

$30, Honeywell, Inc.

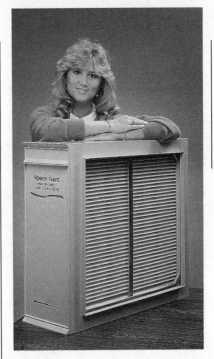

THE SPACE-GARD AIR CLEANER

This air cleaner packs 78.6 square feet of folded synthetic fabric into a 20"x25"x9" cartridge. Simple in design, it requires no electricity and actually improves in efficiency as it collects dust. Annual maintenance consists of removing the dirty cartridge and sliding in a new one. The Space-Gard effectively removes particles down to just below one micron, just what the doctor ordered for cleaning up pollen and cigarette smoke. –J.S.

$300 to $350 (including installation)
Research Products Corporation

HOME MANAGER

How smart is your home? Not as smart as it would be with a Home Manager. This computerized home system controls lights, appliances, heating, air conditioning, and security systems. Using it to send command signals over your existing house wiring, you can program any electrical device to turn on and off on a preprogrammed schedule.

Home Manager can save water by operating sprinklers at night. It can help keep you safe by sensing natural gas fumes, sounding an alarm, and turning off the gas. Home Manager saves energy by monitoring temperatures throughout the house, individually regulating and scheduling each room. You heat and cool spaces only when they are occupied.

As sophisticated as it is, Home Manager is easily operated from a touch-sensitive video screen display. It shows your home's floor plan and prompts you with simple instructions. –J.S.

$6,500 to $17,000 (includes installation in new or existing homes),
Unity Systems, Inc.

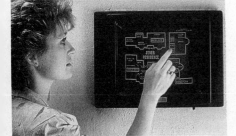

Each year the amount of energy that leaks through American windows equals the energy in the oil that flows through the Alaskan pipeline.

New Life for An Old Flame

> *The challenge to making wood heat environmentally sound is to burn cleanly — and to plant more trees.*

BACK IN THE DAYS OF OPEC oil embargoes and long gas lines, home heating with wood experienced a sudden — almost overnight — renaissance. Nearly five million people bought wood stoves in 1979 alone. Stove makers churned out units based on century-old designs with little regard for efficiency or emissions.

Homeowners caught up in the craze paid little attention to stove performance since even the least efficient units could save them hundreds of dollars in fuel bills. Most were happy to burn three or four cords to avoid turning up the thermostat. By the beginning of the 1980s the amount of energy produced by wood eclipsed that of nuclear power. It displaced millions of gallons of foreign oil.

Unfortunately, the millions of inefficient stoves — being used by a new generation of inexperienced owners — caused severe pollution problems. It got so bad in some places that new stoves were banned. Missoula, Montana, had "no burn" days when its air got too dirty.

By 1984 various states, led by Oregon, began setting clean-burning standards. Finally the Environmental Protection Agency (EPA) established tough regulations — so strict, in fact, that it now regards the resulting modern breed of wood stoves as important weapons in battling the greenhouse effect.

And that's good news because, after all, so many of us had turned to wood burning because we wanted to help the environment. The last thing we wanted was to make things worse.

Just how efficient are these new stoves? Soon after we installed our state-of-the-art heater a few years ago, a neighbor asked if we had given up burning wood. He hadn't noticed the tall smoke plume rising from our chimney anymore, he said. The emissions are that dramatically much cleaner.

Indeed, the best wood heaters have overall efficiencies of nearly 80 percent. Compare this to the 50 percent of the older airtight stove and the 30 percent of a Franklin stove. It's like comparing a new Lexus with a Model T. Even some modern metal fireplaces are as efficient as airtight stoves.

STOVES

Today's wood-burning heaters are clean, efficient, and handsome enough for any modern living room or den. All the models included here meet strict Phase II EPA standards.

THE JØTUL ALPHA

It doesn't look like Grandma's wood stove (more like a *USA Today* newsstand) and doesn't burn like one either (it's about 25% more efficient than Grandma's). But the Jøtul Alpha is as rugged and practical as the stoves of yesteryear. It features heavy-duty cast-iron construction and a sizable glass door that, unlike most, stays clean for fire viewing.

This wood burner has several other things going for it, too. It is a double-walled convection stove. This means that hot air circulates around the stove, leaving the outside warm — not hot — to the touch. As a bonus, the Alpha can be placed closer to walls — as little as seven inches away as opposed to the typical 20 to 36 inches. Its six-quart capacity ash pan cuts down on the dirty job of emptying ashes. Logs are loaded from the front, and the door is wide enough to hold a sizable 20-incher.

Made in Norway, the Alpha features an internal catalytic combustor that burns fire gases to reduce pollution. It's a midsized stove, able to heat about 1,000 square feet without much trouble. –S.M.

$1,395 - $1,735, Jøtul USA

Each U.S. citizen produces four to six pounds of solid waste per day, for a national total of 179 to 268 million tons per year.

THE JØTUL #8TDC

Jøtul, the world's largest manufacturer of wood heaters, designed this stove expressly for the American market in 1984. Its style was so universally appealing that it is now the company's best-selling stove worldwide. There's nothing too fancy here: the cast-iron #8TDC features traditional American design copied from colonial cabinetry. Its combustion system is fairly straightforward, too, with an internal catalytic combustor to produce a clean burn. The only drawback is its curved door, which prevents the loading of larger logs once you've put one or two in.

You'll get an eight- to ten-hour burn out of the #8TDC. Heat output ranges from 6,000 to 49,000 Btu, and it heats a well-insulated 1,400-square-foot home adequately. *–S.M.*

$1,245 - $1,535, Jøtul USA

VERMONT CASTINGS RESOLUTE ACCLAIM

Started by two Vermonters at the height of the first OPEC oil embargo, Vermont Castings has been a pacesetter in developing clean-burning technology. Its cast-iron stoves are the Cadillacs of the industry, combining Yankee know-how with traditional Early American styling. The Resolute Acclaim is our favorite. It is efficient (67.4% in government ratings) and produces just a whisper of smoke (5.1 grams per hour).

The Resolute can crank out the heat, producing 40,000 Btu per hour — enough to heat a well-insulated 1,600-square-foot home. For those times when romance is more important than heat, the Resolute Acclaim instantly transforms into an open fireplace; the door unhitches in a flash, and you can install a clip-in spark screen to protect the ambience.

An enamel stove, the Resolute features shaker grates, a back-saving top-loading option, and a reversible flue collar that allows venting from either the top or back. *– S.M.*

About $1,425, Vermont Castings

"The problems of pollution should be addressed today, not left to boil over on another generation." — *The Christian Science Monitor*

Catalytics Come Home

Some of the most efficient stoves use catalytic combustion, similar in concept to your car's catalytic converter. Catalytic combustors for wood heaters reduce pollutants (mainly dustlike particulates) by nearly 80 percent. Not only that, but they also squeeze more heat from less wood, with efficiency typically increased by a whopping 15 to 20 percentage points. They also reduce creosote buildup — the wood burner's nemesis — by 90 percent. In short, a clean-burning catalytic heater means less expense and fewer trips to the woodpile.

Catalytic combustors work by burning smoke (which, after all, is just incompletely burned gas) — igniting it as it heads out of the stove. Combustion efficiency in a catalytic stove has been recorded as high as 97 percent.

Wood heater catalysts, the materials used by the catalytic combustors, have a limited life — about two years in cold climates, four in milder areas where less wood is burned over the course of a winter. They also can die an early death by "poisoning." This occurs when the catalyst is contaminated by a foreign substance, such as burning plastic.

There are several noncatalytic designs among EPA-certified stoves. However, most acceptable noncatalytic models have small fireboxes and a limited range of heat because they are designed to burn short, high-temperature fires for clean combustion. On the plus side, they tend to be easier to operate, and there is no expensive catalyst to replace at $100 to $225 each.

EPA WOOD HEATER CERTIFICATION

All new wood heaters sold in the United States must now be EPA-certified that they meet minimum efficiency standards. Tougher "Phase II" regulations are slated to go into effect in 1992. Although pollution control has added $100 to $200 to the average price of a new EPA-certified stove, you can easily recoup that money and more in reduced wood use and chimney cleaning. And, of course, our environment benefits, too.

Look for the EPA "hang tag" on the heater to make apples-to-apples comparisons. The tag will specify the heater's emission rate and its efficiency range.

Old-fashioned fireplaces remain unregulated; only designs with variable air supply and heat controls must comply with the new standards.

For a complete list of EPA-certified heaters, write: Stove List, U.S. Environmental Protection Agency.

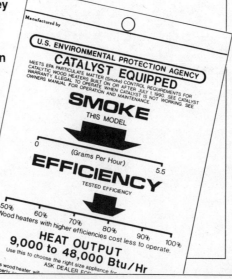

STOVES

THE WATERFORD 104 MK II

If you're yearning for a stove that's simple to use, basic in design, and cheap, here's a bit of nostalgia that meets the EPA's clean-burning requirements. The Waterford 104 MK II is perfect for the rec room, garage, or shop. It's a no-nonsense stove employing the box design that was the standard for the Shakers as well as the Scandinavians. Made in Ireland, this little powerhouse can heat about 750 square feet comfortably. It's rated 70.3% efficient in tests for the Oregon Department of Environmental Quality and emits just 3.1 grams of smoke per hour. Black only. –S.M.

$498, Waterford Irish Stoves

What You Can Do

✔ If you have an older, conventional stove, consider adding a catalytic device. But get good advice first because their effectiveness varies widely depending on design, installation, and methods of operation. Internal add-on combustors are more effective than stovepipe models but may nullify the heater's warranty.

THE PIAZZETTA 905

Wood stoves can be ugly. This one is a work of art. Inside, it features a cast-iron firebox that teams with a smart noncatalytic design with an automatic thermostat to provide constant, clean-burning heat. Outside it boasts a handcrafted Majolica finish in seven brilliant colors.

The ceramic exterior provides more than good looks, too; it absorbs heat and gently releases it hours after the fire has died down. Air inlets located at the top and bottom of the stove provide constant air circulation around the firebox, and the stove never gets sizzling hot (reassuring in homes with small children). It's not cheap, but then again, quality seldom is. – *S.M.*

About $1,695, BSW Inc.

THE LOPI E'LAN

It used to be so simple. Wood stoves were black, square, and ugly. But who cared? As long as you were putting the screws to OPEC and saving a couple hundred bucks, the black tank in the middle of the living room was a statement of self-sufficiency. It wasn't supposed to look good too.

Eventually the novelty of wood heat wore off, and stove designers went to work making stoves that looked good and still provided cozy heat. The Lopi E'lan is a classic, and it's a first in contemporary design. Its curved glass front gives it modern flair, and it has a combustion design to match.

The E'lan's wide expanse of glass is kept clean by a unique air-wash system that prevents the smoky fog that develops in most stoves. Made of steel, its no-maintenance enamel finish keeps the stove bright. Perfect for a room or two, producing anywhere from 11,700 to 26,300 Btu per hour, but don't count on it for much more heat than that. The E'lan's noncatalytic design features simple one-touch operation. –*S.M.*

About $1,600
E'lan Mfg./Travis Industries

THE ELMIRA OVAL WOOD COOKSTOVE

Every wood-burner junky dreams of owning an Elmira Oval. This is the grande dame of wood cookstoves with its nickel plating, porcelain oven, and polished cast-iron cooking surface. The company began making these in the mid-1970s for the sizable Amish community near its Ontario, Canada, plant and since has made several key improvements in the stove for the American market. Doors are tight fitting. Spin-style draft controls give you the option of a lazy cooking fire or a hot oven. And a gasketed firebox makes the stove a wood miser.

Cookstoves are exempt from EPA emissions testing, but this unit is a clean burner just the same. It burns either wood or coal in a large airtight firebox and can heat the kitchen and another room or two. Invest in the optional water jacket for supplemental water heating; this stove throws off so much heat it will provide the extra hot water with little effort. –*S.M.*

$3,195
Elmira Stove and Fireplace Mfg.

In 628 communities across the country collecting household hazardous waste, only 1% to 5% of the citizens contributed.

FIREPLACES & INSERTS

RUEGG PRISMA FIREPLACE

Most of us have a soft spot for fireplaces, but as a heater an open hearth performs abominably. It has a monstrous appetite for wood, is extremely drafty, and may backpuff, leaving the living room smelling like smoked bacon.

The Swiss-built Ruegg Prisma has none of these drawbacks. And hold on to your bellows . . . it's about as efficient as the wood stoves of the late 1970s. Made of steel, it features firebrick guts and a quiet fan. Because of its size, duct requirements, and heat output (it can keep a 1,200-square-foot area warm by itself), this fireplace should be considered only if you're planning a new house or adding on a room. It burns most efficiently when its full-view thermal glass door is closed. Romantics will be pleased to know that the door glides out of view, up into the unit, when you want to hear the snap, crackle, and pop of the fire. –S.M.

About $3,485, Ruegg Fireplaces

VERMONT CASTINGS WINTERWARM FIREPLACE INSERT

Forget tiny glass doors. Forget adding a funky grate. If you're serious about transforming your classic brick fireplace into an efficient and minimally polluting heater, you'll need to install what's called a fireplace insert. Until the Vermont Castings WinterWarm came along, however, this usually meant losing the ambience and glow of the fireplace. This insert is a stylish compromise. The technology is the same as that used in high-tech stoves; catalytic combustors give the unit a 78.3% efficiency rating. As a bonus, the catalytics provide an extended burn time — up to nine hours for each load of wood.

The WinterWarm features all the bells and whistles you'd expect on a top-of-the-line heater, including a stay-clean glass door, fans, and even an ash bin. –S.M.

About $1,700, Vermont Castings

What You Can Do

✔ Close dampers when not using your fireplace.

✔ Even when they're closed, many dampers leave a gap of an inch or more. Stuff the gap with insulation and save up to $5 a year in lost heated or cooled air.

✔ Better yet, equip the front of your fireplace with a glass door — it's a real energy saver.

A bleached-pulp mill generates roughly 50 tons of chlorinated poisons every day.

TESS 148 FIREPLACE

The TESS 148 boasts a souped-up, Rumford-style fire chamber with a heat-storing area above it. Dense refractory bricks positioned in a zigzag maze force gases to release their heat on their way up the chimney. This energy is stored in the masonry mass, where it gradually and steadily releases heat into the room.

The 148 looks just like a traditional fireplace from the outside. Its main advantage, however, is that it is easy to build. All components are pre-engineered and stack on one another. We've seen an experienced mason with a helper install the refractory component core of a TESS fireplace in one afternoon. It costs about what you'd pay for a traditional (and far less efficient) fireplace. –S.M.

About $5,000 (installed)
Thermal Energy Storage Systems Inc.

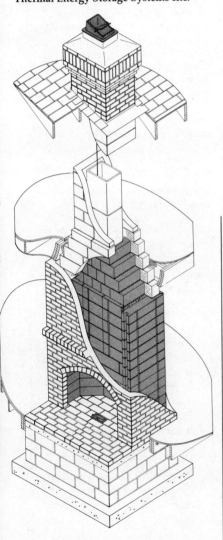

THE TULIKIVI

Long before glasnost, a fireplace popular in Siberia and the chillier parts of Eastern Europe had been gaining interest in America. The Russian or Finnish fireplace, generally made of stone, brick, or tile, features a small firebox and a labyrinth of channels above its fire chamber. As 2,000° F fires roar in the firebox, the masonry innards above it soak up heat and radiate it slowly and evenly throughout the house. Since wood is burned at short, hot intervals, combustion is clean. Warmed masonry slowly provides cozy heat for hours before the next fire is required. The drawbacks: each must be custom-built by an experienced mason, and fire viewing is virtually nonexistent (not exactly the kind of fireplace you'd put a bear rug in front of).

The TuliKivi from Finland is a ready-made Russian fireplace built of smooth, heat-retaining soapstone. It features a "contra flow" design with an energy efficiency of nearly 60% and an airtight glass door. If you have kids, this hybrid fireplace/stove should be appealing; the soapstone never gets hot to the touch. Several different models are available, including cookstoves and bake ovens. –S.M.

About $6,000
The New Alberene Stone Co.

We each throw out an average of ten times our own weight in trash every year (about 1/2 ton per person).

Clean Pellet Fuel

Another breakthrough development in clean wood burning is the pellet-burning stove. Pellet fuel is made of wood scraps that have been pulverized, dried, and compressed into tiny cylinders resembling rabbit food. It is sold in 50-pound bags. Because pellet fuel contains little moisture and has a lot of surface area, it burns with more than 80 percent efficiency.

Although features vary among pellet heaters, they work like this: You fill a reservoir on the stove with 80 pounds or so of pellets, then kindle a blaze in the small firebox. An electric auger gradually trickles a few pellets at a time onto the fire, and a fan forces air into the firebox. The result is a small, intense blaze that burns incredibly cleanly. By adjusting the pellet flow, you control the heat output and the time between reservoir refills. Many pellet stoves don't need chimneys; UL-approved models simply vent out through the wall with a special metal vent.

The stoves are still generally hard to find and, more important, so is the fuel. But should a reliable fuel distribution system develop close by, you'll be glad you checked this out.

For more information and a current list of pellet stove manufacturers, order the "Buying Guide to Pellet Stoves" from Biomass Publications of America.

— *Steven Maviglio*

YOU SHOULD KNOW

The decomposition of trees in the forest puts as much harmful carbon dioxide into the atmosphere as burning the wood, only then we miss using the heat and saving oil and coal. Also, the new tree that replaces the one being burned in your stove absorbs 10 to 20 times as much carbon dioxide as the burning creates. The keys are to burn cleanly and to plant more trees.

CENTRAL HEATER

THE DUMONT TEMPEST WOOD-FIRED CENTRAL HEATER

The Dumont Tempest is the best-kept secret in wood heating, and we can't quite figure out why, because it is head and shoulders above every other wood-fired central heater on the market. The Tempest, developed by University of Maine wood guru Dick Hill, burns so cleanly that it produces absolutely no creosote.

What the Tempest does make plenty of, however, is hot water. A neighbor who has three teenagers also has one of these; he reports no shortage of hot water, even in summer. The unit squeezes heat from wood through a system of heat storage and high-temperature combustion. Light a fire in the unit after work, keep it going until bedtime, and the Tempest will produce enough heat for the house for 24 hours — and provide all your hot water as well. It has a built-in oil or gas backup option, just in case. Pricey, but worth it. – *S.M.*

About $6,500
Dumont Stoker Corp.

What You Can Do

✔ Don't use your wood stove as a household incinerator. Burning colored paper, plastics, gift wraps, painted wood, and even synthetic fireplace logs can destroy your catalytic combustor. Since they produce harmful air pollutants and toxic ashes, these materials shouldn't be burned in conventional stoves either. (See page 20 for more information about burning trash in wood stoves and fireplaces.)

PELLET HEATER

PYRO INDUSTRIES WHITFIELD WP-2

Convenience was not always a word associated with wood heating. It is now, thanks to pellet heaters that offer flames without the fuss. No room in the yard for cordwood? Pellets come in bags. Don't like the dust and dirtiness of wood? Pellets generate neither. Tired of rolling out of the La-Z-Boy to feed the stove? A single 80-pound feeding can run a pellet stove like the Whitfield WP-2 from Pyro for 16 hours at a respectable 40,000 Btu per hour.

You don't get the roaring flames of a conventional wood stove; the flame is more like that of two packs of cigarettes burning at once. But you do get 80% efficiency and almost no pollution or creosote. Pyro Industries is the most established manufacturer in the still-young pellet stove business. *–S.M.*

About $1,900
Pyro Industries Inc.

ACCESSORIES

PENNSYLVANIA FIREBACKS

Squeeze extra heat out of your fireplace the way the colonists did. Cast-iron firebacks absorb and reflect heat. They also protect bricks from excess heat. Weighing 45 pounds, Pennsylvania Firebacks, available in 17 different designs, are sand-molded the old-fashioned way. 18^1/$_2$"Wx19"Hx^3/$_4$" thick. *–S.M.*

$155, Pennsylvania Firebacks Inc.

THE CONDAR PROBE THERMOSTAT

If you already own a stove, there is one sure way to minimize pollution: Burn short, hot fires. Trying to set the Olympic record for all-night burns causes your stove to smoke wood instead of burn it. The Condar Probe Thermostat provides a quick check of the temperature of gases leaving your stove. Color coding lets you know when you're burning for maximum efficiency. Installs with one drill hole in the stovepipe. *– S.M.*

About $15, Condar Co.

In our urban forests, about four trees die or are removed for each new one planted.

Your Planet, Your Home

Y OUR HOME. It's one of your most precious possessions. It's also one of the most dangerous. Your home can harm the environment more than any other single thing you have or do.

The most damage is done by the energy your home uses. Over the course of 50 years, 50,000 gallons of oil — or the equivalent in coal or nuclear fuel used by the power plant — is likely to go toward your heating, cooling, and lighting needs. But you can do better than that. Energy conservation design and products, and smart use of the sun's energy, can slash energy bills in new homes to less than 25 percent of those for most houses being built today. And they'll go right on working for decades, saving energy and dollars and avoiding pollution.

The building products you use can also harm the environment — and your family. The chemical CFCs in rigid foam insulation break down protective ozone in the atmosphere. The hydrocarbons in solvent-based paints, stains, and preservatives pollute the air both when they're made and when they're used. And the construction process itself creates tons of solid waste.

Here, too, environmental alternatives can make a big difference. Cellulose insulation, for example, is made of recycled newspaper. And some fiberglass insulation materials are made predominately from the glass you recycle.

Consider the possibilities.

> *A typical "naked" window in central Ohio costs home owners $1.50 per square foot per year in lost oil heat or $2.93 for electric heat.*

Good News from Yesterday's Newspaper

When your Sunday paper is recycled, chances are it ends up as cellulose — an insulation material that has some big environmental benefits. Cellulose is more energy efficient than fiberglass, and it is treated for fire safety — usually with environmentally safe borax. As loose-fill attic insulation, cellulose also costs less than fiberglass, which can be harmful to human eyes, skin, and lungs.

We've long been proponents of loose-fill attic insulation: nice, simple, easy. And now there's a new type: K-13 or wet-spray cellulose for insulating during new construction.

LIVOS PLANTCHEMISTRY

Livos offers a complete line of environmentally safe and people-friendly alternatives to toxic solvents, paints, and other finishes and wood preservatives (see page 52). The products are imported from Germany and are quite expensive. Available by mail order. – A.W.

Livos PlantChemistry

What You Can Do

✔ Spruce up instead of cutting cedar and redwoods down. Plain old native spruce (or pine) clapboards can be a fine alternative to more expensive cedar and redwood being cut from the last remaining stands of virgin forest in the continental U.S. If you're planning to paint or stain the wood (opaque stains are best), and if you have used care to avoid moisture problems in the walls, spruce should hold up almost as well as cedar or redwood, for much less money. Pine is fine, too, if you let it dry several months to allow the pores to open up before finishing.

Fifteen percent of all energy consumed in the U.S. is used to heat and cool our homes and to heat household water.

AURO NATURAL PLANT CHEMISTRY

Like Livos, Auro is a product line from Germany, where a burgeoning movement called "Baubiologie" supports a totally natural indoor environment. Its adherents shun all synthetics, including polyester clothes, petroleum-based paints and finishes, plywood, and the like.

Auro offers a full line of natural, nontoxic finishes, paints, wood preservatives, oils, and even tile and wood adhesives; the company says it's the only one that uses "non-petroleum, non-crude oil, and nonplastic ingredients." Like Livos products, these are not cheap. Expect to pay $30 to $40 per quart for lacquers, varnishes, and shellacs, and over $10 per quart for some paints. But the feel and smell of a space finished with these products is worth the price. *–A.W.*

Sinan Company (U.S. distributor)

INSULATION MATERIALS

AIR-KRETE INSULATION

This is the insulation material favored by builders specializing in safe, nontoxic construction. It is made from magnesium silicate and contains no chemicals that can "outgas" (give off air pollutants). More expensive than most insulation materials, it is mixed with air and sprayed into open wall cavities by a licensed contractor. The resulting brittle foam is weak, but once covered, insulates well and is totally nonflammable. *–A.W.*

Air-Krete

EXPANDED POLYSTYRENE (EPS) FOAM INSULATION

Expanded polystyrene, or EPS, isn't a *great* product and isn't the perfect alternative to the earlier forms of insulation that were very damaging to the earth's ozone layer. But it's a lot better. Unfortunately, it is foamed with pentane, which is released into the atmosphere and contributes to smog and ground-level ozone pollution. Dozens of companies make it, and some building supply stores stock it. *–A.W.*

ICYNENE "INSEALATION"

Here's a great alternative to atmosphere-harming polyurethane insulation. It is foamed in with carbon dioxide instead of CFCs, so it will not harm the earth's ozone layer. A licensed installer sprays the Insealation in place inside a wall or ceiling space. Unlike urethane, it remains relatively soft and flexible, enabling it to expand and contract with the structure throughout the year. The R-value (insulation rating) of 4.3 per inch isn't quite as high as sprayed urethane foam, but it never goes down, as urethane does when the CFC gas leaks out. Insealation is a Canadian product, only recently available in the U.S. *–A.W.*

Icynene

If the U.S. were still operating at 1973 efficiency levels, we would have pumped 50% more carbon dioxide into the air in 1986.

Unlike the blown-in version used for insulating older buildings, wet-spray is installed before the walls are closed in with drywall. A licensed installer sprays a fine mix of aerated cellulose and water-based binder into the cavity. It sticks to the studs and sheathing and fills completely around all wiring and wall penetrations. A contractor then grades the inside surface flush with the inside of the studs.

Wet-spray is a real mess going in, but it usually takes only a day or two to finish an entire house. The cellulose dries in place (wait a few days before closing it in) and insulates to about R-3.5 per inch with almost no air infiltration through it. After insulating the 2"x6" walls of a new office with it, we can leave the heat off for a day in midwinter and hardly notice a drop in temperature.

To find someone who can install wet-spray for you, look in the yellow pages under Insulation Contractors. Before signing a contract, make sure you're getting fully fire-rated cellulose.

Super Windows

It's old news that windows are a major source of energy loss in your home. But now windows are available from most major manufacturers with low-emissivity (low-E) coatings on the glass and with argon gas instead of air between the layers of glass. The argon is less conductive. These windows have an insulation rating of about R-4, roughly twice that of standard double-glazed windows. Their small cost difference and fast payback in energy savings (one or two years) make standard insulated (thermopane) windows obsolete. Ask your window dealer or building supply salesperson about these new windows. And see the reviews on these pages for other ideas to make your home both energy efficient and a good neighbor for the environment.

INSULATION MATERIALS

REMARKABLE COUNTRY HOMES CEDARFOAM PANEL SYSTEM

This insulating panel system provides continuous, uninterrupted superinsulation from footings to ridge. The stress-skin panel is the only one with 100% Cedarfoam, a patented process of impregnating expanded polystyrene foam with a natural, nontoxic insect repellent to keep bugs from nesting in it. Cedarfoam contains no CFCs to destroy the ozone layer.

The panels are equally remarkable in performance; homes using them in northern New England have documented annual heating bills of less than $100. This really helps reduce global warming from fossil fuel consumption.

Cedarfoam panels are designed to be applied to post-and-beam frames. The combination of this age-old timber-framing system with the most up-to-date panel system creates a home of unsurpassed beauty and energy efficiency. You can have the panels customized to your specific location and budget for a minimum of waste and for easy installation.
– *Hank Huber*

Remarc Inc.

HOMING IN ON ECO-BUILDERS

There aren't yet many designer/builders specializing in nontoxic construction. One recognized pioneer in the field is Paul Bierman-Lytle. He uses ecological designs and materials (distributing many himself) and is the closest thing we've found to a national clearinghouse for eco-builders. Write him at the Masters Corp. for information on his mail-order product line, Environmental Outfitters. You'll also find listings in *The Healthy House Catalog* (see review). As a last resort, you might find environmental builders though local hospitals that work with environmentally sensitive people.

Acid rain and global warming could be drastically reduced if more people conserved natural resources.

SEALING IN THE HEAT

PUR FILL OZONE-FRIENDLY FOAM SEALANT

Foam sealant is one of the most important new energy-efficient construction products of the decade. It tightly seals around window and door frames, wall holes, and cracks.

Unfortunately, in the beginning all the foam sealants were made with CFCs. Now that is changing. Pur Fill was the first foam sealant introduced that does not contain CFCs (three others have followed suit: Fomo Products, Polycell from Grace Construction Products, and Touch 'n Foam from Convenience Foam Products). *–A.W.*

Todol Products (U.S. distributor)

FOAM ROPE BACKER ROD

Foam backer rod is the ideal sealer for wide cracks, between logs in log homes, and as a backing for caulking. Insulators Supply Co. offers foam backer rod in $3/8$", $1/2$", and $5/8$" diameters, in small 20' rolls or more economical 250' rolls. The company sells to homeowners as well as contractors, and offers a complete range of insulating and weatherstripping products. *–A.W.*

About 7¢ to 10¢ per foot in smaller coil sizes, Insulators Supply Co.

ELECTRICAL BOX ENCLOSURE

Sealing up air and heat leaks around electrical boxes can be difficult. Even if you're careful to install a vapor barrier and seal it to the boxes, the drywallers are likely to damage it during installation. That problem is all but eliminated with Resource Conservation Technology's Wiring Box Enclosures.

These wide boxes can fit triple-gang boxes, and they provide room above and below the boxes for nailing. Even routing around the boxes by drywallers won't damage them. A flange is provided for sealing the vapor barrier to the box. Comes with instructions. *–A.W.*

**$2.25 each
Resource Conservation Technology**

EPDM CONSTRUCTION GASKETS

During construction, install these gaskets under sills and wall plates and at the perimeter of drywall sheets (between drywall and studs or plates) as an effective temperature, air, and moisture seal.

Resource Conservation Technology has a wide range of EPDM gasket sizes and styles, including 5-inch gaskets specially made for sealing between the foundation and sill. Imported from Sweden, where highest attention is paid to tight construction. *–A.W.*

15¢ to 65¢ per foot in small quantities, Resource Conservation Technology

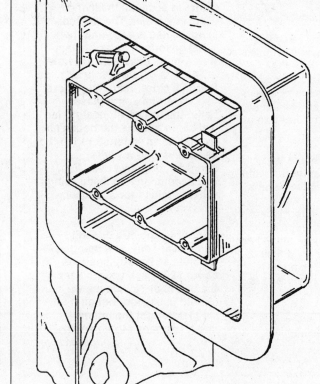

THE HOME THAT HAPPENED TO BE SOLAR

Thirteen years ago my wife and I bought a new home in south-western New Hampshire that contained active and passive solar heating. The mortgage officer asked, "How does it feel to buy something that will be obsolete in ten years?"

My wife, quicker and sharper than I, responded, "Are you telling me that homes will be obsolete in ten years?" As far as we were concerned, this was a house, not a solar house.

Our daughter is now ten years old; to her, the brooklike ripple of water trickling down the glass-covered collectors overhead, though the air temperature is 15° F, sounds as natural as the snap, crackle, and pop of Rice Krispies.

Indeed, living in a home that happens to be solar does create changes in perspective. After a week of sunshine, if I ask my wife in front of visitors, "How's the solar system running?" they look up at the sky and marvel at our dedication to metaphysics. Meanwhile, I'm checking to make sure the water storage is warm enough.

And winter seems different when, even on December 21,

the sun pours through the south glass, reaching the highest point on the back walls of our living and dining rooms.

We've found that our greenhouse gets hot on a sunny day, especially in January when three feet of snow are piled about it. It's such a pleasure to take off my shirt, sit in a beach chair, and absorb vitamin D, amazed that it can be 90° on one side of a piece of glass and 25° on the other.

Standing next to the south glass in our living room are passive, seven-foot-tall, fiberglass tubes that hold 40 gallons of water. They absorb and store heat; they also make wonderful conversation pieces. "No, algae has never grown in them — not even after 13 years." "Yes, some of them still have original water in them." "Yes, they would make delightful fish tanks, but our daughter prefers a tank she can clean, and our cats prefer fish they can reach."

It's 3:15 on December 8. The sun is setting. The greenhouse has dropped to 74° and the cat wants in because the living room is warmer. The roof collector plates are 82° and the 1,800 gallons of solar-heated water in the basement are now at 84°. The outside air is 22°. Soon I'll close insulating doors that cover the south glass. Later, the forced-air heating fan will begin to blow the house air by that warm water stored in the basement, and my wife, daughter, dog, two cats, fish, and accompanying living things will snuggle in for a long winter's nap.

Of course, the sun doesn't shine every day, and using electric heat as backup costs us about $200 each year to keep the house at 70°. Maybe we should use wood; but after all, we just bought the house — and it happened to be solar.
—*Rodger Martin*

SEALING IN THE HEAT

DUPONT TYVEK® HOUSE WRAP

This was the first air-infiltration barrier introduced, and it still seems to be the best wind block that also allows moisture in the wall cavity to pass through.

Tyvek comes in a 200' roll (9' wide) for installation on the outside of the wall sheathing (under exterior siding). Edges should be taped, especially around window and door openings. Properly installed, Tyvek will make a tremendous difference in the overall air-tightness of a building.

We checked with DuPont about use of CFCs in the manufacturing process. Indeed, CFC-11, which is dangerous to the ozone layer, is used as a solvent in the process, but the company claims it recovers and reuses more than 99.9% of the CFC-11 and says it will be replaced with an environmentally safer solvent by 1992. *–A.W.*

From building supply stores nationwide

VENTILATION

ACORN VENT SPACERS

Anyone who has dealt with ice dams will understand the importance of adequate roof ventilation. These are used to provide a continuous air flow channel under the roof sheathing in insulated cathedral ceilings. Simply staple the vent spacers to the sheathing and install batt insulation against them. Because of their design, air can even flow sideways — which can be important for ventilating rafter cavities above and below skylights. We like this product because it's made from recycled paper instead of plastic. *–A.W.*

About 85¢ each for a 4' length
Building Science Engineering

Before ordering from any mail order suppliers, please check with them to determine shipping and handling charges.

"Avoiding danger is no safer in the long run than outright exposure." — *Helen Keller*

HURD INSOL-8 SUPER WINDOW

Hurd Millwork's new R-8 Super Window has two layers of glass and two low-E suspended plastic Heat Mirror™ films — a total of three air spaces. The spaces are filled with a proprietary low-conductivity gas mix. At the edges, where heat loss

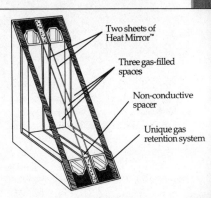

Two sheets of Heat Mirror™

Three gas-filled spaces

Non-conductive spacer

Unique gas retention system

through the aluminum glazing spacer is becoming more and more of a concern in standard windows, Hurd now has an insulating edge spacer between the two plastic films. When you take into account sunlight that enters a house through the glass as well as heat loss, the InSol-8 will actually save more energy than an R-19, well-insulated wall. Available in casement window styles. Cost is 25% to 30% higher than Hurd's current top-of-the line Heat Mirror™ windows. –A.W.

Hurd Millwork

WINDOW QUILT® INSULATING WINDOW BLINDS

Appropriate Technology Corporation pioneered interior window insulation in the mid-1970s with its convenient roll-down insulating blind. The basic product is still the same, but it's now available in lots of designer colors, and the mechanical components (track, pulleys, etc.) are much improved from earlier versions. Window Quilt® more than doubles the total R-value of a standard double-glazed window from R-2 to R-5.2, and it will greatly cut down on air infiltration through the window, too. For summertime use the insulating blind can be used to prevent unwanted heat gain. –A.W.

Cost of Window Quilt® varies greatly depending on the size of the window. For a 6' sliding glass door, suggested retail cost is about $13 per square foot.
Appropriate Technology Corp.

What You Can Do

✔ Write the World Bank to protest their funding of development projects that destroy rain forests. Encourage funding instead for projects promoting sustainable development.

An estimated two billion scrap tires have accumulated in dumps, ravines, and roadsides across the United States.

Building with the Best

What materials should you use in your new home or building project? A good rule of thumb: Stick to natural materials. This means mostly wood, but it can also include ceramic, stucco, stone, or brick.

With flooring, we vote for wood again. Asphalt and vinyl tiles are derived from petroleum and don't last very long, while wood is renewable. Other good picks are stone, brick, ceramic tile, or terrazzo tile, a mosaic flooring made from granite or marble. Brick and tile require a lot of energy to produce, but they last forever with little upkeep.

Make sure the wooden cabinets, counters, and trim are made of solid wood. Avoid particleboard and plywood, if possible, because they contain formaldehyde, which will leak into the air that you breathe. Or seal the exposed edges.

Woods to Watch For: Saving Tropical Rain Forests

Stay away from tropical wood. Once a tropical tree is harvested, it's gone and is unlikely to be replaced.

Most of the tropical hardwoods are from rain forests in the Philippines, Malaysia, Indonesia, South America, and West Africa — but they're bought by consumers in North America, Europe, and Japan. As alternatives, here are some do's and don'ts . . .

Do not buy:

Tropical hardwoods: African walnut, ebony, greenwood, mahogany, rosewood, teak, tulipwood.

Temperate hardwoods: Redwood and cedar (sometimes considered softwoods).

Do buy:

Temperate hardwoods: Alder, apple, ash, aspen, beech, birch, black walnut, cherry, chestnut, elm, hickory, larch, maple, oak, pear, pine, poplar, sycamore.

Temperate softwoods: Pine, spruce, hemlock, and Douglas fir are good alternatives to temperate hardwoods. But be aware of toxic chemicals used to improve their durability.

— *Alex Wilson*

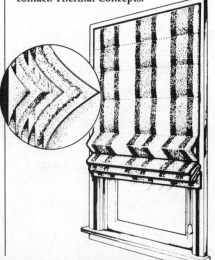

What You Can Do

✔ Don't throw paints, thinners, solvents, varnishes, wood preservatives, or glue down the drain or storm sewer or into the trash. They can eventually leach into the soil and water.

✔ Share leftover paint with others — neighbors, friends, relatives, churches, theatrical groups, high schools, community service organizations, etc. Be sure the paint is in its original container with label intact.

✔ Contain the spill of oil-based paint, solvent, or other hazardous chemical to a small area and soak it up with cat litter, sawdust, wood ash, or soil. Put the material into a plastic pail or other noncorroding container, but don't use a broom or mop (you'd be contaminating them). Volumes greater than a couple of gallons should be taken to a hazardous waste collection.

SMART SHADE™ BY COMFORTEX

Here's another great window-insulating product, complete with solar-powered remote-control motorized opener. Unlike Window Quilt®, Smart Shade™ opens in an accordion fashion, with the insulation provided by the air space between the 2 layers. With the optional metalized coating on 1 of the layers, Smart Shade™ will boost the total R-value of a double-glazed window from about R-2 to R-4.2.

Comfortex also makes the Oasis Sun Shade™, which operates on the same principle but uses a material that blocks most of the sunlight, while allowing some view to the outside. Available through many drapery and interior decorating companies. –A.W.

$8-$12/sq. ft., Comfortex

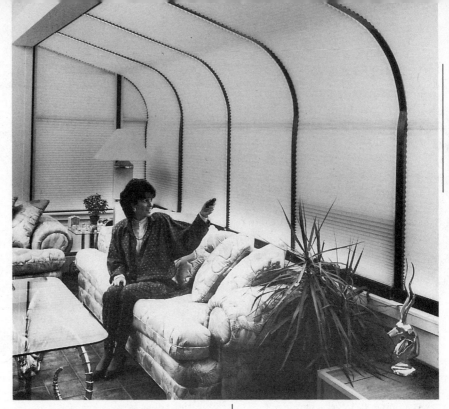

SUNEYE™ INNOVATIVE WINDOW WITH INSULATING SHUTTER

From the creative mind of solar pioneer and inventor Leandre Poisson comes this innovative passive solar window/shutter system. Suneye features insulated (double-layer) fiberglass tubes that serve as windows, with aluminum-faced insulation panels that pivot inside the tubes. When the panels are all the way open, full light comes into the building; when closed, the system provides between R-10 and R-20, depending on the insulation material you select (the company offers several choices).

Perhaps its most unusual feature is its ability either to direct all or part of the available sunlight into the building or to reflect it away, depending on your needs. Suneye windows can be installed horizontally or vertically in walls or overhead as skylights. They can be used singly or in clusters. –A.W.

$450 per unit (about 2'x5') Solar Survival

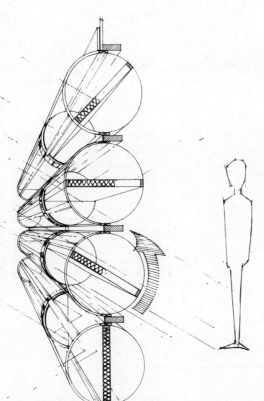

PASSIVE SOLAR DESIGN

Passive solar design is such a good idea that it cannot be left out of the discussion of environmentally smart building. If you carefully plan window placement and building materials, your house can collect and store clean, free solar energy, enabling you to cut heating costs dramatically, increase comfort, and use new, exciting design elements like skylights and greenhouses.

What You Can Do

✔ Never burn particleboard, plywood, or treated wood, because this can give off toxic fumes. Instead, treat all of these items as hazardous waste and take them to a hazardous waste collection.

If 50% of the waste in New York City were recycled, taxpayers would save $456 million annually.

SOLAR PATHFINDER

Is this a good solar site? Is it better over there? One look through this solar site analysis instrument gives immediate, accurate information about year-round potential. You actually see when your site is shaded by trees or buildings. Use it any time of day, any day of the year, clear or cloudy, to quantify shading. Takes the guesswork out of tree trimming to improve solar exposure. While fundamentally easy to use, initial setup and data analysis require following detailed instructions. *–J.W. & S.M.*

$144 (includes carrying case & stand), Solar Pathways Inc.

SOLAR-L-FOIL

Would you believe nighttime solar heating? That's in effect what you get when you apply this "selective surface" to the exterior glass side of a thermal-storage concrete wall. Like space-age wallpaper, this thin self-adhesive black-chrome copper foil acts like a one-way solar sponge, absorbing sunlight during the day and giving it back slowly all night, significantly increasing the amount of energy you save.

Of course your heat storage wall must be properly sized and oriented for maximum effect. Installation requires close attention to detail. Combine it with south-facing windows for daytime solar heating and you'll have an elegantly simple, low maintenance, passive solar heating system. We chose this product for our own homes. *–J.W. & S.M.*

$2.35 per sq. ft., MTI Solar Inc.

SOLAR WATER HEATING

These solar water heaters are our favorites. Give them serious consideration if you have 3 or more people in your home and your site has good southern exposure. Properly sized, they'll save 60% to 80% on your hot-water bill, giving you a return on your investment comparable to that of a good municipal bond. *–A.W.*

COPPER CRICKET SOLAR WATER HEATER

This completely passive solar water heater not only is elegantly simple but also is reliable and reasonably priced. Selected by *Popular Science* as one of the 100 best new technical products of 1989.

The Copper Cricket operates without electricity, using the same pumping action you see in a perking coffeepot to move solar heated liquids through the system. A methanol-water antifreeze fluid (our only environmental reservation about the system) boils in a flatplate solar collector — usually roof mounted. The boiling action "pumps" solar-heated fluids down to a heat exchanger under the regular hot water tank and back up to the collector again. The heat exchanger transfers the solar heat to your hot water tank.

This tank can be as much as 36' below the collector, so you can put it in the basement. (Previous passive systems required the tank to be higher than the collector, a very inconvenient place for a 500-pound tank.) Alternatively, other systems use electric pumps, which add cost and complexity.

The Copper Cricket can be used in both new and existing homes.

With no moving parts, it's very reliable. And you get a 10-year limited warranty. This is an impressive system. *–Hank Huber*

**$1,400 to $1,800
Sage Advance Corporation**

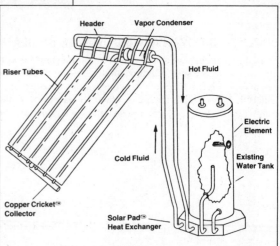

CORNELL 480 PASSIVE SOLAR WATER HEATER

Hooray! A problem-free solar water heater. We love the simplicity of these batch-style water heaters. No moving parts, troublesome pumps, or complicated controls — cold in, hot out. Even in cloudy weather it will warm the water and reduce your backup water heater's energy consumption. High-performance insulation, absorber, and glazing make this 42-gallon unit freeze proof. Easier to retrofit than many active systems, these units are also ideal for integrating into new home construction. And solar-powered showers do feel better! We wish all solar systems were this reliable and maintenance free. *–J.W. & S.M.*

$995 wholesale FOB, Sun Heating Manufacturing Company

If the U.S. recycled just half of the newsprint consumed each year, it would divert almost six million tons of paper from landfills.

RESOURCE-EFFICIENT HOUSING GUIDE: A SELECT ANNOTATED BIBLIOGRAPHY OF HELPFUL ORGANIZATIONS, 1989 EDITION

By Robert Sardinsky. Even before you get into it, a look at the table of contents tells you that this book is packed. It covers more than 125 resource-efficient (notice it's not just energy-efficient) housing-related periodicals, organizations, catalogues, and source books — books on design, construction, and retrofitting; energy-efficient house plans; resource-efficient landscape and site design; even energy-efficient appliances. The list goes on to include sources for help with using renewable energy, financing energy efficiency, shopping for and building resource-efficient housing, and much more. A must for anyone interested in, active in, or teaching about resource-efficient housing. *–Jennifer A. Adams*

$15, Rocky Mountain Institute

Completely revised and expanded 1990 EDITION

THE HEALTHY HOUSE CATALOG

This directory is a must for anyone interested in indoor air quality. It holds a wealth of information on everything from removal of lead paint to heat-recovery ventilation to non-toxic construction. Includes products and services, in-depth articles, helpful tips, and interesting facts. Published annually. Approximately 200 pages. *–A.W.*

$20, Housing Resource Center

THE HEALTHY HOUSE

By John Bower. A most interesting, thought-provoking book about building and living in a healthy, harmonious, and ecologically sound home. Very useful tips throughout and extensive resources at the end. Be prepared for a rather "spiritual" emphasis. About 400 pages. 1989. *–A.W.*

$17.95, Carol Publishing Group

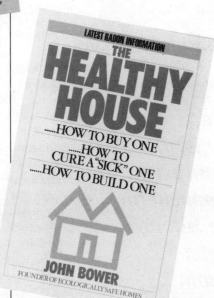

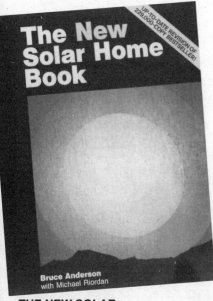

THE NEW SOLAR HOME BOOK

By Bruce Anderson. This 1987 best-seller is a practical, easy-to-follow guide that's just right for anyone who's interested in heating with either passive or active solar energy. Shows you how to site your house for maximum solar gain, do heat-loss calculations, and much more. 204 pages. *–A.W.*

$16.95, Brick House Publishing Co.

What You Can Do

✔ Let used turpentine or brush cleaners sit in a closed container until the paint particles settle. Pour off the clear liquid for reuse. Add cat litter to the remainder and let it dry completely. It is still a hazardous waste, but there is less to dispose of. (See page 38 for information on disposing of hazardous waste.)

YOU SHOULD KNOW

At the current rate of use, by the year 2000, half the world's tropical forests will have been razed for timber and for agriculture. — The Canadian Green Consumer Guide

Recycling saves 64% of the energy used to make paper from virgin wood pulp.

Let the Sun Shine In

I T'S THE DEAD OF WINTER, yet all around me are flourishing plants; the sun is warm on my face, and the temperature is a balmy 78°. Warm moist air envelopes me, and the sweet scent of flowers and herbs is everywhere.

An island in the South Pacific? Nope, it's a sunspace overlooking my backyard in New Hampshire.

Living with Sunshine

Thousands of homeowners across the country have discovered the many psychological, ecological, and economic benefits of adding a sunspace or greenhouse to their homes. I can't think of anything that quite compares to looking out on a snow-covered countryside from inside a sunspace on a cold winter day (except perhaps a rum swizzle in the Bahamas). A few hours a week in a sunny room can dissolve the wintertime blues. And with proper design and solar orientation, a sunspace/greenhouse can also reduce the amount of oil, gas, wood, or electricity required to heat your home.

Imagine harvesting fresh vegetables and herbs for an evening dinner and sitting down to a table adorned with homegrown flowers . . . while there's snow on the ground. All without the herbicides, pesticides, diesel-powered farm equipment, transportation, and refrigeration required for supermarket food.

A sunspace is a part- or full-time living space. It may be a family room, dining room, sitting room, or breakfast nook. Many homeowners are quite content to use their sun rooms only on sunny days. Others use them all the time, adding heat as needed. Either way, it's usually better to separate the sun room from the house with a door. (No use heating an empty sunspace to 65° F at two o'clock in the morning). Houseplants will do quite well with night temps in the 40° to 50° F range.

> *Sunspace. Sun'spās, n. A warm, bright environment for people, plants, and pets; solarium; sun room; solar room; greenhouse.*

A variety of options from Sunplace, Inc.

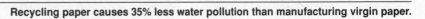

Getting Oriented

For maximum performance try to have the sunspace face within 30 degrees east or west of true south. Keep in mind, though, that a more westerly exposure will be baked by the hot afternoon summer sun.

Energy Give and Take

Should thermal storage — such as concrete, ceramic tile, or water-filled cylinders — be incorporated into your sun room? This is probably the most misunderstood design element in sunspace construction. Basically, thermal storage is used to absorb solar energy during the day to help keep the sunspace itself a little warmer at night. For family room sunspaces, thermal storage eliminates the need for backup heat in the evening. If, on the other hand, the sunspace is only for daytime sitting, you don't need thermal storage. Instead, concentrate on letting your sun room pass the maximum available extra heat to the rest of the house while the sun shines.

Greenhouses

While a sunspace is used primarily by people, a greenhouse is used mostly by plants. Greenhouse operation and design can be quite different from those of a sunspace.

Greenhouses can be freestanding, which gives them the potential advantages of unshadowed locations and the best possible orientation to the sun. The disadvantages of making them freestanding include the outdoor trip to the greenhouse and the loss of excess solar heat to the outside rather than to your living space.

Here thermal storage is an absolute necessity to help maintain minimum temperatures in the 35° to 50° F range. And backup heat is a must for greenhouses in almost all areas of the U.S. The glazing (the glass or plastic envelope that lets the sun in) may be different than for attached sunspaces. Instead of clear glass or plastic, many professional growers prefer foggy translucent glazing; this diffuses sunlight over the entire area, producing more uniform growth and eliminating the "hot spots" common with clear windows. Of course, if you want a view, translucent glazing won't work.

A Gain in the Glass

New types of glass do a much better job at keeping heat in than those available just a few years ago. Some sunspace manufacturers now offer specially coated glass with R-values approaching 5 or more. See page 150 for more information about these exciting types of glass.

Standard (thermopane) insulated glass rates R-2. For sunspaces and greenhouses using auxiliary heat, look for high-performance glass. It is well worth investing an additional ten to 20 percent in the initial cost of a sunspace for lifetime returns of lower heating costs.

THE VEGETABLE FACTORY® SUN PORCH™

The Sun Porch is perfect for a part-time living space where extra heat isn't needed or is kept to a minimum. You can easily convert it from a sunspace to a summer room by replacing the glazing with interchangeable screens.

Some of its best features: The continuous full-length screened ridge vents are operated by a pole, or you can purchase an automatic heat-operated mechanism. The Sun Porch comes with gutter and downspouts. And you can take advantage of some optional features such as exterior-mounted sun shades and awning windows.

But be aware that the Sun Porch must be carefully constructed, especially when it comes to caulking. One owner had to completely remove the roof panels and recaulk in order to stop leaking. Also, the aluminum baked enamel finish is not thermally broken.

Although no foundation is needed and you and a friend might be able to build the sunspace in a weekend (it's been done), don't count on it. It took Pamela Ward and her husband, not amateur builders, a full week. "The directions were very hard to understand," she says. "It was a long, often frustrating experience." –T.M.

Glazing: Roof-insulated GE Lexan® Thermoclear®, bronze tinted. Wall-insulated Plexiglas® DR ®, clear
Guarantee: 5 years, prorated
Accessories: Fans, heaters, growing aids, benches
$4,195 (for nominal 9'x12' attached unit; $39 per sq. ft.) $6,855 (for nominal 9'x12½' freestanding unit; $61 per sq. ft.)
The Vegetable Factory, Inc.

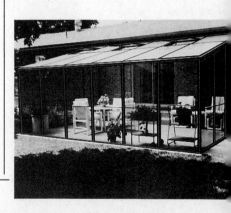

SUN ROOM COMPANY SUNSPACE

You'll find superior workmanship in every Sun Room Company sunspace, from intricate Victorian to classic Colonial to precise Contemporary. The ultimate in redwood-framed sunspaces, every unit is handmade by Amish craftsmen.

The concealed ridge vent system is standard, but exterior mounted sun screens are optional. You can also opt for straight or curved eaves, French doors, all kinds of roof pitches, etched and stained glass, arched grids . . . and you can have the entire thing custom designed. What more could you want? Only a professional crew can install one of these. And plan for a foundation. –T.M.

Glazing: $7/8$" insulated, clear glass
Guarantee: 10 years, full
$9,800 (for nominal 9'x11' attached unit with ridge vent system, swing door, and screen door; $99 per sq. ft.)
Sun Room Company, Inc.

Keeping Your Cool

If the sunspace or greenhouse is to be used during the summer months, pay careful attention to its ability to prevent unbearable over-heating. Many sunspaces have tinted or reflective glazing in the roof to block most of the hot summer sun. Operable windows and/or doors (with screens) are a must. Ventilation fans or movable roof vents can effectively exhaust heat, too. You might even supply some natural shade by growing sunflowers in front of the greenhouse or letting morning glories cover a trellis mounted a few inches from the glazing.

Getting Framed

Sunspaces and greenhouses are either aluminum or wood framed. Wood offers a warm, natural appearance; because cedar and redwood resist moisture, cracking, and warping, they are especially popular choices. Because aluminum is strong, lightweight, and requires little or no maintenance, it's the best choice for high-moisture uses such as greenhouses. If winter heat loss is a factor, make sure the aluminum extrusions are "thermally broken" — isolated from contact with the cold outdoors. Some manufacturers offer sunspaces with wood as the interior framing and aluminum glazing caps on the exterior.

One more consideration: Wood is a renewable resource (assuming the industries logging and processing cedar and redwood replenish their harvests). Aluminum is a non-renewable, non-biodegradable (but recyclable) material manufactured with or mined from Mother Earth.

Go for It!

With the many choices available to the sunspace or greenhouse shopper, you'll have to carefully review features to decide which most suit your uses and your pocketbook. Compare quality, check prices, talk it over with solar space veterans, and have fun visiting some solar spaces. Somewhere out there is a backyard winter retreat just right for you, your family, your plants, and your budget.   — *Tom Minnon*

SUN TALK

When you review the manufacturer's literature, pay particular attention to the following points:

• *Will you need to provide a foundation?* Some sunspaces and greenhouses that use plastic glazing can simply be set on landscape timbers and anchored to the ground. One with glass windows will most likely need a foundation or concrete piers to prevent movement from frost heaving.

• *Who pays the freight from the factory to your home?* This can add hundreds of dollars to the price.

• *Can you install the structure yourself?* Some manufactured rooms are designed specifically for the do-it-yourselfer. Most are best left to qualified installation crews.

• *What about the guarantee?* A guarantee can range from one to ten years. Many manufacturers offer a full replacement policy over the term of the guarantee. Others have prorated guarantees based on how long you've owned the structure. (Of course, Murphy's Law dictates that nothing ever goes wrong until the day after the guarantee expires!)

GREENHOUSE

NORTHERN LIGHT™ GREENHOUSE

The Northern Light is the ultimate greenhouse for growing plants. Owner Janet Helgemoe says, "It's fantastic! I've thoroughly enjoyed it!"

The glossy white north wall and mirrored roof reflect light back onto your plants, and the saltbox shape is designed to provide the greatest possible amount of light in the winter. In the freestanding unit you'll find an insulated and reflective north roof and wall areas. Other features? Roof and front wall panels automatically open with a temperature-sensitive mechanism. Plus, the mill finish, aluminum frame is thermally isolated. You can opt for an exterior summer sun shade, if necessary. Janet Helgemoe says it's a snap to heat, and snow slides off easily — a definite plus in snow country!

No foundation is required. Two people can put this structure together in about two days — a nice weekend project for you and a friend! Then sit back and enjoy *The Growing Connection*, a quarterly gardening newsletter that comes free with your greenhouse.

Quality, durability, and value make the Northern Light one of the best home greenhouses available. –*T.M.*

In recent years Americans have received almost two million tons of junk mail every year.

Glazing: Exterior is Dupont Tedlar 400SE (translucent). Interior is Melinex 071.
Guarantee: 100% money-back guarantee for 6 months. Full guarantee on structure for 5 years. Full guarantee on glazing for 10 years.
Accessories: Fans, heaters, shelving, books, videos, irrigation systems
$3,395 (for nominal 10'x10' attached unit; $34 per sq. ft.)
Northern Light™ Greenhouse

READ MORE ABOUT IT

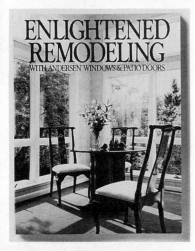

ENLIGHTENED REMODELING WITH ANDERSEN WINDOWS & PATIO DOORS

This booklet is required reading for anyone considering building his own sunspace, room addition, or attic conversion, or simply adding a new window. Although *Enlightened Remodeling* was produced for the Andersen Window people, the information is generic and presented concisely and clearly. Construction sequence photos take you step-by-step through many remodeling and new addition projects. You'll learn about design and planning, structural concerns, cost estimating, and blueprint reading. There's even a section on vital statistics and dimensions (for instance, the width of a room should be no more than 2½ times the window height).

Where else could you discover that the word "window" was derived from "wind eye"? A welcome addition to the building/remodeling home library! –*T.M.*

$6.95, Andersen Window dealers

RESIDENTIAL & COMMERCIAL SUNSPACES, 1990 BUYER'S GUIDE

Don't go sunspace shopping without this excellent guide to more than 100 sunspace manufacturers plus (by state) 350 sunspace builders and dealers. The *Guide* also includes information on what to look for (and look out for) in a sunspace: location, framing, glazing, foundations, cost, hiring a contractor, auxiliary heat, summer shading, and maintenance. This is the "who, what, and where" of the sunspace industry. –*T.M.*

$3.95
Home Buyer Publications, Inc.

SUN ROOM COMPANY, INC.

SPEAKING OF SUN SPOTS

Before you buy, find out as much as you can about the manufacturer and/or dealer of your chosen sunspace. Consider the following:

- Where is the company located? (How high will your shipping costs be?)
- How long have they been in business? (Are they likely to stick around?)
- Is installation available?
- How much manufacturing is done in-house? (Do you have confidence in the quality control? Will replacement parts be available?)
- Does the company have a toll-free customer-service phone line?
- Are accessories — summer shading, fans, heaters, thermal storage, gardening aids, window treatments — available?

Request full literature: installation instructions, owner's manual, guarantees, and — oh yes, prices.

Plugging Into the Sun

Many of these products are also available from catalogues and suppliers listed elsewhere in this section.

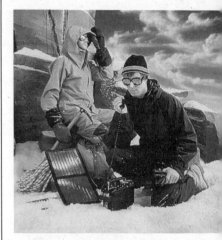

I T SOUNDS ALMOST TOO GOOD to be true: an unlimited supply of power with no strip mining, no pipelines or oil spills, no air pollution, no contribution to global warming or acid rain, and no deadly nuclear waste. Just pure, clean electricity, generated with one of the most elegant and fascinating devices of modern physics — the photovoltaic or PV cell.

Solar cells averaging 25% efficiency and covering just 1% of the land area of the U.S. could supply all of the country's energy.

A PV cell is a remarkable combination of high-tech semiconductor physics and low-tech simplicity and durability. Whenever the sun shines on it, the cell produces electric current — silently and without moving parts. From the most sophisticated communications satellites orbiting the earth to the simplest vaccine refrigerators in Bangladesh, photovoltaics meet power needs without harming the environment.

Photovoltaic technology is environmentally kind at the manufacturing level, too. It starts with silicon, from ordinary sand, and adds extremely safe materials like boron and phosphorus. The amount of energy that it takes to create a PV is far less than what that same PV generates. And while massive use of PVs in large-scale, public-utility-sized PV "farms" would require substantial amounts of land, the U.S. Department of Energy has noted that such farms would actually use less land than current coal-burning plants — when you include in the figuring the land from which that coal is mined.

So why isn't everyone using this miracle source of clean, safe electricity? The technology is extremely promising, but the down side is that PVs require special materials and high-tech manufacturing methods that are expensive and not yet very efficient. While they're already used to pump water, illuminate highway signs, activate train signals, heat remote homes, and fill hundreds of small consumer applications, experts predict it will be at least the turn of the century before PVs will be competitive with old-fashioned power plants.

You don't have to wait, though, to begin benefiting from photovoltaic technology. By using the products reviewed in this section, you can reduce consumption of polluting fossil fuels and help hasten the coming solar age — when clean energy technologies such as photovoltaics will prevail.

— *Alex Wilson*

SUN PAL™ PORTABLE SOLAR GENERATOR

Here's quick and easy power far from home and extension cords. The lightweight and unbreakable Sun Pal™ Portable Solar Generator fits in your backpack, picnic basket, or handbag. Open it up, put it in the sun, and plug in your portable radio, TV, or other small appliance.

The smallest Sun Pal folds to just 6"x10" and produces 2 watts at 6 volts in full sunlight. That's plenty to keep a small battery-powered radio fully charged. For larger radios, TVs, and other equipment, you may need the 6- or 12-watt chargers. The 6-watt model is 6 volts. The largest is 12 watts at 12 volts — ideal for maintaining a charge or recharging a car or boat battery. Other accessories available. Sovonics is a pioneer in PV technology. –*A.W.*

$60 to $200 (depending on size)
Sovonics

The amount of sunlight that strikes the U.S. each year is 500 times more than the energy we use.

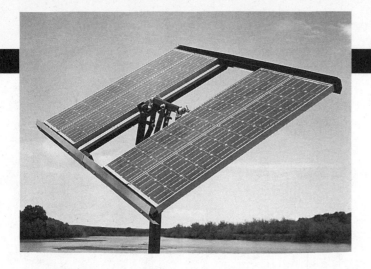

PV TRACK RACK

Like an elegant giant sunflower that turns its face toward the sun, the Track Rack is always adjusting to catch the most solar energy on your expensive photovoltaic panels. It collects up to 40% more than stationary installations — at least in the summer. It is ideal for summer water-pumping needs like garden irrigation and livestock watering. Wintertime gains, however, are often much less significant.

Carefully engineered and constructed of high-quality materials, this modern-looking hardware will last. These trackers work best in sunny climates and will withstand very high winds. *–Johnny Weiss and Steve McCarney*

$330 (2-panel model); also available in 4-, 6-, 8-, and 12-panel models (up to $990); Zomeworks Corporation

SILENT GENERATOR™

PV for your RV! Going off-road? Your tranquil stay at the campground can be ruined by a loud gasoline-powered electric generator used to recharge batteries. Now you can have the power without the noise, pollution, fumes, and vibrations. Solarmetrics provides a power system for any size recreational vehicle (RV), complete with top-quality batteries, PV panels, and controls. The panels mount on your vehicle's roof, out of sight from the ground but in full view of the sun. An optional inverter supplies alternating current for appliances, computers, etc. *–A.W.*

$500 to $4,000, Solarmetrics

ADVANCED HOME POWER SYSTEM

This one is for out-of-the-way homes. The cost to run utility lines on poles to a remote site can be $20,000 a mile. More and more remote home owners are choosing instead to make their own power with photovoltaics.

Photocomm's Advanced Home Power System is equipped with eight 47-watt PV modules, mounting hardware, wiring, controller, inverter (for AC power), batteries and a backup generator. This system can satisfy the electricity needs of a small low-energy house. In an "average" U.S. climate it will provide power to fill all of the following sample demands combined each day: 4 hours of a 15-watt fluorescent light, 8 hours of a 30-watt light, 4 hours of 25-watt incandescent lighting, 5 hours of 35-watt incandescent lighting, 3 hours of color television, 5 minutes of food blender use, 1 hour of vacuuming (per week), and 2 loads of laundry (per week). That's not a lot of power consumption, but you can get by if you're careful. What you cannot have is electric heat, electric hot water, or a standard electric refrigerator.

Such a system is not cheap, but it's worth it when the only alternatives are robbing a bank or heating your water over a fire. Home solar-power systems like this are easy to upgrade with additional panels, batteries, etc. *–A.W.*

$8,000, Photocomm

THE SCIENCE OF THE PV SANDWICH

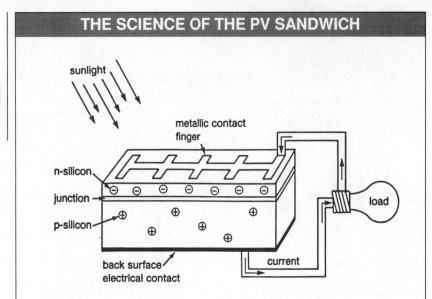

sunlight

metallic contact
finger

n-silicon

junction

p-silicon

back surface
electrical contact

load

current

A photovoltaic cell is a wafer-thin sandwich of materials with varying electrical properties. The side facing up reacts to sunlight, or any light, by giving off electrons. These flow to the collector cell on the other side. A one-way "junction" between the two sides keeps the electrons from flowing back. As a result, a charge builds up, in effect creating a miniature "battery" with positive and negative sides. Connect a wire between the two and voilà! Flowing electricity! Connect more cells together, and you get more power. It's that simple.

PV PRODUCTS

DELUXE SOLAR FLASHLIGHT

There are quite a few solar flashlights on the market, but this one is expressly designed for rugged use. It is unique in that the batteries themselves contain the PV cells: sunlight shines through the clear plastic flashlight barrel to keep them charged. A belt clip allows charging while you hike. Built to military specs, this is no cheap light. –A.W.

$45, Jade Mountain Trading Company

SOLAR LANTERN

This tough solar-powered light was used at the base camp on the first winter climb of K-2, the world's second-tallest mountain. At 3.3 pounds, it's a good hefty lantern — definitely not a toy. The Solar Lantern has a 6-watt fluorescent bulb that puts out about as much light as a 25-watt incandescent light bulb — certainly enough to read by in your tent on those warm summer nights in the woods. Then strap it on top of your pack or canoe the next day or tie it to your tent for recharging.

On a full charge, the Solar Lantern provides up to five hours of light. Even with daily partial discharge, the built-in batteries should last for years. If you always store the Solar Lantern in a sunny place, the batteries will last longer and always be ready to go. It can be kept charged through a bedroom window or through the rear window of a car. –A.W.

About $100, Heliopower

The No. 1 exports out of the ports of Boston and New York City are scrap paper and scrap metal.

PV PRODUCTS

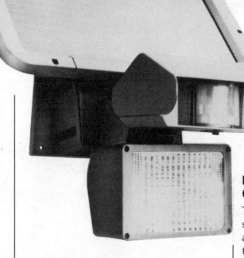

PARMAK SOLAR FENCE CHARGER

Keeping the family cow or horse where you want her is a cinch with this PV-powered fence charger. Just mount it on a fence post with the PV panel facing south. With enough battery power to operate for 21 days in total darkness, you shouldn't have any trouble keeping it going even through a long dark winter. No promises made for keeping goats out of the roses, though. –A.W.

About $185
Widely available in farm stores and most renewable energy catalogues

DIGILITE™ SOLAR HOUSE NUMBER LIGHT

With the Digilite you can light up your house numbers without using old-fashioned electricity. A small PV module and battery light up the highly visible 4" numbers. Just four hours of sunlight will provide three full nights of illuminated numbers. A photosensor turns the Digilite on at dusk and off at dawn. The unit mounts in the ground or on a wall, and an 8-foot wire connects the PV module to the lighted numbers. If the three AA NiCd batteries ever wear out, you can replace them; the lamps will last indefinitely. –A.W.

About $90, Sunergy

SOLAR SENTINEL™ OUTDOOR SECURITY LIGHT

The Solar Sentinel uses a PV panel to charge a battery during the day, and at night a special infrared motion detector switches on a bright halogen security light when it senses motion within about 75 feet, scaring away would-be intruders or lighting your way out to the recycling bins. It will stay on for as long as three minutes after the motion stops.

As with other PV lights, there are no wires or calls to an electrician. Mount the panel in sunlight up to 12 feet from the light. On a full charge, the Solar Sentinel will turn on up to 120 times. –A.W.

About $140, Sunergy

MIGHTY MULE SOLAR GATE OPENER

This item is proving to be a great seller in suburbia as well as in farm and ranch country. A PV panel keeps the battery charged. You can open the gate from your vehicle using the remote controller. The rugged hydraulics will easily open and close gates up to 16 feet wide, weighing up to several hundred pounds. Can also be opened manually. –A.W.

About $800
Jade Mountain or Photocomm

NEW BREEZE HOME COOLING SYSTEM

Air-conditioning is most important when the sun is shining, right? Well, why not use solar power to provide that cool air? The New Breeze is a PV-powered evaporative cooler, a form of air-conditioning that makes most sense in dry climates, such as the Southwest. It won't function well with relative humidity over 75%.

A 48-watt PV panel is used to power the atomizer pump and fan. The PV panel acts as a "smart thermostat" — when the sun is its brightest, the unit provides the most cooling. In addition to adding cool moisture to your house, it also filters out dust, pollen, and some pollutants. An optional battery-storage package allows the unit to work at night, too. –A.W.

About $430; optional PV panel $350 to $450
Photocomm

Nine percent of U.S. energy comes from renewable sources, especially hydropower and wood.

(Left) A photovoltaic first: The Carlisle House in Massachusetts, by Steve Strong Associates.

(Bottom) Photovoltaics power the Caltrans snow removal station in California.

Packaging accounts for 50% of the volume and 30% of the weight of all municipal waste.

PV CATALOGUES & OTHER SUPPLIERS

PHOTOCOMM, INC.

Probably the largest supplier of PV equipment in the world. A distributor for numerous products, the company also manufactures some equipment itself. With experience supplying thousands of remote home PV systems, these folks know what they're talking about. Fifty-page full-color catalogue available. –A.W.

REAL GOODS TRADING COMPANY

At 320 pages, *The Real Goods Alternative Energy Sourcebook* is the most comprehensive catalogue of PV equipment and components, energy-efficient lighting, and appliances available. Loaded with valuable information, such as how to figure lighting system sizes. Cover price is $10. –A.W.

MORE PV SUPPLIERS

These suppliers offer a full line of PV equipment and components, including energy-efficient lighting and appliances:

Jade Mountain Import-Export Co.

Alternative Energy Engineering

Sunnyside Solar

Sunelco

Backwoods Solar Electric Systems

READ MORE ABOUT IT

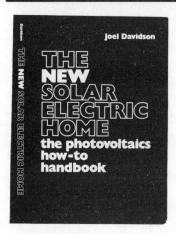

THE NEW SOLAR ELECTRIC HOME

By Joel Davidson. A great start for anyone serious about building a PV-powered home. –A.W.

$18.95, Aatec Publications, 1987

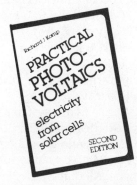

PRACTICAL PHOTOVOLTAICS

By Richard Komp. This book is geared toward the do-it-yourselfer. Nowhere else will you get as much information on assembling your own PV modules. Excellent information on how PV cells work. –A.W.

$16.95, Aatec Publications, 1984

THE SOLAR ELECTRIC INDEPENDENT HOME BOOK

By Fowler Solar Electric. Excellent how-to on photovoltaics for the remote home. Detailed information on wiring and components. –A.W.

$15.95, Fowler Solar Electric

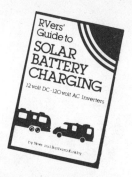

RV-ERS' GUIDE TO SOLAR BATTERY CHARGING

By Noel and Barbara Kirkby. Written by experienced RV travelers who needed a better way to charge their batteries. Lots of practical experience presented here. –A.W.

$12.95, Aatec Publications, 1987

HOME POWER MAGAZINE

This is the only publication we know of devoted exclusively to home power in remote locations. Includes practical, how-to articles on photovoltaics, hydropower, wind, and all system components needed in remote homes. Published bimonthly. –A.W.

$6 annual subscription Home Power

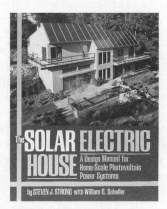

THE SOLAR ELECTRIC HOUSE

By Steve Strong. Very good book on PV-powered homes by one of the pioneers. Particularly informative about powering conventional homes with photovoltaics, whether connected to the power company or not.

$19.95, Rodale Press, 1987, or order directly from Steve Strong

---

"We must get past this business of hearing the phrase, 'We need more study.' We must act." — *Robert Redford*

HYDRO POWER

Water Power For Home Electricity

IF YOU DON'T HAVE EASY ACCESS to utility lines but you do have a stream with some vertical drop to it, we may have just the solution to your electricity needs: a "micro-hydro" power system. Used as a battery charger, a small hydro generator costing less than $1,000 can provide as much power as photovoltaic panels that cost ten times as much.

Here's how the system works: Water flows downhill through a buried pipe to a hydro turbine/generator unit. The vertical drop, or head, puts the water under considerable pressure. When the water reaches the bottom of the hill, it shoots through one or more small nozzles to turn the Pelton wheel (or a modified Pelton wheel called a Turgo wheel), which turns the generator to produce electricity.

> *Hydro power supplies 10% to 12% of U.S. electricity.*

The electricity from micro-hydro systems is typically used to charge batteries, just like the electricity from PV panels and wind generators. A lot of hydro generators today are used to supplement PV power systems. All of the micro-hydro systems now on the market can operate with very low flow rates.

Costs for putting in a hydro system vary greatly, depending primarily on the amount of work required in damming the stream and burying pipe. While the hydro unit itself may cost less than $1,000, the installation can easily run $2,000 or more at some sites (still usually less than PV systems). And, like other remote power systems, your hydro system will probably need batteries, a voltage regulator, an inverter (if you want AC electricity), and a backup generator. All of these are additional costs. When the Anderson-Kohlers installed their system in 1980, it cost them $10,000 for all materials. Since they buried the pipe and installed the equipment themselves, they had no labor costs.

Before getting started with a micro-hydro system, you should contact your state Fish and Wildlife Service or Environmental Department; you may need a permit to change the flow of a stream.

For more information on hydro systems, check with one of the manufacturers listed here, or contact one of the independent power catalogue companies listed in the Photovoltaics section on page 169.

— *Alex Wilson*

listed in the Photovoltaics section on page 169.

LIVING WITH A MICRO-HYDRO SYSTEM

Since 1980 our private power plant — a Pelton wheel and 70 feet of head — has produced more than enough electricity for our family of four . . . most of the time. During the dry summer months, we anxiously eye the sky looking for black clouds, but we rely on eight PV panels and good ol' energy conservation.

It's stressful to yo-yo constantly between abundance and drought, so recently we plugged into our local utility. Only as a backup, mind you. We purchased a Gentran transfer switch (about $250 at your local electrical parts store), a delightful gadget that lets some or all of the circuits switch between the hydro system and the power company.

I still love the thrill of turning on a light and knowing I'm using renewable energy. But now Joe can run his power tools without blowing the circuits, and we can freeze our garden produce without worrying about cleaning out the freezer in time for the dry season.

Would we do it again? Absolutely. After ten years we've worked out most of the bugs so that the system requires only minimal maintenance — an occasional greasing of the turbine and sweeping of leaves away from the pipe intake. We've needed to replace only the batteries.

And the best part is not feeling hostage to the fossil fuel industry!   —*Mona Anderson*

Fully 35% of the earth's land surface is in various stages of desertification.

HYDRO POWER PRODUCTS

HYDROCHARGER I AND II

These are the smallest and simplest micro-hydro systems on the market — but they pack a lot of bang for the buck. Depending on the stream flow and feet of head, Hydrocharger I can equal the power output of five to ten 40-watt PV panels; Hydrocharger II can equal the output from more than 25 PV panels. The Hydrochargers are all-in-one systems for fast, easy hookup and low maintenance. They use permanent magnetic generators. Costs do not include installation and other system components (batteries, wiring, inverter, etc.). –A.W.

$600 Hydrocharger I;
$900 Hydrocharger II
Photocomm, Inc.

POWERHOUSE PAUL'S STREAM TURBINE

Along with Don Harris of Harris Hydro, Paul Cunningham is the only other full-time manufacturer of micro-hydro systems. He, too, makes each machine himself. The Powerhouse Paul's Stream Turbine, like the Harris system, uses an automotive-type alternator, but the turbine is somewhat different. Instead of a Pelton wheel, it uses a Turgo wheel, which allows a larger-diameter jet of water. In addition to manufacturing the Powerhouse Paul, the company makes turbines for Photocomm's Hydrochargers. –A.W.

$700 to $1,400, Energy Systems and Designs

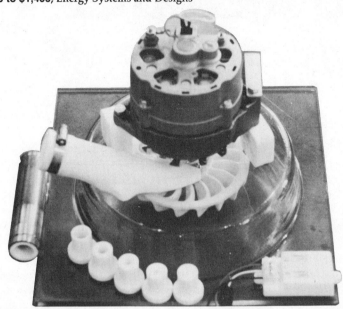

HARRIS HYDRO SYSTEM

Use these for larger hydro systems with 40 to 600 feet of head and up to a 200-gallon-per-minute flow. This system generates up to 1.5 kilowatts of continuous power from 600 feet of head and a 30-gallon-per-minute (gpm) flow or from 200 feet of head and a 100-gpm flow. In more typical stream conditions (75 feet of head and a 20-gpm flow) the Harris will crank out 125 watts. (Remember that, unlike PV panels, a hydro system operates around the clock, whenever the water's flowing.)

Don Harris makes every one of his quality machines himself. Each system includes an individually balanced Pelton-type wheel cast from silicon bronze. An automotive-type alternator is used for power generation. Costs depend on the number of nozzles in the Pelton turbine housing and the type of alternator and voltage regulator used. Pipe, wiring, controls, batteries, and inverter can add $4,000 for large systems. –A.W.

$700 to $1,400, Harris Hydro

HARRIS HYDRO

On the Road To a Better World

W E BLAMED EXXON when the *Valdez* spilled 11 million gallons of crude oil into Alaska's Prince William Sound in the spring of 1989. But we neglected to acknowledge our collective obsession with cars — and their insatiable thirst for oil — as the root of the problem.

No nation in the world uses more oil than the U.S. or wastes it so carelessly — mostly because of our persistent addiction to driving private vehicles to get just about anywhere, whether it's across the country or to the corner store. At the rate we're squandering this precious, non-renewable resource — which nature took millions of years to create — the world supply of oil will be completely spent in just 30 years.

First, the Bad News

Every mile you drive uses precious petroleum and creates poisonous pollution. Even the blacktopping of roads adds to air pollution. Ironically, a simple ride in the country can actually prove harmful to nature!

The average car in America dumps its own weight in carbon dioxide into the atmosphere every year.

Automobiles being what they are, no model is entirely clean. But we'll tell you how to make the best of an imperfect situation by showing how to buy an efficient car and identifying those cars with the best and worst fuel economy. Then we'll check out how you can help the environment and your pocketbook by improving your car's operation and maintenance. We'll also examine the prospects for better fuels and some simple, too-often-overlooked alternatives to conventional motoring. But first a little motivation.

Driving Is a Dirty Business

In case you didn't know . . . Each of the millions of autos on the road today puts a slew of poisonous chemicals into the air we all need to breathe. According to the EPA, your exhaust fumes contain:

Carbon dioxide. Burning just one gallon of gas creates 22 pounds of this, the major contributor to global warming.

What You Can Do

✔ Look for low-solvent or water-based auto paints, de-icers, and engine cleaners that are free of earth-warming CFCs. Some common auto supplies, especially paints, are environmental toxins.

✔ Fill up your tank at service stations that have sleeves or hoods on their gas pumps to protect you and the atmosphere from poisonous vapors such as benzene.

EASY RACER HPV (HUMAN-POWERED VEHICLE)

The 18-speed Easy Racer HPV cuts wind resistance by 30%, allowing you to travel faster and farther with less fatigue. Pedaling from a slightly reclined position increases your comfort because your back is fully supported, your arms are relaxed, and your neck is straight. Like the Hammacher Schlemmer model, this high-tech bicycle is made of lightweight but strong aircraft-grade steel. The Easy Racer is shipped in 2 boxes with all controls hooked up and adjusted, so it takes only 30 to 45 minutes to assemble. –L.H.

$1,795, Sharper Image

JADE MOUNTAIN FOLDING BICYCLE

Now you'll have no excuse to leave your bicycle behind when you go traveling. This collapsible single-speed 2-wheeler fits easily into a car trunk, recreational vehicle, or boat compartment. The bike is simple but fully equipped with coaster brakes, a carrier rack, reflectors, a tool pouch, and other standard features. Weighs 34 pounds and comes in a blue enamel finish over a steel frame. –L.H.

$160, Jade Mountain

FOLDING BICYCLE

This ingenious folding bicycle has 3 speeds. Though it can support a rider weighing up to 250 pounds, it folds down quickly to one-eighth the size of a full-size bike (28"x18"x9") so it fits in your car trunk or even under a train seat. Features include a center pull brake; luggage rack; front, rear, and side reflectors; a chain guard; kick stand; and vinyl carrying bag. This bike weighs only 28 pounds. And unlike others, you don't have to take it apart to fold it. –L.H.

$299.50, Dahon California, Inc.

The annual contribution of rubber tires to the waste stream dropped from 2.3 to 1.7 million tons from 1975 to 1986.

Hydrocarbons. Cars emit half of the nation's total hydrocarbons, which come from partially burned fuel. Hydrocarbons are a "greenhouse gas," which contribute to global warming.

These nasty compounds also create a ground-level ozone smog, which should not be confused with the ozone layer in the upper atmosphere that protects us from harmful sun rays. Ground-level ozone is a serious lung irritant. Children and asthmatics are particularly susceptible. In addition, ground-level ozone damages plants and forests and can reduce crop yields by as much as one-third.

Benzene. This toxic, flammable hydrocarbon causes leukemia.

Nitrogen oxide. This gas will kill you if you inhale it in an enclosed place. It also causes acid rain, which kills lakes and trees.

Particulates, or Soot. Particulates reduce visibility, damage plants, blacken buildings, and possibly contribute to cancer and other diseases.

Lead. This element is an ingredient in the gasoline used by older cars. If absorbed in substantial quantities, lead can seriously damage the brain and central nervous system.

It All Adds Up

With so many pollutants dumped into our thin atmosphere, it's no wonder that 150 million Americans — more than half the nation's population — live in areas in which the EPA's smog limits were exceeded at least once in 1988. Most of these areas are in the Northeast and other urban centers such as Los Angeles and Houston. The accumulation is so bad that back in 1981 the space shuttle *Columbia* spotted a large plume of carbon monoxide drifting off the East Coast.

And it's not just the air that's at stake. Roads take up space. Each time a new highway is built, more acres of land and life are smothered under asphalt.

It's true that cars have become more efficient since the OPEC oil crisis of 1973, which spurred consumers to worry about their wallets as much as the environment. The phaseout of leaded gas and the use of catalytic converters — which convert hydrocarbons and carbon monoxide into water vapor and carbon dioxide — have helped. So have "leanburn" engines, which use more air and less fuel than average engines.

But still more can and must be done. Technology exists for cars to get nearly 100 miles per gallon. Yes, 100! For example, Toyota's prototype AXV weighs in at 98 mpg. This nearly doubles today's best. Such cars, among other things, use more lightweight materials, such as reinforced plastic and aluminum body parts and ceramic engine parts. (Whether that plastic can be recycled is another issue.)

Despite efficiency improvements, the EPA predicts that by 1994, motor vehicle emissions will increase for the first time since 1970, simply because there are more people on the road driving more miles.

The Hog and the Chickadee

Of course, in addition to its effect on the environment, car fuel economy has an enormous effect on the all-important pocketbook. Take, for example, the Chevrolet Corsica and the Rolls-Royce Bentley, two mid-size passenger cars on opposite ends of the fuel-efficiency spectrum. The EPA estimates that the Corsica, with its five-speed manual transmission and four-cylinder engine, achieves a respectable 24 miles per gallon in the city and 34 on the highway. The Bentley, by comparison, with an automatic transmission and eight cylinders, rates ten miles per gallon in the city and 13 on the highway. Assuming 15,000 miles per

What You Can Do

✔ To get the best mileage, inflate tires to the maximum pressure indicated on the sidewall; an estimated 50 percent or more of the tires on the road are under inflated.

✔ Check your tire pressure before driving long distances. Under-inflated tires wear out faster and cost four percent more in fuel.

✔ Keep your engine tuned up, especially if you notice a drop in your car's fuel efficiency. Clogged fuel filters make your car use more gas. Get a tune-up every 7,500 miles.

✔ If you've had a tune-up but fuel economy isn't what it used to be, have your car's fuel injector checked. It may be staying open all the time, the result of dirt or a damaged part.

✔ If you feel your car should be getting better fuel economy, have the thermostat checked. A cold-running engine will dramatically reduce fuel efficiency. Engine temperature is controlled by a thermostat valve.

✔ Replace old hoses in your car's air conditioner every three years so that ozone-depleting CFCs won't leak out. Ask your service station to use CFC recovery equipment when repairing auto air conditioners.

✔ Slow down. A difference of just ten miles per hour — from 65 to 55 — cuts your fuel consumption by 15 to 30 percent and reduces nitrogen oxide emissions. The average car gets the best mileage at 40 mph.

ALTERNATIVES TO INTERNAL COMBUSTION

What You Can Do

✔ To conserve water, cut down on car washing. Shut off the water flow from the hose while soaping your car.

✔ If your antifreeze is less than two years old, try to reuse it. Check its protection level first. Then strain it through a clean rag before replacing it.

THE LAND ROWER

Pedaling not your style? Then check out the Land Rower, a 3-wheeled vehicle that is powered by rowing, using the same stroke and muscle groups that you use in a quality rowing shell. The only differences are that the Land Rower is forward facing, and its variable geometry steering adds to its stability and maneuverability. Not only is the Land Rower light (55 pounds) and quick (over 30 miles per hour), but it also gives you a great aerobic workout, conditioning your heart and lungs while exercising your legs, back, abdomen, and arms. –L.H.

$1,875, LandRower Inc.

THE VOLT BOAT

Here's an alternative to the standard motor boat and its noise pollution: the Volt Boat, powered by a 12-volt "deep-cycle" battery. The Volt Boat will power 2 or 3 passengers at speeds up to 10 miles per hour. It has 5 forward and 3 reverse speeds and draws less than a foot of water, which makes it easy to maneuver through hard-to-reach or shallow areas. This boat, 12' long and 90 pounds, is made of a durable weather-resistant plastic that's lighter than fiberglass. Standard features include 2 padded, folding Bass seats, navigation lights, cockpit cover, carpeting, electric bilge pump, and a flag to wave in the breeze. The battery runs 6 to 8 hours before it needs recharging. –L.H.

$1,650, Real Goods Trading Company

OVER TIRED

Americans generate scrap tires at a rate of 240 million a year. An estimated two billion have accumulated in dumps, ravines, and roadsides across the country.

What can be done? Shredded tires can be added to asphalt pavement, extending its life four to five times. In Modesto, California, old tires are used as fuel for electrical power generation. Recycled tire rubber can also be used for making new tires, adhesives, wire and pipe insulation, brake linings, conveyor belts, carpet padding, roofing, hoses, sporting goods, and more.

A recycled tire material called Tirecycle, added to virgin rubber, can reduce a rubber manufacturer's costs by 20 to 50 percent. Producing recycled rubber requires 71 percent less energy in manufacturing than producing virgin rubber. Most tires contain less than 10 percent recycled rubber; this could easily be increased to 30 percent. Support tire dealers and local and regional organizations involved in recycling tires for products or energy.

Packaging accounts for 50% of all paper produced in the U.S., 90% of all glass, and 11% of aluminum.

year, the Corsica uses about $500 in gas each year, while the Bentley uses about $1,500 worth. Driving the Corsica would save you almost $1,000 in fuel costs each year over the Bentley.

Those who can't afford a Rolls may take comfort in the knowledge that the Bentley is one of many automobiles subject to the EPA's "gas-guzzler" tax (in effect since 1980). Any model that gets fewer than 22.5 miles on a gallon of gas is taxed from $500 (for lesser offenders) to $3,850 for the really heavy drinkers.

The Right Stuff

Assuming you're now sufficiently inspired to be counted among the more ecological drivers on the road, here's what to look for in your next set of wheels (from *The Car Book* by Jack Gillis; Harper & Row, Publishers, Inc.; © Jack Gillis).

Transmission. Generally, manual transmissions are more efficient than automatic ones. A four-speed manual transmission can give you up to 6.5 more miles per gallon than a three-speed automatic. A fifth gear adds to the advantage. An overdrive feature can save gas in both types — three percent for manuals and nine percent for automatics.

Engine size also affects fuel economy. The smaller the engine, the better your mileage. Of course, there's a trade-off in power.

Tires. Radial tires can give you three to seven percent better mileage than regular bias-ply tires. They last longer and help your car handle the road better, too. Steel-belted tires are generally the most efficient. If all the cars in the U.S. were equipped with the most efficient tires possible, the fuel savings would be 400,000 barrels of oil per day.

Cruise control. Driving at a constant speed uses less fuel than changing speed often, so this feature can help you save gas.

Air-conditioning. An air conditioner makes your car less efficient because it adds weight and robs the engine of some of its power to operate. This can decrease your fuel economy by eight to twelve percent or up to three miles per gallon in city driving. Auto air conditioners also use 25 percent of the chlorofluorocarbons in the U.S.

On the highway, however, an air-conditioned car does just as well as a car with all the windows rolled down, because of added wind resistance. Consider buying a cutoff switch, which automatically turns off the air conditioner during quick acceleration. This can improve the fuel economy of air-conditioned cars by about four percent. Also, light colored cars and white interiors are considerably cooler.

Trim and power options. A trim package can include decorative features, soundproofing, and undercoating. Power options include power steering, brakes, seats, windows, and roofs. All of these add to the weight of your car and reduce gas mileage. If the weight of your car increases by ten percent, your fuel economy will drop by four percent.

Origin of manufacture. Consider where your new car is coming from. The farther away, the greater the resources used to transport and deliver it. Obviously, it takes more energy to get a car manufactured in Japan to the U.S. showroom than one made in Detroit.

Gasoline "saving" devices. Sorry to say, with few exceptions they don't work. The EPA has tested nearly 100 air and vapor bleeders, fuel-line devices, fuel and oil additives, and mixture enhancers — and found that only six of the products improved a car's fuel economy, with just marginal improvements — so marginal that fuel "savings" did not justify the costs of the products.

What You Can Do

✔ Never pour used oil or transmission fluid down the drain, into the sewer, or onto the ground. Just one quart of oil can contaminate up to 250,000 gallons of drinking water. Used auto fluids can be recycled by your auto mechanic or service station, along with old car batteries.

✔ Support service stations that recycle! And take old antifreeze and brake fluid to a hazardous-waste collection site.

✔ Dispose of your used motor oil by taking it to a service station. Try to find one that sends used oil back for recycling.

✔ Try windshield washer fluid and antifreeze revitalizers, among other products from Chief Auto Parts, Inc., labeled as "environmentally safe and biodegradable."

✔ Or make your own windshield washer fluid by combining three parts white vinegar to one part water. This solution will keep windows ice free.

✔ If you spill antifreeze or other vehicle fluids, wipe them up and dilute the area with water. Be careful: antifreeze has a sweet smell and taste that can attract animals and children, but it is toxic.

THE MISER'S DERBY

MAKE & NAME OF CAR	ENGINE SIZE in liters/ no. cylinders	TRANSMISSION TYPE	MPG city/hwy	ANNUAL FUEL COST based on 15,000 miles/year
The Chickadees				
Geo Metro XFI	1 L, 3 cyl	man 5-spd	53/58	$259
Geo Metro LSI	1 L, 3 cyl	man 5-spd	46/50	296
Geo Metro	1 L, 3 cyl	man 5-spd	46/50	296
Suzuki Swift	1 L, 3 cyl	man 5-spd	46/50	296
Honda Civic CRX HF	1.5 L, 4 cyl	man 5-spd	43/49	320
The Hogs				
Lamborghini Countach	5.2 L, 12 cyl	man 5-spd	6/10	$2,250
Chevrolet C 1500	7.4 L, 8 cyl	auto 3-spd	10/11	1,715
Rolls Bentley	6.8 L, 8 cyl	auto 3-spd	10/13	1,565
Rolls Corniche III	6.8 L, 8 cyl	auto 3-spd	10/13	1,565
Rolls Bentley Eight/Mulsan	6.8 L, 8 cyl	auto 3-spd	10/13	1,565
Rolls Silver Spirit II/Spur	6.8 L, 8 cyl	auto 3-spd	10/13	1,565
Dodge B350 Wagon	5.9 L, 8 cyl	auto 4-spd	10/13	1,565

Now, we bet you're thinking you could never pay for a Lamborghini anyway (let alone the gas) or wondering how you're going to fit your kids, the puppy, and the groceries into a two-seater. Hold your horsepower. We know different people need different things from their wheels. So we've compiled a chart of the best and worst vehicles of all types, according to the EPA.

MAKE & NAME OF CAR	ENGINE SIZE in liters no. cylinders	TRANSMISSION TYPE	MPG city/hwy
Two Seaters — Best			
Honda Civic CRX HF	1.5 L, 4 cyl	man 5-spd	43/49
Honda Civic CRX	1.5 L, 4 cyl	man 5-spd	32/35
Two Seaters — Worst			
Lamborghini Countach	5.2 L, 12 cyl	man 5-spd	6/10
Ferrari Testarossa	4.9 L, 12 cyl	man 5-spd	10/15
Mini-Compact Cars — Best			
Volkswagen Cabriolet	1.8 L, 4 cyl	man 5-spd	25/32
Volkswagen Cabriolet	1.8 L, 4 cyl	auto 3-spd	23/28
Mini-Compact Cars — Worst			
Porsche 928 S4	5 L, 8 cyl	man 5-spd	13/19
Maserati 222 E	2.8 L, 6 cyl	auto lockup, 4-spd	15/18
Porsche 928 S4	5 L, 8 cyl	auto 4-spd	15/19
Maserati 222 E	2.8 L, 6 cyl	man 5-spd	15/20
Subcompact Cars — Best			
Geo Metro XFI	1 L, 3 cyl	man 5-spd	53/58
Geo Metro LSI	1 L, 3 cyl	man 5-spd	46/50
Geo Metro	1 L, 3 cyl	man 5-spd	46/50
Suzuki Swift	1 L, 3 cyl	man 5-spd	46/50
Daihatsu Charade	1 L, 3 cyl	man 5-spd	38/42
Subcompact Cars — Worst			
Rolls Bentley	6.8 L, 8 cyl	auto 3-spd	10/13
Rolls Corniche III	6.8 L, 8 cyl	auto 3-spd	10/13
Maserati 430	2.8 L, 6 cyl	auto lockup, 4-spd	15/18
Maserati 430	2.8 L, 6 cyl	man 5-spd	15/20
Chevrolet Camaro	5.7 L, 8 cyl	auto lockup, 4-spd	16/24

Honda Civic CRX HF

Suzuki Swift

One gallon of gasoline can contaminate 750,000 gallons of drinking water.

Volkswagen Jetta

Ford Escort

Saab 9000

THE MISER'S DERBY continued

MAKE & NAME OF CAR	ENGINE SIZE in liters no. cylinders	TRANSMISSION TYPE	MPG city/hwy
Compact Cars — Best			
Volkswagen Jetta	1.6 L, 4 cyl	man 5-spd	37/43
Ford Escort	1.9 L, 4 cyl	man 4-spd	32/42
Isuzu Stylus	1.6 L, 4 cyl	man 5-spd	32/37
Pontiac LeMans	1.6 L, 4 cyl	man 5-spd	31/40
Compact Cars — Worst			
BMW 535 I	3.4 L, 6 cyl	auto lockup, 4-spd	15/21
Volvo 780	2.8 L, 6 cyl	auto 4-spd	17/21
Jaguar	4 L, 6 cyl	auto lockup, 4-spd	17/22
Mid-Size Cars — Best			
Chevrolet Corsica	2.2 L, 4 cyl	man 5-spd	24/34
Plymouth Acclaim	2.5 L, 4 cyl	man 5-spd	24/32
Dodge Spirit	2.5 L, 4 cyl	man 5-spd	24/32
Mazda 626/MX-6	2.2 L, 4 cyl	man 5-spd	24/31
Mid-Size Cars — Worst			
Rolls Bentley Eight/ Mulsan	6.8 L, 8 cyl	auto 3-spd	10/13
Rolls Silver Spirit II/Spur	6.8 L, 8 cyl	auto 3-spd	10/13
BMW 750 IL	5 L, 12 cyl	auto lockup, 4-spd	12/18
Audi V8	3.6 L, 8 cyl	auto lockup, 4-spd	14/18
Maserati 228	2.8 L, 6 cyl	man 5-spd	14/19
Large Cars — Best			
Saab 9000	2 L, 4 cyl	man 5-spd	21/28
Chevrolet Caprice	4.3 L, 6 cyl	auto lockup, 4-spd	19/27
Large Cars — Worst			
Cadillac Brougham	5.7 L, 8 cyl	auto lockup, 4-spd	14/21
Cadillac Fleetwood/ DeVille	4.5 L, 8 cyl	auto lockup, 4-spd	16/25
Small Station Wagons — Best			
Honda Civic	1.5 L, 4 cyl	man 5-spd	31/34
Dodge/Plymouth Colt	1.5 L, 4 cyl	man 5-spd	28/34
Mitsubishi Mirage	1.5 L, 4 cyl	man 5-spd	28/34
Toyota Corolla	1.6 L, 4 cyl	man 5-spd	28/33
Small Station Wagons — Worst			
Toyota Camry	2.5 L, 6 cyl	auto lockup, 4-spd	19/25
Chevrolet Cavalier	3.1 L, 6 cyl	man 5-spd	19/28
Mid-Size Station Wagons — Best			
Chevrolet Celebrity	2.5 L, 4 cyl	auto lockup, 3-spd	23/31
Mid-Size Station Wagons — Worst			
Audi Quattro	2.2 L, 5 cyl	man 5 spd	17/24
Large Station Wagons all have the same mpg			17/24
2 WD Small Pickups — Best			
Ford Ranger	2.3 L, 4 cyl	man 5-spd	24/29
GMC S15	2.5 L, 4 cyl	man 5-spd	23/27
Nissan Hardbody	2.4 L, 4 cyl	man 5-spd	23/27
Chevrolet S10	2.5 L, 4 cyl	man 5-spd	23/27

In the United States, on average, an acre of trees is cut down every five seconds.

THE MISER'S DERBY continued

MAKE & NAME OF CAR	ENGINE SIZE in liters no. cylinders	TRANSMISSION TYPE	MPG city/hwy
2 WD Small Pickups — Worst			
Ford Ranger	2.9 L, 6 cyl	auto lockup, 4-spd	17/21
GMC S15	4.3 L, 6 cyl	man 5-spd	17/23
Chevrolet S10	4.3 L, 6 cyl	man 5-spd	17/23
2 WD Large Pickups — Best			
Toyota Truck	2.4 L, 4 cyl	man 4-spd	23/28
Dodge Dakota	2.5 L, 4 cyl	man 5-spd	21/28
2 WD Large Pickups — Worst			
Chevrolet C 1500	7.4 L, 8 cyl	auto 3-spd	10/11
Dodge D100/D150/D250	5.9 L, 8 cyl	man 4-spd w/ creeper first gear	10/14
4 WD Large Pickups — Best			
Jeep Comanche	2.5 L, 4 cyl	man 4-spd	20/24
Mitsubishi Truck	2.4 L, 4 cyl	man 5-spd	19/22
Toyota	2.4 L, 4 cyl	man 5-spd	19/22
4 WD Large Pickups — Worst			
Dodge W100/ W150/W250	5.90 L, 8 cyl	man 4-spd w/ creeper first gear	10/14
Cargo Vans — Best			
Chevrolet Astro 2 WD	2.5 L, 4 cyl	man 5-spd	21/26
GMC Safari 2 WD	2.5 L, 4 cyl	man 5-spd	21/26
Cargo Vans — Worst			
Dodge B350 Van 2 WD	5.9 L, 8 cyl	auto 4-spd	11/14
Ford E150/E250 Econoline	5.8 L, 8 cyl	auto lockup, 4-spd	11/15
Passenger Vans — Best			
Nissan Van	2.4 L, 4 cyl	man 5-spd	18/21
Mitsubishi Wagon	2.4 L, 4 cyl	auto lockup, 4-spd	18/21
Passenger Vans — Worst			
Dodge B350 Wagon	5.9 L, 8 cyl	auto 4-spd	10/13
Dodge B150/B250 Wagon	5.9 L, 8 cyl	auto 4-spd	11/13
2 WD Special Purpose — Best			
Suzuki Sidekick	1.6 L, 4 cyl	man 5-spd	27/28
Plymouth Voyager	2.5 L, 4 cyl	man 5-spd	22/28
Dodge Caravan	2.5 L, 4 cyl	man 5-spd	22/28
2 WD Special Purpose — Worst			
Dodge AD150 Ramcharger	5.9 L, 8 cyl	auto 4-spd	12/14
4 WD Special Purpose — Best			
Suzuki Samurai	1.3 L, 4 cyl	man 5-spd	28/29
Suzuki Sidekick	1.6 L, 4 cyl	man 5-spd	26/28
4 WD Special Purpose — Worst			
Dodge AW150 Ramcharger	5.9 L, 8 cyl	man 4-spd w/ creeper first gear	10/14
Jeep Grand Wagoneer	5.9 L, 8 cyl	auto 3-spd	11/13

Honda Civic Wagon

Ford Ranger

Toyota Truck

YOU SHOULD KNOW

Motor vehicles use almost two-thirds of all the oil consumed in the U.S.

Changing to a low-flow shower head saves approximately 27¢ of water a day and 51¢ of electricity for a family of four.

Alternative Fuels:
Around the Corner and Down the Road

There's no such thing as an ecological car — especially when the car runs on gasoline. None of the fuels that can power automobiles is completely benign, but gasoline may be the worst. The EPA estimates that toxic fumes from gasoline are responsible for about 1,800 cancer cases a year. And did you know that your car engine pollutes even when it isn't running, because the sun's heat causes some gasoline to evaporate?

From a strictly environmental standpoint, the best thing you could do is not drive at all, and we wholeheartedly support using alternatives whenever possible. But accepting the fact that society as we've structured it would collapse without cars, here's a look at some fuels that are potential gasoline substitutes.

Diesel: Some Good, Some Bad

Cars that run on diesel fuel instead of gasoline generally get more miles per gallon and last longer. Diesel cars are lead free and give off less carbon monoxide and fewer hydrocarbons. But they also produce more particulates, nitrogen oxides, and sulfur dioxides than gasoline engines that have pollution-control devices. And they're noisier. Not a real alternative.

"Reformulated Gasoline":
Same Cookie, New Recipe

This option is popular with both the oil and auto industries. The idea is to alter the composition of gasoline to reduce the toxic emissions of older cars, which produce more than their share of pollutants. This cleaner gasoline can cut emissions from cars made before 1975 by four to nine percent.

The advantage of cleaner gasoline is that it doesn't require costly, time-consuming engine conversions. But given the magnitude of the problem we face, its environmental gains, while worthy, are a drop in the bucket.

Natural Gas: A Clean Burn

Natural gas is a high-octane fuel that is already used for cooking and heating. Because it burns more completely than gasoline, natural gas creates much less pollution, cutting emissions of hydrocarbons and carbon monoxide by 40 to 90 percent and carbon dioxide emissions by 30 percent. Natural gas is lead free and emits almost no toxic formaldehyde. And it is cheaper than gasoline — about 70¢ for the same amount of energy you'd get from a gallon of gasoline. Cars that run on natural gas are expected to cost about $800 more than conventional cars. However, that cost, or the cost of converting the car you already own, could be made up in fuel savings.

Unfortunately, natural gas probably isn't practical for the average passenger car driver living outside urban areas. With natural gas, you'd have to refuel much more often than with gasoline (about every 100 miles or so) or weigh down your car with extra, bulky fuel tanks. Also, although there's plenty right now, natural gas is not a renewable resource.

What You Can Do

✔ If you sail, motor, or fish offshore or in lakes, clean up all waste, including fishing line, so aquatic creatures and birds won't swallow trash or become entangled and suffer.

✔ Never discharge boat sewage closer than three miles from shore.

✔ Better yet, use pump-out facilities back in port; if none exists in your area, get involved and see that local officials arrange to provide this service.

✔ Use only approved chemicals in boat holding tanks or other systems.

✔ Don't spill gasoline or oil — just one cup in sensitive areas can kill many thousands of baby quahogs.

✔ Clean, scrape, and paint your boat away from water. Avoid or cut down on cleaners and antifouling compounds.

If every car in the U.S. were equipped with the most efficient tires, the fuel savings would be 400,000 barrels of oil per day.

SUMMARY OF FUEL COMPARISONS

Although no alternative energy source presents the perfect replacement for gasoline, the push to find one (or several) is likely to continue, as indeed it must. Here's the current state of the debate:

DIESEL
Pro: Lower carbon monoxide and hydrocarbon emissions.
Con: Higher emissions of particulates, nitrous oxides, sulfur dioxides.

REFORMULATED GASOLINE
Pro: Slightly lower exhaust emissions for cars made before 1975; requires no engine conversion.
Con: Environmental gains are minimal.

NATURAL GAS
Pro: Clean burning, substantially lower exhaust emissions; relatively abundant supply; cheaper than gasoline.
Con: Need to refuel often; not a renewable resource.

METHANOL
Pro: Lower exhaust emissions, especially for hydrocarbons (though not as low as natural gas or ethanol); lower output of carbon dioxide, unless derived from coal.
Con: Double the output of carbon dioxide if derived from coal; higher emissions of formaldehyde; cars more expensive to buy and run.

ETHANOL
Pro: Cleaner burning, substantially lower exhaust emissions than gasoline (except for carbon dioxide); made from renewable resources.
Con: Emits toxic aldehydes; twice the cost of gasoline; requires vast amounts of agricultural land for production.

ELECTRICITY
Pro: Emits no pollutants. If electricity is made from clean, renewable resources, environmental impact is minimal.
Con: If electricity comes from a coal plant, greater carbon dioxide emissions than those produced by a gasoline-powered car; if electricity is made from nuclear fuel, radioactive-waste problem intensifies. Batteries require six to eight hours' recharging for every 60 to 100 miles.

HYDROGEN
Pro: Emits no pollutants; 15 to 45 percent more efficient than gasoline. Environmental impact depends on source of electricity to separate hydrogen.
Con: Fuel needs excessive storage capacity; engine costs could double. Practical use decades away.

What You Can Do

✔ Remove unnecessary articles from your car. Each 100 pounds of weight decreases fuel efficiency by one percent.

✔ Avoid short trips when possible. They use more gas because your car is usually cold. For the first mile or two, a cold vehicle gets only 30 to 40 percent of the mileage it gets when it is warmed up.

✔ Drive smoothly. Gradually changing speeds saves gas. Avoid sudden stops and starts.

✔ When possible, time trips to avoid idling in congested traffic, a real waste of gas. Just 30 seconds of idling can use more gas than it takes to start your car. Turn off the engine at drive-up banks or while waiting to pick up the kids.

ANNUAL FUEL COSTS

The Annual Fuel Costs chart will help you estimate how much you will save by buying a more efficient car. The costs are based on 15,000 miles of driving per year.

EST MPG	DOLLARS PER GALLON		
	1.45	1.25	1.05
50	435	375	315
45	483	416	350
40	544	469	394
35	622	536	450
30	724	624	525
25	870	750	630
20	1088	938	788
15	1451	1251	1050
10	2175	1875	1575

One auto repainting job can release 25 pints of harmful solvents into the atmosphere, which adds to smog and forest damage.

Methanol: Panacea or Pandora's Box?

Much has been made of methanol as the most likely successor to gasoline. Proponents tout methanol as cleaner burning than gasoline (though not as clean as natural gas). Compared to gasoline, methanol can cut the emission of hydrocarbons and carbon monoxide in half. Except in its coal-derived form, which actually doubles carbon dioxide emissions, it also reduces the emission of carbon dioxide by ten percent.

Methanol also would require less engine conversion than some other fuels. Already, it has been blended with gasoline (up to five percent). And a fuel blend known as M85 — 85 percent methanol and 15 percent gasoline — is seen by many as the fuel of the future.

Using M85 would require an engine conversion for today's autos. But the Big Three domestic auto makers — Chrysler, Ford, and General Motors — already have a jump on production of their first generation of "flexible-fuel" cars, due out in 1993.

The flexible-fuel car would be able to run on any mixture of gasoline and methanol. A fuel sensor in the engine would determine the fuel mix and feed that information to an on-board microchip (computer), which would adjust the fuel injection and spark timing for greatest efficiency.

Though cars that run on methanol would have 20 percent more horsepower and faster acceleration than gasoline-powered cars, they would also be more expensive to buy and run. They would sell for about $300 to $2,000 more. And mile for mile, methanol would cost noticeably more than gasoline until prices evened out around the turn of the century.

Methanol has its critics. They say it would be inconvenient to fill up twice as often as with gasoline. And because methanol erodes some kinds of plastics and metals, you'd have to be especially careful not to spill it on your car or tire while filling. Also, methanol emits about five times the amount of formaldehyde, a suspected carcinogen, as gasoline.

Nevertheless, federal and state governments seem convinced that developing methanol is the best alternative to gasoline, probably because it is relatively easy to produce from abundant natural gas. You may be able to judge methanol's assets and flaws for yourself, in the not-too-distant future.

Ethanol: Moonshine in Your Fuel Tank?

Ethanol, called "grain alcohol" because it is derived primarily from corn, is methanol's cleaner cousin. Though it emits carbon dioxide and toxic aldehydes, ethanol burns more cleanly than methanol and has a higher energy content. It is also less corrosive than methanol.

Ethanol is already in use in small amounts, having first been added to domestic gasoline supplies during the 1973 oil crisis. Today it supplies half of the auto fuel used in Brazil.

Unlike methanol, ethanol can be made entirely from renewable resources — not only corn, but also sugar cane or wood. But it does have some serious practical drawbacks: it is very expensive (about twice the cost of gasoline) and requires a vast area of agricultural land for production. Even if the nation's entire corn crop were made into ethanol, that would supply only 20 percent of our motor-vehicle fuel needs at current levels of efficiency.

What You Can Do

✔ Drive less. Walk more. Bike more. Or carpool. And take the train! Or at least the bus. Public transportation is much more efficient than single- or double-passenger cars, gallon for gallon.

✔ Van pool, and reduce hydrocarbons, carbon monoxide, and nitrogen oxide up to 80 percent.

✔ Ride the bus. Doing so can reduce hydrocarbons by almost 90 percent and carbon monoxide by more than 75 percent from the emissions created if each passenger were instead riding in a single-passenger car. In the same way, buses can reduce nitrogen oxide and particulate emissions by ten or 15 percent.

IN TRAINING FOR A BETTER ENVIRONMENT

Consider . . .

• When everyone on an average train ride is traveling by train in place of a single-occupancy car, the result is that hydrocarbons and carbon monoxide emissions are cut by more than 99 percent, nitrogen oxide by more than 60 percent, and particulates by more than 90 percent. And commuter trains use about one-sixth as much energy per passenger as single-occupancy cars.

• Trains are the most efficient and inexpensive way to move large numbers of people and goods because they can carry more people and goods at one time than any other mode of transportation. If the trains are electrically powered, the only pollution they create comes from the power plants that generate the electricity.

• Trains are cost effective, too, when you compare the cost of upkeep of rails and train cars

to the upkeep, frequent expansion, and new construction of roads. In fact, trains can help to reduce the continual expansion, repaving, and disruption associated with roads.

• Every cubic yard of highway macadam contains 240 pounds of oil-based asphalt. Steel rails, rock rail beds, and wooden ties contain no oil. At 55 percent capacity a nine-car, long-haul train with one engine gets 98.5 passenger miles per gallon. By comparison, automobiles average 59 passenger miles per gallon (averaging two to three passengers), while airplanes get 27 passenger miles per gallon.

• During the 1980s more than a dozen cities throughout the country successfully established Light Rail Transit systems for their commuters. New LRT systems like the ones in San Diego, California, and Portland, Oregon, have attracted strong ridership, proved to be cost effective,

and encouraged more energy-efficient land-use patterns.

You'd think that with a "track" record like this, trains would be a preferred mode of transit throughout the nation — both in rural areas where long distances can isolate people without cars and in cities that cry out for better air and less traffic congestion.

FLIGHTS OF FANCY

Then there's the human-powered aircraft. In April 1988 a Greek bicycling champion named Kanellos Kanellopoulos flew (pedaled) an aircraft 72 miles across the Mediterranean Sea before crashing into the water 20 feet short of the landing area.

The aircraft was named Daedalus after the legendary

ancient Greek engineer who escaped from a prison by flying on wings of feathers and wax. The modern-day Daedalus is something like a glider powered by pedals, which in turn spin a propeller. Naturally, this mode of commuting is still in its infancy. But so was the horseless carriage at one time. Who knows what tomorrow will bring?

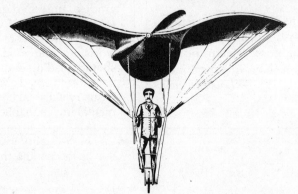

YOU SHOULD KNOW

In 1947, when we had passenger trains everywhere carrying people and mail in an energy-efficient system, the U.S. exported 164 million barrels of oil and imported 159 million. Thirty years later, when the rail system was in decline, the U.S. exported 88 million barrels and imported three billion barrels.

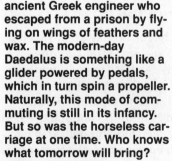

"Unless we change our direction, we are likely to end up where we are headed." — *old Chinese proverb*

A Plug for the Electric Car

Presently, the electric car is the cleanest alternative to gasoline because it is quiet and produces no nasty emissions at all. And it would be ideal in city traffic because it uses no energy when idling or braking.

But the electric car's environmental soundness depends entirely on how its electricity is produced. If it came from nonpolluting, renewable sources such as solar, wind, or hydro power, the electric car would be very ecological indeed. But if the electricity came from a coal plant, carbon dioxide emission would be greater than that caused by a gasoline-powered car. And if the source were nuclear power, the world's radioactive waste disposal problem would only be intensified.

Then there's the problem of storing the electricity. The lead-acid batteries used in today's experimental electric cars (such as the BMW prototype, Elektro) can weigh up to half a ton and require six to eight hours of recharging every 60 to 100 miles.

Electric cart marketed by Real Goods Trading Company.

Hydrogen: A Good Thing Down the Road

The fuel with the most promise, but the furthest away in developmental terms, is hydrogen. As a compressed gas or liquid, hydrogen could be used to power an engine much like today's models, while providing 15 to 45 percent more energy efficiency than gasoline.

Because the hydrogen would be produced by separating water molecules through electricity, it would emit almost no pollutants — primarily steam. And if the electricity were generated with renewable resources rather than fossil fuels, the overall environmental impact of the hydrogen car would be minimal.

The hydrogen-powered car has a long way to go before it is road ready. The cost of making and storing hydrogen is high, and the very low temperature requirements of the car's fuel injection system could double the cost of an engine. But when it leaves the lab, we'll meet it at the door.

— *Leda Hartman*

CHECKING YOUR FUEL ECONOMY

It is always helpful to have some idea of how many miles per gallon your car is getting so you can check the effectiveness of any improvement measures you take. Here's how to determine your car's actual MPG.

- **When filling up, note the present odometer reading.**

- **Don't refill until your tank is nearly empty. Then write down the odometer reading again and the number of gallons it takes to fill the tank.**

- **Subtract the first odometer reading from the second. Divide the result by the number of gallons of gas you just bought. This is your miles per gallon.**

You'll get the most accurate estimate if you repeat these steps several times, because a variety of factors can affect fuel economy, including weather, your car's condition, and road and traffic differences.

What You Can Do

✔ If you have an older car without a catalytic converter, try Arco's new grade of unleaded gasoline for just that type of vehicle. This new product reduces emissions, and good sales should goad other oil companies concerned about the industry's dismal environmental image to follow suit.

✔ Use high-quality motor oil; it lasts longer and therefore is less wasteful.

In a 1986 Roper poll 37% of the respondents said they couldn't get along without aluminum foil, 45% without Scotch tape.

TWO WHEELS ARE BETTER THAN FOUR

Next time you make a short trip, remember your bike. Making a ten-mile round trip on your bicycle three days per week, instead of making that same trip by car, eliminates a half ton of poisonous carbon dioxide each year!

The problem we face here in the U.S. is that people — and government policies — don't take the bicycle seriously as a form of transportation. Although the Netherlands is a very different country from the U.S., consider: It has 12,000 miles of established bicycle paths and half the trips in that country are made on two wheels instead of four. Amsterdam even keeps specially designated bicycles around town for free public use: You simply get on, ride to where you're going, get off, and leave the bike on the curb for the next person. No one rips off the bikes because they don't need to — there's always one around to use.

If you're an urban dweller who's considering commuting by bike, you shouldn't necessarily be scared off by worries about breathing in congested air. A study of 35 New York City couriers in 1989 showed that carbon monoxide levels in their blood were actually slightly lower at the end of a work day than at the beginning. The average evening level was .87 percent, well below the accepted safety standard of two percent. Although the study didn't measure other toxins in the blood, it

suggested that exercising actually may have helped the couriers eliminate the carbon monoxide they were exposed to.

In order for bicycles to get the recognition and use that they deserve — as the most healthful, ecological, and efficient alternative on the road — we need to change our transportation and land-use policies. We need to encourage bicycle use, as is done in Europe, by creating special bicycle travel lanes and parking areas and devising traffic regulations and licenses for riders, for safety and to prevent theft.

SOLAR ROLLERS

When you're considering alternatives to conventional cars, how about a solar car? Solar cars are just as user friendly as gasoline-powered ones. They work like this: Photovoltaic solar cells, usually mounted on the roof, convert sunlight into electricity. The electricity is fed into an electric motor, which turns the car wheels or is stored in batteries to power the car at night or under cloud cover.

There are a variety of solar car designs, including one with a combination solar collector and sail. So far, solar car publicity has centered mainly around racing. The original Tour de Sol race, which has been held annually in Switzerland since 1985, has led to other competitions in the U.S. and Australia. In these races the cars cover hundreds of miles over a period of days and accelerate to speeds of more than 60 miles per hour.

STEVE LOWE

The winner of the Australian race, the Sunraycer by GM, exhibited some intriguing possibilities. It beat all the other cars hands down; when the Sunraycer reached the finish line, its nearest rival was 600 miles behind. It is made of a lightweight synthetic

material stronger than steel and runs on three specially designed, aerodynamic bicycle wheels. The Sunraycer has a tiny, high-efficiency engine of just two horsepower, which allows the car to go as fast as 65 miles per hour using only 1,000 watts of electricity — about the same amount of power as a hand-held blow-dryer. In gasoline equivalents, that's 300 miles per gallon!

STEVE LOWE

The potential advantages of the solar car — the fact that it doesn't create smog or need petroleum to run — have spurred true believers to keep on working. When you consider the fact that most people commute an average of ten to 20 miles a day and that with existing technology a full day of sun will store up to 50 miles of power, you can believe the possibilities are there.

America would save $1 billion in imported oil a year if only 10% of the population rode bikes to work.

Earthship Safaris

ECOTOURING, the earth-friendly "alternative safari" — is catching on big in the 1990s. Over two million Americans each year choose vacations in the wild, shooting exotic birds and beasts not with guns but with cameras, following in the footsteps of Lowell Thomas, Marlin Perkins, and Jacques Cousteau.

> *The primary goal of most wildlife preserves is the long-term conservation of habitats and species. It is not to provide tourists with the best photo opportunities.*

Today the adventurous traveler can, with a little luck and luggage, get to any continent or country in the world within 24 hours. But the current explosion of access has brought serious new concerns about the impact of all this human traffic on wilderness areas and native peoples: Humans tend to disturb the peace of natural places, befoul the environment with waste, upset and endanger animal life in numerous ways, and interfere with the local community.

It's not surprising, then, that for many years conservation organizations denounced as just another form of pollution any programs for travel into the world's pristine natural areas to view wildlife. Today, however, environmentally sensitive tourism can provide a vital source of income for the people who live in wilderness areas, thus creating a key incentive for preserving those areas.

A perfect example is the rain forests of Central and South America. Soundly run tourism based on the attraction of a pristine forest can offer its owners an alternative to clear-cutting for, say, farming. On the other hand, if the development that inevitably accompanies burgeoning tourism is poorly planned and executed, the inevitable result will be the death of both the wilderness and the wilderness travel industry. Much is at stake.

Ecotourism, although not precisely defined, is a term used to describe travel into wilderness areas that maximizes the potential of saving those areas in their pristine condition for generations to come.

An Ecotour by Any Other Name

Just because a travel tour is called "ecotourism" doesn't mean that it is. The term has become very popular, but it can have little meaning if a tour provider using the word doesn't adhere to sound environmental principles. Some operators make meager donations to reserves and for-

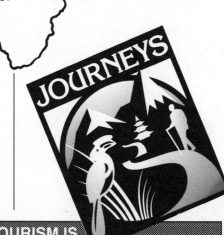

Africa under a rainbow

JOURNEYS

Journeys has a unique approach to its programs — designing them around the group of people who sign up. It cares about the environment, actively working with wildlife experts to make sure its travelers do not adversely impact the area. Everyone we spoke with agreed that the service and programs are good.

ECOTOURISM IS

Excursions into areas untouched by man to see birds, mammals, reptiles, amphibians, and flora living free in natural habitats. These trips include photo safaris, snorkeling, and diving trips (without spearfishing).

• **Trips to relatively undeveloped archaeological sites.**

• **Volunteer research and work programs, with participation in ongoing research in the natural sciences and archaeology. Or volunteer work repairing trails or building facilities at national parks, research stations, etc.**

• **Educational travel programs that have specific objectives such as teaching the principles of tropical ecology.**

• **Consumptive ecotravel may include some types of research where specimens of plants and/or animals are taken. Hunting and fishing would also be included in this category.**

ECOTOURISM IS NOT

Ecotourism generally does not include sports-related outings like mountain climbing, skiing, camping, or hiking. Nor does it include family recreation and day-trip activities like picnicking or general nature studies. These activities may not necessarily be harmful to the environment — although they can be — but they are usually carried out in parks and recreation areas rather than in pristine reserves.

What You Can Do

If ecotourism is not in your stars, but camping and hiking are, here are some ways to keep your impact on the environment minimal.

✔ "Pack it in, pack it out" is a well-known backpacking rule. Try to leave a convenient pack pocket available for carrying out litter you find along the trail.

✔ Give yourself enough time at the end of the day to find a camping site that will notice your presence the least.

✔ Bone up on the types of wildlife you are likely to meet. The more you know, the better you can observe without disrupting them.

✔ Most backpackers prefer to have no contact with others. To lessen your visibility, use gear and wear clothing that blends in with the landscape.

✔ Read either of two good books on enjoying the outdoors in environmentally sensitive ways: *Soft Paths*, by Bruce Hampton and David Cole (Stackpole Books), or *Backwoods Ethics*, by Laura and Guy Waterman (Stone Wall Press).
                                            –Ellen Ruggles

eign conservation organizations to prove how much they "care." One company with a poor environmental reputation has purchased a small piece of woods in Costa Rica and advertises it as a "virgin rain forest preserve." So don't use these gestures to measure the ecological commitment of a tour provider.

How can you recognize a true ecotour operator and select a good ecotour? Here are some important tips to keep in mind.

Who's in Charge Here?

Only about one in 20 nonprofit organizations has program coordinators who know anything about travel, the locations that are being visited, or wildlife conservation.

Just because a tour company advertises in *Audubon*, don't assume it is ecologically oriented or even reputable. Often large companies will create a subagency with a more acceptable sounding name that includes "nature," "conservation," "adventure," or even "ecotour." They buy programs or itineraries outright or possibly work with operators in the country where a nature reserve exists. They pick dates, add their markup, create the advertising, and sell the packaged product to eager conservationists like you. Frequently no staff with scientific, natural history, or conservation training is involved.

Indeed, even a tour offered by your local zoo, museum, or university is no more likely to be an ecotour than one from a travel company, because such groups rarely organize the tours themselves. Instead, they are usually only the marketing vehicle for the tour operators. The tour receives the direct or implied endorsement of the organization, which receives either a direct donation from each traveler or, hidden in the price, a kickback per passenger.

Happily, there are a few true ecotour operators that do care about and support conservation, that are reputable in planning and carrying out eco-sensitive policies, and that responsibly practice appropriate restraints when taking travelers into natural areas.

Are Ecotours Expensive?

Yes, because they are difficult to arrange. In addition to communi-cation costs to remote, often foreign locations, organizers must pay large insurance fees. This covers liability for accident and injury to travelers, plus "agent insurance" against unforeseen calamities (such as unscrupulous ground operators skipping back into the jungle after receiving their setup money from the U.S. It happens.).

"I'll Do It Myself!"

What if you do contact directly the land operator in the country you wish to visit? Chances are you may save a little, especially if you have access to a fax machine, but be aware that you may get lost in the shuffle, you won't get group discounts, and you won't have anyone to complain to if reservations aren't what you expected. Besides, have you ever tried to call Lima, Peru, during the day? Average tries before success usually run around 50. Other countries are even worse, and the chance of getting an English-speaking person on the other end is about one in ten! Qué pasa! Then can you describe exactly where it is you want to go (in Spanish or Chinese), figure out how to get there, and coordinate air and land travel schedules (trains, ferries, buses)?

ECOTOUR OPERATORS

Moderately Recommended

These companies often have good programs, but they are not always careful about the conservation measures their tours use. Services range from very good to just acceptable.

VOYAGERS

The service is excellent and so are the educational materials. In most places the operators are good, but do check; the quality is not consistent.

INTERNATIONAL EXPEDITIONS, INC.

Excellent itineraries, and many zoos and conservation groups use its services. But sometimes the programs and service are sloppy — poor pre-departure services, poor follow-through with travelers. The airline ticketing services are very weak. Be sure your actual itinerary will be the same as what was published. The best programs are in the Peruvian Amazon, Kenya, Belize, and Costa Rica.

FUN SAFARIS

Excellent African programs, but stay away from its tours in other countries. It hasn't reviewed or changed methods for viewing wildlife, and it is not always in keeping with strict conservation standards. Although the programs vary in quality, most are successful.

WOOD STAR TOURS

Provides small, limited birding programs and uses good operators to develop its programs. It may be overzealous at times in chasing down birds, but generally has a good reputation.

JOSEPH VANOS PHOTO SAFARIS

Programs are good, but all too often guides give in to demands by participants — at the expense of wildlife. Service is fine.

© JOEL SIMON/SOCIETY EXPEDITIONS

VOYAGERS INTERNATIONAL

From Zodiac landing craft, expedition travelers photograph seal pups and king penguins in South Georgia Islands.

WATCH OUT FOR DETOURS

We once received nearly identical itineraries from two different operators. The only difference: $300. Investigation revealed that the cheaper tour was operated by a taxi driver who had copied the itinerary of the other organizer, a legitimate licensed land operator. Buyer beware!

How Do I Pick a True Ecotour Operator?

- *Know where you want to go, and why.* Ecotourism isn't for everyone, and you really may want more general outdoor recreation.
- *Do not call or visit your friendly travel agents.* They are experts at making computerized reservations, not at getting you into the real, primitive backwater areas of the Amazon basin.
- *Compare.* Pick up several of your wildlife conservation, zoo, or museum magazines, and ask for itineraries from the wildlife or cultural companies that advertise in those publications.
- *Check the local reputation of your tour organization.* Find out who the land operator is within the country or area of your destination. Get names of authorities who issue permits to land operators to use the reserves. Write or fax them for info on your potential guides. (Don't call if language barriers are a problem.)

Evaluating Ecotour Itineraries

Consider the following:

- *How much of the time will you actually be viewing wildlife?* Mornings are very important. Time in cities, "for shopping," is usually a cost-cutting measure for the operator.
- *How many days will you have in each locality?* The more days, the greater the experience and opportunity to see the often elusive wildlife. It will also minimize the tiring effects of traveling.
- *How much bus, air, and train travel are involved?* Is all airfare and transportation included in the price? Are the logistics well planned? Get a map and check it out. Are there double-backs? How much of the country do you get to see? Are there long drives with little opportunity for viewing as you try to get from place to place?
- *How many people are in the group?* More than 15 is fine in a museum, where stuffed critters can't run and hide, but not in the bush! Most large cruise-ship programs are not good ecotours. They are usually short-staffed considering the large number of travelers and tend to offer very superficial experiences.
- *Who is leading the programs?* Do you have an expert local guide? What is his/her expertise? Check for affiliations with local conservation efforts. Are wildlife reserve or park personnel present in each location to be visited?
- *What meals are included?* Read the tour itinerary word for word. Tours that don't include meals while in cities are more economical, and you might appreciate the time away from the group.
- *When should you go?* Check the seasonality of the aspects of nature you wish to experience or observe. You wouldn't go to Alaska in January to see nesting geese or to Hawaii to see the migrating whales after they've come and gone.
- *What can you believe?* No true ecotour organizer can guarantee what you will see. Itineraries that promise you will see certain species are either misleading or violating ecotour principles.
- *What else should you ask for?* Ask about activities and the species that may be observed. Request logs from past trips and referrals to past participants, and call some of them. Ask about liability insurance and the providing companies.

ECOTOUR OPERATORS

SOCIETY EXPEDITIONS, INC.

If you want to see the "wilds" without too much effort or sweat, this group offers good natural history and cultural cruises. It is becoming more concerned about the large numbers of people that it dumps onto one location and is trying to find ways to reduce the impact. The organization also generously donates to conservation projects. The service is excellent, but the guides on board the ships are sometimes not well qualified. It's best if you travel with an organization that has blocked space and provides additional guidance.

EARTHWATCH

This is the program if you want to volunteer for research projects. However, those we spoke with had from excellent to downright poor experiences. To be sure yours is on the excellent end, ask to see a study plan for the project, ask who will be responsible for your daily care, and try to see a previous report of the researcher you'll be working with. It's difficult for a researcher to take care of volunteers and do a big research project at the same time. Have a clear idea of what you'll be doing and how you'll be tied into the project being researched. High cost.

VICTOR EMANUEL NATURE TOURS

Excellent programs, specializing in birding. Unfortunately it uses U.S. guides, who, while good, take away work from the operators who live where the tours are. This group makes donations and supports ecotour ethics, but does little to ensure that bird-watching practices on trips do not bother the birds. Some leaders try to see the birds at any cost.

An Earthwatch volunteer examines leathery turtle eggs, threatened by poachers.

A fast-growing tree can recycle more than 26 pounds of carbon dioxide each year.

EARTHWATCH

Society Expeditions Cruises Inc.

VICTOR EMANUEL NATURE TOURS, INC.

An Earthwatch volunteer helps with a study of orangutans in Borneo.

EARTHWATCH

EARTHWATCH/KEN MIYATA

Earthwatch volunteer Jeff Trelegan measures a leatherback turtle coming ashore to lay her eggs.

What Should I Expect?

- *After making a deposit, you should receive information useful in preparing for your departure.* This includes what to bring; detailed natural history, geographical, anthropological, and cultural background on the country; and sites you'll visit. If you don't get this material, get your money back.
- *Expect nice hotel accommodations in the cities.* However, avoid large luxury hotels on or near the wilderness sites you wish to visit. Often the experience is like trying to get through Disney World at the height of the tourist season. Living in the more rustic areas adds to your nature experience. There's a place on the Amazon in Peru where visitors sleep under a thatched-roofed platform on mattresses under mosquito netting, with no electricity or plumbing. This is one of the most highly rated experiences on the trip.
- *Look for informed tour operators.* Knowledge about conservation, wildlife, and the ecosystem they are working in is difficult to fake. It can reflect long-term commitment to environmental awareness. Of course, longevity in the business alone is hardly proof of that commitment. Lots of older travel companies remain as unecological and unscrupulous as ever.

The Rules of the Road

Ultimately, the success or failure of ecotourism will be determined by how the ecotourists affect an indigenous ecosystem or culture — for better or worse.

Many times have I interceded on an expedition when a traveler has offered to pay the guide a considerable sum to ensure that certain animals were photographed up close, even though it might jeopardize a nest or violate park rules. One very prominent zoo traveler paid a considerable amount to obtain illegal trinkets made of crocodile teeth and to get a guide to collect sacred artifacts from villagers — after the group itself had agreed to do neither. It nearly cost the guide her job.

Think invisible. The heart of ecotourism is minimizing the impact of your visit. To do this, your tour guide should understand the natural dynamics of the ecosystem you are entering, as well as the official regulations covering the area.

And you should respect what he tells you. — *Ray E. Ashton, Jr.*

Not Recommended

The following operators are not recommended for one or more of these reasons:

- Poor quality of the program and/or operator at the site.
- Disregard for conservation and appropriate ecotourism practices.
- Lack of knowledge about the places visited. Poor service.

Baja Expeditions, Inc., San Diego, California

Ecotour Expeditions, Cambridge, Massachusetts

Global Adventures, Boulder, Colorado

Holbrook Travel, Gainesville, Florida

Paul Beaver, Amazon Tours, Largo, Florida

Travel Learn, Cambridge, Massachusetts

SOCIETY EXPEDITIONS/COURTESY WOLFGANG KAEHLER

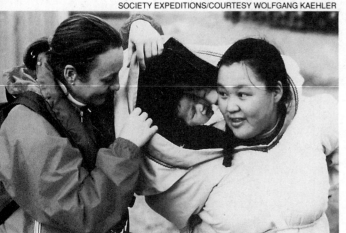

At Eskimo Point in Hudson Bay, a Society Expeditions traveler peeks inside the hood of an Inuit woman's parka or *amautik*. The word *amautik* means "to carry."

Society Expeditions travelers walk among the *moai* statues of Easter Island.

SOCIETY EXPEDITIONS/ART WO

What You Can Do

✔ Know the rules of behavior: Stay on trails. Approach wildlife according to regulations. Avoid approaching or doing anything that startles animals.

✔ Follow the rules. Some animals consider people food, and a number of over zealous bird-watchers have met their end in the wild. We know of one birder who was consumed by a Komodo dragon. Another wandered off the road a couple of steps to confront a mother tiger and cubs, a fatal breach of the rules.

✔ "Take only photographs and leave only foot prints." If you look under logs or rocks for little critters, carefully put them back. Of course, don't litter. Carry out everything man-made, especially non-biodegradables.

✔ Where appropriate, your donations to wildlife reserves or their support organizations can be very helpful. Ask your guide how best to give money.

✔ Never buy items, including exotic meals, that are made from any part of wildlife. Feathers come to market when birds are shot; they aren't just picked off the ground. Nor are claws, teeth, or skins taken from animals that died naturally. When you buy animal remains, you create the market and a reason for someone to go out and collect them, usually illegally.

✔ Insist on small accommodations that fit the atmosphere, not giant luxury hotels. Large facilities, such as a large swimming pool in a dry savanna, can be a tremendous drain on local resources.

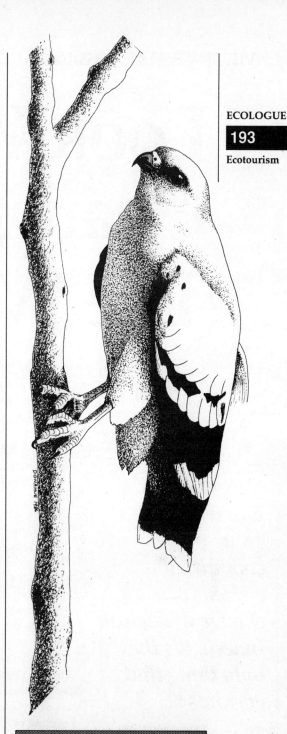

NO MORE UGLY AMERICANS

Tourists seem to have a difficult time switching from wildlife viewing to visiting the homes of fellow humans. We commit too many unthinking improprieties. Remember:

• Cultural values are relative and so are wealth and poverty. It is condescending to consider a native village "poor" because it lacks a movie theater or a family "deprived" because it has no television.

• Treat people with dignity at all times. Mentally do a role reversal and think about how you would feel or react if a guest were to do just what you were thinking of doing.

• Be sensitive to native customs. Enter dwellings and religious structures only when invited or when instructed by your guide. Do not touch or photograph anything or anyone without permission. Don't offer money unless it is customary to do so.

• Be careful offering gifts. They can be taken as handouts or bribes.

• Learn about traditional dignified bartering. Americans are not comfortable with bartering, but most of the world is. Be fair. It's a small world after all.

NO GLOP IS TOO SMALL

A friend of mine who rafted the Grand Canyon told me how meticulous his guide was. He saw him pick up a tiny glop of strawberry jam that dripped from someone's sandwich. Evidently his ten years of experience convinced him that no effort to preserve nature the way he found it was excessive. –*Bruce Anderson*

The ink used on plastic bags contains cadmium, a toxic heavy metal. When the bags are incinerated, heavy metals spew into the air.

Look Who's Changing The World

I N 1987 I LIVED NEAR A BEAUTIFUL, undeveloped peninsula on Cape Cod. The shoreline was littered with construction materials and plastic throwaways. I enlisted my family in a cleanup effort, and when we picked up the final plastic several weeks later, it felt great.

Perhaps you too have had enough of polluted beaches, filthy air, mountains of garbage, and dying forests. Perhaps you want to see some changes and you want to help, but you don't have a lot of time and aren't even sure where to start. If so, you're in good company. And that's just the point. Almost all environmental organizations have enjoyed tremendous growth over the past decade. By adding your voice to those of the millions of other Americans who share your concerns, you can make a difference.

> *"Never doubt that a small group of committed citizens can change the world. Indeed, it's the only thing that ever has."*
>
> — MARGARET MEAD

What exactly is the point of joining an environmental organization? That's easy. If, like me, you care about specific causes but don't have a lot of time to do much, you can quickly send in some money! If, also like me, you sometimes feel guilty that you're not as conscientious as you should be in what you buy or recycle, maybe you can salve your conscience by supporting one of these organizations. Finally, your support is your vote of thanks. It lets the many people in the organization know that you appreciate and honor them for their efforts.

Your membership *matters.* These organizations are doing the work that we want them to do, and they need our money to do it. Also, wind-testing politicians look at the membership numbers of the groups who lobby them and think of the votes they need to get reelected. So your membership counts that way, too.

We hope these reviews of our 30 or so favorite groups will help you pick one or two. We've included many that we've worked with; others we chose after reviewing information they provided. Finally, we picked those that captured our hearts and minds. We've given you just the basics. Many groups have several membership levels and packages.

—*John Quinney*

GLOBAL RELEAF, AMERICAN FORESTRY ASSOCIATION

A past issue of AFA's magazine, *American Forests,* featured a striking photograph of Madagascar on its cover. Not the island of verdant forests and clove-scented air we might imagine, but Madagascar as much of it is today — a treeless moonscape, empty of trees and life. AFA has been publicizing this kind of destruction and doing something about it since 1875.

These days, AFA is best known for the Global Releaf program, an ambitious effort to improve the earth's environment through more and better trees and forests. For $1.50 it'll send you its *Global Releaf Action Guide* ($1.50), a call to plant and care for trees. Just three trees properly planted around your home can cut air-conditioning bills by 10 to 50 percent and help purify the air and remove carbon dioxide. There's lots more in this guide, too.

AFA memberships are $24. For this you receive six issues of *American Forests,* opportunities to join others in tree-planting projects and policy reform, advice and information on tree-planting and tree care, educational tours, and discounts on books, gifts, and services. *–J.Q.*

Household hazardous-waste collection costs an average of $100 per person — usually money from town budgets or corporate sponsors.

ANAI

An offspring of the New Alchemy Institute, ANAI is based on a 450-acre farm, half still in virgin forest, in the canton of Talamanca in Costa Rica. Its agroforestry project involves 1,300 farmers in 26 communities who have to date planted 1.5 million trees and other plants to produce new crops for commercial and home use. ANAI provides plant materials, technical assistance, information, and assistance with processing and marketing. In a second project ANAI is helping several hundred farmers gain title to their lands and is also managing a 30,000-acre wildlife refuge. Both projects owe their success to a combination of local knowledge, respect for community problems, an appreciation of tropical ecology, and hard work.

ANAI is incorporated as a U.S. nonprofit organization and so contributions are tax deductible. Rather than offer memberships, ANAI will supply its annual report in return for contributions of $25 or more. –J.Q.

BIO-INTEGRAL RESOURCE CENTER

There are ugly insects crawling all over your carpet . . . Japanese beetles on your roses . . . ants in your kitchen. You want to get rid of them without risking your health or damaging the environment. Where can you get the best advice? From our experience, the Bio-Integral Resource Center (BIRC) is the place to start.

Founded in 1978, BIRC bases its work on the principles of integrated pest management or IPM, an effective, economical, and safe way to solve pest problems. BIRC's staff have impressive qualifications and years of experience with IPM. It boasts a 10,000-volume library, a well-equipped laboratory, and a 40-acre field station. It publishes two journals: the *IPM Practitioner* (*IPMP*), for scientists, researchers, and farmers, and the *Common Sense Pest Control Quarterly* (*CSPCQ*) that focuses on practical information for solving pest problems in your garden, home, school, and community.

For $25, $30, or $45/year, BIRC offers Professional (includes *IPMP*), Associate (includes *CSPCQ*), and Dual memberships (includes *IPMP* and *CSPCQ*). Associate and Dual members can write or call BIRC for advice on solving specific pest problems. There is no charge for the "easy answers" — and the BIRC staff have hundreds of easy answers. They will also research more complex problems on a consulting basis. Try the organization. –J.Q.

CO-OP AMERICA

Do you want to change our economic system? Or correct economic, environmental, and social abuses? Then consider joining Co-op America. Co-op America is a nonprofit membership association that supports a socially responsible, cooperative economy through information, services, catalogues, and magazines.

Here's what that means. As a member, you'll receive Co-op America's catalogue, from which you can buy environmentally friendly products. You can make travel arrangements through Co-op America's Responsible Travel Service or use its *Financial Planning Guide* for advice on financial decisions. With the *Boycott Action News*, you can keep up to date on boycott campaigns.

Memberships are available for $20. In addition to the above benefits, you will also receive Co-op America's quarterly newsletter, *Building Economic Alternatives*, access to health insurance plans, and a listing of hundreds of progressive businesses, co-ops, and nonprofit organizations. –J.Q.

EARTH ISLAND INSTITUTE

Earth Island Institute is lean and action oriented. Take its Save-the-Dolphins Project. To start the project, Earth Island placed an undercover marine biologist with a video camera on a Central American tuna boat for three months. You may have seen the results on the network news — dozens of dolphins cruelly slaughtered for the sake of a few tuna. This was the sad fate of 150,000 dolphins each year. Earth Island followed up this dramatic exposure with a letter-writing campaign, a boycott on canned tuna, and a series of full-page newspaper ads. The fight paid off when major tuna companies announced that they would no longer purchase tuna from fishermen whose practices involved killing the dolphins.

Earth Island puts this same activism to work in helping the people of Central America save tropical rain forests and in building worldwide concern over unnecessary dam projects. It's all described in the excellent quarterly, *Earth Island Journal*, which comes with membership dues of $25. –J.Q.

ENVIRONMENTAL ACTION FOUNDATION

Earth Day 1970 left us with many legacies. One was Environmental Action, founded by the Earth Day organizers to promote environmental protection through research, public education, organizing assistance, and legal action. Currently it is working on toxics, energy, and solid waste.

SWAP, the Solid Waste Alternatives Project, is a good example of Environmental Action's work. SWAP favors producing less and recycling more as solutions to solid-waste problems. Working with SWAP, the cities of Minneapolis and St. Paul passed an ordinance to allow only recyclable packaging on store shelves.

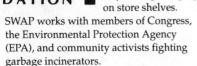

SWAP works with members of Congress, the Environmental Protection Agency (EPA), and community activists fighting garbage incinerators.

Environmental Action publishes several newsletters — including *Environmental Action Power Line* and *Wasteline* — as well as reports and books. Membership in its affiliate, Environmental Action, Inc., is $20 and includes a subscription to *Environmental Action*, which is very well done. –J.Q.

ENVIRONMENTAL DEFENSE FUND

The Environmental Defense Fund focuses its research on acid rain, global warming, ocean pollution, preserving the Antarctic, wildlife and habitat, rain forest preservation, solid wastes, heavy metals and human health, water supplies, and more. Ten years ago, for example, EDF had the foresight to urge utilities to invest in conservation and alternative energy instead of new power plants. Merging ecology with industry's economic biases is complex — but a potent force for positive change. Accomplishing this is where EDF, with its battery of scientists, lawyers, and economists, shines. EDF memberships are $20. Members receive the bimonthly magazine, *EDF Letter*, with news of all EDF's activities. –J.Q.

GLOBAL TOMORROW COALITION

What a remarkable experience we had attending the Globescope Pacific Assembly! Organized by the Global Tomorrow Coalition (GTC), this event attracted hundreds of environmentalists, CEOs of major corporations, high school students, politicians, members of the armed forces, and community organizers. Our mission was to produce an agenda for sustainable development in the United States. We were astonished by the depth and breadth of commitment to environmental values and moved by the passion of Jimmy Carter, the eloquence of Dennis Weaver, the style of Ted Turner, and the leadership of others.

GTC is a national nonprofit alliance of organizations and individuals committed to acting today to assure a more sustainable, equitable global tomorrow. Founded in 1981, GTC unites more than 110 U.S. organizations representing over eight million Americans.

GTC reaches an amazing number of people: Its excellent book, *A Citizen's Guide to Sustainable Development*, is used by more than 100 colleges and universities. Over 20,000 children and teachers have field-tested GTC education materials. More than six million citizens have been reached by the Globescope process.

Individual memberships are $35. Members receive GTC publications and periodic bulletins on GTC activities and events. –J.Q.

GREEN COMMITTEES OF CORRESPONDENCE, CLEARINGHOUSE

The global environment is in a mess. You feel that most governments and political parties do not share your ecological values. So what other alternatives are there? In Europe, and especially in West Germany, the Greens have emerged as a significant political party. Their numbers have grown in each election over the past few years, and Greens now sit in European parliaments and hold the balance of power in some local, county, and provincial governments. In this country the Greens have been organizing since 1984, especially at the local level.

Key values adopted by the Green Committees of Correspondence include: ecological wisdom, grassroots democracy, personal and social responsibility, nonviolence, decentralization, community-based economics, postpatriarchal values, respect for diversity, global responsibility, and future focus/sustainability. Hardly mainstream American, the Greens are, nonetheless, committed to building an alternative political structure for this country.

The Greens are most active in local politics. To check it out, you can become a supporting member of the Green Committees of Correspondence for an annual contribution of $25. You'll receive two quarterly publications, *Greener Times* and *Green Synthesis*, bibliographies and other information, notices of Green gatherings, and support for your local organizing efforts. –J.Q.

GATHERING OF THE GREEN

Seventh Generation's Field Guide to More Than 100 Environmental Groups is available from them for $2.

The World Environmental Directory (ask for it in your local library) lists environmental organizations, environmental data-base services, government agencies, and more.

The National Wildlife Federation publishes an annual *Conservation Directory* ($18) to more than 1,800 environmental organizations.

ings, and savings on future tree purchases.

The foundation is doing a lot to promote Trees for America . . . special TV programs . . . free "Grow Your Own Tree" kits for schools . . . "Tree City USA" titles awarded to cities and towns active in caring for their trees . . . and reviving the celebration of Arbor Day in thousands of school districts. –J.Q.

GREENPEACE

We've all seen pictures of Greenpeace activists. They parachute off smokestacks, sail into nuclear test zones, and put their bodies on the line. They get results. When France ended atmospheric nuclear testing in 1974, Greenpeace received much of the credit. The group was also active, along with other organizations, in convincing the European Community to ban the import of white seal fur products harvested in bloody carnage off Newfoundland and in decreasing the known annual harvest of whales from 25,000 in 1975 to 1,000 in 1988. Of late, Greenpeace has enjoyed increasing public support, and in America it now has more than three million members.

Greenpeace is an international organization with offices in 22 countries. It has a staff of more than 400, a "navy" of nine ships, and thousands of committed volunteers. Greenpeace works for no nukes, elimination of toxics, wildlife preservation, and ocean ecology . . . and to protect the Antarctic, to eliminate air pollution and acid rain, and to curb the killing of Australia's kangaroos. Although Greenpeace engages in lobbying and education, it focuses on direct action. Through dramatic actions well photographed and publicized, it is able to get results. In this, Greenpeace is unsurpassed.

Membership is $15 and includes the excellent *Greenpeace Magazine*. –J.Q.

INTERNATIONAL FUND FOR ANIMAL WELFARE

As any animal lover knows, one of the saddest realities of life is that many of the animals we share this earth with fall prey to cruel human hands. In 1966 IFAW founder Brian Davies traveled to the Magdalen Islands in the Gulf of St. Lawrence and witnessed the senseless clubbing deaths of harp seal pups. This horrific sight prompted the beginning of IFAW and his two-decade "Crusade for Seals."

Now over 600,000 members strong, IFAW's campaigns include combating the slaughter of African elephants and poaching of Australian kangaroos, informing the public of the needless tragedy of cosmetic testing on animals, educating farmers in Peru in shearing methods to obtain wool from the beautiful vicuna without killing them . . . and more.

As part of its 20th anniversary celebration, IFAW is initiating an important and ambitious campaign called "Assurance for Animals." This project will establish a multimillion dollar endowment fund for animals so that IFAW's efforts will be ensured of continuing into the 21st century.

There is no minimum membership fee, but members are encouraged to contribute to various campaigns outlined in frequent newsletters and updates. *–Amy Huckins*

NATIONAL ARBOR DAY FOUNDATION

"Each generation takes the Earth as trustees. We ought to bequeath to posterity as many forests and orchards as we have exhausted and consumed." So said J. Sterling Morton in 1872 when first proposing a tree-planting holiday to be called Arbor Day. By 1894 Arbor Day was celebrated in every state.

It costs nothing to get involved in the foundation's most recent effort, Trees for America. Just ask to join and you'll receive ten free trees, selected for their suitability to your region. Plant them. Then for only $10, become a member of National Arbor Day, and receive a copy of *Tree Book*, a terrific introduction to planting and caring for trees. You'll also receive the bimonthly magazine *Arbor Day*, invitations to special out-

National Audubon Society
Americans Committed to Conservation

NATIONAL AUDUBON SOCIETY

Since its founding in 1905 the National Audubon Society has, in its own words, "approached conservation and environmental issues in a manner reflected by nature itself. With balance. Audubon believes that the requirements of a flourishing economy and those of a flourishing environment need not conflict." Not surprisingly, this approach has earned Audubon a respected position in scientific and political circles. With active research and education programs on acid rain, toxic-waste disposal, forest management, habitat preservation, and energy conservation, Audubon has become much more than a group of naturalists and bird lovers. Few organizations do more to save the balance and beauty of nature.

You'll see that dedication to balance and beauty in *Audubon*, often called the most beautiful magazine in the world. In our experience, it is. Simply exquisite. And *Audubon*'s writers are no slouches either! Add news about Audubon's many programs and a nice mix of controversy, criticism, philosophy, and news, and you get, quite simply, one of the best magazines going.

Membership in the National Audubon Society begins at $20 and includes six issues of the magazine, local chapter membership, and many travel and educational opportunities. For an additional $9 you can be plugged into Audubon's network of conservation activists, with the chance to work directly on Audubon's projects. — J.Q.

Planners and educators must dispel the myth that conservation is exclusively a short-term strategy to alleviate immediate crises.

NATIONAL WILDLIFE FEDERATION

The list of activities of this 5.8 million member organization is impressive. It includes: a Nature Education Catalog with videos, books, puzzles, and discovery kits for children of all ages; NatureScope, an environmental education series for grades K-8; *Class Action Guide*, a publication with action-oriented suggestions for helping the environment; wildlife camps in North Carolina, Colorado, and Washington; and the Institute for Wildlife Research, a clearinghouse for information on a broad range of wildlife species. NWF's Resources Conservation Department, staffed by teams of lobbyists, attorneys, scientists, and resource specialists, works on such issues as conservation of fish and wildlife habitat, promotion of energy conservation and renewable resources, regulation of toxic and hazardous wastes, protection and wise use of public lands, and development of a sound national water policy.

With the membership price of $20, you'll receive the excellent magazine *National Wildlife*, and many other benefits. And you'll be supporting the organization with perhaps the most clout on Capitol Hill of any environmental organization. –J.Q.

NATURAL RESOURCES DEFENSE COUNCIL

You can thank Meryl Streep, apples, and Alar for propelling the National Resources Defense Council (NRDC) into public view in 1989. In case you missed it, NRDC led and won the campaign to prevent the suspected cancer-causing chemical, Alar, from being used on apples. In the process they awakened an entire industry to the public's concerns about pesticides. But NRDC's interests and achievements range far beyond Alar.

For 20 years NRDC has worked to protect our air, our water, and our food supplies — through legal action, hard-hitting research, and persistent advocacy. It has an excellent reputation. According to the *Washington Monthly*, "EPA staff members say NRDC lawyers know more about the Clean Air Act than anyone else, including most EPA lawyers." Its environmental lawyers are among the best in the country — they received almost $1 million in court-awarded fees in one year alone.

NRDC members receive *The Amicus Journal* of environmental thought and opinion and the in-house publication *NRDC Newsline*, plus updates on NRDC's work. All for $10. –J.Q.

NATURE CONSERVANCY

The Nature Conservancy has a remarkable record. Since its formation in 1951, it has been preserving land. Not just any land, but areas that must be saved because of their ecological significance or the distinctive wildlife they contain. To date, it has protected nearly 3¹/₂ million acres in all 50 states, the Virgin Islands, Canada, the Caribbean, and Latin America. That's about equal to the land area of Delaware and Rhode Island combined!

The Conservancy often competes with private interests in the real estate market, an expensive venture for a nonprofit organization that depends on grants and contributions. Fortunately, owners often give land to the Conservancy in return for tax advantages or because they support the

Conservancy's mission. Most of the land it acquires is protected. Some is exchanged for more desirable parcels, and sometimes Conservancy land is turned over to other conservation organizations. Today, the Nature Conservancy owns and cares for more than 1,000 sanctuaries.

Membership dues are $15 yearly. Members receive the Conservancy's attractive full-color bimonthly magazine, bulletins and briefings on local projects, invitations to field trips and special events, and more. The Nature Conservancy is unlikely to be controversial; it is certain to continue quietly saving and caring for our planet's most beautiful and threatened lands. –J.Q.

NEW ALCHEMY INSTITUTE

In its 20 years New Alchemy has achieved a distinguished record in ecological design. New Alchemy researchers developed some of the first solar greenhouses — known as bioshelters — to produce vegetables, herbs, flowers, and fish year-round, using sunshine as the only heat source and beneficial insects in place of pesticides. They developed new, highly productive fish-raising techniques, designed and built a greenhouse heated by compost windrows, and created a superinsulated auditorium warmed mainly by body heat and light bulbs.

The institute's recent research has focused on sustainable agriculture — ways for farmers to produce food economically without losing soil, polluting water, or using chemicals. Equally important are education programs that feature tours of the market gardens, greenhouses, and facilities, a college-level semester program, short courses, and innovative and highly successful science programs for young students.

Becoming a member (for $35) is the best way to learn more about New Alchemy's work. Membership benefits include a subscription to the *New Alchemy Quarterly*, free admission to the site, and a generous discount on education programs and on books and products in the institute's catalogue. Heartily recommended. –J.Q.

PROJECT LIGHTHAWK

In flying over much of the Pacific Northwest, Lighthawk has found that Forest Service estimates of the amount of old growth forest are up to 50 percent too high. The forests are there on the maps, but from the air all that remain are the scars of clear cuts.

Lighthawk is good at what it does. In 1988 executive director Michael Stewartt spent three days flying Dan Janzen, the ecologist behind the restoration of the Guanacaste National Park in Costa Rica, over a 200-square-mile area. Janzen's assessment: "I was able to get work done in a few hours that I hadn't been able to accomplish over the last ten years with other pilots."

Lighthawk uses resources carefully. It recruits the services of qualified aircraft owner-pilots willing to volunteer their time and their planes. Its brochures are printed on recycled paper — we received materials in an envelope previously used by someone in the U.S. House of Representatives. Services are all either free or provided at minimal cost. Clients have included the Nature Conservancy, the Wilderness Society, and the Oregon Natural Resources Council. Russell Train, president of the World Wildlife Fund says, ". . . I've seen few projects anywhere as cost effective as Project Lighthawk." Memberships start at $35 and include a subscription to the newsletter. –J.Q.

RAINFOREST ACTION NETWORK

Burger King used to buy beef that was produced on tropical lands that were once rain forests. It was cheap for Burger King — but expensive for the earth. In 1987 the Rainforest Action Network (RAN), in its first direct-action campaign, led a national boycott of Burger King. It was successful. Burger King stopped importing rain forest beef. We all became more aware of our role in rain forest destruction — and of the purchasing power we had to bring about change.

RAN's goal is to protect tropical rain forests and the human rights of those living in and around these forests. It emphasizes networking and citizen action through the 120-plus Rainforest Action Groups (RAGs) in North America. Contact RAN to find a RAG near you.

RAN's current campaigns focus on forcing the World Bank to stop funding rain forest destruction and to protect tropical rain forests in Hawaii, Puerto Rico, the Virgin Islands, and U.S. Trust Territories in the Pacific.

Regular memberships are $25. Benefits include a subscription to *Rainforest Action Network Alerts*, published monthly, and occasional reports. As a RAN member you'll have lots of ways to act for rain forest preservation. RAN will tell you which rain forest products to boycott and where your protest letters should be sent. It will also provide a bibliography and list of books, tapes, and T-shirts that you can purchase to help support the work. –J.Q.

RENEW AMERICA

Remember when there was an oil crisis? When there was lots of interest and government support for solar energy, and an organization called Solar Lobby was formed to promote the celebration of "Sun Day" around the world? All this happened in the late seventies. Times change and organizations must, too. So today, Solar Lobby is doing business as Renew America, an educational forum and network dedicated to the development of a safe and sustainable environment.

It is probably best known these days for its annual publication, *State of the States*. Since 1987 Renew America has ranked each state's performance in dealing with five or six key environmental problems. It's a great way to measure progress and to highlight areas that need improvement. Topics reported include food safety, drinking water, forest management, recycling, indoor pollution, and highway safety. Useful information to take to your state politicians.

Memberships are $25. Benefits include a subscription to the quarterly *Renew America Report* and two years' worth of *State of the States*. –J.Q.

PROGRAMME FOR BELIZE

How can one person help to stop the destruction of tropical rain forests? The Programme for Belize is purchasing 110,000 acres of tropical forest in Belize (formerly British Honduras). Then it's asking individuals to donate $50 an acre, for which they receive a certificate of appreciation, toward that purchase. The program was started with funds from the Massachusetts Audubon Society and is sponsored by the Nature Conservancy through a formal operating agreement with the Belize Ministry of Agriculture, Forestry, and Fisheries. Together with other donated lands this program will make the "Rio Bravo" tropical forest a model of balanced wildlife conservation, agro-forestry development, research, and tourism. What a perfect gift for that person on your list who has everything!
— *Penny Uhlendorf*

ROCKY MOUNTAIN INSTITUTE

Reading the Rocky Mountain Institute's (RMI) newsletter leaves me breathless — and full of admiration for this lively young organization founded by Amory and Hunter Lovins in 1982. Amory Lovins has been a passionate, articulate, and remarkably skilled advocate for energy-efficient technologies for many years now. *The Wall Street Journal* recently selected him as one of "the rising stars, the leaders of tomorrow."

Lovins's organization, RMI, says its official goal is to "foster the efficient and sustainable use of resources as a path to global security." Its work is focused in five areas: energy, water, economic renewal, agriculture, and security. It is best known for its energy work. Using an "end-use/least-cost" approach it has been able to convince utilities, local governments, corporate officers, and politicians that saving energy saves money and protects the environment.

RMI doesn't offer memberships. For a contribution of at least $10, however, you will receive the quarterly newsletter and an extensive publications list. Many of its publications are highly technical. –J.Q.

SAVE-THE-REDWOODS LEAGUE

Redwoods are awesome trees. Once referred to by John Steinbeck as "ambassadors from another time," redwoods can live to be 2,000 years old. The world's tallest measured tree is a 367.8-foot redwood in the Tall Trees Grove in Redwood National Park. Thanks to the Save-the-Redwoods League, more than 250,000 acres of the finest redwood forests have been protected from logging and destruction.

Save-the-Redwoods League has been successful, in part, because of partnerships with the California State Park Commis-

sion, the National Park Service, and other agencies. Often money raised by the League — $43 million since 1918 — has been matched by federal and state funds. Thus, there are now 32 California Redwood state parks in addition to the 78,000 acres in Redwood National Park.

The League has 40,000 members, and you can join for as little as $5. Members receive twice-yearly bulletins and regular updates on the league's activities. –J.Q.

SIERRA CLUB

"If wilderness is to be saved, people must come to love it." This simple truth guided John Muir when he founded the Sierra Club in 1892. It's the same today. Each year the Sierra Club hosts thousands of outings for its members. Many are free or low cost. They include day hikes, backpacking, skiing, mountain trekking, bird watching, and more — all helping people experience wilderness. The Sierra Club is also the world's largest conservation publisher: calendars, nature books, and environmental texts, plus *Sierra*, its bimonthly members' magazine.

But more than this, the Sierra Club fights to protect the earth's wild places. It has helped protect 8.5 million wilderness acres in 21 states . . . lobbied for a new toxic-waste cleanup bill . . . and pushed the Clean Water Act into law in 1988. Since 1979 the Sierra Club has been instrumental in convincing Congress to enact over 100 laws to protect wilderness and the environment.

As a Sierra Club member, you can experience the grandeur and diversity of wilderness lands, receive special discounts on books, and learn to love the world of *Sierra*. Regular memberships begin at $33 for individuals, $41 for couples. –J.Q.

TREEPEOPLE

In 1969 Andy Lipkis began planting smog-resistant trees to replace those he saw dying around Los Angeles. From this simple and effective action, TreePeople was born. Since then it has been responsible for planting, directly or indirectly, 170 million trees around the country.

But TreePeople is about much more than trees. Early on it learned that if young trees are not cared for they die. It learned to involve community members and volunteers in this work. Today, TreePeople teaches individuals to recognize the power they have to change and improve the environment. Trees are the medium it uses to demonstrate that power.

And it's been effective. In 1981 TreePeople set out to inspire Los Angeles residents to plant one million trees before the 1984 Summer Olympics. They succeeded. How? By bringing individuals, community groups, corporations, and government agencies together. Recently, it has rescued 70,000 surplus fruit trees from nurseries and distributed them to low-income families.

If you're in Los Angeles, visit the 45-acre headquarters in Coldwater Canyon Park and consider becoming a volunteer. Or become a member for $25. You'll receive its bimonthly newsletter, *Seedling News*, and six free tree seedlings each year. –J.Q.

WORLDWATCH INSTITUTE

If you only want to read one magazine on the global environment, read *World Watch*. Now in its third year, this is the place to go for solid and highly readable information on trends in food production, energy use, climate change, toxics, and more. It's not all bad news, either. Each issue includes several environmental success stories. The magazine's stated purpose is quite clear: "Few magazines seek to change the course of history. This one does. Our goal is to help reverse the environmental trends that are undermining the human prospect." To subscribe, send $20 to the Worldwatch Institute.

Since 1975 researchers at the Worldwatch Institute have analyzed and described the global environment. The widely respected institute often testifies before Congress and in international forums. In January each year it publishes *State of the World,* an "annual physical" measuring the earth's vital signs. In *State of the World 1990* we learned about the problem of rising seas, the world's precarious food situation, and the role of the bicycle in modern transportation systems. The institute's writing combines scientific rigor with excellent style. No easy task. It also publishes *Worldwatch Papers,* each one a gold mine of information on topics ranging from population control to recycling and energy-efficiency to tree planting.

To tap into this rich resource, send $25 for a *World Watch* subscription. In return you'll receive the current edition of *State of the World* and a year's worth of *Worldwatch Papers.* A great bargain. –*J.Q.*

WORLD WILDLIFE FUND

With more than 670,000 members in the United States and two million around the world, plus an annual budget pushing $30 million, the World Wildlife Fund (WWF) is one of the larger groups on our list. It has a correspondingly ambitious mission: to protect the earth's endangered wildlife and wildlands and to safeguard the natural resources upon which all life depends.

WWF's symbol is the giant panda, one of the world's most endangered species. It was endangered when WWF was formed 30 years ago. It's stiil threatened. Soon,

the giant panda may exist only in zoos, in books, and on WWF's literature, a tragic symbol of life at the beginning of the 21st century. The giant panda is, sadly, not alone. At current extinction rates, we may destroy 20% of the earth's plant and animal species by the year 2000.

To date, WWF has sponsored more than 1,400 projects in 100 countries. It has helped create almost 200 national parks and reserves . . . taught practical methods of soil conservation and forest farming . . . trained park rangers . . . sponsored university wildlife programs in developing countries . . . and much, much more.

If you want to help save forests and wildlife, you can become a member for $15. You'll receive a host of benefits: WWF's members-only newsletter, invitations to special events and project sites, and frequent updates on WWF projects. –*J.Q.*

ZERO POPULATION GROWTH

ZPG's activities center on a special theme: "ZPG . . . for Earth's sake." Our expanding population is the root cause of all our environmental problems. More of us on the planet means more demand for goods and services — and greater threats to our water, our air, and our soil. Zero popula-

tion growth — the point at which population size stays the same from year to year — is needed now more than at any time in the past.

ZPG has been leading this effort for more than 20 years. It is active at the grassroots level, in our classrooms, with the media, and on Capitol Hill. The ZPG video, "World Population," is a graphic depiction of population growth from 1 A.D. to the present and a projection for the next 60 years. *Making a Difference* lists 150 things we can each do for the earth's sake. ZPG has published *USA by Numbers,* it offers workshops for teachers, and it has devised an urban stress test to examine how cities are coping with population pressures. And that's just a small sample. These folks produce the goods!

Memberships start at $20. You will receive the *ZPG Reporter,* with excellent coverage of population issues. If you want to be an activist, ask for *The Activist* and join ZPG to make things happen. –*J.Q.*

What You Can Do

How, specifically, can you support your chosen group? Here are some possibilities.

✔ Become a member.

✔ Donate money.

✔ Volunteer by answering phones, leading tours for the public, etc.

✔ Participate in programs — measuring the acidity of local ponds, restoring a degraded river, staffing a recycling center.

✔ Lead by serving on a committee or a board.

✔ Be an activist: write letters to politicians, newspapers, and businesspeople; demonstrate; boycott; run for office.

Manufacturing recycled paper produces 74% less air pollution than manufacturing paper from virgin wood pulp.

In Business For a World That Works

IF YOU'RE DOING YOUR PART in your everyday life to help the environment, are there things that you can encourage your employer to do? You bet there are.

The new thinking says that economic development and environmental protection are not mutually exclusive. On the contrary, they must actually work together if we are to have a better world.

In this section we'll suggest ways to make the most of this dynamic situation and to make your own workplace cleaner and more energy efficient — which, after all, means more profitable. We'll also examine the market trends that bode well for the earth's future, and our own.

Cleaning Up Your Act

Let's start simply. Of course, many of the products and ideas suggested elsewhere in this book — recycling aids, cleaners, energy-saving devices, and so on — can be applied to the workplace. But beyond that, here are some relatively easy changes you and your coworkers can make to minimize the waste of energy or materials.

> *In 1988 American Telephone and Telegraph saved $1 million in trash disposal costs and realized a $365,000 profit from recycling.*

- Reuse office supplies as much as possible. (See other information on recycling, pages 16-41).
- Use "continuous use" envelopes for interoffice mail.
- Collect flawed copies from copy machines and use for scratch paper, or staple stacks of scrap paper together and distribute them to all office workers. Some printers will even make pads out of your scrap paper.
- Shred scrap paper and old newspapers for packing material. You can also reuse packing that you receive, particularly those plastic foam "peanuts" and pellets, some of which contain CFCs that destroy the earth's protective ozone layer.

JUST THINKING

"We need another and a wiser and perhaps more mystical concept of animals . . . . In a world older and more complete than ours they move finished and complete, gifted with extensions of the senses we have lost or never attained, living by voices we shall never hear. They are not brethren, they are not underlings; they are other nations, caught with ourselves in the net of life and time, prisoners of the splendour and travail of the earth."

— *Henry Beston*, The Outermost House

100% recycled

Copy Paper (100% recycled paper): $49.50 (case of 5,000 sheets)

Shredded Paper Cushioning: $44.50 (50-lb. box)

100% recycled

Legal Pads (100% recycled paper): $69.50 (case of 6 dozen)

Cellulose Wadding Cushioning: $59.75 (25-lb. roll)

Shock-Absorbing Cushioning Paper: $29.50 (600' roll)

Wood Excelsior Flexible Cushioning Material: $26.95 (25-lb. bale)

Excelsior Cushioning Pads: $44.50 to $47.50 (depending on size, 100 pads)

Padded Mailing Bags (60 percent recycled material, no plastic, biodegradable, 10 different sizes): $35.75 to $98.50 (depending on size, 50 to 500 bags)

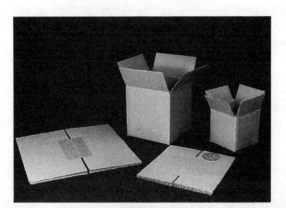

Sturdy Corrugated Shipping Boxes (100% recycled paper): 30¢ to $4.73 (depending on size, unit price per 1,000)

Pressure-Sensitive Box Sealing Tape (biodegradable): $22.95 (2 in. x 55 yd., 6 rolls)

Gummed Box Sealing Tape: $31.95 (3"x600')

Gummed Tape Dispenser (with preset measuring device): $295

Americans throw away enough office and writing paper each year to build a wall 12 feet high from Los Angeles to New York City.

- Label your outgoing packages or stamp them with messages that point with pride to your recycling efforts and encourage other companies to do the same.
- In kitchens and cafeterias, use washable dishes and silverware, not disposables. Substitute mugs and spoons for throwaway coffee cups and stir sticks. Use cloth coffee filters instead of paper ones.
- Turn down the heat at night and on weekends.
- Raise environmental awareness and get good PR by publicizing your environmental efforts and suggestions in company newsletters and local and industry papers.

In addition, encourage your employer to try the following:

- Purchase materials in bulk and avoid overpackaged goods.
- Make sure lights have accessible switches so they can be turned off when not in use.
- In bathrooms, install reusable cloth roll towels and water-saving flush toilets.
- Invest in a free or low-cost energy audit from the utility company (or a private firm) to maximize energy efficiency.
- Sponsor and help publicize used appliance swaps, recycling awareness programs, and community hazardous-waste collection days.
- If the business has company cars, use fuel-efficient models with good pollution-control devices. In cities use bicycle couriers when possible, and install a bike rack outside the office to encourage employees to pedal to work.
- Share, borrow, or rent tools or equipment that aren't used often.
- Save purchasing and disposal costs by swapping manufacturing by-products: chemicals, solvents, and other would-be, one-way pollutants.
- Consider investing in automatic thermostats.

And for the health and safety of employees:

- Monitor the radon levels in all office buildings.
- Establish a nonsmoking policy or a designated smoking area.

Work Shouldn't Be a Hazard to Your Health

While you're making the earth a healthier place, don't ignore your own physical well-being. Here are some tips to consider:

- Use white or yellow commercial glues; in general, they're the safest types. When possible, substitute paper clips, staples, or rubber bands for processed liquids in plastic containers. And never inhale anything that doesn't smell like fresh air.
- Use water-based correction fluid (the kind intended for copies) instead of petroleum-based ones.
- Purchase water-based pens and markers, available at most art and office supply stores.
- Have your printing jobs done with vegetable-oil-based inks (such as those made from soybean oil) rather than petroleum-based varieties. Soy ink rubs off less, is environmentally cleaner to produce and dispose of, is easier to clean off presses, and is safer for press operators to use.

Out of the Trash Can

Each year most businesses throw away thousands of tons of paper that could be reprocessed to make more office paper, newsprint, and many other paper goods. Recycling much of that would-be garbage has many advantages. Not only do you show you care about the environ-

OFFICE-PAPER RECYCLING SYSTEM HOLDERS

Made of recycled corrugated fiberboard (a paper product) with 3 collection sections. Holds 2 to 3 days' worth of office-generated paper. Suitable for desktop use. Printed logo says, "I'm a Recycler." An economical, attractive way to get recycling started. –W.S.

$6.95 (each 3-compartment bin); $23.95 for 3 bins including postage and handling, Seventh Generation

PAPER PAL

Made of corrugated plastic, this file has a wire bracket that hangs on either the inside or outside of an office trash can. Fits nearly any 13½" or taller wastebasket of any shape. Holds 1 to 2 days' worth of office paper. –W.S.

$6.49
White River Paper Company

DUO-FILE RECYCLING FILE

Most suitable for desktop use, but can also be placed next to the wastebasket on the floor. A 1-piece unit with 2 large sections to hold different grades or sizes of paper for recycling. Each section holds 2 to 4 days' worth of paper. Comes in recycled, corrugated fiberboard (a paper product) or plastic. –W.S.

$5.95
White River Paper Company

The average person in an office discards 175 pounds of valuable high-grade paper a year.

STEEL RECYCLING BIN

Meant to be used primarily for paper and cans. Holds a 19-gallon polypropylene mesh bag (washable, sanitary, and permanent) and has a 15"x1" slot for paper and 3 1/2" diameter slot for aluminum cans. Attractive, utilitarian, and vandal and trash proof. –W.S.

White River Paper Company

PLASTIC STACKING BINS

Hold 11 gallons of material. Come in sets of 3 and a variety of colors. Made of recycled plastic. –W.S.

$9.99 to $14.99
White River Paper Company

JUST THINKING

"I am utterly convinced that most of the great environmental struggles will either be won or lost in the 1990s. By the next century it will be too late."

—*Thomas Lovejoy, Smithsonian Institution*

FIVE EASY STEPS TO STARTING COMPANY RECYCLING

The following guidelines will be useful to start a recycling program at your workplace.

• **Establish a coordinator for the program. This person will be responsible for implementing the program and will act as a liaison between management, employees, the maintenance staff, and the wastepaper buyer.**

• **Shop around for a reputable wastepaper buyer. When you've found one, develop a contract that will specify which types of materials the buyer will accept and in what quantities.**

• **In general, the most acceptable types of wastepaper are letterhead paper, typing paper, and writing tablet paper. A** good rule of thumb for estimating quantities is that each office employee will produce about half a pound of paper per day.

• **Develop the separation and collection system. With this system each employee separates recyclable paper from other trash and stores it in a desktop container or folder. The employee then empties the desktop container into a central collection container. The maintenance staff takes it from there to a central storage area, where the wastepaper buyer picks it up.**

• **Several weeks before the program is scheduled to start, begin an education campaign that informs all involved about its goals and methods. Stress** how important it is for each person to participate.

• **Monitor the program. Let other employees know how it is going, reporting its success and soliciting ideas for improvements. Use in-house newsletters, memos, posters. Encourage feedback.**

100% recycled

ment and set an example in your community, but your company also reduces its trash disposal costs and can even profit by selling recycled and used paper goods.

More and more businesses have begun to capitalize on these benefits. State and local governments as well as private companies are now successfully running their own internal recycling programs. County government offices in Fairfax County, Virginia, for example, have reduced their trash output by more than half. And in 1988 American Telephone and Telegraph saved $1 million in trash disposal costs — and realized a $365,000 profit from recycling.

Looking to the Future

No doubt, if businesses don't make the necessary changes toward environmentally sound practices on their own, government will soon impose changes in the form of stricter regulations. And for some companies, the medicine may be hard to swallow.

In smog-bound Los Angeles, for example, comprehensive pollution-reduction legislation would enforce tough emissions controls on businesses from bakeries to breweries, staggered work hours, mandatory ride sharing, and the elimination of free parking. Such an approach is not extremist; it simply recognizes the crisis in our environment.

Given the proper responses, the environmental crisis does not have to imply all bad news. Creative, innovative approaches promise a variety of new opportunities and markets. Consider:

- Ten years ago, only a handful of cleanup companies across the country were equipped to dispose of toxic waste. Now the EPA estimates there are more than 1,600 hazardous-waste processing facilities in the U.S.
- In South Carolina one company recycles 100 million pounds of two-liter plastic soft drink bottles each year. It transforms the stuff into everything from fiberfill for ski parkas to scouring pads and auto parts.
- A Portsmouth, New Hampshire, firm, Environmental Resource Return Corporation, recycles up to 500 tons of building rubble, concrete, and asphalt per day. It also makes old wood, brush, tree stumps, and yard waste into wood chips and composted soil.
- In Los Angeles, where landfills are stuffed to capacity, officials have struck an innovative recycling deal with China. The city will ship office trash such as pink message slips, reports, and lunch sacks to China, which has a paper shortage. There the materials will be recycled into lower-grade printing and writing paper.

The new opportunities in business are also a direct result of smart market response. Look at the successes of the Japanese auto industry. While American auto makers spent much of the last two decades fighting pollution control regulations in Congress and court, the Japanese capitalized on them by making cars with greater efficiency and reduced emissions. The results are well known: Japanese domination of the automobile industry.

Your business can be environmentally savvy too, and your employer doesn't have to move into this relatively uncharted territory alone. Already, there are many consultants available to help businesses save energy, tread lightly on the earth, and make money, too. If you encourage your company to get out there on the cutting edge of positive environmental change, the world will salute you — and probably buy your company's products as well.
— *Leda Hartman*

EARTH CARE PAPER

This Wisconsin company carries everything from holiday greeting cards to computer paper — all recycled. All prices can be discounted for larger orders. Here are some samples of its products. (All Earth Care reviews by Leda Hartman.)

LETTERHEAD AND ENVELOPES

In a variety of colors and textures. The paper also comes in larger sheets and rolls for printing jobs.

**Letterhead: $7.35 to $15.60 (depending on texture; package of 500 sheets)
Envelopes: $12.25 to $28.25 (depending on texture; box of 500)**

COPY-BOND

Suitable for high-speed copy machines and all-purpose office paper. Recycled content of 50% to 70%.

$6 to $9.95 (depending on size; 500 sheets)

ECO PLUS COMPUTER PAPER

Made entirely from postconsumer waste such as phone books and newsprint. Might be the most ecological computer greenbar paper manufactured today.

$44.60 (2,600 sheets 11"x15")

BOND-QUALITY COMPUTER PAPER

In a variety of forms, all at least 50% recycled.

**Greenbar Bond: $57 (2,750 sheets 11"x15")
White Bond: $42.45 (3,500 sheets 9$\frac{1}{2}$"x11")
White Bond Clean Edge: $17.80 (1,000 sheets 9$\frac{1}{2}$"x11")**

BUSINESS ENVELOPES

These white envelopes contain 50% to 70% recycled fiber. Window envelope uses glassine, a clear paper product similar to tracing paper. Brown Kraft envelopes are sturdy and 100% recycled.

White Business Envelopes: $12.25 (box of 500)
White Regular Envelopes: $11.15 (box of 500)
White Window Envelopes: $14.50 (box of 500)
Brown Kraft Envelopes: $13.15 to $19.30 (depending on size, box of 250)

MINIMUM IMPACT PAPER

Light cream-colored paper that varies slightly in color; suitable for letterhead, envelopes, newsletters, brochures, and copying. Made from wastepaper that isn't de-inked or bleached. Also, this recycling process uses less water and fewer chemicals and produces less solid waste than the standard recycling process. One hundred percent recycled.

Letterhead: $5.95 to $11.90 (depending on size, package of 500)
Envelopes: $12 to $13.20 (depending on size, package of 500)

LEADING YOUR CORPORATE LEADERS

In addition to making everyday business practices more environmentally sound, you can encourage your company to commit to a policy of environmental responsibility. Here are a number of inspiring examples:

• **The Body Shop,** a British chain of personal care stores that sells naturally based cosmetics and body products in recycled packages, sends environmental messages to shoppers through posters and window displays and actively supports environmental organizations such as Greenpeace.
• **Patagonia,** a U.S. maker of outdoor wear, uses its catalogue to recognize individual environmental activists and publicize more than 100 environmental organizations. Since 1984 Patagonia has donated ten percent of its pretax profits to such groups.
• **Clean Harbors, Inc.,** a $100 million hazardous-waste disposal company in Massachusetts, buys only paper drinking cups instead of polystyrene, uses biodegradable hand soap, and purchases recycled paper for stationery. The company doesn't even put road salt on its parking lot, relying instead on snowplowing.

How can you push your company in the right direction? For starters:

• Lobby the management to create a committee to monitor your company's environmental performance.
• Suggest purchasing policies that take into account the environmental records of your vendors.
• Try to discourage the company pension plan from investing in businesses that harm the environment. See pages 208-11 for help with investing in environmentally conscious companies.

WHISTLE-BLOWING

Wouldn't it be nice if every business had the best interests of the earth at heart? But we know that's not the case. If the company you work for is knowingly harming people or the environment and your efforts to right matters have been resisted, you may want to consider informing the public and/or the appropriate authorities of the company's offensive practices. But think hard first. Evaluate the risks. You may get fired for blowing the whistle. And you may get blacklisted from other businesses as well.

But there may also be rewards, both personal and public, for doing what you believe is right. If you decide to go ahead, consider these suggestions:

• Weigh the risks.

• Get advice from a lawyer, union, professional association, state agencies, other workers you can trust, or other whistle-blowers.

• Check your rights under the law, and find out how you are protected or vulnerable.

• Do your homework. If you don't have all your facts and evidence straight, your risk may be for nothing. You could even get sued.

• Send your information where it will get the best results. Decide whether you should work through the system, talking to company superiors of increasing importance until you're heard, or whether you should go directly to the media or the government. Decide whether you want to supply the information anonymously. Consider your timing; a change of administration, for instance, might improve your chances of success.

• Be persistent. In many cases it takes years to get violations corrected.

Hot paper cups cost only about 1.5¢ more than foam cups, and they are biodegradable.

Doing Well By Doing Good

> *"Environmental investing" combines personal gain with planetary gain.*

IN A RAPIDLY SHRINKING WORLD, everything we buy makes a difference to the environment — personal products, household appliances . . . even corporate stocks. Your choices about financial security directly affect the well-being of people everywhere and of the planet itself. The more money you control, the more your potential influence.

So when you invest, you are also voting. How do you want to vote? How do you want your money to be used in relation to the environment? You'll probably feel better about your private nest egg if you know that the people using it aren't harming the earth.

The good news is that you can vote your conscience without compromising the return on your investments. In recent years a wide range of new companies, investment funds, and environmental ventures have sprung up — all designed to satisfy the most demanding investment criteria. Better yet, with the enormous amount of research being done on socially and ecologically sound investments, sound advice is plentiful. So no longer is there any reason to fear that companies that meet your tough standards of behavior will fare worse financially than unconcerned companies.

In fact, the big investment action in the 1990s will be in "clean" companies. Their products are finding a large, rapidly growing market, while their services are desperately needed to clean up the mess we've made. Many of the largest and most sophisticated investment firms have moved environmental stocks to the top of their favored lists.

Will your modest drop in the bucket of the financial marketplace really make a positive difference? You bet it will! According to *Fortune* magazine, business executives and investment bankers are especially sensitive to trends affecting their ability to compete internationally for the flow of cash that funds new ventures, products, and plant expansions. If industry leaders sense that the American investor is taking a serious view of each and every company's environmental record, you will see a rapid change of attitude toward the values in which you believe so strongly. You'd better believe that money talks!

Poland recently declared five villages unfit for human habitation because of extremely high levels of heavy metals in the air and soil.

FREEDOM ENVIRONMENTAL FUND

This fund raised $45 million in its initial offering and began investing in November 1989. Sixty-five percent of its assets are in companies that focus on cleaning up the environment. The minimum investment is $1,000. The maximum sales fee is 4.5% plus a 0.5% annual fee. –R.K.

Performance: NA (started in November 1989)
Freedom Capital Management

NEW ALTERNATIVES FUND

This is a socially concerned mutual fund. Investments include companies involved in recycling, conservation, clean water, and a variety of forms of alternate energy. The fund was the top-performing fund in the natural resources group of *Lipper's Mutual Fund Guide* for the five years ending September 29, 1989; average annual total return after deducting sales charges was 17.26%. New Alternatives avoids petroleum and nuclear energy companies and looks for firms engaged in conservation, resource recovery, and alternate energy sources. The minimum investment is $2,650. The maximum sales fee is 5.66%. Literature printed on recycled paper. –R.K.

Performance: 1988, 23.9%; 1989, 26%, New Alternatives Fund, Inc.

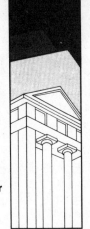

PARNASSUS FUND

With a total return of 42.4%, Parnassus was the top-ranked mutual fund in 1988, according to the Lipper Analytical Service Corporation. It finished 1989 with $23 million in net assets. Its focus is on technology and cyclical stocks (industries that rise and fall with predictable regularity). –R.K.

Performance: 1988, 42.4%; 1989, 2.78%, Parnassus Fund

PAX WORLD FUND

Organized in 1970, Pax World is a mutual fund with both economic and social investment criteria. It was the first social responsibility fund to stress investment in non-war-related industries. It invests in such industries as health care, education, pollution control, food, retail, housing, renewable energy, leisure time, and others. The minimum investment is $250. –R.K.

Performance: 1988, 11.65%; 1989, 24.92%, Pax World Fund, Inc.

SFT ENVIRONMENTAL AWARENESS FUND

This long-term investment fund was converted from a general to an environ-mental awareness fund in November 1988. At least 65% of the funds are invested in narrowly defined pollution control and environmental companies. The minimum investment is $1,000. The maximum sales fee is 5% plus a 0.35% annual sales fee. –R.K.

Performance: 1988, NA (started at year's end); 1989, 31%, SFT Inc.

SOCIALLY RESPONSIBLE BANKING FUND

Vermont's second-largest bank, with assets of approximately $700 million and 26 offices around Vermont, has a socially responsible fund for loans in affordable housing, environmental and conservation projects, family farming, education, and small business development. With a minimum investment of $500 in certificates of deposit or new money market accounts, you can specify that your money be deposited in the S.R.B. fund. Deposits exceed $33 million. The bank publishes a quarterly newsletter called *The Good Investor*. –R.K.

Performance: not applicable to a banking fund, since money is deposited with a fixed interest rate
Vermont National Bank

THE VALDEZ PRINCIPLES: GOOD NEWS FROM BAD

"Eager to work with business, many environmentalists are moving from confrontation to the best kind of collaboration. In September [of 1989] an ad hoc combination of institutional investors, controlling $150 billion of assets (including representatives of public pension funds) and environmental groups, promulgated the Valdez Principles, named for the year's most catalytic environmental accident. The principles ask companies to reduce waste, use resources prudently, market safe products and take responsibility for past harm. They also call for an environmentalist on each corporate board and an annual public audit of a company's environmental progress.

The group asked corporations to subscribe to the principles, with the implicit suggestion that investments could eventually be contingent on compliance. Companies already engaged in friendly discussions include DuPont, specialty chemical maker H. B. Fuller, and Polaroid, among others." — *David Kirkpatrick, Fortune* magazine, © 1990 The Time Inc. Magazine Company. All rights reserved.

Ask the company you are considering investing in whether they subscribe to the Valdez Principles. Contact the Coalition for Environmentally Responsible Economies (CERES) for more details.

WORKING ASSETS MONEY FUND

This is a money market mutual fund. Working Assets looks for companies in higher education, small business, family farming, and energy conservation. It screens out military contractors, nuclear power companies, companies doing business in South Africa, and companies with a record of environmental violations or job discrimination. The minimum investment is $1,000. Its assets at the beginning of 1990 were $188 million. –R.K.

Performance: 1988, 6.67%; 1989, 8.43%
Working Assets Funding Service

Chlorofluorocarbon concentrations in the atmosphere are increasing by 5% to 7% every year.

Policymakers and governments are also sensitive to the winds of change blowing through the investment community. From Europe's democratic and green revolutions, to the dismantling of apartheid in South Africa, to the massive response of millions of environmentally concerned Americans on Earth Day 1990, it is the will of the people that, when demonstrated, is shaking up the status quo.

Heightened Awareness, Heightened Prices?

The tremendous optimism regarding environmental investments may push their prices higher than they should be. Just be aware of this and realize that government regulations, which can significantly affect environmental industries such as toxic-landfill cleanups and pollution-control equipment, may be slower to come than most people think. Your best response to this concern is to proceed with caution and remain diversified, favoring companies that show concern for their customers and employees, as well as for the environment.

When "Clean" Gets Muddy

There are many mutual funds claiming to be "environmental." Be careful! Many of them include companies that are involved in some way in the environment but are not necessarily helping to improve it. For example, many environmentalists harshly criticize some companies because they don't trust the technology (such as waste incineration) the companies use or because the companies may make or sell environmental products but may not operate in an environmentally aware manner. So satisfy yourself that the "environmental" mutual fund or company you are about to invest in meets *your* definition of that word.

One, Two, Three, Buy

The first important steps for environmental investing are exactly the same as for any sound investing:
- Set realistic goals.
- Develop a comprehensive plan.
- Choose advisers and investments carefully.
- Periodically review and revise your strategy.

If you follow these guidelines, your environmental investments will be a natural outgrowth of intelligent financial management, not an altruistic sacrifice of your hard-earned assets. You can always find good places to donate your money; you don't want your investments to become contributions.

— *Rick Katzenberg*

AN EARTH-WISE INVESTMENT

Make a gift of $5,000 in cash or securities to the Nature Conservancy — an environmental protection land trust — and receive a lifetime income through its gift annuity program. The Conservancy will pay a fixed quarterly or annual sum for the rest of your life. A gift annuity provides excellent tax and income benefits to you as well as vital resources to the Nature Conservancy for natural areas preservation. You may schedule benefits to begin at a future date to help supplement your income, a portion of which may be tax exempt. See more about the Conservancy on page 198.

—*R.K.*

SOCIALLY RESPONSIBLE INVESTMENT GROUP, INC.

SRI provides investment management services for institutions and individuals. It uses a "social screen" to weed out corporations with poor environmental or labor records or heavy participation in certain morally questionable industries, such as tobacco or defense. In the 36 months ending 12/31/88, the SRI achieved a 13.5% return (Standard & Poors 500 posted a 13.3% return). In 1989 SRI's total return was 16.40%. Minimum account size is $200,000. –R.K.

SOCIAL INVESTMENT FORUM

The Forum is a nonprofit professional association for investors and professionals interested in social investing. It informs the public about the social impact of investments and provides information about individuals and institutions; thus, you can consider social criteria when making investment decisions. For $8 it sells an 80-page guide to socially responsible investment services. –R.K.

What You Can Do

✔ Ask corporations in which you are a shareholder to print annual reports, brochures, and catalogues on recycled paper. Many do, including RCA, Texaco, Coca-Cola, Consolidated Edison, and AT&T.

✔ Order your next personal checks from Message! Check Corporation. When you order 200 personal checks from this company for $14, it donates $1 to $1.50, split between its two environmental clients, Greenpeace and the National Audubon Society. In 1989 the contributions from this process exceeded $50,000. Message! works with your present checking-account system at any U.S. financial institution. Satisfaction is guaranteed. Write or call for sample checks and ordering instructions.

AFFINITY CARDS FOR DOWN-TO-EARTH INTEREST

Affinity Cards are special Visa cards or MasterCards that direct a portion of your purchase payments and annual fee to a designated charitable organization. Interest rates on these cards are slightly higher than average, but by early 1990 the cards had generated more than $100,000 for the National Audubon Society and $800,000 for the National Wildlife Federation. Some examples:

• **Working Assets Visa (800-634-5452) works for peace, human rights, and the environment. Every time you use your card it donates 5¢ to one of those causes. The 1989 total was** $218,000. **As a cardholder, you vote on how to allocate the funds among the groups annually.**

• **Bank of New England's cards (800-548-4783) donate to Defenders of Wildlife to help fund programs that protect wildlife and the habitat it needs to survive.**

• **Bank of Montreal and Canada Trust Affinity MasterCards have provided more than $45,000 to environmental groups in the U.S. and over $50,000 in Canada through 1989.**

READ MORE ABOUT IT

A SOCIALLY RESPONSIBLE FINANCING PLANNING GUIDE

By Cindy Mitlo-Shartel. This booklet advises readers on the principles of social investing, provides information on personal financial planning, offers a work sheet to help you organize your investment strategy, and has an excellent list of resources you can go to for further information. –R.K.

$5 (19 pages), Co-op America, 1988

THE CLEAN YIELD NEWSLETTER

The Clean Yield is published monthly as a stock market newsletter for investors who would like to make timely and profitable investments in publicly traded companies that pass certain social responsibility tests. –R.K.

$85/yr., The Clean Yield

THE WALL STREET GREEN REVIEW

This monthly newsletter tracks companies that fall into two environmental categories: waste services and alternative resources. It advocates a long-term investment strategy. –R.K.

$48/yr., Wall Street Green Review

YOU SHOULD KNOW

The amount of money that is invested on the basis of social criteria increased tenfold from 1984 to 1988, climbing to $450 billion.

— *Social Investment Forum*

We can save 3,700 pounds of lumber and 24,000 gallons of water by recycling one ton of paper.

Our Earth, Ourselves

THE GROUND WE LIVE ON and grow our food in is the earth's skin. How the natural forces in our soil interact is still a mystery to us — and it's a mystery we've forgotten to consider in our rush to industrialize.

The myth of miracle agricultural chemicals is dead. Now we know that synthetic fertilizers, herbicides, insecticides, and pesticides upset natural plant metabolism, create soil imbalances, and kill off living organisms indiscriminately. They remain in our food, leach into our drinking water, and wash into streams and rivers — where they react with bacteria to generate even more toxins.

The Chemical Killers

Healthy lawns, flowers, and vegetables require healthy soil, full of life and life-promoting nutrients. Here are some problems with the old-fashioned, chemical way of doing things.

> *"Whatever befalls the earth, befalls the children of the earth."*
>
> – CHIEF SEATTLE

- Chemical or mineral-salt fertilizers create a brutal environment for all the beneficial, life-sustaining organisms that live in the soil. With their continued use, the soil loses its vitality and plants become more vulnerable to insects. Then they need ever larger amounts of pesticides and herbicides to survive.
- Synthetic fertilizers generally work for only short periods of time because they give off gases and leach into water.
- Most synthetic fertilizers supply only a narrow range of nutrients, principally nitrogen, potassium, and phosphorus. Plants (and people) fed on such a narrow diet cannot be fully healthy.
- Chemical fertilizers change the vitamin and protein content of some crops and ultimately their nutritional value.
- The manufacture of agricultural synthetics uses lavish amounts of fossil fuel.
- Pesticides and herbicides are often carcinogenic. If something kills unwanted plants and insects, it will also have some effect on the plants you are cultivating and eating. We don't know the full carcinogenic effects of over 80 percent of the pesticides we use.

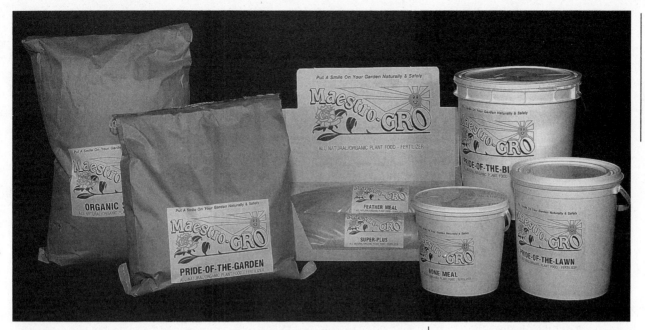

MAESTRO-GRO

Features a full range of fertilizers and soil amendments, including Pride-of-the-Lawn all-purpose lawn and turf food. Free brochure.

NECESSARY TRADING CO.

Necessary has been a leader in the organic gardening and farming field for well over a decade. Its straight-forward catalogue overflows with helpful aids, fertilizers, soil amend-ments, compost starters, kelp, and pest control aids. Catalogue $2.

NORTH COUNTRY ORGANICS

A no-frills organization with a strong dedication to healing the ecosystem, North Country has a wide range of or-ganic fertilizers, soil amendments, and bi-ological pest controls for gardeners and farmers. Free catalogue.

GARDENER'S SUPPLY

This lively and colorful free catalogue provides just about every organic or biodegradable garden product available, including fertilizers, pest controls, devices for extending the growing season, and tools to make chores more pleasant and efficient.

JUST THINKING

"Farmers see the light lie down in the dung heap and rise again in the corn."

—Wendell Berry

FEED THE SOIL, NOT THE PLANT

If you build rich soil, your plants will be more productive and far more capable of withstanding pests and diseases, which prey upon weaker plants. Once you've noticed a problem, it's usually too late to start building up the soil. Sure you can side-dress each plant with a handful of compost at midseason or you can spray a seaweed mixture on the leaves, but you really can't do much about the quality of the soil once plants are in the ground.

Add these natural fertilizers, green manures, and enzymes to your shopping list and your plants will thank you with healthy vigorous growth.

FERTILIZERS

Alfalfa meal. Derived entirely from vegetable sources. Ground from untreated alfalfa hay. Full of nitrogen and other nutrients.

Blood meal. From the dried blood of animals processed through slaughterhouses (shunned by some vegetarians). A rich source of nitrogen, often used for quick-growing greens such as spinach and lettuce. Dig or till into the soil to avoid attracting dogs and other animals.

Bonemeal. A favored source of phosphorus, also from slaughterhouses. Contains calcium, trace minerals, and small amounts of nitrogen.

Chilean nitrate. A naturally occurring nitrate of soda from salt beds in Chile. Contains up to 16% nitrogen and is totally soluble.

Cottonseed meal. A low pH for acid-loving plants. High in nitrogen.

Greensand. An iron potassium silicate from ancient beds of sea shells in New Jersey. Has some 30 trace minerals and lots of potassium, which makes for strong stems. (Wood ashes are also a good source of potassium, but don't add too much too fast.)

Holds large amounts of water; helpful in dry climates.

Manure. The organic fertilizer of choice. Not the sanitized cow manure that comes in neat little plastic bags, but heaps of the real stuff, which you've composted with other organic materials.

Manure tea. Made by steeping a burlap bag filled with fresh manure in a large container of water. Apply the resulting brew to the ground around plants to give them a boost just before they start to bloom.

Milorganite. Made from dried sewage sludge by the Milwaukee Metropolitan Sewage District. A prime lawn fertilizer purified by heat and microorganisms, favored by many landscapers and golf course superintendents.

Rock phosphate. Hastens plant maturity, increases fruit development, builds disease resistance, and increases the vitamin content of plants. Add only 35 to 50 pounds of phosphate to a 1,000-square-foot garden. Since the rate of release is slow, that's enough for three to five years.

Seaweed (kelp). A terrific fertilizer, used for many centuries. If you can get the real stuff, rinse the salt off with a garden hose and use it as mulch; in time it will break down and enrich the soil, releasing locked-up minerals. If you are far from the coast, purchase seaweed concentrates or kelp sprays.

Sul-Po-Mag. A blend of sulfur, potassium, and magnesium. Good for gardens that lack these elements but have a sufficient supply of calcium. It increases fruiting and speeds ripening.

GREEN MANURES

These are planted not to harvest but to chop up and mix back into the earth. They also protect valuable topsoil, shielding it from wind and water erosion.

Alfalfa. A deep-rooted legume favored for its high protein and nitrogen content. Also contains calcium, magnesium, and potassium.

Buckwheat. A non-legume grown mostly in the Northeast. Extensive root system and excellent choice for rebuilding poor or acid soils. Also attracts bees to the garden.

Cowpea. A fast-growing legume with powerful roots that can crack open and aerate compacted soils.

Crimson clover. A favored winter legume for improving already fairly good soil. If the soil is poor, sow a crop of cowpea seed first, and after it has enriched the soil, sow a crop of clover.

Legumes. Like clovers, legumes help take nitrogen from the air and fix it in the soil.

Red clover. A legume grown over much of the U.S., but primarily in the North. Easily cultivated, it will hold the soil together over the winter and can be plowed under in the spring.

Rye. A non-legume that tolerates many different soil types, even poor soil. The annual variety lasts until winter frosts. The perennial variety, called winter rye, will germinate late in the season, sometimes even after light frosts. Sow all non-legumes late in the growing season as a winter cover.

Vetches. Legumes that will grow in any reasonably fertile soil. Investigate to see which variety is best for your region.

ORGANIC FERTILIZERS, MAIL ORDER SOURCES

NITRON INDUSTRIES, INC.

Nitron's free glossy catalogue lists a full line of earthworm castings, greensand, compost, limestone, rock phosphate, bonemeal, kelp, cottonseed meal, trace elements, soil enzyme formulas, and fertilizer blends.

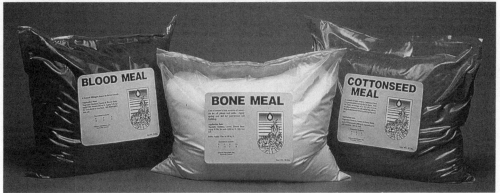

PEACEFUL VALLEY FARM SUPPLY

There's everything here from chicken manure to cocoa bean hulls, rock powders, and compost-fertilizer blends. Catalogue $2.

SAFER, INC.

A company with formidable marketing skills, Safer's biodegradable pest-control materials, fungicides, and weed killers are in hardware stores and garden centers everywhere.

ZOOK & RANCK INC.

Makes Erth-Rite, a composted fertilizer composed of rotted manure, greensand, colloidal and rock phosphates, seaweed meal, and a bacterial starter. Free catalogue. –S.M.

Half of the paper consumed in the U.S. is used solely to wrap and decorate consumer products.

Going Organic

Can your lawns be green and your gardens bountiful without old-fashioned synthetic chemicals? Can our nation's farmers prosper without them? The answer is a resounding "yes."

In the 1970s the Center for the Biology of Natural Systems in St. Louis, Missouri, found that crop yields on 32 well-managed organic farms were comparable to those on farms using old-fashioned chemical methods.

In 1989 the National Academy of Sciences, in a landmark study, concluded that farms using few or no chemicals are often as productive as those that use pesticides and synthetic fertilizers.

On your own piece of land — however small — you too can help heal the planet. Simple, natural, organic methods actually produce healthier lawns and gardens.

BEWARE OF THESE TOXIC GARDEN CHEMICALS

CHEMICAL	USED ON	DANGERS
Carbaryl (Sevin™)	General insecticide for flowers, fruits, vegetables	Loss of appetite and weight, kills bees and beneficial insects
Diazinon (Spectracide™ or KnoxOut™)	Mites and other insects	Disrupts nervous system
Methoxychlor (Marlate™)	Mosquitoes, cockroaches, flies, Japanese beetles	Toxic to bees and fish
Propoxur (Baygon™)	Lawn pests	Probable carcinogen, disrupts nervous system, kills bees
2, 4-D (Weed-B-Gone™ Weed & Feed™)	Most popular home weed killer	Irritates lungs and stomach. Can injure liver, kidneys, nervous system; toxic to bees and fish

Homeowners use on their lawns up to ten times more toxic chemicals per acre than farmers use on their crops.

GREEN BAN FOR PLANTS

Do you wonder if there will ever be a safe garden insecticide? Green Ban has developed just that — a safe insect repellent *plus* plant food. It's available as a spray concentrate that is suitable for both your indoor and outdoor plants. Containing kelp, hedera helix, sage, garlic, and eucalypt oil, it is 100% biodegradable and safe to use on edibles. There's nothing more satisfying than picking your own homegrown flowers and vegetables and knowing how they've been grown. Tester Deborah Giuffre remarks on the "eucalyptic freshness in the atmosphere" in her greenhouse and on how shiny and healthy her plants now look. *–Penny Uhlendorf*

$5.95 (8 fl. oz.); $29 Super Concentrate (1/2 gal.)
The Hummer Nature Works

What You Can Do

✔ Control slugs by placing old boards on the ground. The slugs will gather under them at night, where they will be easy pickings in the morning.

✔ Urge the Environmental Protection Agency and the Food and Drug Administration to step up testing of produce for pesticides and to immediately ban all high-risk pesticides.

SHOO, FLY

Houseflies are a vexation to the human spirit. They carry millions of microorganisms. But flies are only as filthy as the environment they inhabit. Keep a clean house and yard, and not only will you attract fewer flies, but the flies you do attract will also be better groomed, so to speak. If you do have too many flies around, here are a few environmentally benign steps:

• If your compost stinks, turn it with a pitchfork. If it still attracts flies, cover it with a tarp.

• Use fly parasites if you are overwhelmed by flies. Fly parasites are tiny, nonstinging wasps that kill fly pupae and are so small they go unnoticed by humans and livestock. (Available from IPM Laboratories, Inc.)

• Make your own flypaper with honey and yellow paper, and hang it from the ceiling. The color will attract the flies, and the honey will hold them.

• Use purchased flypaper only as a last resort; it is unsanitary and may contain unfriendly chemicals.

BYE-BYE, BEETLES

Striped cucumber beetles can turn an entire patch of squash vines into Irish lace in a week. Hand pick first, or spray them repeatedly with a tea made from pennyroyal, a type of mint. The beetles will vacate for a few days between sprayings, disrupting their breeding cycle and bringing the problem to a gentle end.

Flea beetles are tough to identify; they're only 1/16 inch long. But if your sprouting beans are being gnawed to nothing by these pests, spray a brew of minced garlic and insecticidal soap on the beans. Bye-bye, beetles; hello, peace of mind.

But wait! Stop! Don't step on the big black beetle! Let her live and she'll reward you by dining on those snails, slugs, cutworms, gypsy moths, houseflies, mosquitoes, termites, and gnats you really want to get rid of. Though they may also eat a beneficial insect from time to time, black beetles generally gobble up as many as 100 garden pests a week — a big help. Besides, beetles themselves are tempting morsels for others in a garden's food chain.

Pesticide-Free Pest Control: War or Peace?

It just isn't true that you have to use chemical pesticides. Instead, you can choose from many natural, organic options for handling every insect or pest problem. Just ask your local farmers' supply store.

Your first line of defense is the many creatures in your backyard that help to control insects and diseases; they include lady bird beetles, bees, lacewing larvae (aphid lions), praying mantis, dragonflies, spiders, toads, garter snakes, and birds. Learn to identify these allies, and let them be. They are your garden's best friends.

Many organic gardeners have found that they can control unwanted insects by turning loose their natural predators. But beware! Natural pest controls, too, can be abused. An overdose or an improperly timed application can destroy the delicate balance in a garden or an orchard.

Be certain you have correctly identified the offending insect or disease. Then apply the spray or dust just where it is needed to take care of a specific problem. In doing so, you will be doing your best to spare the beneficial bugs in the neighborhood.

Bat Patrol

There's another backyard creature that can be your ally, too. Slipping swiftly through the inky blackness of night, bats descend upon suburbia, open their menacing mouths, and bite. But they are not biting humans or pets; rather, they are chowing down on insects — as many as 3,000 a night. You couldn't ask for a better neighbor! Along with other winged visitors to the garden, such as purple martins and wrens, bats are one of the most effective natural controls available.

Misled by the wild mythology of bats, many people needlessly crush, trap, or poison them. For information on how to live at peace with bats — and to encourage their predations on insects — contact Bat Conservation International.

ANIMAL & BIRD REPELLENTS

You may never see them, but their handiwork is unmistakable. Nothing is more discouraging than to walk out to the lawn or garden and discover that gophers and moles have been using their big buck teeth to chew through garden plants, gnaw root systems, lacerate flower bulbs, and trash lawns. They are models of destructive efficiency.

We've heard of successful assaults using traps or combining water, dishwashing soap, and castor oil, then pouring the mixture into the burrows. Or try setting soda pop bottles into the critters' holes, taking care to leave the tops of the bottles above ground. As breezes pass over the bottle mouths, the eerie sound that's created disconcerts the rodents below and may convince them to relocate. If all else fails, you may want to turn to these high tech solutions:

THE MOLE MOVER

Buried underground and inaudible to humans, the Mole Mover is an expensive but effective way to discourage moles, voles, mice, and gophers. It sends out a highly annoying (to animal pests), ultrasonic vibration every two minutes. –S.M.

$89, Gardener's Supply

BIG EYES BIRD REPELLER

The Scare-Eye balloon is a basketball-sized blue, red, and yellow contraption, fashioned from heavy-gauge vinyl. Hung from a pole or a tree, the eye floats above the garden, clearly visible to any critters contemplating a snack. These have been strikingly effective protecting Japanese rice crops. This one guards a circle with an 85-foot diameter. –S.M.

$12.50, Hartmann's Plantation, Inc.

GOPHERIT II

A foot-long stake is set into the ground, and using four AA batteries, it emits its nasty underground sounds every 15 seconds or so. One GoPherIt II stake protects about 1,000 square yards of lawn or garden. –S.M.

$49.95, Ryans by Mail

RODENT ROCKS

This is a somewhat less expensive approach to ridding yourself of moles and mice. Rodent Rocks are porous lava rocks soaked in an herbal formula containing garlic and onions. When buried, the rocks give off a pungent, repelling odor. –S.M.

$8.95 (for a package of about 60 Rodent Rocks), Gardener's Supply

FRENCH SCARE CAT

Silhouetted against the backdrop of the garden, the sinister French Scare Cat, with its fiendish, shimmering marble eyes, crouches in perpetual readiness. French gardeners have used "scarecats" for years and found them to be an elegant and humane way to ward off birds, rabbits, and other marauders. –S.M.

$15, Gardener's Eden

Harvesting Brazil nuts can bring in 20 times more money than clearing forests to raise beef or crops.

A GUIDE TO NATURAL PESTICIDES

The following ingredients are natural pesticides.

Garlic. An effective deterrent for most leaf-munching insects when planted among susceptible crops or when made into a spray (put in a blender with water). Has antibiotic powers and can be used to control downy mildew, cucumber and bean rust, early blight of tomato, and bacterial blight of beans.

Pyrethrum (extract of chrysanthemum). Paralyzes on contact dozens of fruit and vegetable pests such as leafhoppers, aphids, and cabbage loopers. Must be sprayed directly on the bugs, which will revive completely if not hit with a lethal dose. Therefore often combined with rotenone. Do not use near waterways: toxic to aquatic life and breaks down slowly.

Rotenone. Extract from roots of several plants. Available as 1% or 5% dust or wettable powder or as liquid formulated with other botanicals such as pyrethrum or ryania. Kills many insects, including Mexican bean beetles, cabbageworms, and flea beetles. Moderately toxic to humans and animals. Wear a protective mask while applying the dust.

Ryania. Made from stems of a South American shrub. Doesn't kill insects outright, but makes them sick so they can't eat the treated crop. Highly selective; kills only a few pest species such as the European corn borer, codling moth, and cranberry fruit worm. Somewhat less toxic to humans than rotenone, but breaks down slowly so remains effective longer. Apply well before harvest so no residues remain on food.

Sabadilla. Made from seeds of a South American lily containing toxic substances that rapidly decompose when exposed to light. Use to control lice, leafhoppers, squash bugs, striped cucumber beetles, and chinch bugs. Irritating to mucous membranes; wear a mask while applying. Toxic to honeybees; apply during evening hours.

Soap. A time-tested method of controlling soft-bodied garden pests such as aphids, whitefly, and spider mites. Mix biodegradable soaps, like dishwashing detergent, in a 2% solution, and then spray. Harmless to beneficial insects like honeybees, ladybugs, and parasitic wasps.

Tobacco water. A potent natural pest control that can be poisonous to humans and can injure the nervous system. Use only when all else fails, and wear protective clothing. Soak a large handful of tobacco in four quarts of warm water for 24 hours. Dilute mixture with water until the color of weak tea, then spray on infested plants. Bugs immediately recognize that tobacco will do them no good, and they keep away. Most effective against small, soft-bodied insects such as aphids, but will also kill beneficial insects. Do not use on roses.

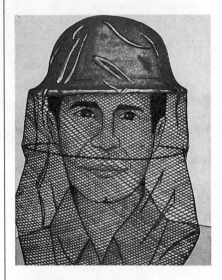
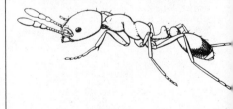
Americans suffer 20 to 90 million cases of illness due to contaminated food each year.

BUG-OFF BUG SUIT

When a head net just isn't enough and it's too hot for long sleeves, try Bug-Off, a 100% nylon mesh suit that is lightweight, flexible, and relatively comfortable. Handsome with bright red and yellow trim, elastic cuffs, high-quality zippers, and a protective hood. The suit is ideal for children — and for the child in all of us. –S.M.

$28 Children's small, medium, and large; $35 Adult suit; $19.95 Adult shirt, Bug-Off Creative Clothing

JAPANESE BEETLES + CHICKENS = EGGS

By sheer accident I discovered a cure for my Japanese beetle plague: chickens. Our six Easter chicks were originally, of course, for my five year old, but what scavengers they turned out to be! In the spring they dined on the beetle grubs in the lawn; in the summer, they ate the live beetles. Only a few dozen beetles escaped them compared with the thousands in previous summers.

— *Bruce Anderson*

INSECT REPELLENTS

Many insect repellents contain R-11, which has come under fire recently since lab studies raised questions about its potent health effects.

Another major issue regarding insect repellents is that the EPA requires all products labeled as insect repellents — even those with active ingredients such as the highly potent DEET — to be tested on animals. Some companies get around this requirement by labeling their products as something other than insect repellents.

Pennyroyal, common in bug repellents, can burn the eyes and mucous membranes and cause other harmful side effects through breathing or skin absorption. Keep it away from children and pregnant women.

LAKON HERBALS BYGONE BUGS

Contains oils of eucalyptus, peppermint, birch, rosemary, and Australian tea. A vegetable-oil base extends protection time. Does not contain pennyroyal or citronella. The company claims it's safe for children and pregnant women. –*Lonny Brown*

$3.99 (2 oz.), Lakon Herbals

WEEDS OF WORTH HERBAL INSECT DETERRENT

"Perfected in New England swamps," the promotional copy says. Contains pennyroyal, sassafras, eucalyptus, citronella, tansy, sage, rubbing alcohol, spring water, olive oil, and elephant garlic. –*L.B.*

$7.95 (4 oz.) Weeds of Worth Ltd.

GREEN BAN FOR PEOPLE

Finally — an herbal alternative to chemical insect repellents. Green Ban for People (tested in the Australian rain forest) contains citronella, pennyroyal, sassafras, cajuput, lavender, and bergamot in a base of calendula, soy, and tea tree oils. Our tester Joe Kohler even uses it indoors — just because he loves the smell! The Regular Formula will protect the whole family against such pests as mosquitoes, fleas, no-see-'ems, chiggers, and leeches. Adults braving badly infested areas, or needing longer-lasting protection, should use Double Strength. –*P.U.*

**$5.95 Regular Strength (2.5 fl. oz.); $6.95 Double Strength (2.5 fl. oz.)
The Hummer Nature Works**

GREEN BAN
For People

The Herbal Alternative to Chemical Insect Repellant

Tested in the Australian rainforest.
A little goes a long way.

75 ml 2½ fl oz

If Americans reduced their intake of meat by ten percent, 60,000,000 people could be adequately fed by the grain that would be saved.

Water, Water — Everywhere?

While organic gardeners are trying to save their gardens from insect pests, they're also trying to save the environment from further harm in other ways. They know that when we use hoses or sprinklers to water our lawns, we are being wildly extravagant. Gallons of water evaporate — some of it before it even hits the ground — and much falls where it's not needed: on walkways, between plant rows, on thirsty weeds. This leads to further damming of unspoiled valleys.

Is there another way to share a dwindling fresh water supply with our cultivated plant neighbors? Yes! In fact, you can choose from many clever tools and techniques to conserve water.

- *Build your lawn and garden soil organically.* High-quality organic soil retains moisture, and healthy plants are far more capable of withstanding drought.
- *Mulch heavily.* Place thick layers of compost, mulch hay, or grass clippings around each shrub and plant. Mulch reduces evaporation of moisture, and when it is finally turned into the soil, it adds even more organic matter.
- *Use shrubs and ground cover rather than grass.* They require less maintenance and less water and provide year-round greenery. Examples include thyme and vinca.
- *Select grass, shrub, and crop varieties that require less water and are drought resistant,* such as:

Perennials — Black-eyed Susan, coreopsis, edelweiss, gaillardia, globe thistle, lavender, yarrow.

Annuals — Celosia, cleome, cosmos, daylily, gazania, marigold, morning glory, nicotiana, portulaca, strawflower, sunflower, verbena, zinnia.

Shrubs — Aucuba, barberry, cotoneaster, crape myrtle, euonymus, juniper, nandina, privet, wild lilac.

Ground covers — Crown vetch, ice plant, sedum, sempervivum.

Consult further with your nursery about plants native to your environment, or from similar climates, that require little watering.
- *Divert roof runoff.* Even in the driest of summers, some rain falls. By running gutter downspouts into a covered barrel or cistern, you can use rainwater by the bucketful whenever the garden needs it. "Soft" (low-mineral) rainwater can also be used for laundry, dishes, and bathing. Don't drink it. Cover and store in the shade to protect it from evaporation.
- *Check outdoor water systems from end to end for leaks.* Examine spigots, hose lines, and connections. Most systems leak a little, but carefully assembling all parts according to manufacturer's instructions will help.
- *Water after sunset or before 9 A.M. to avoid evaporation.* Use a timer to avoid overwatering.
- *Water lawns only when grass doesn't spring back if stepped on.*
- *Put moisture directly where it can be used most efficiently.* Aim your hose or preferably your watering can at the roots of plants, or use trickle irrigation.

LAWN AND GARDEN IRRIGATION SYSTEMS

If water is plentiful, lawns will certainly appreciate a good soaking every ten days or so. If you sprinkle too often, the roots remain shallow.

Where water is expensive or in short supply, however, consider installing a drip irrigation system. Drip systems are costly and require annual tinkering, but they save time and water.

Because dripped water concentrates in small areas, it penetrates deeply and quickly — a foot deep in 15 minutes. Soluble fertilizers can be mixed in so as to distribute nutrients at the same time.

All you need is a water source — a water faucet or a gravity-fed system from plastic or metal rain barrels. And one of the items on the facing page . . .

Before ordering from any mail order suppliers, please check with them to determine shipping and handling charges.

CLAY POT CONSERVATION

For over 2,000 years the Chinese people have used a clay-pot system to save water while caring for trees and shrubs. The system is elegantly simple:

1. Dig a hole beside each tree or shrub to be irrigated.

2. Place a naturally porous, unglazed earthenware pot or jug in the hole, and cover to prevent evaporation.

3. When the tree or shrub needs water, fill the pot, and it will slowly pass the water to the roots.

IRRIGRO SYSTEMS

All of these kits are based on porous plastic tubing that gently weeps water to plant roots, allowing them to continually absorb water. The Starter T-Kit has enough tubing and fittings to irrigate 200 square feet, and it can be expanded. The Automatic Garden System waters 400 square feet. Beware of confusing instructions, however. Although the company's product literature is thorough, it includes a confusing hodgepodge of facts, figures, and sales hype. –S.M.

$19.95 The Starter T-Kit; $34.95 The Automatic Garden System
The International Irrigation Co. (Irrigro)

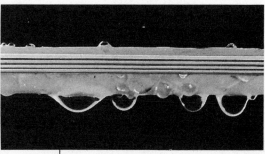

AQUAPORE SOLID STATE WATER TIMER

Program this easy-to-install timing device to automatically switch watering systems on or off at various intervals. It's great for automatic drip systems, but can be easily switched to manual, too. –S.M.

$62, Gardener's Eden

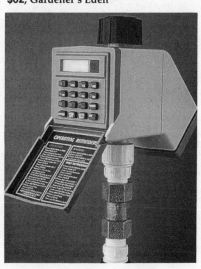

RAINDRIP, INC.

We like Raindrip as the supplier of the most complete line of drip irrigation products. Ask for its catalogue because there are hundreds of little pieces and parts to a complete drip irrigation system. Setting up the system in your garden or yard is an exacting process. Matching the drip rate to each plant and assembling myriads of plastic components is a one-time job. –David Del Porto

GARDENA, INC.

The best water timers and computers are made by Gardena. We like the convenience of setting the water timer to a drip irrigation system at night before going to sleep. No hassle, and you minimize water loss through daytime evaporation. –D.D.P.

What You Can Do

✔ Watch what you pour into your kitchen drain; it's your personal connection to the world of water. Never simply pour out substances such as garden chemicals, solvents, paints, or oils. Dispose of them carefully in accordance with the manufacturer's instructions.

Green Lawns, Green Planet

Lawn care is the most popular gardening activity in North America, far outpacing vegetable or flower gardening. There's just something about looking out over a vibrant, green yard that appeals to the American soul. Unfortunately, until recently much of that green was maintained by applying synthetic substances, an estimated five to ten pounds of chemicals per acre of lawn each year.

But you can have a green, healthy lawn when you balance air, water, and nutrients so that beneficial bacteria and earthworms thrive in the soil. Here's what you need to consider:

- *Air.* Life in the soil under your lawn needs air. A dethatching machine will remove plant matter that may be smothering the grass. An aerator will break up hard soils. Both are available at rental stores and hardware shops.
- *Water.* Healthy soil rich in organic matter tends to hold water in the right proportion and produces deep-rooted grass with increased drought resistance. Really soak your lawn for at least an hour every ten days or so (better for your lawn and water supply than merely sprinkling the surface daily).
- *Nutrients.* Test your soil every two years for critical nutrients such as nitrogen, potassium, and phosphorus, and correct for deficiencies. County extension agencies usually charge $5 to $7 for a soil sample test that will tell you what your soil is like and what it needs.
- *Lawn length.* Keep your grass fairly tall (2.5 inches or more). Taller grass grows thick, conserves moisture, squeezes out weeds, and roots deeply.

Which Grass Is Best for You?

It's far easier to have a beautiful, healthy lawn without chemical fertilizers if you plant the right variety of grass. Consider the specific conditions of your area, talk to neighbors, and ask local garden centers before making a choice of grass seed. Here are some possibilities (see map).

Northeast and Pacific Northwest. Fylking, Baron, Park, and Newport are varieties of Kentucky bluegrass. These grasses appear dry and brown in the heat of summer, but resume a vibrant green color when cool days return. For variety, health, and a longer green season, mix a little clover seed in when you plant.

Southeast, Southwest, California. What the bluegrasses do for the North, the Bermuda grasses do for these regions. Tifflawn is one popular variety of Bermuda grass, deep green, fine in texture, vigorous, and very disease resistant. Better yet are the zoysia grasses developed in recent years, which surpass the performance of many Bermuda grasses.

West and Midwest. In arid regions only buffalo grass, gama grass, and a few other desert species will succeed, unless enough water is available to support Northeast varieties.

YOU SHOULD KNOW

A lawn punctuated with ant hills is not necessarily unhealthy. The sight may disturb some homeowners, but ants are actually quite beneficial, aerating the lawn naturally. (Lawn ants are not the ones that invade the house.) Letting the grass grow a little longer will camouflage most ant colonies and help conserve water.

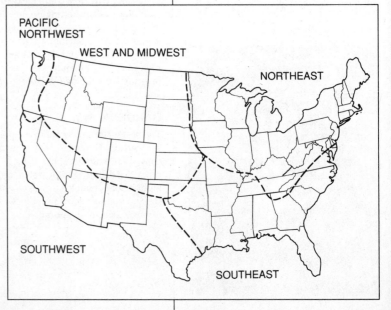

REEL MOWERS: MUSCLE VS. MOTOR

Improvements in materials and design have made reel mowers lighter and easier to maneuver than the prehistoric monsters you may remember. Plus, they are quieter and conserve energy, and their scissor-action is kinder and gentler to the grass. A terrific way to slow lawn moisture evaporation in hot weather. The one major drawback of reel mowers is that they can't handle tall grass. On the other hand, they don't cost much!

Simple, handsome, and easy to use, the hand mowers from the American Lawn Mower Co. require a minimum of maintenance and will give years of good, nonpolluting service. The company makes 12 basic mowers, ranging from the economy model with plastic wheels and untempered blades, to a deluxe version with a heavy-duty frame and chrome-plated hub caps. –S.M.

From under $70 to over $100 for the top of the line
The American Lawn Mower Co.; Vermont Country Store; Alsto Co. Handy Helpers

What You Can Do

✔ For your organic garden, select a site that receives at least six hours of direct sun each day. Avoid poorly drained areas.

✔ Build the soil steadily by adding well-rotted organic matter — leaves, composted garbage, manure — whatever nature provides. The soil is the foundation of everything that happens in the garden; the better your foundation, the greater your successes.

✔ Be careful about timing. Sow seeds or plant seedlings too early or too late, and your plants will be unnecessarily vulnerable. Vigorous growth is often a plant's best defense.

✔ Locate your plants where they will prosper. Don't force them to live in situations that don't suit them. A rose that is grown against a house, for example, will inevitably suffer from mildew.

✔ Take a daily stroll through the garden. How are things coming along? The sooner you notice a problem, the easier it is to correct it.

✔ Keep a jar in hand as you survey your garden, and sweep any unwanted insects into the container. Be careful not to eliminate beneficial insects.

Considering Compost

The compost heap is the heart of the organic garden. No matter what your garden soil is like, compost will improve its structure and — by adding nitrogen, phosphorus, and potassium — boost its fertility. It can be safely used on vegetables, flowers, shrubs, and lawns.

Compost is organic waste — leaves, grass clippings, garbage, manure, shredded newspaper (black ink only), whatever — that has broken down. It's best made like lasagna! Layer the materials as you go, covering kitchen scraps (except meat and grease) with soil, leaves, or trimmings, and every so often adding a shovelful of manure or lime. Turn the pile after two months or so to speed up the process.

Composting: The Hot & Cold of It

Aerobic or "hot composting" involves storing biodegradable materials in a drumlike container or some other vessel where it can be frequently turned and mixed. Turning introduces a steady supply of air, creating a slow, ecological oven in which millions of bacteria can thrive and break down the wastes into humus. Aerobic compost can reach temperatures of 150° to 170° F — hot enough to destroy weed seeds, pests, and disease-promoting organisms. But it requires a lot of attention and work.

Anaerobic composting is slower than the aerobic method and rarely destroys weed seeds or disease spores. But it is easier. The gardener simply designates a spot for the pile or digs a hole in the ground, then tosses the waste into it. In this inglorious heap, bacteria and fungi have their disintegrating way.

Composting is also a brilliant means of managing biodegradable household waste. Many towns and cities have begun composting programs, too.

COMPOST BINS

Compost bins are easy and inexpensive to build out of wooden pallets, scrap lumber, or even a hoop of old chicken wire. Many gardening books and magazines have construction plans. But if you have neither the time nor the inclination, then consider commercially manufactured compost bins. They are neat, attractive, and generally unobtrusive. Plus the store-bought variety makes compost quickly and usually gets hot enough to kill weed seeds.

If your yard and garden are sizable, you'll want one or two large bins. But if you have a small yard and few table scraps, then a barrel composter is a reasonable option. Keep in mind that the best hot compost piles must be at least one cubic yard in volume.

THE DOUBLE NOTCH COMPOSTER

One of the best of the commercially available bins. Made of natural, no-maintenance white cedar, it blends in with the colors and textures of nature. It's easy to assemble with a notched construction system that gives it strength and stability, and there are ventilation slots on all four sides. It measures 27"x27"x26" and is made in the U.S. –S.M.

$54.95, The Plow and Hearth

THE CONFESSION OF A COMPOST HEAP HERETIC

I must confess that I am a compost heap heretic. I use the "Random Method": compost haphazardly, like the forest does. A pile of leaves here, a bucket of ashes there, some table scraps . . . everything takes its own sweet time, and so do I. Even without faithfully layering, amending, inoculating, and turning as prescribed in gardening manuals, Mother Nature inevitably rewards me with a beautiful heap of organic fertilizer.

Drawbacks to the lazy approach? It takes far longer to transform the stuff to the point where it's usable, weed seeds may persist, and the level of microbial life never gets particularly high. I accept the trade-offs for the convenience of less work. *–S.M.*

THE BLACKWALL GREEN MAGIC 500 COMPOST TUMBLER

The bin is loaded in the usual way, but instead of having to bend your back and turn the heap with a shovel or a pitchfork, you just spin it. By spinning it once a day, an easy chore, you can transform up to 8 cubic feet of organic matter into compost in about three weeks. –S.M.

$99.95, Gardener's Supply

What You Can Do

✔ If you're building a compost heap, keep the compost moist, but not wet; it should feel like a squeezed-out sponge.

✔ You can compost in tight quarters, even in cities. Just keep the bins tightly closed.

✔ Remember the watchwords of composting: "Layer, moisten, and turn."

✔ Never include fish or meat scraps, grease, oil, bones, or milk products in the compost. They will foul the heap and attract vermin. And of course, omit all plastic, glass, foil, or metal.

✔ Pick up a carton of fishing worms and set them free in your compost heap. They'll think they've gone to worm heaven, and your compost will break down swiftly and thoroughly.

THE WIRE COMPOST BIN

Simplicity itself, this bin has four coated, 10-gauge, galvanized-steel wire sides that, when assembled, fence in 25 cubic feet of yard and garden refuse. There's no top, so you may want to place a tarp over it to prevent rain from leaching out valuable nutrients. This bin is less attractive than the enclosed bins, but it's also less expensive than most. –S.M.

$49.95, Gardener's Supply

INSTANT COMPOST

Mary Perlmutter of the Canadian Organic Growers has devised a nifty way to make small amounts of instant compost. She churns up her few kitchen scraps in a blender with a cup of water and pours the rich tea directly on her garden and houseplants. "It makes wonderful plant food," she says. "It doesn't smell and it's out of your way immediately."

Plant a Tree — Save a Planet

You've got your garden pests under control without using harsh chemicals. You're conserving water, you're working on your yard, and you've started a compost pile. What else can you do, literally in your own backyard, to help preserve the environment? Plant a tree.

From mowers to furnaces to automobiles, almost every modern energy-consuming device uses combustion to generate power. Combustion eats up oxygen and gives off carbon dioxide; trees, however, do the opposite. A fast-growing tree can recycle more than 26 pounds of carbon dioxide each year, and it does this whether it's growing in your yard or in a rain forest.

Trees around your home decrease water runoff and increase natural cooling. For every tree you plant you'll save money in heating and cooling costs, help stop soil erosion, and reduce air pollution.

Deciduous trees (maples, oaks, sweet gum) can provide summer cooling. The air beneath large trees can be as much as five to ten degrees cooler than the air above. An evergreen wind screen can help on northern exposures. They should be 30 feet from the house and two to six feet apart, depending on the species.

Tree Farming

Tree farmers are people who own forestland and who recognize the importance of managing the land wisely. The American Tree Farm System is a nationwide community of nearly 60,000 landowners. Each member generally owns a minimum of ten acres of forestland. To qualify, landowners must have improved their land with activities such as tree planting or the enhancement of wildlife habitat. They must also have their land inspected by one of the 10,000 foresters who donate time to the Tree Farm System.

A free inspection of your woodlands for their potential as a tree farm can be arranged by your state forest service, forestry association, or tree farm committee. County extension service agents can also recommend foresters to inspect property.

Backyard Tree Farms

So you'd like to be a tree farmer, but you have fewer than ten acres? Well, if you live in Louisiana, Washington, Vermont, or New Hampshire, you may qualify as a Backyard Tree Farmer. Those four states are pioneering an ambitious program for forest and wildlife management that supports small acreage owners — a population far bigger than that of the larger owners. If you live in one of the four pioneering states, ask your county extension agent how to connect with the program. If not, contact your county extension agency and talk up the idea of starting a Backyard Tree Farmer program in your state.

BAT HOUSES

Bats are a wonderful natural insect control. They like to live in old trees, caves, and barns, but not all of us have those handy. These bat houses are a perfect substitute. Made of 3/4" yellow cypress, they'll last for years. The small version will hold 20, the large 30. Hangholes, mounting instructions, and fascinating bat facts are included. –S.M.

$42.95 (large, modified for greater protection from predators); $2.25 (construction plans for small and large modified sizes)
Bat Conservation International

ACTIONS SPEAK LOUDER . . .

Applied Energy Services of Arlington, Virginia, set an earth-healing precedent in 1988 with plans to plant enough trees in the rain forests of Guatemala to absorb the amount of CO_2 that its new coal-fired energy plant was generating in Connecticut. "Given the scientific consensus on the seriousness of the global warming problem," the company president said, "we decided that it was time to stop talking and to act."

BIRDHOUSES

No more rotting or loose screws, no more chewed entranceways. Finally there are birdhouses available that not only blend well into the environment and are safe for the healthy development of baby birds, but also are built to last. Made in Germany from a unique mixture of sawdust, concrete, and clay, these birdhouses are completely rot-, squirrel-, and predator-proof and should last over 20 years. The roof and sides are covered with a nontoxic brown paint to shed water easily, and the front panel, which can be interchanged with varying hole sizes to attract your garden favorites, removes for annual cleaning. A friend from Harvard, Massachusetts, proudly claims that when she hung her new birdhouse, a wren moved in within one hour!

Available in 11 models, including free-hanging (which are suspended from branches up to 5" in diameter), tree-trunk or building mounted, and open swallow boxes. –P.U.

$19.95 (wren and bluebird size) to $42.95 (owl or wood duck size); $12.95 Open Swallow Box
The Kinsman Company, Inc.

FLOWFORMS: ART IN THE SERVICE OF NATURE

Water trapped in long, straight pipes for days and weeks stagnates and "dies." Flowforms — sculptured vessels designed to carry water in a rhythmical, pulsating, figure-eight pattern — help water oxygenate and cleanse itself. While Flowforms are aesthetically pleasing in their own right, they are also educational and therapeutic, calming the nerves and refreshing the senses. Where they have been used near fish ladders, more than the usual numbers of fish are found in the eddy.

The forms can be custom designed, but several standard Flowforms are available in a variety of materials for use in gardens, parks, plazas, or architectural settings. –S.M.

Waterforms, Inc.

"This time, like all times, is a very good one if we but know what to do with it." —Emerson

In Search of Seedlings

Forty-four of the 50 states have tree nurseries that make seedlings available for reforestation projects. When the annual needs of those reforestation projects have been met, most states make the surplus seedlings available at low cost, not for home landscaping, but for civic and demonstration projects. For information on the availability of seedlings, contact the division of your state government responsible for forests and public lands.

Free Trees

Skip the local nursery and save a bundle by scouting the wooded areas of your yard, or a friend's, for small seedling trees to transplant. When you find one, dig an ample root ball, and replant the baby tree as soon as possible.

Have a favorite evergreen? Take a cutting in early spring and place it immediately in a plastic bag filled with half peat moss, half sand. Moisten the mixture, close the bag, and in a couple of weeks roots should begin to sprout. At that point, repot the cutting into a richer soil mix, and tend it until it reaches transplant size.

Urban Trees: The Bad News

Some scientists believe that urban trees, growing in close proximity to high concentrations of carbon dioxide, may be even more effective in cleaning the air than rural trees. They help keep city streets cool on hot summer days with their shade, and they work incessantly to purify the air. But development, pollution, disease, insects, aging, and physical abuse are rapidly killing urban trees. In too many American cities, harsh open gaps have replaced the green splendor of the vanishing urban trees. Only one tree is planted for every four lost. Many newly planted trees die because of insufficient care and inadequate space.

Urban Trees: The Good News

Through its Global ReLeaf Project, the American Forestry Association is working to reforest the cities. It publishes a citizen action guide entitled *Save Our Urban Trees*. To get a copy, contact the American Forestry Association. See page 194 for more information about the AFA.

JUST THINKING

"The soil is like a bank account. You must put in and put in and wait for the interest to grow before you start making withdrawals. Who has a bank account anywhere where you can only withdraw and never deposit?"

–Don Eligio Panti

YOU SHOULD KNOW

As we enter the 1990s, less than half of the planet's original acreage of tropical rain forest is left. Imagine a giant stomping through a rain forest, with huge feet that obliterate an area the size of a football field every 30 seconds. This is the rate at which tropical rain forests are disappearing all over the world. This "giant" manifests itself in the form of fires half the size of California burning at any given time in developing countries such as Brazil.

According to the American Forestry Association, there are at least 100 million energy-efficient tree planting sites available around American homes and in our towns and cities. Planting trees in that many sites could offset carbon dioxide emissions by 33 million tons a year, helping to stabilize the world climate.

THE TEAK PIQUE

Some U.S. companies selling garden furniture tout their policy of importing teak only from plantations such as those in Thailand and Burma, rather than from virgin rain forests. But it takes 50 to 100 years to grow a Tectyona grandis to a size sufficient for harvest, and according to sources from the Thai Department of Agriculture, most plantation trees have not yet reached harvest size. Even if/when plantations are able to fill the demand for teak, they cannot create the balanced diversity of life that currently exists in rain forests.

Fortunately, it's not necessary to buy teak to get handsome, durable lawn furniture. The Adirondack Chair is another option.

What You Can Do

✔ Do not buy products made of rosewood, mahogany, teak, liana, or other tropical woods from the "fueling stations" of migrant songbirds.

✔ While you're creating a backyard wildlife preserve, don't forget what you like to eat. It's an age-old tradition, setting out perennial trees, shrubs, and other plants that will produce backyard, or even front-yard, food year after year. Edible plants can be beautiful as well as tasty. And, of course, the more fresh food we grow for ourselves, the less we must depend on energy-eating transportation systems to bring the food to us from far away.

KARL PETZKE, ©1989 SMITH AND HAWKEN

THE ADIRONDACK CHAIR
This unfinished light red cedar chair never needs to be sealed, sanded, or painted. It's weather resistant, will improve in appearance as time goes by, and is ultra-comfortable. –S.M.

$139-$169, Smith and Hawken

ENZYMES

Without enzymes, your soil and seeds sit in a sorry, soggy heap. In recent years some organic gardeners sprayed commercially prepared enzymes on their soil. The results? Improved soil composition, vigorous root growth, and increased disease resistance. While expensive, they may be worth the investment.

NITRON
This natural enzyme conditioner can help to detoxify soils that have previously been treated with chemical fertilizers. And it comes with a money-back guarantee. –S.M.

$9.50 (1 qt. for 2,500 sq. ft.)
Nitron Industries, Inc.

Naturally Native

When you purchase new trees or shrubs for your yard, ask the nursery about native plant species, those most naturally adapted to your area's climate and conditions. These will grow stronger, be less susceptible to disease, and be less likely to require treatment with chemicals. They will also avoid the problems that come with certain exotic plants, which were imported for gardens and have escaped into the wild; the exotic species are now crowding out native species that are valuable to wildlife.

An obsession with perfect, artificial landscaping wastes energy and offends native wildlife. Leave some dead or dying trees standing for the woodpeckers and owls. And instead of hauling all your brush off to the local landfill or chipping it for mulch, pile some in a back corner of your lot as an inviting habitat for birds and rabbits.

— *Steven S. H. McFadden*

BENEFICIAL ORGANISMS

SUPPLIERS OF BENEFICIAL ORGANISMS

You can have your bugs bug other bugs instead of bugging you! Too good to be true? Not at all. Send for this comprehensive listing of companies that supply beneficial organisms. Updated every few years, the list specifies more than 50 mail order companies that supply predatory insects, mites, snails, and disease organisms. –S.M.

Free
Biological Control Services Program, California Department of Food and Agriculture

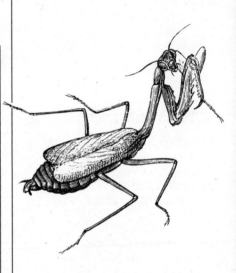

YOU SHOULD KNOW

Much of the chemical fertilizer we put on our lawns ends up in neighboring bodies of water. This often causes plant life to grow wildly and choke off the oxygen needed by fish and other aquatic life. The resulting "eutrophication" is killing many of our ponds and lakes.

You can use black-and-white newspapers as mulch without fear of toxins in the ink, thanks to an ecological industry-wide policy established in 1980. Colored printed papers, however, such as the comic sections, use heavy-metal inks — not good for garden soil. Don't even use the ashes after burning colored papers.

According to a 1987 National Research Council study, nearly 1.4 million people in the U.S. will develop cancer over their lifetimes due to pesticide residues on foods.

Railroad ties and utility poles, often used to make barbecue pits and garden fences, are likely treated with pesticides such as pentachlorophenol, creosote, and arsenic to kill the microorganisms that invade wood. Recognized as carcinogenic by the Environmental Protection Agency, these chemicals can cause cancer and birth defects as well as blood, liver, and skin diseases. Instead, use brick and stone.

The average modern farm uses over a barrel of oil to produce a ton of grain. The more food we grow close to home, the less fuel must be used to transport it to us.

What You Can Do

✔ Learn about rotation, interplanting, and companion planting, time-tested ways of preventing serious pest problems.

✔ Sow cover crops, like red clover or winter rye, to nourish the soil between growing seasons.

SUPPLIERS OF BENEFICIAL INSECTS

Send for a price list before ordering, and include a self-addressed, stamped envelope. Most suppliers also make commercial quantities available.

BENEFICIAL INSECTARY
Beneficial insects and fly parasites, ladybugs, and organic products.

BENEFICIAL INSECT SALES, INC.
Beneficial insects and organic products.

BIOLOGIC
Scanmask nematodes and other beneficial nematodes and organic products.

GROWING NATURALLY
A variety of beneficial insects.

IPM LABORATORIES, INC.
A good source of a variety of insect predators, like mites and fly parasites.

RINGER CORPORATION
A broad range of biological controls, especially for the lawn.

W. ATLEE BURPEE COMPANY
Beneficial insects and organic products.

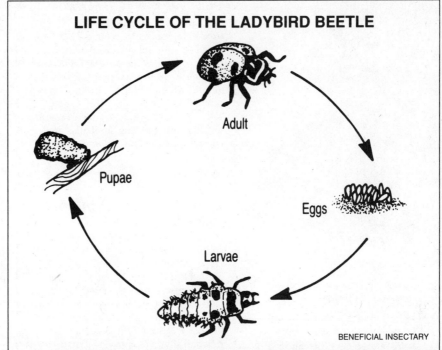

LIFE CYCLE OF THE LADYBIRD BEETLE

Adult

Pupae

Eggs

Larvae

BENEFICIAL INSECTARY

GARDENING VIDEOS

THE VICTORY GARDEN VEGETABLE VIDEO SERIES
Spawned from the famous "Victory Garden" television series, this full-color video has 31 segments and an index that directs viewers to the subjects they are interested in. It's intended as a full course for home gardeners, geared not only for beginners but also for those with some experience. Host Bob Thomson, however, frequently employs petro-chemical-based fertilizers and pesticides. –*S.M.*

$24.95, Crown Video

JUST THINKING

"A weed is a plant whose virtues have not yet been discovered."
—*Ralph Waldo Emerson*

THE ENCYCLOPEDIA OF NATURAL INSECT AND DISEASE CONTROL

You won't find a more systematic and comprehensive guide for growing plants without using toxic chemicals. Each possible pest or disease has its own entry, with detailed information on how to identify the culprit, and what natural steps to take to heal the plant. Color plates depict the most common pests and diseases to make identification even more sure. When you're ready to take action, you can turn to the pages of this encyclopedia for hundreds of specific remedies. –S.M.

$30, Rodale Press

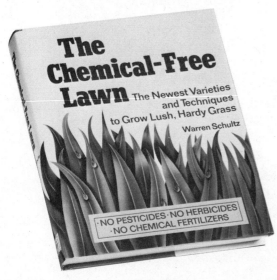

THE CHEMICAL-FREE LAWN: THE NEWEST VARIETIES AND TECHNIQUES TO GROW LUSH, HARDY GRASS

By Warren Schultz. After reading this book, you'll be convinced that eliminating chemicals doesn't mean settling for an inferior lawn. This interesting and well-organized book is chockablock full of detail, facts, comparisons, and tips. –S.M.

$14.95 (paperback); $21.95 (hardback), Rodale Press

BUILDING A HEALTHY LAWN

By Gardener's Supply. Here's another excellent resource for creating and maintaining a beautiful lawn without using toxic chemicals. "There are 900 billion organisms living in a cubic foot of soil," the authors write, "and they can work for you rather than against you." The 168-page softcover book includes chapters on seeding, mowing, watering, fertilizing, and controlling weeds, insects, and diseases. –S.M.

$9.95, Gardener's Supply

EARTH PONDS: THE COUNTRY POND MAKER'S GUIDE

By Tim Matson. For an elegant yet eminently practical resource, turn to *Earth Ponds*. It's amply illustrated with black-and-white photographs and shows the steps necessary to create a pond. It also takes you through the seasons of a pond's life, where still waters are a magnet for life and a mirror for the sky. You'll find practical advice plus an extensive list of resources. –S.M.

$9.95, The Countryman Press, 1982

LET IT ROT!

By Stu Campbell. A modern composting classic! For the ins and outs and ups and downs of how to rot your waste in high style, these are the pages to turn. It's all here, from an entertaining philosophical discussion of composting to specific information on location, structure, additives, watering, turning, and the other details of compost care. One of the best features of the book is the number of composting options that it presents. –S.M.

$7.95, Garden Way Publishing, Storey Communications, Inc., 1975

THE RODALE GUIDE TO COMPOSTING

By Jerry Minnich, Marjorie Hunt, and the editors of *Organic Gardening* magazine. As with other Rodale publications, this is a competent and comprehensive (405 pp.) hardback resource for the novice and a handy reference guide for the experienced. Detailed information on methods, equipment, and raw materials. –S.M.

$14.95, Rodale Press

One leaky faucet dripping a drop of water a second wastes 20 gallons per day.

DESIGNING AND MAINTAINING YOUR EDIBLE LANDSCAPE NATURALLY

By Robert Kourik. A handsome volume of 370 pages full of useful perspectives, ideas, tips, and resources for transforming your grounds into beautiful and bountiful landscapes. The most complete resource available on this topic, it's written by an "edible landscape" pioneer. –S.M.

$16.95
The New Alchemy Institute, 1986

ORGANIC GARDENING MAGAZINE

The standard resource for the beginner from the leader in organic gardening. *Organic Gardening* is generally written in an anecdotal style, with color photographs and illustrations showing gardeners just how to do it. After subscribing for a few years, some readers complain that they find little truly new information, just different angles on tools and techniques they are already familiar with. But for the first few years at least, *Organic Gardening* magazine is a terrific support for gardeners. –S.M.

$13.97 a year, Rodale Press

TREES: A CELEBRATION

By Jill Fairchild. This gorgeous collection of stories, articles, essays, poems, and ruminations about trees includes works by such celebrated authors as La Fontaine, Thoreau, Chekhov, Aldous Huxley, Hans Christian Andersen, and Hermann Hesse. My favorite is the inspiring "The Man Who Planted Trees" by Jean Giono. –S.M.

$15.95, Available in bookstores

ORGANIC GARDENING MAGAZINE

RODALE'S ENCYCLOPEDIA OF ORGANIC GARDENING

The basic, cover-all-the-bases reference book for organic gardeners, with 1,236 packed pages. Entries are alphabetized for easy reference. This volume does a solid job of exploring the tools, techniques, and nuances of the organic approach to working with nature. –S.M.

$34.95, Rodale Press

GARDEN INSECT, DISEASE & WEED IDENTIFICATION GUIDE

By Miranda Smith and Anna Carr. Choose this as a companion to the Encyclopedia. It tells how to identify the good guys and the bad guys, and it reminds us — and we do need reminding — that there really are very few harmful insects. In fact, not only are most insects harmless, but they are also a crucial aid in the decomposition of organic matter, in helping to keep weeds in check, and in pollinating almost every fruit, flower, and vegetable. Includes 97 color photos of the worst pests, and black and white drawings of many other insects, plus the wild plants we call weeds. 1988. 336 pages. –S.M.

$16.95, Rodale Press

THE ORCHARD ALMANAC: A SPRAYSAVER GUIDE

By Stephen Page and Joseph Smillie. A valuable guide if you have fruit trees and want to control insects and diseases without chemical sprays. Although it focuses primarily on apples, the techniques are adaptable to other crops. –S.M.

$10 (paperback)
The New Alchemy Institute, 1986

The Earth Is What You Eat

THE FOOD YOU EAT AFFECTS not just your health, but also the earth's. Massive irrigation programs are draining rivers and sucking underground water supplies dry. In many areas of the Midwest, wells have been contaminated by fertilizers and pesticides. All over the country, farmers have been driven out of business, partially because they can't afford to pay for the huge amount of energy it takes to keep their crops irrigated. Food packaging accounts for the bulk of the product packaging — especially plastics — clogging our landfills.

It's no wonder that the earth is what you eat.

We can't blame our grocery stores or restaurants for this entirely: they respond to what we buy. So we are in control. We can improve our health and the earth's by buying different food. Here are some ideas.

Here's the Beef

One-third of American land is devoted to grazing. More than one-half of U.S. farmland is planted with livestock feed, and one-half of all water consumed on farms goes to livestock (mostly cattle). Animal agriculture is responsible for 85 percent of topsoil loss and 260 million acres of forest destruction. The same amount of fossil fuel used to generate protein will produce four times the amount of grain protein as it will meat protein. Experts agree that soy products are a much more ecological source of protein than meat.

There is considerable evidence linking antibiotic use in cattle to salmonella food poisoning in humans, caused by superresistant bacteria. Officially, half of all antibiotics produced in 1985 were fed to animals, and penicillin and tetracycline are sometimes used illegally. The European Economic Community has banned all U.S. beef because it contains hormones.

One alternative is Coleman Natural Beef, which is labeled free of hormones and antibiotics, and is available in A&P, Grand Union, and Purity Supreme supermarkets. In addition, Americans for Safe Food maintains a list of retailers and producers of meat raised without drugs.

> *To produce one pound of steak from steers raised in feed lots costs five pounds of grain, 2,500 gallons of water, the equivalent of one gallon of gasoline, and about 33 pounds of eroded topsoil.*

BEFORE YOU GRAB THAT SHOPPING CART

Contact the following resources to help you get your supermarket working with local farmers.
- **Public Market Collaborative**
- **Greenbelt Alliance**
- **New England Small Farms Institute**
- **New York Food & Agriculture Network**
- **Agriculture Task Force**

Also try these reliable and reputable mail order sources.
- *Wine:* Chartrand Imports
- *Meat (Kosher):* Organic Kosher Cattle Co., Inc.
- *Grains:* Living Farms or Natural Way Mills, Inc.
- *Miscellaneous or Full-Line Products:* Walnut Acres or Farmers Wholesale Cooperative

Organically grown French wine from Chartrand Imports.

BILL MUTCH, COURTESY CHARTRAND IMPORTS

Twenty vegetarians can be fed on the amount of land needed to feed one meat-consuming person.

What You Can Do

✔ Avoid plastic packaging and containers whenever possible. They are non-recyclable and can contaminate food, especially when warmed along with them.

✔ Buy products in safe and recyclable cardboard. Fifty percent of the cardboard packages found in supermarkets are made from recycled paper, including products from Quaker Oats, Kellogg, Ralston Purina, and General Foods.

✔ Request your supermarket to provide pesticide-free produce, and support the call for growers to phase out pesticides by the year 2000.

✔ Patronize stores with the greatest variety of healthy products, especially produce. Talk to the produce manager about where the items come from and what literature is available to back up any claims.

✔ Request that prepared meats and cheese at the deli counter be wrapped in "modern" paper, which is still used for wrapping fish in most stores, rather than old-fashioned foam and plastic wrap.

✔ Buy in bulk to reduce packaging requirements and save energy-consuming shopping trips. Single-serving containers are wasteful and expensive.

✔ Buy foods without chemical additives or preservatives, which have a high environmental impact on production as well as on the land. Stay away from highly processed foods.

✔ Use the influence and purchasing power of your state and local school systems to improve food quality. Get them to replace candy machines with fruit dispensers.

✔ Purchase locally grown produce. It doesn't require unsafe preservatives or energy-intensive long-distance transportation. It also helps decentralize food production and counter the problems of large-scale monoculture, including mass susceptibility to pests, increased reliance on pesticides, and water shortages.

✔ If you can't buy organically grown fruits or vegetables, wash produce thoroughly at home. One-quarter cup of white vinegar in a gallon of water makes a good wash to remove oil-based chemicals. Or use a mild solution of phosphate-free dish detergent to remove wax and other residues. Peeling the skin will eliminate pesticide residues that remain on the surface; however, residues that have seeped into fruits or vegetables will remain.

✔ Get used to the idea of purchasing food that is not picture perfect. Much of our pesticide use is solely to enhance appearance and has no positive taste or nutrition value. Indeed, beware of perfect-looking produce. Nature rarely produces flawless fruits or vegetables. Often the most picturesque specimens have had their appearance enhanced with chemicals and waxes.

✔ Grow your own food, even a small amount, to save on transportation energy consumption. Support local family farms and farmers' markets when possible.

Something's Fishy

Fish is the only animal food that is not government inspected for safety. The Centers for Disease Control state that 24 percent of all food-borne illness outbreaks are caused by eating contaminated fish. Many groups are calling for legislation that would require strict sanitation requirements at every point of handling, mandatory inspection, and comprehensive education on properly handling and preparing seafood.

The War of the Labels — Going Organic

Most of us now realize that man-made chemicals harm our bodies. The problem is to decipher such ambiguous marketing terms as "natural," "organic," "lite," "low sodium," "low calorie," "high fiber," "low fat," "cholesterol," and dozens of other claims and come-ons used by the industry more to seduce than to inform the shopper.

Take the word "organic." After decades of consideration, no federal agency has made a ruling about its use, so 17 states and 40 certification groups have tried to define it. The best a shopper can do is look for specific compliance statements such as this one, found on Amy's Kitchen Organic Vegetable Pot Pies:

"Organically grown and processed in accordance with section 26569,11 of the California Health and Safety Code."

Generally, "organic" refers to foods completely free of synthetic chemicals used either as fertilizers, pesticides, animal feed supplements, or added ingredients. Often a field has to be chemical free for a minimum of three years to be considered "organic." Testing, regulation, and enforcement are even looser than the definitions of the term.

The term "natural" is also little more than a faddish labeling gimmick. In fact, a product labeled "100% natural" without further explanation should be suspect. Instead, look for labeling that specifies what is *not* inside, like this, from Hain Naturals™ Vegetarian Vegetable Soup:

"No preservatives. No artificial ingredients. No MSG or processed sugar. No modified starches."

Most unusual, and to its great credit, Hain also volunteers the following enlightening information about the can itself:

"Special Cans — Hain uses only special enameled containers that have a welded lead-solder-free seam."

This is the type of integrity that earns trust and support for a food company. In fact, when we find such products, we don't even consider the price. (We gladly paid $2.35 for this 19-ounce can of soup in a local health food store — fully three times the Campbell's Soup equivalent!)

The Hot Issue of Food Irradiation

For those in search of organic foods, one especially hot debate is the irradiation of food, particularly produce. This procedure subjects food items to low levels of radioactive cobalt 60 and cesium-137, which kill bacteria and extend shelf life. The FDA has sanctioned test sales of irradiated foods, though the long-term effects are not yet known. Opponents fear that the procedure produces harmful chemicals, creates carcinogenic by-products, destroys vital nutrients, and helps the nuclear industry to justify its existence. The state of Maine has banned the sale of irradiated food completely.

If you want to avoid irradiated food, don't purchase any products with the "radura" symbol — a stylized flower enclosed in a circle.

— *Lonny Brown with David Litwak and Paula Perlis*

THE GOLDBECKS' GUIDE TO GOOD FOOD

By Nikki and David Goldbeck. From cereal to condiments, this is the definitive guide to eating wholesome, healthy food. *–Lonny Brown*

$9.95, New American Library, 1987

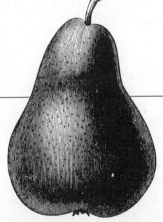

What You Can Do

✔ Buy organically. As consumer demand for chemical-free fruits and vegetables increases, they become more widely available. Supermarket managers get the message, and they convey it through distributors to the farmers.

✔ Avoid artificial colorings. There are far too many to be sure that they're all safe. Many are carcinogenic.

✔ Use cheesecloth or moist cotton towels, rather than plastic bags, to store produce in the refrigerator.

✔ If you purchase beverages with six-pack plastic yokes, cut each circle so that it cannot harm wildlife if it is disposed of improperly.

✔ When barbecuing, use regular charcoal instead of the chemicalized self-lighting kind. Light coals with paper and wood kindling. Barbecuing pollutes the air, and lighter fluid compounds the problem. Be aware that burnt meat can be carcinogenic.

✔ Eat fruit, nature's perfect snack! It comes in its own self-preserving, edible or biodegradable packaging and provides the best complement of fresh nutrients.

✔ Learn vegetarian recipes.

✔ Support companies that don't pollute or damage the environment or test products on animals. Avoid buying endangered species products such as swordfish.

✔ Tell your representatives in government that you want full-disclosure ingredient laws and adequate regulatory oversight.

Nearly a third of the trash we generate is empty containers and packages.

What You Can Do

✔ Boycott plants, animals, or products made from over-exploited species, such as furs, ivory, reptile skin, or tortoise shell.

✔ Send for *Environmental Product Shopping List,* for $2 from Pennsylvania Resources Council, to find out which packages are made from recycled paper.

✔ Patronize businesses, such as Body Shop cosmetics and Ben & Jerry's Ice Cream, that have policies designed to promote sustainable rain forest use.

✔ Write to product manufacturers and tell them when you like or dislike their packages or products. Companies need to hear that consumers are concerned about waste and recyclability. Inform manufacturers of your disapproval of excess packaging.

✔ Encourage outlets to approach suppliers and manufacturers to adjust their packaging to environmental concerns. Point to the positive examples of Walmart, Loblaws, and D'Agostino's.

✔ Examine the stores' own waste-removal systems, and urge them to participate in municipal recycling efforts.

✔ Recognize retailers' positive environmental efforts with letters to the editors of local papers, with civic awards, and most of all, with your patronage.

✔ Ask retailers to publicize a policy of recycling paper and plastic grocery sacks. They may even be able to buy them back for a few cents each and still save money over the cost of one-way supplying.

SHOPPING FOR A BETTER WORLD

Each year we spend thousands of dollars shopping for food and household products. But do the corporations we buy from share our values? How can we find out? This pocket-sized consumer guide rates over 1,800 supermarket and health food products in 11 social criteria, including the environment. You won't want to head to the supermarket without it!

You can use this guide with confidence. Since 1968 the Council on Economic Priorities has published more than 1,000 books, reports, and newsletters on corporate responsibility. It has looked at subjects as diverse as air pollution, child care, toxic wastes, and arms control, and its research has been factual and fair — and, therefore, an effective tool for change in the hands of stockholders, voters, and activists.

For those who want to do more than buy the book, council memberships range from $15 for folks with limited income to a donor membership for $100. For the regular $25 membership (and the $15 fee) you will receive a monthly newsletter and *Shopping for a Better World.*
–John Quinney

$5.95
Council on Economic Priorities

SHOPPING FOR A BETTER WORLD

A QUICK & EASY GUIDE
TO SOCIALLY RESPONSIBLE SUPERMARKET SHOPPING

Updated & Expanded
1990 EDITION

COUNCIL ON ECONOMIC PRIORITIES

Company or Product	Abbr.	$	♀										refuses cans
									No	No	✔	✔	
CRACKERS & BREAD PRODUCTS									No	No	✔	✔	
Ann Page	GAP	?	✔	✔	No	✔	✔	✔	No	No	✔	✘	
Arnold	CPC	✘	✔	✔	No	✔	✔	✔	No	No	✔	✘	cigarettes
Barbara's Bakery#	BARB	?	✔	✔	No	✔	✔	?	No	Yes*	✘	✔	
Better Cheddars	RJR	✔	✔	✔	No	?	✔	✔	No	No	✔	✘	cigarettes
Chicken Helper	GIS	✔+	✔	✔	No	✔	✔	?	No	Yes*	✘	✘	
Classic	RJR	✔	✔	✔	No	?	✔	✔	No	No	✔	✔	
Colonial	BUD	✔+	✔	✔	No	✔	✔	✔	No	Yes●	✔	✔	
Corn Flake Crumbs	K	✔	✔	✔	No	?	✔	✔	No	No	✔	✘	
Devonsheer	CPC	✘	✔	✔	No	✔	✔	✘	No	No	?	?	
El Molino#	AMH	?	✔	✔	No	?	✔	✔	No	Yes	✘	?	
Entenmann's	MO	✘	✔	✔	No	?	✔	✔					

SHOPPING FOR A CLEANER WORLD

Shopping for a Better World includes ratings of specific companies in terms of their sensitivity to the environmental impact of their products. Here's how some major companies (100 employees or more) stack up:

✔ = Top Rating
✔ = Middle Rating
✘ = Bottom Rating

COMPANY	Rating
Anheuser-Busch	✔
Ben & Jerry's	✔
Colgate-Palmolive	✔
General Electric	✘
Hershey Food Corp.	✔
Johnson & Johnson	✔
Minnesota Mining & Manu.	✔
Ocean Spray Cranberries	✘
RJR Nabisco	✘
Scott Paper	✘

Fifty-one percent of Americans would buy organically grown food even if they had to pay a little extra.

Ecologue Source Directory

To order a product reviewed in *Ecologue*, first find the name of the company that carries that product; it's noted at the end of the review. Then look in the listings below, under the chapter in which you found the product; companies are listed alphabetically within each chapter. Before ordering from any of these companies, please call them to confirm the availability and price of the product you want, and to find out how much to enclose for postage and handling.

RECYCLING

American Things, Box 250, Cherry Hill Rd., Harrisville, NH 03450; (603) 827-3811

Bag Connection, Inc., P.O. Box 817, Newburg, OR 97132; (800) 62-BAG-IT

H.T. Berry Co., 50 North St., Canton, MA 02021; (617) 828-6000

Better Environment, Inc., 480 Clinton Ave., Albany, NY 12206; (518) 426-4987

Cancelor Corporation, 6 Parker Rd., Arlington, MA 02174; (617) 643-4851

Chef's Catalog, 3215 Commercial Ave., Northbrook, IL 60062; (800) 338-3232

Conservatree Paper Co., 10 Lombard St., Suite 250, San Francisco, CA 94111; (800) 522-9200

Co-op America, 49 The Meadows Park, Colchester, VT 05446; (802) 655-2975

Dano Enterprises, 75 Commercial St., Plainview, NY 11803; (516) 349-7300

Direct Marketing Assoc., 11 W. 42nd St., P.O. Box 3861, New York, NY 10163; (212) 689-4977

Earth Care Paper, P.O. Box 3335, Madison, WI 53704; (608) 256-5522

Ecco Bella, 6 Provost Sq., Suite 602, Caldwell, NJ 07006; (800) 888-5320

Environmental Hazards Management Institute, 10 Newmarket Rd., P.O. Box 932, Durham, NH 03824; (603) 868-1496

M. Evans & Co., 216 E. 49th St., New York, NY 10017; (212) 688-2810

Gardener's Supply, 128 Intervale Rd., Burlington, VT 05401; (802) 863-1700

Granite Lake Pottery, Inc., P.O. Box 236, Munsonville, NH 03457; (603) 847-9908

Nichols Garden Nursery, Inc., 1190 North Pacific Highway, Albany, OR 97321; (503) 928-9280

Old-House Journal Corp., 435 Ninth St., Brooklyn, NY 11215; (800) 274-9909

Paper Service Ltd., P.O. Box 45, Hinsdale, NH 03451; (603) 239-4934

Plow and Hearth, 301 Madison Rd., Orange, VA 22960; (800) 627-1712

Recycled Paper Co., Inc., 185 Corey Rd., Boston, MA 02146; (617) 277-9901

Seventh Generation, Colchester, VT 05446-1672; (800) 456-1177

Signature Art, P.O. Box 801, Wilder, VT 05088; (802) 295-3291

Spectrum International, Inc., P.O. Box 353, Shrewsbury, NJ 07702; (201) 747-1313

Lillian Vernon, 510 S. Fulton Ave., Mount Vernon, NY 10550; (914) 633-6300

White River Paper Co., P.O. Box 455, White River Junction, VT 05001; (800) 225-0079

Windsor Barrel Works, P.O. Box 47, Kempton, PA 19529; (215) 756-4344

Windstar Foundation, 2317 Snowmass Creek Rd., Snowmass, CO 81654; (800) 669-4777

HOUSEHOLD CLEANERS

Allens Naturally, P.O. Box 339, Farmington, MI 48332-0339; (313) 453-5410

Chip Distribution, 1139 Dominguiz St. Unit E, Carson, CA 90746; (213) 603-1114

Co-op America, 49 The Meadows Park, Colchester, VT 05446; (802) 655-2975

Garden Way Publishing, Storey Communications, Inc., 1476 Massachusetts Ave., North Adams, MA 01247; (800) 827-8673

Lion & Lamb Cruelty-Free Products, Inc., 29-28 41st Ave., Suite 813, Long Island City, NY 11101; (718) 361-5757

Livos PlantChemistry, 1365 Rufima Circle, Santa Fe, NM 87501; (800) 621-2591

Mercantile Food Co., P.O. Box 1140, Georgetown, CT 06829; (203) 544-9891

Mountain Fresh, P.O. Box 40516, Grand Junction, CO 81504; (303) 434-8491

Murphy-Phoenix Co., P.O. Box 22930, Cleveland, OH 44122; (216) 831-0404

C.W. Parker Co., 1415 Second Ave., Des Moines, IA 50314; (515) 243-6610

Seventh Generation, Colchester, VT 05446-1672; (800) 456-1177

Shaklee, 444 Market St., San Francisco, CA 94111; (415) 954-2007

Simon & Schuster, Rockefeller Cntr., 1230 Ave. of Americas, New York, NY 10020

Williams Sonoma, P.O. Box 7456, San Francisco, CA 94120; (415) 421-4555

OTHER HOUSEHOLD

Abbeon Cal, Inc., 123-73 OpGray Ave., Santa Barbara, CA 93101-1895; (805) 966-0810

Co-op America, 49 The Meadows Park, Colchester, VT 05446; (802) 655-2975

Hummer Nature Works, Reagan Wells Canyon, Box 122, Uvalde, TX 78801; (512) 232-6167

Kinsman Company, Inc., River Rd., Point Pleasant, PA 18950; (215) 297-5613

Livos PlantChemistry, 1365 Rufima Circle, Santa Fe, NM 87501; (800) 621-2591

Co-op America, 49 The Meadows Park, Colchester, VT 05446; (802) 655-2975

Garden Way Publishing, Storey Communications, Inc., 1476 Massachusetts Ave., North Adams, MA 01247; (800) 827-8673

Lion & Lamb Cruelty-Free Products, Inc., 29-28 41st Ave., Suite 813, Long Island City, NY 11101; (718) 361-5757

Melitta USA, 1401 Berlin Rd., Cherry Hill, NJ 08003; (609) 428-7202

Rockline, Inc., Box 1007, Sheboygan, WI 53082-1007; (800) 558-7790

Vermont Country Store, P.O. Box 3000, Manchester, VT 05255; (802) 362-2400

Lillian Vernon, 510 S. Fulton Ave., Mount Vernon, NY 10550; (914) 633-6300

Williams Sonoma, P.O. Box 7456, San Francisco, CA 94120; (415) 421-4555

CLOTHING

Artek, P.O. Box 145, Antrim, NH 03440; (603) 588-6825

BATTERIES

Environmental Action Coalition, 625 Broadway, New York, NY 10012; (212) 677-1601

Mercury Refining Co., 790 Watervliet-Shaker Rd., Latham, NY 12110; (800) 833-3505

Panasonic, P.O. Box 1511, Secaucus, NJ 07094; (201) 392-4675

Solarex Consumer Products Division, P.O. Box 6008, Rockville, MD 20850; (800) 521-SOLAR

SunWatt, RFD, Box 751, Addison, ME 04606; (207) 497-2204

PERSONAL CARE

Aubrey Organics, 4419 Manhattan Ave., Tampa, FL 33614; (813) 876-4879

Aura Cacia, P.O. Box 399, Weaverville, CA 96093; (916) 623-4999

Auromere Ayurvedic Imports, 1291 Weber St., Pomona, CA 91768; (714) 629-8255

Autumn-Harp, Inc., 28 Rockydale Rd., Bristol, VT 05443; (802) 453-4807

Alexandra Avery, 68183 Northrup Creek Rd., Birkenfeld/Clatskanie, OR 97016; (503) 755-2446

Bare Escentuals, Inc., 104 Cooper Court, Los Gatos, CA 95030; (800) 227-3788

Body Shop, 45 Horsehill Rd., Cedar Knolls, NJ 07927-2003; (800) 541-2535

Borlind of Germany, P.O. Box 1487, New London, NH 03257; (800) 447-7024

Dr. Bronner All-One-God-Faith, Inc., Box 28, Escondido, CA 92025; (619) 743-2211

Clearly Natural, P.O. Box 13973, Petaluma, CA 94975; (707) 762-5815

Crown Publishers, Inc., 201 E. 50th St., New York, NY 10022

Desert Essence, P.O. Box 588, Topanga, CA 90290; (800) 727-2714

Earthen Joys, 1412 11th St., Astoria, OR 97130; (800) 451-4540

Ecco Bella, 6 Provost Square, Suite 602, Caldwell, NJ 07006; (800) 888-5320

Feather River Company, 133 Copeland, Petaluma, CA 94952; (707) 778-7627

Ida Grae Nature's Colors Cosmetics, 424 La Verne, Mill Valley, CA 94941; (415) 388-6101

Dr. Hauschka Biodynamic Formulations, Meadowbrook Herb Garden, Rte. 138, Wyoming, RI 02898; (401) 539-7037

Home Health Products, 1160-A Millers Lane, P.O. Box 3130, Virginia Beach, VA 23454; (800) 468-7313

I & M Natural Skincare, P.O. Box 691, Station 'C', Toronto, ONT M6J 3S1, Canada; (416) 367-0679

InterNatural, P.O. Box 680, Shaker St., S. Sutton, NH 03273; (800) 446-4903

Jurlique, Inc., 37 Commercial Blvd., Suite 110, Novato, CA 94949; (800) 462-0666

Keats Publishing, Inc., 36 Grove St., New Canaan, CT 06840; (203) 966-8721

Keeper Co., Inc., P.O. Box 20023, Cincinnati, OH 45220; (513) 221-1464

Lakon Herbals, Box 252, Montpelier, VT 05602; (802) 223-5563

Liberty Distributing, P.O. Box 33115, Portland, OR 97233; (800) 289-2427

Lion & Lamb Cruelty-Free Products, Inc., 29-28 41st Ave., Suite 813, Long Island City, NY 11101; (718) 361-5757

Meadowbrook Herb Garden, Rte. 138, Wyoming, RI 02898; (401) 539-7603

Mountain Ocean, P.O. Box 951, Boulder, CO 80306; (303) 444-2781

Nature's Gate Herbal Cosmetics, Chatsworth, CA 91311; (818) 882-2951

New England Anti-Vivisection Society, 333 Washington St., Suite 850, Boston, MA 02108; (617) 523-6020

Organica Press, 4419 N. Manhattan Ave., Tampa, FL 33614; (813) 876-4879

Paul Penders Co./D&P Products, Inc., 1340 Commerce St., Petaluma, CA 94954; (707) 763-5828

People for the Ethical Treatment of Animals, P.O. Box 42516, Washington, DC 20015; (301) 770-7444

Walter Rau/Speick, Meadowbrook Herb Garden, P.O. Box 407, Rte. 138, Wyoming, RI 02898; (401) 539-7603

Real Purity & Co., 6825 Carpenter Rd., Ypsilanti, MI 48197; (313) 572-9066

Red Rose Gallerie, P.O. Box 1859, Burlingame, CA 94011-1859; (415) 579-7300

Reviva Labs, Inc., 705 Hopkins Rd., Haddonfield, NJ 08033; (609) 428-3885

Self-Care Catalog, P.O. Box 130, Mandeville, LA 70470-0130; (800) 345-3371

Seventh Generation, Colchester, VT 05446-1672; (800) 456-1177

Tom's of Maine, Inc., P.O. Box 710, Railroad Ave., Kennebunk, ME 04043; (207) 985-2944

Tonialg/Bristol Productions, Inc., P.O. Box 599, Pawtucket, RI 02862; (401) 272-0380

Weleda, Inc., 841 S. Main St., P.O. Box 769, Spring Valley, NY 10977; (914) 352-6145

Wishing Well Distributing, P.O. Box 529, Graton, CA 95444; (707) 823-9310

BABY CARE

Autumn-Harp, Inc., 28 Rockydale Rd., Bristol, VT 05443; (802) 453-4807

Baby Bunz & Co., P.O. Box 1717, Sebastopol, CA 95473; (707) 829-5347

Biobottoms Fresh Air Wear, P.O. Box 6009, Petaluma, CA 94953; (707) 778-7945

Bumkins Family Products, 1945 E. Watkins, Phoenix, AZ 85034; (800) 553-9302

Diap-Air, P.O. Box 103, Upton, NY 11973; (516) 474-4875

Diaperraps, P.O. Box 3050, Granada Hills, CA 91394; (800) 251-4321

R. Duck Company, 650 Ward Dr., Suite H, Santa Barbara, CA 93111; (800) 422-DUCK

Earth's Best, P.O. Box 887, Middlebury, VT 05753; (800) 442-4221

Lovely Essentials, P.O. Box 7C, St. Francis, KY 40062; (502) 865-5501

National Association of Diaper Services, 2017 Walnut St., Philadelphia, PA 19103, (215) 569-3650

Natural Baby Co., RD 1, Box 160 S, Titusville, NJ 08560; (609) 737-2895

Seventh Generation, Colchester, VT 05446-1672; (800) 456-1177

Simply Pure Foods, RFD 3, Box 99, Bangor, ME 04401; (800) IAM-PURE (426-7873)

Tom's of Maine, Inc., P.O. Box 710, Railroad Ave., Kennebunk, ME 04043; (207) 985-2944

PET CARE

Animail Pet Care Products, 2515 E. 43rd St., Box 23547, Chattanooga, TN 37422-3547; (800) 255-3723

Cedar-äl Products, Inc., RFD #1, Box 6, Clallam Bay, WA 98326; (800) 431-3444

Elexis Animal Pet Care Products/Sporting Dog Specialties, 1989 Transit Way, Brockport, NY 14420; (716) 352-1232

Hummer Nature Works, Reagan Wells Canyon, Box 122, Uvalde, TX 78801; (512) 232-6167

Lion & Lamb Cruelty-Free Products, Inc., 29-28 41st Ave., Suite 813, Long Island City, NY 11101; (718) 361-5757

Pedigree: The Pet Catalog, 1989 Transit Way, Brockport, NY 14420; (716) 637-1431

Safer, Inc., 189 Wells Ave., Newton, MA 02159; (800) 423-7544

EDUCATION/FUN

Aerie Design, 141 Blackberry Inn, S. Weaverville, NC 28787; (704) 645-3285

Animal Town, P.O. Box 485, Healdsburg, CA 95448; (800) 445-8642

Boomer's Attitude T-Shirts, P.O. Box 929, Folly Beach, SC 29439; (803) 588-9585

California Pacific Designs, Box 2660, Alameda, CA 94501; (415) 521-7914

Children for Old Growth, Box 1090, Redway, CA 95560; (707) 923-3617

Cousteau Society, 930 W. 21st St., Norfolk, VA 23517; (804) 627-1144

Dawn Publications, 14618 Tyler Foote Rd., Nevada City, CA 95959; (800) 545-7475

Dell Publishing, Dell Readers Service, P.O. Box 5057, Des Plaines, IL 60017; (800) 255-4133

Earth Flag Co., P.O. Box 108, Middleville, NJ 07855; (800) 421-FLAG

Earthwise Consumer, P.O. Box 1506, Mill Valley, CA 94942; (415) 383-5892

Earthworks Press, Box 25, 1400 Shattuck Ave., Berkeley, CA 94709; (415) 841-5866

Environmental Defense Fund, 257 Park Ave. S, New York, NY 10010; (212) 505-2100

Gaia Catalog, 1400 Shattuck Ave., North Berkeley, CA 94709; (800) 543-8431

Geode Educational Options, P.O. Box 106, 301 S. Church St., West Chester, PA 19381; (215) 692-0413

Greenpeace, 1436 U St. NW, Washington, DC 20009; (202) 462-1177

Gryphon House, Inc., 3706 Otis St., Mt. Rainier, MD 20712; (301) 779-6200

HearthSong, P.O. Box B, Sebastopol, CA 95473; (800) 325-2502

International Wildlife Coalition, 634 North Falmouth Hwy., P.O. Box 388, North Falmouth, MA 02556-0388; (508) 654-9980

Klutz Press, 2121 Staunton Court, Palo Alto, CA 94306; (415) 857-0888

Livos PlantChemistry, 1365 Rufima Circle, Santa Fe, NM 87501; (800) 621-2591

William Morrow & Co., 105 Madison Ave., New York, NY 10016; (212) 213-7777

Music for Little People, 1144 Redway Dr., Redway, CA 95560; (707) 923-3991

National Geographic Society, P.O. Box 2895, Washington, DC 20013-9990; (202) 857-7000

National Wildlife Federation, 1412 16th St. NW, Washington, DC 20036-2266; (800) 432-6564

Nature Company, 750 Hearst Ave., P.O. Box 2310, Berkeley, CA 94702; (800) 227-1114

W.W. Norton & Co., 500 Fifth Ave., New York, NY 10110; (800) 233-4830

One Person's Impact, P.O. Box 751, Westborough, MA 01581; (508) 478-3716

Penguin Books, 40 W. 23rd St., New York, NY 10010; (212) 337-5200

Project Learning Tree (PLT), 1250 Connecticut Ave. NW, Suite 320-FG, Washington, DC 20036; (202) 463-2468

Seventh Generation, Colchester, VT 05446-1672; (800) 456-1177

Sierra Club, 730 Polk St., San Francisco, CA 94109; (415) 981-8634

Wildlife Education Ltd., P.O. Box 85271, Suite 6, San Diego, CA 92138; (800) 334-8152

Wildlife Games, P.O. Box 247, Ivy, VA 22945; (804) 972-7016

Windstar Foundation, 2317 Snowmass Creek Rd., Snowmass, CO 81654; (800) 669-4777

Winterland Productions, 100 Harrison St., San Francisco, CA 94105-1605; (800) 521-5511

Young Naturalist Foundation, 59 Front St. E, Toronto, ONT M5E 1B3, Canada; (416) 868-6001

Zoo Books, Box 85271, Suite 6, San Diego, CA 92138; (619) 299-5034

RADON

Air Chek, Inc., 180 Glenn Bridge Rd., Box 2000, Arden, NC 28704; (800) AIR-CHEK

Environmental Protection Agency, 401 M St. SW, Washington, DC 20460; (800) 633-8372

Lowry Engineering, Inc., P.O. Box 189, Unity, ME 04988; (207) 948-3790

North East Environmental Products, Inc., 17 Technology Dr., West Lebanon, NH 03784; (603) 298-7061

Tech/Ops Landauer, Inc., 2 Science Rd., Glenwood, IL 60425; (800) 528-8327

WATER PURIFICATION

Ametek Plymouth Products Div., 502 Indiana Ave., Sheboygan, WI 53081; (414) 457-9435

Amway Corporation, 7575 Fulton St. E, Ada, MI 49355-0001; (616) 676-7948

Coast Filtration, Box 699, Brea, CA 92621; (714) 990-4602

Culligan, c/o Beatrice Water Conditioning, 1 Culligan Parkway, Northbrook, IL 60062; (800) 428-2828

Ecowater, P.O. Box 64420, St. Paul, MN 55164; (612) 739-5330

Electrolux Water Systems, Inc., 325 Riverside Ave., Westport, CT 06880; (800) 356-8740

Enting Water Conditioning, 3249 Dryden Rd., Dayton, OH 45439; (800) 435-0787

Everpure, Inc., 660 North Blackhawk Dr., Westmont, IL 60559; (800) 942-1153

Hurley Chicago Co., Inc., 12621 S. Laramie Ave., Alsip, IL 60658-3225; (708) 388-9222

Sears, Sears Tower, Chicago, IL 60684; (312) 875-2500

Shaklee, 444 Market St., San Francisco, CA 94111; (415) 954-2007

Watertest, 33 S. Commercial St., Manchester, NH 03101; (800) 426-8378

WATER CONSERVATION

Clivus Multrum, 21 Canal St., Lawrence, MA 01840-1801; (508) 794-1700

Crane Plumbing, 1235 Hartrey St., Evanston, IL 60202; (708) 864-9777

Ecological Water Products, 1341 W. Main Rd., Middletown, RI 02840; (401) 849-4004

Envirovac, Inc., 1260 Turret Dr., Rockford, IL 61111; (815) 654-8300

Fowler Bathroom Products/Gemini Bath & Kitchen, 4733 E. Broadway, Tucson, AZ 85711; (602) 750-8433

IFO Water Management Products, 2882 Love Creek Rd., Avery, CA 95224; (209) 795-1758

Mansfield Plumbing Products, 150 First St., Perrysville, OH 44864; (419) 938-5211

Microphor, P.O. Box 1460, 452 E. Hill Rd., Willits, CA 95490; (800) 358-8280

Minnco, 1016 St. Margaret Dr., Cape St. Claire, MD 21401

Nepon (WCS Sys., Inc., Importer), Damonmill Sq., Concord, MA 01742; (508) 369-3951

O'Ryan Industries, 9400 N.E. 130th Ave., Vancouver, WA 98682; (206) 892-0447

Seventh Generation, Colchester, VT 05446-1672; (800) 456-1177

Sun-Mar Corp., 900 Hertel Ave., Buffalo, NY 14216; (416) 332-1314

Vakuumplast AB (WCS Sys., Inc., Importer), Damonmill Sq., Concord, MA 01742; (508) 369-3951

Water Conservation Systems, Inc., Damonmill Sq., Concord, MA 01742; (508) 369-3951

FUEL SAVERS

Brookstone, 5 Vose Farm Rd., Peterborough, NH 03458; (603) 924-9541

Cal-K, Inc., 7411 Laurel Canyon Blvd., North Hollywood, CA 91605; (818) 503-0733

Colonial Garden Kitchens, P.O. Box 66, Hanover, PA 17333-0066; (800) 752-5552

Deflect-O Corp., P.O. Box 50057, Indianapolis, IN 46250; (317) 849-9555

Frost King Thermwell Products Co., Inc., Paterson, NJ 07524; (201) 684-5000

Hall's Christmas Tree Farms, Inc., Outer Pine St., Dover-Foxcroft, ME 04426; (800) 447-1217, x111

Heartland Products International, P.O. Box 777, Valley City, OK 73118; (800) 437-4700

Honeywell, Inc., Honeywell Plaza, Minneapolis, MN 55408; (800) 328-5111

Macklanburg/Duncan, 4041 N. Sante Fe, Oklahoma City, OK 73118; (405) 528-4411

Massachusetts Audubon Society, Educational Resources Office, Lincoln, MA 01773; (800) 289-9504

Niagara Conservation Corp., 230 Route 206, Flanders, NJ 07836; (201) 927-4545

People's Energy Resource Cooperative, 354 Waverly St., Framingham, MA 01701; (508) 879-8572

Real Goods Trading Company, 966 Mazzoni St., #4B, Ukiah, CA 95482; (800) 762-7325

Resource Conservation Technology, 2633 N. Calvert St., Baltimore, MD 21218; (301) 366-1146

Rocky Mountain Institute, 1739 Snowmass Creek Rd., Snowmass, CO 81654-9199; (303) 927-3851

Rodale Press, 33 E. Minor St., Emmaus, PA 18098; (800) 441-7761

Seventh Generation, Colchester, VT 05446-1672; (800) 456-1177

Solar Components Corporation, 121 Valley St., Manchester, NH 03103; (603) 668-8186

Styro-Dome Corp., P.O. Box 220, Yorktown Heights, NY 10598; (800) 52-STYRO

United Textile & Supply Co., 5175 Commerce Dr., Baldwin Park, CA 91706; (800) 456-6282

Viking Products/Trend Manufacturing of America, Inc., P.O. Box 51106, Jackson Beach, FL 32240-1106; (800) 624-8198

We Care, Inc., P.O. Box 873, Pierre, SD 57501; (605) 224-5304

1,000 PENNIES FOR YOUR THOUGHTS!

See the other side of this page

1,000 PENNIES FOR YOUR THOUGHTS!

Send Me Your Thoughts About Environmental Products and I'll Send You
2 ECOLOGUE/*UPDATES* — a $10.00 value — for free!
—*Bruce Anderson*

**ECOLOGUE/
UPDATE**

Dear **ECOLOGUE** Reader,

Because you purchased **ECOLOGUE**, you are entitled to 2 free editions of **ECOLOGUE/*UPDATE*** (valued at $5.00 each) that will keep your book current long after you've bought it. All you need to do to receive them is to send me at least one of your thoughts about environmental products.

What's an **ECOLOGUE/*UPDATE*?**
It's just like **ECOLOGUE** itself, with the latest and hottest information about environmental products. Every few months, we will produce an all-new **UPDATE** packed with:

- timely reviews of new products
- the latest results of our product testing
- up-to-date price changes, ordering addresses, and phone numbers
- breaking research results on what is and isn't environmentally safe
- helpful environmental product and services advertising
- lifestyle tips and mindbending environmental facts
- and more

Here's All You Do
Just send me at least one comment or idea on any one (or more) of the following:

- Your opinion of **ECOLOGUE**. How can we make it better next time?
- Your experience using **ECOLOGUE** products. Do you agree or disagree with our reviews of them?
- Your experience dealing with **ECOLOGUE** companies. Were they courteous? How was their service? How did they fall down environmentally in their packaging, literature, etc.? (Please be specific.)
- What suggestions do you have for new products? For mind bending facts (the notes at the bottom of each page)? For "What You Can Do's"? For inspirational quotes? For additional companies that make or sell environmentally safe products?
- What product categories are you most interested in learning more about?

Write to me on a separate sheet of paper or use one of the reply forms below. If you have a question that needs an answer, include a stamped, self-addressed envelope. With your thoughts and ideas, we can make the **ECOLOGUE/*UPDATES*** even better, and together we can help make sure that someday all products are environmentally safe.

Sincerely,

Bruce Anderson

Bruce Anderson, President
International Environment Group, Inc.

Dear Bruce,

Please send me 2 editions of **ECOLOGUE** /*UPDATE* — a $10.00 value — free!

Here are my thoughts: _____

_____

_____

_____

Name _____

Address _____

_____

_____

Phone number(s) (optional) _____

Mail to: Bruce Anderson, President, International Environment Group, Inc. (IEG),
Box 71 NA, 71 Sargent Camp Road, Peterborough, NH 03458

Dear Bruce,

Please send me 2 editions of **ECOLOGUE** /*UPDATE* — a $10.00 value — free!

Here are my thoughts: _____

_____

_____

_____

Name _____

Address _____

_____

_____

Phone number(s) (optional) _____

Mail to: Bruce Anderson, President, International Environment Group, Inc. (IEG),
Box 71 NA, 71 Sargent Camp Road, Peterborough, NH 03458

Windstar Foundation, 2317 Snowmass Creek Rd., Snowmass, CO 81654; (800) 669-4777

LIGHTING

American Scientific Lighting Corp., 112 Cortelyou Rd., Brooklyn, NY 11218; (718) 851-4577

A Brighter Way, P.O. Box 18446, Austin, TX 78700; (800) 369-9360

Energy Federation, Inc. (EFI), 354 Waverly St., Framingham, MA 01701; (508) 875-4921

Lightolier, 100 Lighting Way, Secaucus, NJ 07098-1508; (201) 864-3000

Osram Corporation, 110 Bracken Rd., Montgomery, NY 12549; (800) 431-9980

Panasonic, One Panasonic Way, Secaucus, NJ 07094; (201) 348-5304

Real Goods Trading Company, 966 Mazzoni St., #4B, Ukiah, CA 95482; (800) 762-7325

Rising Sun Enterprises, P.O. Box 586, Old Snowmass, CO 81654; (303) 927-8051

Staff Lighting, P.O. Box 1020 Rte. 9-W, Highland, NY 12528; (914) 691-6262

Watt Watcher, P.O. Box 2058, Santa Clara, CA 95050; (408) 988-5331

APPLIANCES

American Council for an Energy-Efficient Economy, 1001 Connecticut Ave. NW, Suite 535, Washington, DC 20036; (202) 429-8873

Brookstone, 5 Vose Farm Rd., Peterborough, NH 03458; (603) 924-9541

Clevlab, P.O. Box 2647, Littleton, CO 80161; (303) 730-1769

Deflect-O Corp., P.O. Box 50057, Indianapolis, IN 46250; (317) 849-9555

DLR Design & Development Corp., 44105 Leeann Lane, Canton, MI 48187; (313) 459-0754

Plow and Hearth, 301 Madison Rd., Orange, VA 22960; (800) 627-1712

Lehman's, 4779 Kidron Rd., P.O. Box 41, Kidron, OH 44636; (216) 857-5441

Real Goods Trading Company, 966 Mazzoni St., #4B, Ukiah, CA 95482; (800) 762-7325

Sunfrost, P.O. Box 1101, Arcata, CA 95521; (707) 822-9095

Tarzian West, 194 Seventh Ave., Brooklyn, NY 11215; (718) 788-4213

Vermont Country Store, P.O. Box 3000, Manchester, VT 05255; (802) 362-2400

HEATING & AIR CONDITIONING

Airxchange, 401 VFW Dr., Rockland, MA 02370; (617) 871-4816

Arvin Air, 500 S. 15th St., Phoenix, AZ 85034; (602) 257-0060

Carrier Corp., Consumer Relations Dept., P.O. Box 4808, Syracuse, NY 13221; (800) CARRIER

Energy Kinetics, Molasses Hill Rd., RD 1, Box 103, Lebanon, NJ 08833; (800) 323-2006

Engineering Development Incorporated, 4850 Northpark Dr., Colorado Springs, CO 80918; (800) 777-VENT

Honeywell, Inc., Honeywell Plaza, Minneapolis, MN 55408; (800) 328-5111

Infloor Heating Systems, 920 Hamel Rd., P.O. Box 253, Hamel, MN 55340; (612) 478-6477

Research Products Corporation, P.O. Box 1467, Madison, WI 53701; (800) 356-9652

Trianco-Heatmaker, Inc., 111 York Ave., Randolph, MA 02368; (617) 961-1660

Unity Systems, Inc., 2606 Spring St., Redwood City, CA 94063; (800) 55-UNITY

WaterFurnace International, Inc., 4307 Arden Dr., Fort Wayne, IN 46804; (219) 432-5667

Yukon Energy Corporation, 378 W. County Rd. D, St. Paul, MN 55112; (612) 633-3115

WOOD HEAT

Biomass Publications of America, P.O. Box 69333, Portland, OR 97201

BSW, Inc., 4680 E. Second St., Benicia, CA 94510; (800) 237-8682

Condar Co., P.O. Box 287, Garrettsville, OH 44231; (216) 527-4343

Dumont Stoker Corp., P.O. Box 149, Monmouth, ME 04259; (207) 933-4811

E'lan Mfg./Travis Industries, 10850 117th Pl. NE, Kirkland, WA 98033; (206) 827-9505

Elmira Stove & Fireplace Mfg., 145 Northfield Dr., Waterloo, ONT N21 5J3, Canada; (519) 747-5443

EPA Stationary Source Compliance Div., 401 M St. SW, Washington, DC 20460; (800) 633-8372

Jøtul USA, P.O. Box 1157-B, Portland, ME 04104; (207) 797-5912

New Alberene Stone Co., P.O. Box 300, Schuyler, VA 22969; (804) 831-2228

Pennsylvania Firebacks, Inc., 308 Elm Ave., North Wales, PA 19154; (215) 699-0805

Pyro Industries, Inc., 11625 Airport Rd., Everett, WA 98204; (206) 348-0400

Ruegg Fireplaces, 976 Rte. 22, Bridgewater, NJ 08807; (201) 526-0309

Thermal Energy Storage Systems, Inc., RR 1, Box 3, Beanville Rd., Randolph, VT 05060; (800) 323-TESS

Vermont Castings, Prince St., Randolph, VT 05060; (802) 728-3181

Waterford Irish Stoves, Inc., River Mill Complex, 85 Mechanic St., Lebanon, NH 03766; (603) 448-2385

ENVIRONMENTAL CONSTRUCTION

Air-Krete Inc., P.O. Box 380, Weedsport, NY 13166; (315) 834-6609

Appropriate Technology Corp., P.O. Box 975, Brattleboro, VT 05302; (802) 257-4501

Brick House Publishing Co., 11 Thoreau Rd., P.O. Box 134, Acton, MA 01920; (508) 635-9800

Building Science Engineering, 85 Depot Rd., Harvard, MA 01451; (508) 456-6950

Carol Publishing Group, 120 Enterprise Ave., Secaucus, NJ 07094; (201) 866-0490

Comfortex Corp., P.O. Box 728, Cohoes, NY 12047; (800) 843-4151

Housing Resource Center, 4115 Bridge Ave., Cleveland, OH 44113-0857; (216) 961-4646

Hurd Millwork, 575 S. Whelen Ave., Medford, WI 54451; (715) 748-2011

Icynene, Inc., 376 Watline Ave., Mississauga, ONT L4Z 1X2, Canada; (416) 890-7325

Insulators Supply Co., 220 Sixth St. NW, Cedar Rapids, MI 52405-4902; (800) 247-3381

Livos PlantChemistry, 1365 Rufima Circle, Santa Fe, NM 87501; (800) 621-2591

Masters Corp., P.O. Box 514, 12 Burtis Ave., New Canaan, CT 06840; (203) 966-3541

MTI Solar, Inc., 220 Churchill Ave., Somerset, NJ 08873; (201) 463-0876

Remarc, Inc., Kricket Smith-Gary, RR 1, Newchester Rd., Hill, NH 03243; (603) 934-6888

Resource Conservation Technology, 2633 N. Calvert St., Baltimore, MD 21218; (301) 366-1146

Rocky Mountain Institute, 1739 Snowmass Creek Rd., Snowmass, CO 81654-9199; (303) 927-3851

Sage Advance Corp., 1001 Bertelsen Rd., Suite A, Eugene, OR 97402; (503) 485-1947

Sinan Company, P.O. Box 857, Davis, CA 95617-0857; (916) 753-3104

Solar Pathways, Inc., 31 Caparral Circle, Glenwood Springs, CO 81601; (303) 945-6503

Solar Survival, Box 250, Cherry Hill Rd., Harrisville, NH 03450; (603) 827-3811

Sun Heating Mfg. Co., P.O. Box 1120, San Juan Pueblo, NM 87566; (505) 852-2622

Thermal Concepts, 8521 Van Bussum Rd., Eagle River, WI 54521; (715) 479-8681

Todol Products, P.O. Box 398, Natick, MA 01760; (508) 879-7741

Warm Products, 11232 120th St. NE, #112, Kirkland, WA 98033; (800) 234-WARM

SUNSPACES

Andersen Corporation, Inc., Bayport, MN 55003; (800) 426-4261

Home Buyer Publications, Inc., 4451 Brookfield Corp. Dr., Suite 101, Chantilly, VA 22021; (800) 826-3893

Northern Light Greenhouse, 128 Intervale Rd., Burlington, VT 05401; (800) 356-4769

Sun Room Company, Inc., 322 E. Main St., P.O. Box 301, Leola, PA 17540; (800) 426-2737

Sunplace, Inc., P.O. Box 17019, Baltimore, MD 21203-7019; (800) 877-7901

Vegetable Factory, Inc., 71 Vanderbilt Ave., New York, NY 10169; (800) 221-2550

PHOTOVOLTAICS

Aatec Publications, P.O. Box 7119, Ann Arbor, MI 48107; (313) 995-1470

Alternative Energy Engineering, P.O. Box 339, Redway, CA 95560; (800) 777-6609

Backwoods Solar Electric Systems, 8530 Rapid Lighting Creek Rd., Sandpoint, ID 83864; (208) 263-4290

Fowler Solar Electric, 13 Bashan Hill Rd., Worthington, MA 01098; (413) 238-5974

Heliopower/Fran Maher, Inc., 1390 Valley Rd., Stirling, NJ 07980; (800) 34-HELIO

Home Power Magazine, P.O. Box 130, Hornbrook, CA 96044; (916) 475-3179

Jade Mountain, P.O. Box 4616, Boulder, CO 80306; (800) 442-1972

Photocomm, Inc., 930 Idaho Maryland Rd., Grass Valley, CA 95945; (800) 544-6466

Real Goods Trading Company, 966 Mazzoni St., #4B, Ukiah, CA 95482; (800) 762-7325

Rodale Press, 33 E. Minor St., Emmaus, PA 18098; (800) 441-7761

Solarmetrics, 140 Bouchard St., Manchester, NH 03103; (603) 668-3216

Sovonics Solar Systems, 1100 W. Maple Rd., Troy, MI 48084; (313) 362-4170

Steve Strong Design, P.O. Box 143, Still River, MA 01467; (617) 456-6855

Sunelco, P.O. Box 1499, 100 Skeels St., Hamilton, MT 59840; (406) 363-6924

Sunergy, P.O. Box 177, Princeton, NJ 08542; (609) 799-8800

Sunnyside Solar, RD 4, Box 808, Green River Rd., Brattleboro, VT 05301; (800) 346-3230

Zomeworks Corporation, 1011-A Sawmill Rd. NW, Albuquerque, NM 87125; (505) 242-5354

HYDRO POWER

Energy Systems and Designs, P.O. Box 1557, Sussex, NB E0E1P0, Canada; (506) 433-3151

Harris Hydro, 635 Swanton Rd., Davenport, CA 95017; (408) 425-7652

Photocomm, Inc., 930 Idaho Maryland Rd., Grass Valley, CA 95945; (800) 544-6466

TRANSPORTATION

Dahon California, Inc., 901 Corporate Center Dr., Suite 508, Monterey Park, CA 91754; (213) 264-1688

Hammacher Schlemmer, Dept. 99108, 212 W. Superior, Chicago, IL 60610; (800) 543-3366

Harper & Row, 10 E. 53rd St., New York, NY 10022; (212) 207-7000

Jade Mountain, P.O. Box 4616, Boulder, CO 80306; (800) 442-1972

LandRower, Inc., 4928 S. Fifth W., Idaho Falls, ID 83401; (208) 524-3712

Real Goods Trading Company, 966 Mazzoni St., #4B, Ukiah, CA 95482; (800) 762-7325

Sharper Image, P.O. Box 7031, San Francisco, CA 94120-7031; (800) 344-4444

ECOTOURISM

Alaska Wildland Adventures, P.O. Box 259, Trout Lake, WA 98650; (800) 334-8730

Cowabunga Safaris, Private Bag 4863, Gage Center Sta., Topeka, KS 66604-0408; (913) 272-7604

Earthwatch, 680 Mt. Auburn St., Box 403, Watertown, MA 02272; (617) 926-8200

Victor Emanuel Nature Tours, P.O. Box 33008, Austin, TX 78764; (800) 328-VENT

Fun Safaris, P.O. Box 178, Bloomingdale, IL 60108-0178; (708) 893-2545

International Expeditions, Inc., 1776 Independence Court, Birmingham, AL 35216; (800) 633-4734

Journeys, 3516 NE 155th, Suite A, Seattle, WA 98155; (800) 345-4453

Mountain Travel, 6420 Fairmount Ave., El Cerrito, CA 94530-3606; (800) 227-2384

Sobek Expeditions, P.O. Box 1089, Angels Camp, CA 95222; (800) 777-7939

Society Expeditions, Inc., 3131 Elliott Ave., Suite 700, Seattle, WA 98121; (206) 285-9400

Stackpole Books, Cameron and Kelker St., P.O. Box 1831, Harrisburg, PA 17105

Stone Wall Press, 1241 30th St. NW, Washington, DC 20007

Joseph Vanos Photo Safaris, P.O. Box 655, Vashon Island, WA 98070; (206) 463-5383

Voyagers International, P.O. Box 915, Ithaca, NY 14851; (607) 257-3091

Wood Star Tours, 908 S. Massachusetts Ave., De Land, FL 32724; (904) 736-0327

ENVIRONMENTAL ORGANIZATIONS

American Forestry Association, P.O. Box 2000, Washington, DC 20013; (800) 323-1560

ANAI, 1176 Bryson Rd., Franklin, NC 28734

Bio-Integral Resource Center, P.O. Box 7414, Berkeley, CA 94707; (415) 524-2567

Co-op America, 49 The Meadows Park, Colchester, VT 05446; (802) 655-2975

Earth Island Institute, 300 Broadway, Suite 28, San Francisco, CA 94133; (415) 788-3666

Environmental Action Foundation, 1525 New Hampshire Ave. NW, Washington, DC 20036; (202) 745-4870

Environmental Defense Fund, 257 Park Ave. S, New York, NY 10010; (212) 505-2100

Global Tomorrow Coalition, 1325 G St. NW, Suite 915, Washington, DC 20005; (202) 628-4016

Green Committees of Correspondence Clearinghouse, P.O. Box 30208, Kansas City, MO 64112; (816) 931-9366

Greenpeace, 1436 U St. NW, Washington, DC 20009; (202) 462-1177

International Fund for Animal Welfare, 411 Main St., Yarmouth Port, MA 02675; (508) 362-2649

National Arbor Day Foundation, 100 Arbor Ave., Nebraska City, NE 68410; (402) 474-5655

National Audubon Society, 950 Third Ave., New York, NY 10022; (212) 546-9100

National Wildlife Federation, 1412 16th St. NW, Washington, DC 20036-2266; (800) 432-6564

Natural Resources Defense Council, 40 W. 20th St., New York, NY 10011; (212) 727-2700

Nature Conservancy, 1815 N. Lynn St., Arlington, VA 22209; (703) 841-5300

New Alchemy Institute, 237 Hatchville Rd., East Falmouth, MA 02536; (508) 564-6301

Project Lighthawk, P.O. Box 8163, Sante Fe, NM 87504; (505) 982-9656

Rainforest Action Network, 301 Broadway, Suite A, San Francisco, CA 94133; (415) 398-4404

Renew America, 1400 16th St. NW, Suite 710, Washington, DC 20036; (202) 232-2252

Rocky Mountain Institute, 1739 Snowmass Creek Rd., Snowmass, CO 81654-9199; (303) 927-3851

Save-the-Redwoods League, 114 Sansome St., San Francisco, CA 94104; (415) 362-2352

Seventh Generation, Colchester, VT 05446-1672; (800) 456-1177

Sierra Club, 730 Polk St., San Francisco, CA 94109; (415) 981-8634

TreePeople, 12601 Mulholland Dr., Beverly Hills, CA 90210; (818) 753-4600

Worldwatch Institute, 1776 Massachusetts Ave. NW, Washington, DC 20036; (202) 452-1999

World Wildlife Fund, 1250 24th St. NW, Washington, DC 20037; (202) 293-4800

Zero Population Growth, 1400 16th St. NW, Suite 320, Washington, DC 20036; (202) 332-2200

ON THE JOB

Bio-Pax/Diversified Packaging, 1265 Pine Hill Dr., Annapolis, MD 21401; (301) 974-4411

Earth Care Paper, P.O. Box 3335, Madison, WI 53704; (608) 256-5522

Seventh Generation, Colchester, VT 05446-1672; (800) 456-1177

White River Paper Co., P.O. Box 455, White River Junction, VT 05001; (800) 225-0079

ENVIRONMENTAL INVESTING

Calvert Group, 4550 Montgomery Ave., Suite 1000 N, Bethesda, MD 20814; (800) 368-2748

Clean Yield Newsletter, Box 1880, Greensboro Bend, VT 05842; (802) 533-7178

Clean Yield Asset Management, Inc., 224 State St., Portsmouth, NH 03801-9850; (603) 436-0820

Coalition for Environmentally Responsible Economies, c/o Social Investment Forum, 711 Atlantic Ave., Boston, MA 02111; (617) 451-3252

Co-op America, 49 The Meadows Park, Colchester, VT 05446; (802) 655-2975

Dreyfus Mutual Funds, c/o Bank of New York, P.O. Box 12135, Newark, NJ 07101; (800) 645-6561, x2141

A.G. Edwards & Sons, Inc., Nobles Island, Portsmouth, NH 03801; (603) 430-8000

Ethical Investments, Inc., 430 First Ave. N, #204, Minneapolis, MN 55401; (612) 339-3939

Fidelity Distributors Corp., 82 Devonshire St., L7B, Boston, MA 02109; (617) 570-5994

Freedom Capital Management, 1 Beacon St., Fourth Floor, Boston, MA 02108; (800) 225-6258

Ron Freund & Associates, 835 Judson St., Suite 507, Evanston, IL 60242; (312) 869-2424

Message! Check Corp., P.O. Box 3206, Seattle, WA 98114; (206) 324-7792

Nature Conservancy, 1815 N. Lynn St., Arlington, VA 22209; (703) 841-5300

New Alternatives Fund, Inc., 295 Northern Blvd., Great Neck, NY 11021; (516) 466-0808

Parnassus Fund, 244 California St., San Francisco, CA 94111; (415) 362-3505

Pax World Fund, Inc., 224 State St., Portsmouth, NH 03801; (603) 431-8022

SFT, Inc., 1016 W. Eighth Ave., Suite D, King of Prussia, PA 19046; (800) 523-2004

Social Investment Forum, 711 Atlantic Ave., Boston, MA 02111; (617) 451-3252

Socially Responsible Investment Group, Candler Bldg., Suite 622, 127 Peach Tree St. NE, Atlanta, GA 30303; (404) 577-3635

Vermont National Bank, P.O. Box 804, Brattleboro, VT 05301; (800) 544-7108, x2414

Wall Street Green Review, 24861 Alicia Parkway, #C-293, Laguna Hills, CA 92653; (714) 588-9863

Working Assets Funding Service, 230 California St., San Francisco, CA 94111; (800) 533-3863

ORGANIC YARD & GARDEN

Alsto Company Handy Helpers, Rte. 150 E, P.O. Box 1267, Galesburg, IL 61401; (800) 447-0048

American Forestry Association, P.O. Box 2000, Washington, DC 20013; (800) 323-1560

American Lawn Mower Company, P.O. Box 369, Shelbyville, IN 46176; (800) 457-1049

Bat Conservation International, Inc., P.O. Box 162603, Austin, TX 78716; (512) 327-9721

Beneficial Insectary, 14751 Oak Run Rd., Oak Run, CA 96069; (916) 472-3715

Beneficial Insect Sales, Inc., P.O. Box 40634, Memphis, TN 38174; (901) 276-8341

BioLogic, 18056 Springtown Rd., P.O. Box 177, Willow Hill, PA 17271; (717) 349-2789

Biological Control Services Program, California Dept. of Agriculture, 3288 Meadowview Rd., Sacramento, CA 95832; (916) 445-9280

Bug-Off Creative Clothing, P.O. Box 367, Hancock, NH 03449; (603) 563-8305

W. Atlee Burpee Company, 300 Park Ave., Warminster, PA 18794; (215) 674-9633

Co-op America, 49 The Meadows Park, Colchester, VT 05446; (802) 655-2975

Countryman Press, P.O. Box 175, Woodstock, VT 05091; (802) 457-1049

Crown Video, Div. of Crown Publishers, Inc., 201 E. 50th St., New York, NY 10022; (212) 572-2359

Environmental Protection Agency, 401 M St. SW, Washington, DC 20460; (800) 633-8372

Farm Tech Service, Inc., RD 1, Box 256, Mt. Joy, PA 17552; (717) 653-9670

Food & Drug Administration, 5600 Fishers Ln., Rockville, MD 20857; (301) 443-1544

Gardena, Inc., 6031 Culligan Way, Minnetonka, MN 55345; (612) 933-2445

Gardener's Eden, 100 N. Point St., San Francisco, CA 94133; (415) 421-4242

Gardener's Supply, 128 Intervale Rd., Burlington, VT 05401; (802) 863-1700

Garden Way Publishing, Storey Communications, Inc., 1476 Massachusetts Ave., North Adams, MA 01247; (800) 833-6990

Growing Naturally, P.O. Box 54, Pineville, PA 18946

Handsome Rewards, 19465 Brennan Ave., Perris, CA 92379; (714) 943-2023

Hartmann's Plantation, Inc., 310 60th St., P.O. Box E, Grand Junction, MI 49056; (616) 253-4281

Hummer Nature Works, Reagan Wells Canyon, Box 122, Uvalde, TX 78801; (512) 232-6167

International Irrigation Company (Irrigo), LPO 160, 1555 Third Ave., Niagara Falls, NY 14304; (416) 688-4090

IPM Laboratories, Inc., Main St., Locke, NY 13092-0099; (315) 497-3129

Kinsman Company, Inc., River Rd., Point Pleasant, PA 18950; (215) 297-5613

Lakon Herbals, Box 252, Montpelier, VT 05602; (802) 223-5563

Maestro-Gro, P.O. Box 310, Lowell, AR 72745; (501) 770-6154

National Audubon Society, 950 Third Ave., New York, NY 10022; (212) 546-9100

National Wildlife Federation, 1412 16th St. NW, Washington, DC 20036-2266; (800) 432-6564

Necessary Trading Co., 7140 Main St., New Castle, VA 24127; (703) 864-5103

New Alchemy Institute, 237 Hatchville Rd., East Falmouth, MA 02536; (508) 564-6301

Nitron Industries, 4605 Johnson Rd., P.O. Box 1447, Fayetteville, AR 72702; (800) 835-0123

North Country Organics, P.O. Box 107, Newbury, VT 05051; (802) 222-4277

Peaceful Valley Farm Supply, P.O. Box 2209, Grass Valley, CA 95945; (916) 272-GROW

Plow and Hearth, 301 Madison Rd., Orange, VA 22960; (800) 627-1712

Raindrip, Inc., 21305 Itasca St., Chatsworth, CA 91311; (800) 222-3747

R Value/West, 150 N. Santa Bonita Ave., Suite 300, Arcadia, CA 91006; (818) 798-4000

Ringer Research Corp., 9959 Valley View Rd., Minneapolis, MN 55344; (612) 941-4180

Rodale Press, 33 E. Minor St., Emmaus, PA 18098; (800) 441-7761

Ryans by Mail, 23010 Lake Forest Dr., Suite D321, Laguna Hills, CA 92653; (800) 950-5432

Safer, Inc., 189 Wells Ave., Newton, MA 02159; (800) 423-7544

Sharper Image, P.O. Box 7031, San Francisco, CA 94120-7031; (800) 344-4444

Smith & Hawken, 25 Corte Madera Ave., Mill Valley, CA 94941; (415) 381-1800

Spalding Laboratories, 760 Printz Rd., Arroyo Grande, CA 93420; (805) 489-5946

Vermont Country Store, P.O. Box 3000, Manchester, VT 05255; (802) 362-2400

Waterforms, Inc., P.O. Box 930, Blue Hill, ME 04614; (207) 374-2383

Weeds of Worth, Ltd., Box 140, Star Route 65, Great Barrington, MA 02130; (413) 229-3348

Zook & Ranck, Inc., RFD 1, Box 243, Gap, PA 17527; (717) 442-4171

GROCERY SHOPPING

Agriculture Task Force, 331 Queen St., Philadelphia, PA 19147; (215) 465-8878

Americans for Safe Food, 1501 16th St. NW, Washington, DC 20036; (202) 332-9110

Center for Science in the Public Interest, 1501 16th St. NW, Washington, DC 20036; (202) 332-9110

Chartrand Imports, P.O. Box 1319, Rockland, ME 04841; (207) 594-7300

Co-op America, 49 The Meadows Park, Colchester, VT 05446; (802) 655-2975

Council on Economic Priorities, 30 Irving Place, New York, NY 10003; (800) U-CAN-HELP

Farmers Wholesale Cooperative, P.O. Box 7446, Olympia, WA 98507; (206) 754-8989

Greenbelt Alliance, 116 New Montgomery, San Francisco, CA 94105; (415) 543-4291

International Alliance for Sustainable Agriculture, 1701 University Ave. SE, Room 202, Minneapolis, MN 55414; (612) 331-1099

Living Farms, Box 50, Tracy, MN 56175; (800) 533-5320

Natural Way Mills, Inc., RR 2, Box 27, Middle River, MN 56737; (218) 222-3677

New American Library, 1633 Broadway, New York, NY 10019

New England Small Farms Institute, P.O. Box 937, Belchertown, MA 01007; (413) 323-4531

New York Food & Agriculture Network, 175 W. 90th St., New York, NY 10025; (212) 724-6862

Organic Kosher Cattle Co., Inc., P.O. Box 355, White Plains, NY 10605; (914) 684-OKAY

Pennsylvania Resources Council, 25 W. Third St., P.O. Box 88, Medina, PA 19063; (215) 565-9131

Public Market Collaborative, 153 Waverly Place, New York, NY 10014; (212) 620-5660

Walnut Acres, Penns Creek, PA 17862; (717) 837-0601

Index

"We will never accomplish
international economic security through arms control alone.
Unless we also eliminate the threat to the world's environment,
global economic security is inconceivable."

— *Soviet President Mikhail Gorbachev*